INTO ADDIE'S ARMS

First in the Left Fork Series—From New York to Left Fork

Into Addie's Arms

Barbara Hood Hopkins

Copyright © 2011 by Barbara Hood Hopkins.

Library of Congress Control Number: 2011914891
ISBN: Hardcover   978-1-4653-3782-5
            Softcover   978-1-4653-3781-8
            Ebook   978-1-4653-3783-2

All rights reserved. No part of this book may be reproduced or transmitted in any form or by any means, electronic or mechanical, including photocopying, recording, or by any information storage and retrieval system, without permission in writing from the copyright owner.

Author's Note: This is a work of fiction. Names, characters, places and incidents are either the product of the author's imagination or are used fictitiously, and any resemblance to actual persons, living or dead, business establishments, events or locales is entirely coincidental.

This book was printed in the United States of America.

To order additional copies of this book, contact:
Xlibris Corporation
1-888-795-4274
www.Xlibris.com
Orders@Xlibris.com
99613

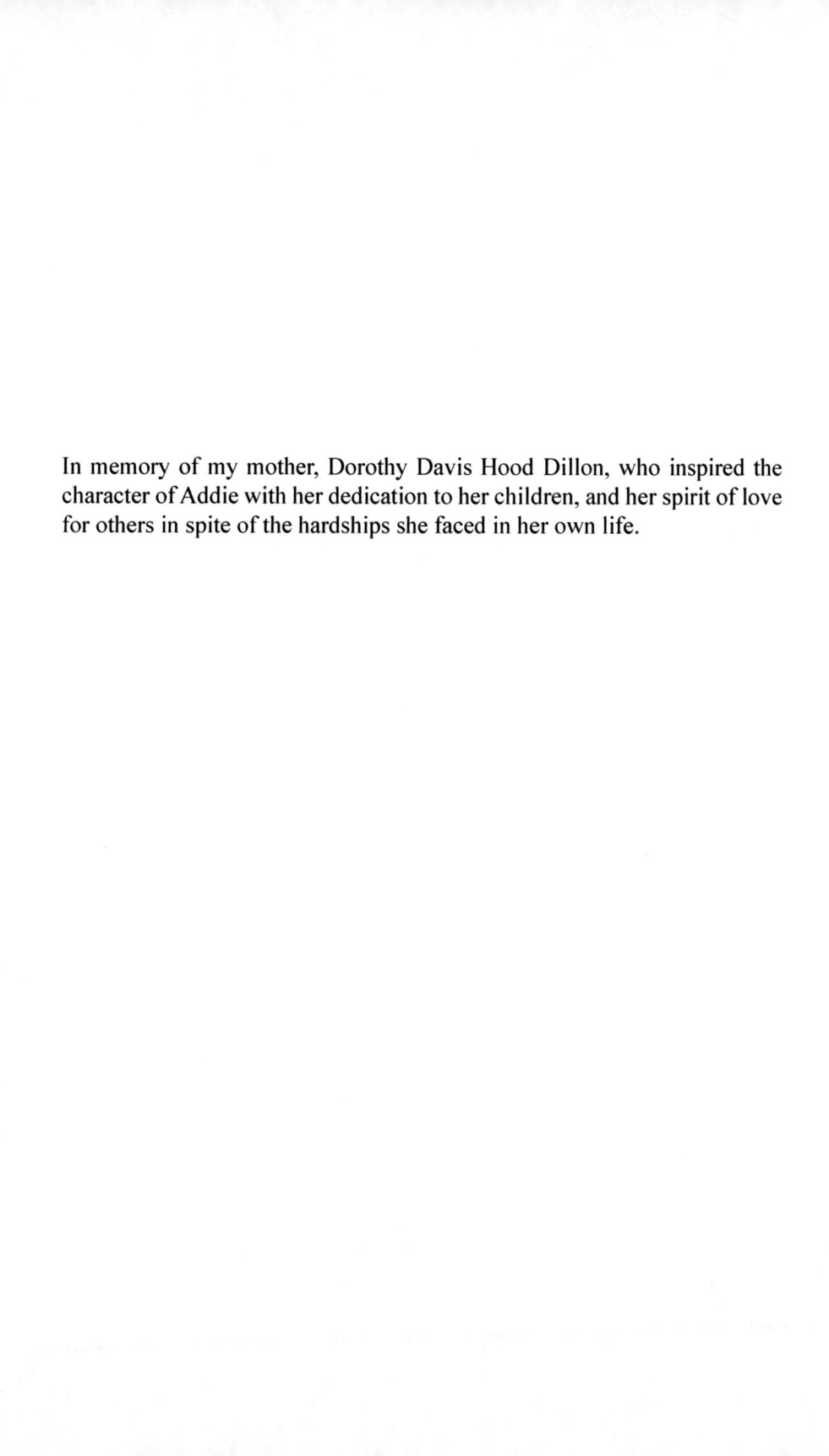

In memory of my mother, Dorothy Davis Hood Dillon, who inspired the character of Addie with her dedication to her children, and her spirit of love for others in spite of the hardships she faced in her own life.

Foreword

Jesus never entered into the equation as the Smith family planned their move from New York City to Left Fork, South Carolina. Career advancement, safe living, peace, and the hope of keeping jobs in the United States for this small town were reasons Mike Smith rationalized as he made his decision to move. However, man's plans are often superseded by God's plan. (Jer. 29:11)

Life well lived is emotional and the formerly one-dimensional life of Mike, Cindy and Mary Margaret Smith becomes complicated immediately after the announcement of this well-intentioned move. Mary Margaret doesn't take the news well, but after time she seems to be coming around. The hope of a peaceful, safe environment for Mary Margaret appears to be coming together as the family engages with two Southern spirit-filled women whose unlikely friendship has spanned decades. Their faith in Jesus Christ is apparent, even though initially unspoken, and they envelope this family with love only dreamed about. However, the first day of school for their daughter shatters this peace, and gives a glimpse of the turmoil that follows as she is harassed by a small group of girls who, even before she arrives, have pledged to shun her very existence and to make certain she doesn't feel welcome. The leader of the group continues the harassment after the rest of the *gang* have apologized and reach out to Mary Margaret in friendship. Allison Kincaid continues to plot and act on revenge.

New dimensions are added to everyday living as two neighbor boys become allies for Mary Margaret; a homeless man who has been living in a tent on the property they purchase makes his presence known; and a business associate's family not only opens their home and friendship to them, but their horses and dogs bring new-found pleasure for Mary Margaret. All of these changes pale in comparison to the change that is made on Mother's Day, 2001 when for the first time this family hears about salvation through Jesus Christ. Yes, they had heard about Jesus, but they hadn't heard about a relationship with him. After an almost unbelievable week of chaos, Mary Margaret takes the lead and brings this family to a decision point that will forever change their lives.

This book tells part of the story of this family. 2001 is a year that forever changed the hearts and minds of not only Americans, but people around the world. This first book will be followed with others as questions left unanswered here continue to be answered and real-life events meld into the daily lives of this fictional family.

I thank the people whose names I have chosen for some of the characters, not to share real-life events, but for the positive influence I have seen them share in the lives of others. This story is truly fictional except for the steps taken to accept Jesus Christ as your Savior. The Holy Bible outlines that the only way to eternity is through faith and belief in Jesus Christ. (John 3:16) It is a free gift, available to all who choose to believe. It is my hope that if you have not already made that decision the words on these pages will somehow cause you to think about it and hopefully take the simple steps necessary to make it a reality.

The writing of this story has been a more than 10-year journey. I must give homage to Oprah and Dr. Phil whose shows regarding bullying inspired me to begin. My mother was very ill at the time and she became engaged with the writing and asked everyday "What's going on with Mary Margaret?" After her death, and the subsequent deaths of my mother-in-law and sister-in-law, the story was put aside. Then a diagnosis of cancer for my husband and a lengthy treatment followed immediately on its heels by a diagnosis of cancer for me, the creativity was temporarily diminished, but the story remained where God had initially placed it, written across my heart. Good health and my faith in Jesus Christ have brought me to this point of publishing these words. While it's my first effort, I can't take much credit. Every day as I sat to write, I was as surprised as I hope you will be with the words that appeared. They seemed to come from someone else, whom I now know was God. He guided me and this is His story. I hope you enjoy it.

To all my family and friends who have shared this journey with me, I give you my utmost thanks. You have listened, read, encouraged and allowed me to dream.

The Announcement

Chapter 1

"Daddy, you choose the first fortune cookie," Mary Margaret insisted as her father slid the Guest Check from under the three, cellophane wrapped cookies on the small, black, rectangular tray the waitress had placed on the table before she took away the leftovers to place them in to-go boxes.

"No, I insist that my best gals go first," he said as he noted the Chinese writing on the check. "It amazes me that Cashew Chicken translates to this," he laughed as he held out the check for Cindy and Mary Margaret to see.

"Let me see what Won Ton Soup looks like," Mary Margaret said moving out of her seat to stand beside her father.

"I guess this must be Won Ton Soup, because we had 3 soups, and the only thing I recognize is the number 3," he replied handing the check to Mary Margaret.

"Would you like to pay the check this time?" he asked his daughter.

"Daddy, you know I don't have enough money," she said handing the check back to him. "Anyway, I want you to take the first cookie. These are special cookies for New Years, and I want you to have the first one," she insisted.

"I'll tell you what, let's let Mama take the first, and I'll take the second. How does that sound?"

"Well, okay. Here, Mama, you choose the first one. You read it and then daddy can choose his and he can read it. I'll go last," Mary Margaret said carrying the tray to her mother's side of the table.

"Let me see," Cindy said breaking the cookie in half and removing the small slip of paper. "I can't read this small print in this dim light. Let me get my glasses."

"I can read it, Mama, but it's still your fortune, okay?"

That's fine, Mary Margaret, this is my fortune for the New Year.

"It says, 'Prosperity will greet you in the new year." Mary Margaret read. "Does that mean you'll be rich this year?"

"I already am rich. With you and Daddy by my side I am the richest person in the world."

"Oh, Mama, prosperity means lots of money. You're going to get lots of money this year."

"What year is this now, Mary Margaret?" her father asked.

"It's 2001," she immediately replied.

"Do you remember last New Year's Day?"

"Well, I know we came here for dinner. We always come here for dinner on New Year's Day. I guess that's our family tradition now, isn't it?

"I hadn't thought of it that way before, but I guess it is. At least there wasn't as much commotion as there was last year."

"There was a lot of commotion last night, Daddy."

"Yes, but last year was a big deal. We went from the 1900's to 2000. Hardly anybody alive had done that before. Not only that, but there were lots of computer fears that went along with the year change. For a long time preceding the turn of the century, changes were taking place to see that the business world continued to operate smoothly."

Mary Margaret was again at her father's side holding the tray for him to make his cookie selection. "Let's see, I think I'll take this one. No, I think I want that one," he said pointing indecisively at the two cookies on the tray.

Mary Margaret giggled, "Choose one, Daddy, please."

"I can't quite decide. You go ahead and choose yours, and then I'll choose mine."

Mary Margaret started to take one, and laughed. "No, Daddy, that's not a choice for you. I really want you to choose your fortune for the New Year."

"Okay, if you insist."

"I insist," she said jumping from foot to foot.

"I choose this one."

"What does it say?" the now impatient child asked.

"It says, 'The new year will bring many changes in your life."

"Wow, that's a good fortune for you," Cindy said reaching over and touching her husband's hand.

Mike Smith glanced at his wife, and they shared a look that only two people who know each other intimately can recognize. It went unnoticed by the child as she sat back in her chair and unwrapped the final cookie.

"Now, it's my turn to ask. What does it say?" Her father asked.

"Watch for pitfalls in the new year," she read. "What are pitfalls anyway?"

"Well, let me see how to put this," her mother said. "It's like . . . No, it's, uh . . ." she stammered not wanting to put a totally negative spin on the fortune.

"It's like this, Mary Margaret," her father interrupted. "Sometimes things don't always go exactly like we want them to, and when that happens, it's called a pitfall."

"Oh, you mean like problems?" she replied.

"Yes, sort of like problems," her mother said.

"I don't usually have problems, so I guess that's not a good fortune for me. It was probably meant for that man over there," she said pointing to an elderly man who was struggling to put his scarf in the arm of his coat, but dropped it on the floor instead.

"Yes, he does seem to be having a pitfall, doesn't he?" her father said marveling at the positive attitude his daughter took in most everything.

I hope she stays positive when she hears the news I have to tell her tomorrow. She only knows New York City, the apartment building we live in and St. Mark's Academy. When I tell her we're moving from here to a small town in South Carolina, she may not be so positive," his mind wandered.

"Thank you for coming, and Happy New Year," the waitress said interrupting his thought to return his credit card and receipt, as she placed the white paper bag filled with to-go boxes on the table.

"Happy New Year to you, too," the Smiths said in unison.

"Mei, did you remember the plastic forks?" Mike Smith inquired of the waitress as she turned to walk away.

"Yes, Mr. Smith, and I put in some fortune cookies, too," she said as she hurried along to another table.

"Are we ready?" he asked his wife and daughter.

"I am," Mary Margaret replied. "I need to make sure I have everything ready for school tomorrow. I can't wait to see Alice. She's been gone so long. It seems like a month since she left."

"Yes, I'm sure it does, but it really has only been a week." Cindy said picking up her coat and handing Mary Margaret's jacket to her.

"Yeah, but she's my soul mate, and I miss her when she's gone," she almost whined.

"I understand that, but you need to think about new friends. It's not good to only have one friend," her mother said.

"Yeah, but she just lives upstairs, and we go to school together. Charlene and Darlene like it when we get together and they can have tea and talk when we come home from school. You like Alice, too, don't you?"

"Of course, I like Alice. She is a very nice girl, and I'm glad she's your friend. It's just that sometimes we need to broaden our horizons and try new things. We need to make changes in our lives."

"I don't like change. I like things just as they are. I like Charlene as my nanny. I like Harry as our doorman. I like St. Mark's Academy. I like Alice, and I like you and daddy. No, I love you, daddy, Alice, and Charlene. I love Darlene, too," the child concluded with such innocence and emphasis that he mother began to worry that the news they were sharing the next morning might be a *pitfall*.

Mike Smith put on his coat after helping Cindy with hers and zipping Mary Margaret's new red parka. He placed his scarf around his neck and searched his pockets for his gloves that Charlene had given him for Christmas. Only one seemed to be in his pocket, and a quick check of the floor revealed the other.

"If you had lost that, you would have had a *pitfall*," Mary Margaret giggled; proud that she had learned a new word.

"Charlene would have been terribly disappointed with me," Mike said as he led his wife and daughter to the door.

"Mr. Smith, don't forget this," Mei called to him as she brought him the paper bag.

"Thank you, Mei. You know me pretty well to watch that I don't leave the *doggie* bag," he smiled taking the bag from the outstretched hand of the waitress.

"You are a good man, Mr. Smith. It is a pleasure to watch after you," she said blushing and bowing slightly.

"Thanks again," he said as he opened the door, and the wind snatched it from his hand nearly slamming it against the wall. "Goodness, that wind is strong. It'll be a cold walk home. Are you all bundled up, Mary

Margaret?" he asked as his daughter tightened the drawstring on the hood of her parka.

"Yes, Daddy, I have my gloves. I wore my new fur lined boots, and my new jacket is really warm."

"How about you, Honey. Will you be warm enough? Do we need to get a taxi instead of walking?"

"No, Mike, no taxis tonight. We need to walk off that big dinner, and anyway, you have a delivery to make," Cindy said pointing at the bag he was carrying.

"You're right. I just didn't want you to be cold."

"I'll be all right, and it's only a couple of blocks."

The wind seemed to howl as they stepped onto the sidewalk. The walk over had been cold, but the wind wasn't so noticeable at their back. Now they were walking into the wind, and small snowflakes had begun to fall.

"Look, it's snowing," Mary Margaret said as she pulled away from her mother's hand to catch snowflakes on her tongue.

"Stay here with us," her father said as she moved a few feet ahead.

"It's okay, Daddy. I love this night because it seems like we're the only people in the world. The sidewalks are empty, and we have them all to ourselves."

How observant she is, he thought. It did seem as though everybody else had stayed home that evening and this small part of the world was for them alone. *Maybe I was hasty in my decision to leave New York. Maybe it is a safe place for Mary Margaret and Cindy. Maybe I don't need to move them to a small town to give them security.*

The wind continued to blow into their faces. Steam rose from around the manhole covers. A few taxis passed by, but the walkers continued. At the first alley Mary Margaret stopped and waited for her parents.

"You wait here," Mike said as he turned into the narrow passageway.

"Mike, be careful," Cindy said worrying every time her husband made this trip.

"Leon, Leon, are you down here?" she heard his voice call.

"Leon, Leon, it's Mike Smith. I have some food for you."

There was no reply.

"Mike, maybe he went to a shelter. Come on back," Cindy called from the corner curb.

"No, he never goes to a shelter. He's probably sleeping. Leon, Leon, come on Buddy, it's me, Mike Smith."

By now he was standing next to the box that Leon called home. He had strategically placed his box out of the wind and next to a building vent that provided him with some warmth. A blue plastic tarpaulin was wrapped around the box, and pieces of blanket could be seen at one end. None of Leon's body was visible.

"Come on, Leon, wake up. I have some food for you," he nearly shouted this time.

"You don't have to yell. I heard you," a voice came from the box.

"Hey, man, I was getting worried about you. Are you all right?"

"Yeah, I'm all right. I just didn't get much sleep last night. You know. It was New Year's Eve and all. I just got to sleep this morning, and the street sweepers started."

"Yeah, it was the same way at our apartment," Mike said, suddenly ashamed that he had complained about his lack of sleep in his comfortable apartment.

"Here, Buddy, I brought you some Chinese, and Mei put in some extra fortune cookies. She knows you like them."

"Thank you," Leon said finally sticking his head from under the covers and into the night air. "I'm not getting out if you don't mind. I got everything all warm in here."

"Yeah, that's great, Leon. I'm glad you're warm. You sure you don't need anything?"

"Yeah, I'm sure. Thanks again for the food, and tell your wife and daughter I said hello."

"I'll do that," Mike said, turning to leave.

"Leon, I have some bad news. Well, it's good news for me, but bad news for our friendship. I'm moving from New York. I'll only be here for a week or so, and then I'll be gone. I'll be back on the weekends for a while and I'll check on you then. I wish you'd think about going back to your family. I know your son would make a place for you. He told me he would."

"I know he would, but I like my place here. Don't worry about me. I do just fine. Nobody bothers me. This is my place, and the people around here leave me alone. I'll be okay. You go on now. I'll eat this while it's still warm and get back to sleep."

"All right. Happy New Year," Mike said automatically.

"Same to you," the voice from the box replied.

Mike returned to the corner and took Cindy's hand. They had only been a few feet apart, but the worlds were separated as far as the moon is from the sun.

"Daddy, was Leon okay?" Mary Margaret asked.

"He was as okay as he can be," her father replied.

The adults walked hand-in-hand in silence as Mary Margaret continued to lead the way. She jumped over cracks in the sidewalk chanting, "Step on a crack, you'll break your mother's back."

The family stopped at the next corner though it wasn't entirely necessary. Even the streets were empty. There were no cars visible for blocks.

"Maybe we *are* the only people in the world," Cindy said remembering Mary Margaret's earlier statement.

"Sometimes I wish we were. Then I wouldn't have to be concerned about my two girls. Maybe we should move to a deserted island. That would be nice," Mike said watching his daughter's every step into the darkness.

"No, Daddy, that wouldn't be nice. I don't want to ever move. I love it here. This is my world, and this is where I always want to be. It's great here," the voice of innocence implored.

Mike Smith was unprepared for the sudden gush of feeling his daughter expressed for their life in New York City. *This is going to be harder than I thought. She's not going to take this news well.* His mind raced.

The decision had been made. He and Cindy had agreed. He was moving his family to Left Fork, South Carolina, a small town about an hour west of Charleston, in a few weeks, and they would be leaving his daughter's beloved city. He knew he had made the right decision. His career goals were being met with this move, and his daughter would adjust, he told himself. "This is the right thing to do. She is only 9 years old. She'll make lots of new friends. All the folks I met there are nice. It is the right thing to do," he said aloud squeezing his wife's hand.

"What did you say, Daddy?"

"Nothing, Dear, I was just thinking out loud."

"Miss Mary Margaret, your nose is as red as your jacket," Harry said holding the door for the family.

"Is it really, Harry? It's really cold out there. My eyes watered, but I kept warm jumping the whole way home."

"You jumped the whole way?" he asked.

"Well, not the whole way. I jumped over the cracks for one whole block and then I skipped, and I tried to catch snowflakes on my tongue."

"Oh, me, if only we could capture a little of our youthful energy and save it for our old age," Harry said wistfully as Mike and Cindy came inside.

"Yes, Harry, that would be wonderful. Did you and Dorothy have a nice New Year's?" Cindy asked politely.

"Yes, ma'm, we did. Dorothy fixed pork and cabbage. She always hides a silver coin in the cabbage, and this year I got the coin in my serving," he said proudly displaying his silver dollar.

"You are going to have a prosperous year," Cindy said, "Or that's what my mother always said."

"Mine, too. I'm already a rich man. I have a good wife and my children are doing well. What more could I ask for?"

"Not much. We just had the same conversation about our life a few minutes ago."

"Harry, my mother's fortune cookie said she was going to have a prosperous New Year, and our family tradition is to eat at a Chinese restaurant on New Year's Day," Mary Margaret said proudly.

"Well, I guess that's as good a tradition as any," Harry laughed as the family got into the elevator.

The door started to close, but Mary Margaret put her hand on it and said, "Harry, my fortune cookie said I had to watch for pitfalls, but I think I got the wrong cookie."

"I'm sure you did, Little One. I'm sure you did."

The apartment was warm after the cold walk. Mary Margaret hurried into her bathroom and got ready for bed. She checked her book bag and placed it beside her bedroom door. Her clothes were all hanging in the closet for her selection in the morning.

Mike and Cindy tapped on the door and came in for their good-night kiss and to tuck their daughter into bed.

As they turned to leave she said, "Happy New Year. I love you. Thank you for a great holiday."

"Happy New Year to you too," her mother said.

"Yes, Mary Margaret, Happy New Year," her father said with a catch in his voice suddenly aware of the maturity his daughter had begun to show. He turned out the light and closed the door never turning around to look at his daughter, lest the tear in his eye give him away.

"She's growing up before our eyes," he said as he and Cindy sat on the living room sofa.

"Yes, she is. It seems like she has matured so much even in the last two weeks," her mother said.

"It's a shame we have to send her out into this world. She is so positive and enthusiastic about life. I'd like to keep her safe from everything unpleasant for all of her life."

"Yes, I wish *pitfalls* would never be a part of her world, and I'm afraid I'm going to bring a big one to her right away."

"I was just thinking the same thing. But you know her. She's always been resilient. She'll be okay. We'll just tell her in the morning that we're moving just like we planned. She'll have a few weeks to get used to the idea. It'll be okay. You just wait. It'll be okay," she repeated, maybe more for herself than her husband.

The voices drifted into Mary Margaret's room, and as they soaked into her sleepy brain, she sat upright and listened. She didn't really intend to eavesdrop, but had she heard what her mother said. She said, "We're moving," Mary Margaret whispered in the silence of her room. "We can't be moving. Mama works here. Daddy works here. I go to school here. Charlene is here. Alice is here. Maybe I'm dreaming."

Somebody flipped on the television, and the only sound was the announcer of the football game. Mary Margaret lay back on her bed. Her mind was racing. "Are they moving without me? Where are they moving? Is Charlene moving with us? I'm not moving without Charlene. No, that's not right. I'm just not moving at all. They can't make me . . . .

Chapter 2

The streets were nearly empty in Left Fork, South Carolina as most families spent New Year's Day together eating collards and black-eyed peas. Traditions run high in this small town, and family is a big tradition. The one person who dared to face the cold mist of the evening went unnoticed.

Darkness hid the small figure as she now slipped from the bushes near the driveway. Her breath was visible in the unseasonably cold air. The thrust of her right hand met with resistance, but the sharp point of the filed ice pick punctured the tire and was met with a slight whoosh of air. She smiled and deftly moved to the rear tire. Again, she plunged the pick into the resistant rubber, and was greeted with the same whoosh. Her excitement rose.

I'll show her, she thought. *She caused me to be grounded for all of the Christmas vacation. She'll see what it feels like when she can't go anywhere in the morning.*

Allison Kincaid moved her agile, 9-year-old, body to the other side of the car and two more times she plunged the sharp pick and was greeted with the sudden and unmistakable sound of escaping air. A dog began to bark, and an outdoor light bathed the area. The living room curtain began to move, but the girl dressed in gray sweatpants and a hooded sweatshirt disappeared into the darkness and was soon back on her own street. She crouched down, slipped around to her bedroom window and climbed inside. Everything was as she had left it. Her television was on, and the form in the bed was untouched. She walked over, pulled back the covers, and threw the pillows onto the floor.

"Good," she said to no one. "I made it happen. Nobody fools with me."

She pulled out her diary and began to journal the events of the day often embellishing the activities. She turned back the pages and reread the entries beginning with Wednesday, December 20, 2000.

> *"I hate Mrs. Calhoun. She thinks she's such a cool principal, but she's not. She's a witch and I hate her. She said I stole a bracelet that Stephanie gave to Jane for Christmas, but that's not true. I found it. Anyway, it was prettier than the one she gave to me. Stephanie likes Jane better than me. She thinks Jane is her best friend, but I know better. I'll get even with them. Just wait and see. I have the whole Christmas vacation to plan everything, and I'll make them all sorry."*

She continued reading, and each day's notes were filled with threats and rantings as the girl stewed at her predicament of being grounded and blamed everything on everyone—accepting no responsibility herself. Yes, she knew the truth. The bracelet was Jane's, but it was gold, not silver like hers, and the stone looked like a diamond. The stone in hers was yellow, and she hated yellow. *Stephanie should have given me the prettiest one*, she thought. *Anyway, Jane shouldn't have left it on her desk.*

Her plan had finally begun to unfold beginning with destroying the tires on the principal's car. She smiled as she hid away the diary and the ice pick in the hole she had cut in her closet wall. Her other valuables were in there, too.

"That's the first one. The rest can wait for now." Allison reached for a pair of scissors on her desk and took a shirt from her closet. The tags hung from the wristband. She cut the plastic string and the tags fell on the floor. She turned the shirt around and cut a slit up the side. As if she was fed by the excitement, she continued cutting the shirt until the waistband looked like fringe. She threw the shirt into her closet and switched channels on the TV.

"Allison, it's time to eat," her mother called from the kitchen.

Allison ignored the call.

Again her mother called, "Allison, come on and eat!" this time the exasperation was surfacing. It had been a long two weeks. When Mrs. Calhoun called her just days before and asked her to come to the school immediately, she had no idea what lay ahead. Allison had always been a strong-willed child, but had never been a bad girl she told herself. Her mind was remembering incidents which alluded to bad behavior on her daughter's part, but Allison always had an excuse and the blame lay with others.

What could be so bad that I have been summoned on the last day before Christmas vacation, the worried mother remembered thinking as she drove to the school. Her question was soon answered when she entered Mrs. Calhoun's office and found her daughter there with the principal.

"Mrs. Kincaid, I'm sorry to have to call you down here like this, but we have a situation that I don't feel can wait until after the Christmas vacation," the mother remembered the conversation. She looked at her daughter, but their eyes never engaged as the little girl was looking at the floor and refused to look up.

As the principal explained, the mother remembered her shock.

"Mrs. Kincaid, it seems that some of the girls in Allison's class exchanged Christmas gifts at lunch."

"Yes, I knew they were going to do that," the mother responded, wondering what was wrong with that.

"Well, after the exchange the students returned to the classroom for the afternoon session, and to watch a movie," the principal continued.

"Yes, I knew they were having a movie today," Mrs. Kincaid said.

"During the movie one of the students, Jane, went to the restroom. When she returned, a bracelet she had gotten as a gift from Stephanie was missing from her desk. Mrs. Stancil stopped the movie and turned on the lights; and all the students searched the room for the missing item," the principal said.

"Yes, but what does all this have to do with Allison?" the now impatient mother asked.

"I'm getting to that, but I wanted to make sure you understood all that transpired leading up to the discovery of the bracelet in Allison's book bag," the principal said sweeping her eyes in Allison's direction.

Mrs. Kincaid sucked air as she heard her daughter being indirectly accused of stealing.

"I'm sure there is some explanation," the outraged parent said. "Why would she have to steal a cheap bracelet? She has fine jewelry. She would have no reason to steal," she concluded now looking in her daughter's direction.

Silence filled the room as the adults looked at the small but defiant figure who sat in the oversized wing-backed chair. The few seconds that passed seemed like an eternity. The final bell rang, and the occupants of the room were momentarily startled. The noise that filled the hall indicated the students were being dismissed and joy filled the voices that could be heard.

"Merry Christmas!"

"Thank you, same to you!"

"Happy New Year!"

"Call me when you get home. Maybe you can come over to my house!"

Greetings were shouted, but the occupants of the principal's office said nothing. Finally, Mrs. Calhoun broke the silence.

"Allison, do you want to explain to your mother how the bracelet got into your book bag, or should I?"

The little girl defiantly maintained her silence.

"Allison, what is the meaning of all this" her mother demanded.

Silence. She said nothing.

"Allison, answer me," the now exasperated woman said.

Still silent, the little girl looked at her mother and curled up the left side of her mouth in a snarl.

"Young lady, haven't I told you not to look at me like that?" the now angry mother shouted.

As the halls were empty by this time, her voice filled the room. Mrs. Calhoun stood.

"Let me try to explain what I believe happened. Jane went to the restroom and left the box containing her bracelet on the shelf under her desk. In the darkness Allison *dropped* her pencil, and when she picked it up, she retrieved the box from Jane's desk. When Jane returned from the restroom, Allison asked to go to the restroom, and she took the small box with her. She removed the bracelet and buried the box under all the paper towels in the trashcan, where we later found it. She returned to the classroom and dropped the bracelet into her book bag which was hanging on the back of her desk," the principal finished.

"Allison, did you do that?" Mrs. Kincaid demanded.

Silence—the girl said nothing. Before her mother could ask again for a response, she finally spoke.

"Nobody would believe me if I said I didn't do it. Nobody ever believes me. Everybody thinks Jane is so perfect," Allison finally said.

"Allison, this has nothing to do with Jane, except that her bracelet was the one missing, and it fell out of your book bag when Davis accidentally knocked it off your desk," Mrs. Calhoun said. "Also, you are the only one from your classroom who went to the restroom after Jane."

Mrs. Kincaid remembered the embarrassment she felt and the sadness with which she looked at her child. Mrs. Calhoun had agreed not to suspend Allison, but her warning that, "Any further infractions to the rules would be dealt with swiftly," rang in her ears.

I dread tomorrow, she thought as she knew her daughter would return to school the next day. *Instead of this being a happy new year, this is one that's starting off all wrong*, she thought as she left the kitchen to go to her daughter's room to demand that she join her and her husband for dinner.

She knocked on the door, but Allison didn't respond. The TV could be heard. She called her daughter's name. Still no response. She tried the knob. It was locked. Fear filled her brain.

"What is going on in there, Young Lady," she frantically shouted. Still no response. She beat on the door with her fist. Still nothing. Her mind raced, *where is the key to the door?* She knew they had a key somewhere. She ran back into the kitchen to search the junk drawer. In the box labeled KEYS she found it. She raced to the bedroom door, which Allison opened as she grabbed for the knob.

Mrs. Kincaid was relieved and infuriated at the same time. "Allison, why didn't you answer the door? You scared me silly."

Allison leaned against the door's edge with her right arm raised and resting on the frame. Her left arm was crossed in front of her body. Her legs were crossed at the ankles. To an outsider looking in, it would appear that the daughter was casually speaking with her mother. However, from the inside the mother's face was revealing the pain she had been experiencing for months as her daughter had become somebody she no longer knew. Not only that, she was somebody she no longer wanted to know.

Mrs. Kincaid's eyes swept past her daughter and into the room. Shock registered on her face. She was not prepared for what she saw. The room showed no resemblance to the rest of the immaculate house. Clothes had been pulled from the drawers and closets and thrown onto the floor. Feathers from a slashed down comforter floated in the air. Books had been pulled from shelves and her daughter had painted her face white and garishly accented the white with large red lips and gashes of black paint where eyebrows should be.

Mrs. Kincaid cried and Allison stared at her. The first day of 2001 had become one neither would soon forget.

Chapter 3

The warmth in the apartment contrasted with the freezing temperature just outside the thin glass of the windows. January 2 brought a snowfall to the city. The windows were steamed. Mary Margaret always looked forward to returning to school after the Christmas break. However, this morning the warmth of the apartment did nothing to penetrate the cold she was feeling inside.

Mike and Cindy were unaware that she had overheard their conversation and their excitement was evident as Mary Margaret came into the kitchen and Mike announced, "Mary Margaret, Mama and I have something to tell you."

Cindy Smith was at her husband's side, and her smile indicated the joy she felt at the new turn their life was about to take.

Mary Margaret took her seat at the table. Her father continued. "I have gotten a promotion at work, and this promotion will require that we move. I will be the new President at a mill in Left Fork, South Carolina."

He said the name Left Fork like it was special, but Mary Margaret felt as though he was spitting the name at her. He was talking in excited tones. She couldn't hear much of what he said. Words occasionally registered with her, "New house, ride a school bus, new friends." What did she care about those things? She loved her apartment. School buses scared her, and her best friend was just a few feet away. Why would she want to leave those things to go somewhere she knew nothing about?

When it became apparent to her mother that Mary Margaret was not taking the news well, she took over the conversation. Also in excited tones she explained, "I have been promised a great job in a nearby hospital."

Mary Margaret silently wondered, *what's wrong with the great job you already have in the hospital where I was born?*

Her mother, too, began a chain of words, which were incomprehensible to Mary Margaret, except in short phrases, "New surroundings, great opportunity, own their own home."

Mary Margaret ate her breakfast in near silence. She had hoped that the conversation she overheard the night before between her parents had been a dream, but this day had brought forth the reality that they were moving.

Don't I have an opinion in any of this, she wondered. She dared not speak for fear of being sick.

Uh, oh, it was too late! She was going to be sick! Her parents were shocked as she bolted from the breakfast table into the bathroom to lose the breakfast she had just consumed.

As the commotion in the bathroom subsided, Mary Margaret's parents decided that it had been too early in the day to break such news. "We're sorry, we should have waited until later in the day," they apologized.

Mary Margaret could be silent no longer, and she shouted, "I don't want to move, and it wouldn't matter if you had told me at midnight, I still would not want to move!" Once she had found her tongue, she continued, "I love where we live. I love Charlene and Darlene, and I love Alice, too. How can you take me away from them? I don't want anything new in my life. I like things the way they are. This is a *pitfall*, and my fortune cookie said I had to watch out for pitfalls. This is bad. This is very, very bad."

By this time her parents decided that she was too upset to go to school that day. Charlene arrived, and they went off to work, leaving Mary Margaret in her care. Charlene didn't seem her usual self either. The day passed in near silence. Mary Margaret stayed in her bed most of the day. She snuggled under the covers and tried as best as she could to be absorbed by the comfort of her surroundings.

Charlene busied herself around the apartment. The festivities of the holidays had made it impossible for her to keep up with her daily chores, and she actually enjoyed the time to put the apartment back in order and to take down the now tired looking Christmas tree.

As the shadows fell across the windows, Mary Margaret woke up from a short nap. She realized that the room had become darker, and that Alice would be home from school. Alice probably wondered why she hadn't been at school. She thought about this and imagined that by this time Darlene would have broken the news that she and her family would be moving. Mary Margaret hoped that Darlene had told Alice, because she just didn't think that she could say the words. Just thinking the words made her sick. *Saying them will probably be deadly*, she thought. She couldn't imagine that worst words could be spoken.

The shadows lengthened, and Mary Margaret smelled the evening meal and heard Charlene in the kitchen. The aroma touched her in the pit of her stomach, and she realized that she was hungry. While she was sick earlier in the day, she had vowed to never eat again, but now that prospect didn't seem likely. She shivered as she got out of bed even though the room was warm. She hadn't realized how much warmer it was under the covers. She put on her robe and peeked out her bedroom door to see if either of her parents was home. Her mother usually arrived first, and her father would be home about an hour later. Nobody was there except Charlene. Maybe she could eat and go back to bed before her parents arrived.

She surprised Charlene as she entered the kitchen. "Is dinner ready?" she softly asked.

Charlene let out a small gasp and turned to look her squarely in the eye. "Dinner will be ready at 7:00 o'clock just like every other day," she announced.

"I want to eat now," Mary Margaret argued.

Charlene held her ground and continued, "It might be a good idea to put on some clothes before your parents arrive."

Mary Margaret was surprised by Charlene's attitude. She had never been abrupt with her before. This was a change. Charlene seemed angry, and it frightened Mary Margaret, who retreated to her room and back into her bed.

Just as darkness fell at about 5:30, Mary Margaret heard her mother's voice. She called out to Mary Margaret and Charlene that she was home. Mary Margaret did not answer, and she could hear a muffled conversation between Charlene and her mother.

Several minutes passed and Mary Margaret lay in the darkness of her room. A sliver of light entered as the door was opened by her mother. She walked softly into the room and sat on the edge of the bed. She could see the tousled hair as Mary Margaret lay with her back to the door. She reached up and combed her fingers through the tangled hair and began trying to explain to her daughter the reason for the move. Mary Margaret was determined that no matter what her mother had to say, she was still opposed.

"It will take some time for you to get used to the idea of moving. It won't happen for a few months, probably around Easter. We'll be taking trips to Left Fork before we move, and you can see for yourself how nice it is. Before long you, too, will like living there," Cindy Smith attempted to explain.

After getting no response from her daughter, and after exhausting all of the arguments in favor of moving, her mother left the room and softly closed the door. A short time later Mary Margaret heard her father, and she could imagine the conversation between her parents. Her father would ask about Mary Margaret, and her mother would explain that she had taken to her bed. Her mother would wonder if maybe moving was a bad idea. At that thought Mary Margaret agreed that it was a terrible idea. However, she knew that her father would disagree and the move would still be on.

She listened to the usual evening noises. Her mother was setting the table, Charlene was putting the pots and pans in the dishwasher, and her father was listening to the evening news. On the surface life seemed the same. The smells from the kitchen had permeated every inch of the apartment, and Mary Margaret's stomach grumbled in its anger of being empty.

She heard the door to the apartment close, and knew that Charlene had gone home. Almost in the same instant her room was flooded with light as her father walked into her room. He strode over to her bed and sat down. He never touched her, and he immediately began talking.

"Mary Margaret, as the head of the household, I have to make certain decisions. I have weighed each of those decisions to come up with answers in the best interests of the entire household—not just mine or your mother's—but I also included you in those decisions. I have made a decision about moving, and I feel it is in the best interest of the entire family. I realize that each member of the family will have to make sacrifices as a result of that decision, but the decision to move has been made, and I hope that you will eventually see that it is a good one. I will do everything possible to make the transition an easy one on this entire family."

"I do ask you for one thing. I need your support at home while I am away working and making a place for us to live. I need to know that you and your mother will be supporting each other in my absence. Please think about that."

Silence filled the room as he finished his lecture. She was afraid to speak because she knew she would cry. Her father realized that the moment was over, and it was time to move on.

"Okay, now, dinner is ready, and you need to please get ready to eat."

His frankness stunned her. Her father had never told her that he needed anything from her. Now he needed her support. The idea of moving still made her sick to her stomach, but she loved her father and mother and liked the feeling of being needed. Mary Margaret got out of bed, went into her bathroom, combed her hair and washed her face. As she looked into the mirror she thought that she looked a little different. *Do I look a little older?*

At dinner with her parents, Mary Margaret ate heartily. She was truly hungry, and Charlene was a wonderful cook. She had baked pork chops, sautéed apples with pecans, and made a warm spinach salad. Everything was delicious. Charlene had left dessert—dishes of warm chocolate pudding, one of Mary Margaret's favorite desserts. She knew by this that Charlene wasn't angry with her as she had thought earlier in the day. Charlene was sad, too.

Her mother told her about Left Fork as the family ate dinner. "It's a small town, with a population of about 3,000 people. Most of the people are

Into Addie's Arms

farmers. The mill is important to the town for steady incomes and its overall economy. It has fallen on hard times as foreign goods come into the United States, and t-shirts made in this country are more expensive. People in other countries work for less money, and the end result is that products can be imported and sold for less money than they can be produced and sold here. The company that daddy works for wants to improve the efficiency of the mill so that people can continue to work for decent wages and benefits and still provide a product that is affordable to the consumer."

Her mother explained that they would be buying a house, hopefully with lots of land. She said that they would consider getting a pet after they had settled in. She also reassured Mary Margaret that they would find a nice nanny there to help take care of her.

The little girl wondered if there could be a nanny outside of New York who knew anything. Charlene and Darlene had been born in Brooklyn and had lived their whole lives in New York. They knew everything. She doubted if they could ever find a suitable nanny. Anyway, she was nearly 10 and wouldn't need a nanny soon. She knew, too, that Charlene was more to her than just a nanny; she was someone Mary Margaret loved.

Her mother told her that she had spoken with someone in the hospital near Left Fork and had been promised a position as a surgical nurse when they moved. She went on to say that she was excited about the change and hoped that Mary Margaret would get caught up in the excitement, too.

"I'll be leaving next Monday to begin work at the mill. I'm going there every Monday and will be back here on Friday evening to spend the week-ends with my girls," her father explained. "You and your mother will be coming down soon to look for a house and to acquaint you with the area. I'm sure you'll love being there. It's a quaint town, and I need to know that I have your support while I'm away." It made her feel important to be needed, but the hurt and loneliness of moving were invading her soul.

After dinner Mary Margaret wiped the steam from the windows and looked down the two stories to the street below. The snow of the night before had melted, and the streets were glistening in the lights as the remaining water had turned to ice. She could imagine the crunch on the sidewalk as people hurried along in the evening chill. She shivered and decided it was time to go to bed. She was exhausted even though she had spent nearly the entire day dozing.

Chapter 4

Sharon Applegate shivered as she left her home that early January morning to walk around the side and up the stairs to the apartment she and her now-deceased husband had renovated for their children to use when they came to visit. Her mind was racing. She couldn't believe she had agreed to rent it to that nice young man from New York City. Her good friend, Sylvia Gilbert, had approached her a couple of weeks earlier and asked if she would consider a short-term rental, probably just until April, or June at the latest, for somebody who was moving to Left Fork to live in while he transitioned and his family looked for a home to buy.

Her friend, Addie, pulled to the curb as she started to open the door. She waited.

"Good morning to you, Addie."

"Same to you, Sharon. I can't believe you're actually doing this," the woman said as she slammed the door to her pick-up truck a second time.

"Well, I said I would, and I'm as good as my word," the petite homeowner responded.

The two women went into the apartment together and Mrs. Applegate put down the cleaning supplies she had brought with her.

"This place is too nice to have some stranger living in it," Addie chastised her friend. "It's no telling what they'll do to it. He may even have wild parties up here," she concluded.

"Maybe he'll invite me to one of them," Mrs. Applegate giggled.

"Well, all I know is that if it was my apartment, I wouldn't rent it to anyone. It's like a museum."

"Addie, he is such a nice young man. His name is Mike Smith. How much more all-American can you get than that. His wife's name is Cindy, and they have one daughter, Mary Margaret. I think it'll be nice to have a child around here for a while. I miss that, and I see my own grandchildren so seldom."

"Don't you begin to imagine a new family up here? They'll be here a few weeks and then, zap, they'll be gone and you'll be lucky to see them in the grocery store," she emphatically concluded.

This thought saddened Mrs. Applegate. She had already begun to imagine them as family, and she hadn't even met the wife and daughter.

"You may be right, Addie, but I have already said I would, so I will. Come on; let's get this place cleaned up. Nobody has been here since last summer. It'll be nice to have somebody here even if it is for such a short time."

Mrs. Applegate took the already clean sheets from the beds and tossed them into the washing machine. Addie started dusting in the living room and moved into the bedrooms. She looked around as she went. Original oil paintings hung on the walls. A crystal chandelier sparkled in the middle of the living room. The finish on the maple cabinets glistened and the stainless steel appliances looked as good as the ones in Rowell's Department Store. Handmade quilts of museum quality were folded and draped over the footboards of the twin beds.

"She'll be sorry. I just know she'll be sorry," the old friend mumbled as she continued through the apartment. "Not me, not me! I wouldn't be fooled by these folks. Everybody knows that New Yorkers aren't our kind of people. Nope, not me! I don't want anything to do with them. Nope, not me."

Mrs. Applegate was cleaning the bathroom and her voice, though a little off key made a joyful noise as it was heard above the flushing toilet.

"Amazing grace, how sweet . . ."

As if a conductor were directing, Addie joined it. The difference was that Addie's voice had perfect pitch. Each note more delightful than the one before. The toilet flushed, and washing machine shook, the vacuum cleaner howled, and the two old friends continued preparing the apartment for new occupants.

Mrs. Applegate silently prayed that her friend was wrong in her assumption, and Addie Jones knew she was assisting her friend in making a big mistake. However, the two friends were in one accord on their music, and the concert continued until the apartment sparkled from stem to stern.

"Let's go to lunch," Mrs. Applegate said when they had finished.

"Okay, we'll go to Grammy's if that's all right with you. On my day off that's one place I can go and know that the food is good and the kitchen is clean," Addie laughed.

The two friends got into Addie's pick-up truck and drove the few blocks for lunch. "Sharon, please reconsider this," the ever-persistent Addie continued. "He may be a serial killer for all you know. He may be looking for a quiet place to hide after committing some horrible crime. I really don't want to attend your funeral because of this."

"Addie, honestly, woman, you are the most untrusting Christian woman I have ever known. Have a little faith!"

"I have faith, lots of faith. It's just New Yorkers I don't trust. Don't you watch the national news at all?"

Yeah, I watch the Today show and that handsome man on there seems a lot like this man. What's his name, Matt? Yeah, that's it. Mike Smith is a lot like him. It will be all right. And, anyway, you're being prejudiced. You of all people shouldn't be prejudiced."

Addie sighed.

Lord, please don't let me be wrong, Mrs. Applegate prayed silently as they parked on the town square.

Chapter 5

Mary Margaret dressed in the uniform of St. Mark's Academy. Her choices were navy slacks, a plaid skirt or jumper and a white blouse with a navy jacket or sweater. She chose the slacks, shirt, sweater, and jacket as the condensation on the windows had frozen during the night. She knew that it would be very cold today. She pondered the ice crystals on the windows as she wasted no time changing from her pajamas into the uniform. Each of the round crystals was magical. No two were the same, and each was a work of art. They reminded her of the crystalline glaze on pottery by Bill Meadows her parents had purchased at a museum around the corner.

Breakfast was on the table when she went into the kitchen. Her oatmeal was steaming at her place, and brown sugar had been sprinkled on top. Her mother had placed raisins in the oatmeal in the shape of a face, and the smile in the oatmeal caused her to smile back. This had always been one of her favorite things. She realized her mother was making an extra effort to cheer her up.

Her father had toast and a cup of steaming coffee. The aroma of the coffee filled the room, and she wondered how something could smell so good and taste so bad. Her one taste of coffee on a previous occasion had proved disgusting, but her parents made it look good as they sipped it with breakfast. Her mother was having oatmeal, too, but the face was missing. The bowl looked sad. Unlike yesterday, nothing was said about moving, and breakfast was unceremoniously finished just as Charlene arrived.

Her parents left at the same time. Mary Margaret and Charlene were left alone, and Charlene began the conversation, "Mary Margaret, I know that you are moving."

As these words came from Charlene's mouth, Mary Margaret's eyes began to burn. Oh, no, she was going to cry. She hated crying. Sure enough, tears began to stream down her face.

Charlene moved closer and began to hug her. While they had been close since she was born, Charlene almost never hugged her anymore. *What is happening here*, Mary Margaret wondered.

Charlene stroked her hair and in a tone that was foreign to her ears, she continued, "I will miss you when you move, but I understand the reason for the move. I expect you to be strong about this decision your parents have made. I feel partly responsible for the person that you have become. I've nurtured you since you came home from the hospital. I've attempted to instill good values in you. Values that I feel are important in my own life; one of which is to respect your parents. I know that changes are frightening, but change can also be good, and I ask you to look for the good things in the changes that are about to take place."

She finished by telling the little girl she had cared for since her birth, "I love you, and hope that you will always have a place for me in your heart."

As quickly as the conversation began, it was over. Charlene announced that it was time to put on their hats and coats. Mary Margaret was stunned at the tenderness shown by her nanny. So stunned, that she followed her orders, got her hat and coat, and followed her down the hall to the elevator feeling more like a robot than the girl she had been just two days earlier. The tears were gone as they trudged into the cold morning air to see Darlene and Alice standing next to the curb hailing a taxi.

When their eyes met, Mary Margaret knew instantly that Alice knew she was moving. There was a sadness hidden behind a forced smile. Alice raised her right, gloved hand and waved an over-enthusiastic hello at Mary Margaret and Charlene. Mary Margaret knew that her parents had instructed her to be *happy*.

The ice under the tires crunched as the taxi pulled to the curb for its small passengers. Charlene instructed the driver with just two words, "St. Mark's", and she handed him some folded bills. He pulled from the curb leaving the two sisters standing there with almost frozen breath coming from their mouths as they talked and with Mary Margaret and Alice alone with him in the taxi. A few awkward moments passed before Mary Margaret spoke first.

"Alice, do you know that I am moving"?

"Yes, I do," was the whispered response.

Neither knew what else to say, and the two girls rode silently on to school.

The day passed without event. The strict discipline was a blessing as she had very little time to think about anything other than the immediate tasks. The day passed quickly, and soon she and Alice were again in a taxi heading home.

As they rode toward the apartment, Alice broke the silence, "Mary Margaret, when are you moving?"

"I'm not sure exactly, but it will be around Easter, and Easter is on April 15. I looked at the calendar last night. It's about three and a half months from now."

"I'm sorry you'll be leaving," Alice told her.

Once again Mary Margaret felt the stinging in her eyes, and knew that tears were close at hand. She smiled in spite of the stinging and through clouded eyes said, "I'm sorry, too."

A strange uncomfortable feeling settled in the taxi between the two small passengers. The change was already happening, and so far nothing felt good about it.

Chapter 6

Mike Smith left the following Monday morning. He kissed Mary Margaret and her mother goodbye, and the doorman was there to help him with his luggage. It appeared as though this was his moving day, and in some ways it was. He was moving toward a new job, home, and way of life.

Sadness filled the apartment as he left early that morning, and Cindy hustled to hide her feelings. She placed the raisins lovingly on Mary Margaret's oatmeal. Even the smiling face in the bowl failed to lift her spirits. Her father traveled frequently, but she always knew that he would be coming back to this home. Now he was going to start a new home for them. She was sad.

Charlene arrived and recognized the mood. She immediately set to her tasks as Mrs. Smith left for work. Mary Margaret walked to the window and wiped away the condensation. She could see her mother as she walked toward the hospital. She soon lost track of her as she mingled with the other people on the sidewalk. She looked up as a jet passed in a sliver of sky visible between the buildings and wondered if her father was on that plane headed to a new place called Left Fork. She wondered if other fathers were on that plane going to make new homes for their families. Sadness weighed on her shoulders.

Charlene announced that it was time for hats and coats, and Mary Margaret was glad. She and Alice had not seen much of each other, and she missed the closeness. Maybe today would be better. When they got on the elevator, Alice and Darlene were already there. They rode down together, and the sisters caught up on last night's news. The girls stood side-by-side and were quiet. The taxi pulled up, the money was handed over, and the girls were whisked away toward school.

"Daddy went to Left Fork this morning, and my mother and I will be going in another week. We have a long week-end for Martin Luther King's birthday, and my parents decided that would be a good time for us to visit. They think it will be a good idea for me to go there as soon as possible, so that I won't think of it as *foreign and frightening*," Mary Margaret said as she repeated her mother's words.

Alice had tears in her eyes as she told her friend, "I'm glad you'll be seeing where you're moving."

A tear rolled down her cheek, and Alice looked out the window, away from Mary Margaret. The rest of the ride was in silence, and Mary Margaret felt an even deeper sadness. She felt like she was losing her best friend, and she was sitting right beside her.

School was a welcome relief from home. She was busy and didn't have to pretend that everything was all right. Fractions were introduced, and the new challenge was a diversion. Math had always been easy for her, and fractions were exciting as she imagined that one-sixth gave you larger pieces of a pie than did one-eighth. She had always heard Charlene say one-half cup and one-fourth teaspoon as she cooked, and now it all began to make sense.

After lunch her teacher announced the science fair. The projects were to be worked on in teams and were to be completed by Easter break. The announcement of the due date made Mary Margaret's stomach seem to jump. She realized that the time frame between now, the second week in January, and Easter break, the middle of April, was growing smaller every day. Her teammates for the project included Alice, Jimmy Meador, and Billy Zitter. Of course, she and Alice would work well together, but Jimmy and Billy were different influences in her life. She had never worked on a group project. *That would be a change*, she thought. Oh, no, there it was again, that word *change*. She wondered if it would ever end.

After the teams were assigned, the groups got together to discuss their project and come up with ideas. Mary Margaret, Alice, Jimmy and Billy were assigned to a group table in the front of the room. They sat there looking at each other, none of them wanting to say the first word.

Mary Margaret couldn't stand the silence any longer and announced to her group, "I'm moving at Easter break." Of course, Alice knew this, and it was news to Jimmy and Billy, but not big news.

Jimmy said, "I've moved 6 times. My father's company moves him almost every year. I've lived in 7 different cities, and I'm only 9 years old." He was not at all impressed.

Billy said, "I've moved 3 times, and it's no big deal. What are we going to do for our science project, anyway?"

They looked over the suggested list, and decided they would study two plants, one of which would be given light 16 hours a day, and one of which would be placed under a box for the entire length of the project and given no light. They would determine which one grew better and why. They wrote down the description of the project on a piece of paper and handed it to the teacher. She approved their project and told them to determine who would be responsible for purchasing the plants, the light, supplying the box, and keeping daily growth records. Mary Margaret and Alice were to pick out two identical plants. The boys would provide the light and the box. They completed a schedule for taking turns making the notes. All of the supplies were to be brought to school the day after the break for Martin Luther King's birthday.

Mary Margaret felt a panic begin when she realized that she would be out of town before the date that the supplies were due. How would she be able to do her share?

That evening she told her mother about the problem with the science fair project supplies.

"I'll ask Charlene to get with Darlene to make arrangements to take you and Alice to get the supplies. They can probably do it on Thursday after school," her mother calmly offered.

On Thursday as planned, Mary Margaret, Alice, Darlene and Charlene went shopping for plants. They needed to find two plants that were almost identical. The boys told them not to get girly plants, whatever that meant. The florist shop was warm and smelled good as they came in from the cold. The smell of carnations and roses mixed with the musty smell of dirt to combine in a pleasant aroma found only in flower shops. The florist pointed them in the direction of potted plants. After looking over the selection, it was agreed that the peace lily was a good choice, and two nearly identical plants were purchased. Each plant had one bloom, and other buds were visible. The girls giggled with excitement as the selections were placed in bags to protect them from the cold on the walk back to the apartment.

Charlene invited Alice and Darlene to come in for hot chocolate. The four of them felt close as they warmed themselves by the radiator and waited for the chocolate to heat. All seemed right with Mary Margaret's world for the first time in many days.

Mother came home and after Charlene left and dinner was completed, she started packing for their trip. Mary Margaret began asking questions. "What's the weather like?"

"It's much warmer there. It's still winter, but the temperature will probably be in the sixties instead of the low teens here."

"It's strange that it's winter and warm. It's always cold here in the winter," Mary Margaret debated.

A look at the Atlas showed Mary Margaret how much further south they would be than in New York. "It's near the Atlantic Ocean, just like New York, however." Cindy explained that the legend showed the distance at 100 miles per inch, and their calculations indicated they would be traveling about 750 miles. Mary Margaret had never been more than 100 miles from home, and that was on their summer vacation to the shore. Despite her attempts to the contrary, excitement was creeping in, and she was anxious to begin the journey.

Cindy was waiting when Mary Margaret arrived from school on Friday. They were leaving immediately to go to the airport. Their flight was leaving at 6:05. Mary Margaret had never flown before; and as the time approached, she began to wonder what it was like, bombarding her mother with questions as each new one popped into her head. "What if I have to go to the bathroom? What if I get sick? What if there were no empty seats on the plane?"

As she expressed these fears to her mother, she patiently had answers for all of them. "The planes have bathrooms."

"Really, how do you flush them?"

Her mother explained, "Just like any other toilet, and there are holding tanks for the waste which are emptied when necessary."

"If you get sick, the flight attendant has little bags for you to be sick in. They are jokingly called barf bags. Don't worry about the seats. I already have boarding passes, and these passes show our seat numbers. We will be sitting in Row 15, seats A and B. One is by the window and one by the aisle. Which one do you think you would like to have?"

Mary Margaret couldn't decide. What would it be like to look from the window in an airplane? Maybe it would scare her. This was all becoming too much for her to take in. That decision would have to wait she finally told her mother.

A man greeted them at the taxi and offered to take their luggage for check in. Cindy accepted his offer, and she handed him her tickets. When he placed the bag on the shelf at the ticket window, she gave him some folded dollar bills.

The ticket agent wrote "Gate 72" on the jacket that held the tickets and returned them to Cindy. They rode on a train inside the airport. They got off at the correct concourse, and her mother kept repeating, "Gate 72, Gate 72" until she saw Gate 72. Several people were sitting there reading newspapers, sleeping, eating hot dogs, playing with babies, and just looking around.

The sign said Charleston, South Carolina—Leaving 6:05. "Mother, this says Charleston, South Carolina, and we're going to Left Fork," Mary Margaret implored nervously.

"We are flying to Charleston, South Carolina, and daddy will be meeting us there. He has a rental car and will be driving us to Left Fork."

Mary Margaret saw from the big clock on the wall that it was 5:25. They would be leaving soon. They took seats with the rest of the people waiting to go to Charleston, South Carolina.

The airport was busy. Mary Margaret watched as people passed by Gate 72. Some were running as though they were late. Others walked by slowly as though they dreaded reaching their destination. Children cried as their parents urged them along. Wheelchairs, being pushed by people in uniforms, passed quickly. The air was filled with noise as announcements were constantly being made. Mary Margaret was caught up in the activity and soon forgot about her own travels.

The announcement was made that boarding had begun for the flight to Charleston, South Carolina. Cindy began picking up their personal belongings and nudged her daughter.

Her heart began to beat a little faster as they walked through a double door and down a hallway that ended at the plane. The flight attendant greeted them and seemed glad that they were there. She looked at their ticket, took part of it, and motioned them into the plane.

They located their seats. Mary Margaret decided that she didn't want to sit by the window right now—maybe later. Her mother put her purse and carry-on bag on the floor under the seat in front of her, and helped Mary Margaret with her seat belt.

The other passengers boarded the plane. Every seat was soon filled. The door to the plane was closed, and the flight attendants came by to see that the seat belts were fastened, and that all belongings were stowed.

The plane began to move slowly. It moved around the airport, and Mary Margaret could see other planes moving also. The plane bounced slightly as it taxied slowly along the tarmac.

She could see people working on the ground. Some were driving little trucks which pulled trailers. Some trailers were filled with luggage, and some were empty. Men and women wearing ear protection and iridescent vests directed the planes as they pulled into or from the airport terminal.

Mary Margaret never realized before that it took so many people to run an airport.

The plane stopped. They were on the runway and Mary Margaret could see planes in front of them. The pilot announced that three planes would take off before them. After slowly inching forward, the sound of engines suddenly roared, and the plane began to move, picking up speed as it rushed down the runway. Mary Margaret felt that her body was being pressed against her seat, and she held on to her mother's hand. Her mother patted her hand and told her everything was all right. She felt a bump, and the plane was rising from the ground.

She fought the urge to cry as her heart beat faster, and the plane got higher. Soon the pull against her body subsided, and she felt as though the plane was floating. She was excited and maybe not as frightened as before. It was dark outside, and all she could see against the window was black. The inside of the plane's cabin was bathed in a soft glow from the overhead lighting.

The flight attendant began making announcements and a bell dinged. Mrs. Smith told her that now she could take off the seat belt, but it was better to keep it on while in the seat. They decided to leave theirs on.

A flight attendant came by and offered soft drinks and a snack. Mary Margaret wasn't sure what to do. She looked to her mother for guidance. She nodded her head in approval. Her mother helped her put down the tray table which was in the back of the seat in front of her. There was so much activity in the plane that her fears vanished.

After an hour her mother offered to change seats with her to allow her to sit by the window. Mary Margaret looked out the window and down to earth below. She saw tiny lights and asked her mother about them.

"Those are lights in and around homes and in stores and hospitals," her mother explained.

They talked about the states they would be flying over. First New York, then Pennsylvania, Maryland, maybe a little of West Virginia, Virginia, North Carolina, and finally South Carolina. The time passed quickly, and the announcement was made that they were preparing for landing in Charleston, South Carolina.

Once again, the sound of the engines changed, and it felt as though the pilot was applying brakes. As Mary Margaret looked out the window, the tiny lights began to get bigger and bigger until she could see the houses as the plane descended. She could make out the windows and everything was getting closer and closer. Suddenly, she felt a BUMP, and the plane seemed to be hurtling down the runway. Her heart jumped, and she looked to her mother for reassurance. She saw no panic in her mother's face, just a calm smile, and they touched hands. She felt the pull against her body until the plane began slowing, slowing, slowing and finally was barely rolling on the runway.

Except for the roar of the engines, the plane's cabin had been nearly silent as it landed, but now the passengers were talking and beginning to move around in their seats, picking up jackets, bags, books, all sorts of personal belongings. The plane taxied to the terminal and when it finally stopped, Mary Margaret heard another ding. Her mother told her it was all right to remove her seatbelt. They gathered their belongings and waited their turn to stand in the aisle and walk toward the front of the plane. The flight attendant smiled at them and wished them well as they left and stepped into another corridor which appeared to be attached to the plane.

They exited the corridor and stepped into the Charleston International Airport terminal. Many people were standing around excitedly waving and smiling at the arriving passengers. One woman ran to a man, and they kissed. An older couple rushed to pick up two children as they came from the corridor and hugged them vigorously. Excitement filled the area, and Mary Margaret held her mother's hand as they walked toward the crowd. Her eyes were searching faces. Her mind was asking many questions. "Where is he? Did he forget about us? Where are we supposed to go if he is not here?"

Just then she saw the wave and the familiar smile of her father. He ran toward them, and her mother and father kissed on the lips right in front of everyone. Before Mary Margaret could be embarrassed, she was immediately picked up by her father and swung into his chest in a bear hug. It felt good to be there, and her panic eased as they walked through the terminal. Her parents were talking as they walked, and she was walking as fast as she could to keep up with their pace but was failing miserably. They finally realized that she was having trouble and slowed down. Each parent held one of her hands, and the three of them walked through the airport to Baggage Claim.

When they arrived, Mary Margaret saw many of the same faces she had seen at the end of the corridor when they left the plane. These people were also waiting on their luggage. They all stood around a metal chute and seemed to be *willing* the luggage to come out as almost all their eyes were focused on the flap in the wall. Suddenly, a bell rang; the chute floor started to move and as if by magic, suitcases began dropping through the flap onto a conveyor belt, moving the luggage along in front of the waiting people. Mary Margaret saw the suitcase her mother had packed for them as it came under the flap and dropped onto the moving carousel. Her father stepped forward, picked it up, and pointed them in the direction of the door.

The car her father had rented was parked in a lot adjacent to the airport. It was dark and the evening air was much warmer than in New York. Mary Margaret's first thought was that it was spring.

The drive to Left Fork took about an hour. In the darkness of their drive, Mary Margaret glimpsed some large, old homes, which reminded her of plantation houses she and Charlene had read about.

"How was your first full week?" Cindy asked her husband.

"It'll take a lot of work to bring the mill up to the standards we want, but I feel it can be done. I like the people working with me, and they are hard workers."

After an hour's drive, filled with small talk and information he had learned throughout the week, Mike Smith pulled up to an old house with a large front porch. The yellow light on the porch was welcoming. The downstairs windows glowed, and the upstairs was dark. He explained, "I live in the upstairs apartment of this house."

They approached the front, and her father turned left before reaching the steps. "I don't use the front door. I use the upstairs entrance, which is around here." They rounded the corner and Mary Margaret could see the same type of yellow light on the second floor beside a door. They climbed the stairs, and her father juggled the suitcase and his keys until he found the right one that opened the door.

They stepped into a room which seemed truly magical as her father turned and flipped the light switch on the wall. A table lamp came on. The room was bathed in soft light which picked up the muted gold and green tones of antique furniture. The large mirror over the fireplace reflected the crystal chandelier in the center of the room. The walls were covered with art work which rivaled what Mary Margaret had seen in museums. It was a breathtakingly beautiful room. Mary Margaret and her mother gasped as they looked around.

After settling in, her father opened the refrigerator and took out a baked chicken and bowl of potato salad. He explained that Mrs. Applegate, the lady who lived downstairs and owned the house, had prepared some food for their arrival. She had insisted that she be allowed to do this to welcome them to Left Fork. They sat down and filled their plates. Mary Margaret realized that she was hungry. She chose a chicken leg, and her mother gave her a spoonful of potato salad. Her father added a homemade roll also furnished by Mrs. Applegate.

They talked about the plans for the weekend. Mr. Smith said that they would be meeting with a realtor on Saturday, who would show them some houses. He had seen a couple of them earlier in the week and already had a favorite.

The meal was followed by warm apple pie and ice cream also provided by Mrs. Applegate. Cindy said that she was anxious to meet this woman who was such a wonderful cook and gracious person.

"Mrs. Applegate is a widow. Her husband owned the local bank before he died. The apartment was originally a part of the home used by Mr. and Mrs. Applegate while they raised their family. After their children grew up and left home; and when Mr. Applegate retired, they decided to make an apartment for their children to use when they visited," Mike explained.

He went on to say that since Mrs. Applegate's children rarely visited in the winter, she had agreed to allow him to rent the apartment until the family moved there at Easter. His fondness for her was clear as he expressed his gratefulness.

"I don't believe I would have rented it to complete strangers," Cindy remarked. "She must be a truly trusting woman."

Mary Margaret wondered what she looked like and wondered if she would meet her tomorrow. She yawned as she carried her dishes to the sink. Her mother looked at her watch and announced, "Young Lady, it is well past your bedtime."

They went into what was to be her bedroom and found twin beds covered with matching handmade quilts. The blue and white squares had contrasting fabric which had been sewn together to depict a little girl wearing a hat. Cindy explained that the pattern on the quilts was the Little Dutch Girl. Small steps had been pushed to side of the high beds. After changing into her pajamas, Mary Margaret climbed up the steps and slipped between the sheets of one of the beds. Her mother folded back the quilt to reveal sheets with beautiful lace around the edges. She explained that this lace probably had been done by Mrs. Applegate. The bed was cozy as Mary Margaret's mother tucked the quilt up under her chin and kissed her good-night.

Chapter 7

Mary Margaret looked around the unfamiliar room and adjusted her mind to where she was when she awoke. This was comfortable and safe, and she remembered that her parents were in the next room. She lay in the bed and listened for sounds that they were awake. She heard nothing, but the smells from the kitchen alerted her that coffee was brewing and bacon was cooking. It was time to get up.

The family had breakfast and dressed for the day with the realtor. Mike Smith suggested that they dress in light layers as the day would be warmer in the afternoon. Starr O'Hara arrived promptly at 10:00 a.m. She was a strikingly beautiful woman with blonde hair, done up in a French twist. Her expensive red suit was adorned on the lapel with diamond-studded pins indicating the name of the realty company she worked for. She wore high heels and carried a large book which she called her multiple listing. Mary Margaret made a mental note to tell Darlene about Starr O'Hara when she got back home.

The grown-ups sat in the living room of the apartment and looked at the multiple listing. They talked about the houses and the areas in which they were located.

Mary Margaret looked out the window and was surprised to see bushes in the yard across the street with large flowers blooming on them. The flowers were a brilliant pink. She interrupted her parents and the realtor to ask about the flowers. Ms. O'Hara told her that they were camellias which bloomed during the winter in the south. Mary Margaret asked permission to go look at them, and her parents told her to be careful crossing the street and to not pick any.

She went outside and was surprised to feel the warmth of the air. The sky was clear blue with a few puffy clouds. The air smelled fresh and clean. As she walked down the stairs on the side of the building, she again felt anxious and realized that she was breathing harder, and her heart was beginning to race. Mary Margaret went around the side of the house to the front and saw a tiny woman bent over working in the flower garden. She wore a large brimmed hat which was adorned with roses. A scarf was wrapped around the hat and tied under the lady's chin. It startled Mary Margaret to see her, and she made a sound as she took in her breath. The lady looked up and smiled a warm smile. Her eyes were as blue as the sky and her cheeks the same color as the roses on her hat. Mary Margaret smiled in spite of herself at the sight.

"Hello, I'm Sharon Applegate and I'd bet my last rose that you are Mary Margaret Smith from New York City," the impish woman greeted her.

Margaret agreed that she indeed was Mary Margaret Smith and was from New York City.

Mrs. Applegate rose up from her squatted position and Mary Margaret was shocked to see that Mrs. Applegate was hardly taller than she. She was indeed tiny at maybe five feet tall. She was wearing a brightly printed blouse with a pale blue sweater over it. Her slacks were navy blue with patches on the knees. She was a sight, unlike any Mary Margaret had seen before, but she was enchanting. Her tiny hand was extended to Mary Margaret, and a reflex allowed Mary Margaret to take it in hers in a grown-up handshake greeting. Mrs. Applegate told Mary Margaret that it was indeed a pleasure to make her acquaintance, and she looked forward to their becoming friends.

Mary Margaret thanked her. "I'm going across the street to look at the camellias. I have never seen flowers bloom outside during the winter."

"Camellias are a southern secret," Mrs. Applegate whispered to Mary Margaret. "I have some growing on the other side of my house, and I will be glad to show them to you." They walked on the sidewalk to a closed gate.

As Mrs. Applegate opened the barrier, Mary Margaret could not help gasping at what she saw. The bushes were half as tall as the house. The leaves were dark green and looked like they were formed from wax. The flowers reminded her of big roses, but the petals were different. She had never seen such beautiful bushes in her life, and definitely never outside in the winter.

Mrs. Applegate immediately pulled her scissors from her pocket and began snipping the flowers. Mary Margaret was in awe of the speed with which she cut and placed them in the basket she was carrying.

Just then Mary Margaret heard the panic of her mother's voice as she called her name. Mrs. Applegate and Mary Margaret came around the corner of the house to see Mrs. Smith on the other side of the street looking frantically left and right. Relief flooded her face as she saw the tiny pair come into view, and they crossed the street to meet her.

Mrs. Applegate explained, "I didn't even give Mary Margaret the chance to cross the street to look at the flowers. I wanted to show her my camellias in the back yard. I am so sorry to have frightened you."

After that explanation, introductions were made between the two women. The brief uneasiness passed.

"I am looking forward to your moving to Left Fork," said Mrs. Applegate.

"We are too," she answered, sneaking a glance at Mary Margaret, who was basking in the warm sun and lost in the loveliness of the neighborhood.

"Thank you for the delicious dinner. Your hospitality is overwhelming. The apartment is more beautiful than anything I have seen in New York. I felt like I never wanted to leave the moment I arrived."

Mrs. Applegate glowed in the compliment, but before she could say anything Starr O'Hara and Mr. Smith came down the stairs. The ladies crossed the street to join them.

The day of house hunting began with small houses in the center of town. It was obvious to Mary Margaret that her mother was not pleased with the selections she had seen until early in the afternoon when they drove up the driveway to a house about a half a mile from town. The house was not visible from the road, and the driveway curved through a wooded area. Suddenly in front of them sat a beautiful two-story white farm-style house. The front porch reached from side to side and the brick steps fanned out from the pristine white railing. Three dormers accented the black roof line on the main part of the house, and a gambrel roof topped the addition on the side. Black shutters outlined both sides of each window and a red front door proudly marked the entrance. Cindy was excited as she hurried from the car onto the porch. A porch swing swayed gently in the warm afternoon sun, and Mary Margaret immediately decided that would be a good place for her.

It was agreed that this was the right choice for the family. It had 4 bedrooms, 4 1/2 bathrooms, and a bright kitchen, which overlooked a pond in the rear. The living room and dining room were on one side of the house, and the family room anchored the other. Mary Margaret's parents were excited as they discussed with Ms. O'Hara the steps that would be taken to buy the house. Mary Margaret's father confessed that he had already seen this house and secretly hoped that it would meet with their approval.

Chapter 8

The man stood motionless in the shadow of a large pine tree trunk as the realtor and her prospective buyers surveyed the house. He had just been leaving the wooded area when he noticed the big, black car drive around the curve in the driveway. He stepped back into the tree line and watched.

He saw the man, a woman he guessed to be the man's wife, and a child. "Well, Hood," he said to himself, "It looks like we may have neighbors. In that case, I guess we'll have to think about movin' on."

He watched the child sit on the swing he had admired from afar, never daring to be so bold as to try it out. His comings and goings over the past few months had been along the tree line and through the woods to come onto the highway away from the driveway. He had deliberately done this so that no attention would be drawn to the stranger being seen regularly in one area. After years of wanderings, he had become adept at eluding trouble. He really wasn't doing anything criminal—just camping in the woods. His tent was well hidden in the deepest part of the woods that separated this home from the adjoining one where the 2 boys lived. Their curiosity had been a concern to him when he selected his present camp site, but they had never come so deep in to the woods to discover him.

After a few minutes the adults came back outside. He watched the wife with interest. He had seen many people look at this property, and he had never seen any wife act like this one. She was happy. She stood back and looked at the house from every angle. She walked down to the large lake and even dipped her hand in the still-cold water. She walked over to the willow and spread her arms.

She likes this house, he thought.

The final giveaway was when they returned to the driveway, and she actually twirled with joy as her husband and the realtor shook hands.

"Yep, it's a done deal," he muttered. I'll be needin' to move on as soon as this old back gets better and I can carry my pack."

He watched as they drove away, and was filled with sadness even though he didn't know them. *Wonder where they're from? I'll bet they're nice folks. Sure seemed like a nice family*, he wondered silently.

After the taillights were out of sight he continued his journey, carrying his kerosene can to town to get another gallon. The nights had been cold, and the trips had been frequent.

"Maybe I'll move on to Florida. It's a lot easier to live there, but I do hate those snakes that crawl into the sleeping bag with you. It sure would be nice to stay right here."

Chapter 9

When they returned to the apartment, Mrs. Applegate met them. She was carrying a large bouquet of camellias in a crystal vase and insisted that they take them upstairs to brighten up the apartment.

"I would like to entertain Mary Margaret this evening if y'all would like to go out to dinner,"

"That's a wonderful idea," Mike accepted, without even asking for other opinions. It was decided, Mary Margaret was spending the evening with Mrs. Applegate, and her parents were going to dinner alone.

Mary Margaret was feeling left out. Nobody asked her what she wanted to do. Maybe she wanted to go out to dinner with her parents. Mrs. Applegate was a nice lady, but she wasn't sure that she knew her well enough to eat with her and spend the evening alone. Nobody except Charlene and Darlene had ever stayed with her when her parents went out. Her mind began to fill with all kinds of questions. *What if an emergency comes up? What if I get sick? What if my parents forgot where I am? Would Mrs. Applegate know what to do?* However, she remained silent.

The family went up to the apartment, and Mary Margaret could feel the sadness return to her body. The day with her parents had been so pleasant and being able to be outside without a heavy coat and boots was wonderful. Now this! Her mood swung to pouting as she went into her bedroom and lay on the bed. She pretended to be asleep when she heard her mother quietly open the door a few minutes later. She lay there until sleep overtook her, and she napped the rest of the afternoon. When she awoke, it was dark.

I wonder if I've slept so long that they didn't go off and leave me. Maybe they decided not to go out after all, she thought.

She got up and went to the bathroom. Then she went into the living room and was surprised to find Mrs. Applegate on the sofa. Mrs. Applegate explained that her parents hadn't wanted to wake her up, so she had come upstairs to wait for *sleeping beauty* to get up. Mary Margaret had mixed feelings about being left here with a stranger. She wasn't pleased, but Mrs. Applegate's good mood lifted her spirits.

She and Mary Margaret ate homemade vegetable soup, a delicious mixture of vegetables and steamy broth. That along with the homemade bread and real butter gave Mary Margaret a sense of wellbeing. It was difficult to remain in a bad mood. Mrs. Applegate was very good company and delighted her with her tales of her own children when they were younger.

After dinner they returned to the living room and Mrs. Applegate picked up a basket from beside the sofa. She opened the top and inside Mary Margaret saw different colored balls of yarn.

"Choose a ball of your favorite color," Mrs. Applegate instructed. There were so many that it was difficult, but Mary Margaret finally decided on light blue. Mrs. Applegate chose a pink ball and reached into the bottom of the basket to retrieve two metal sticks—one for each of them.

"These are crochet hooks, and I would like to teach you to crochet," Mrs. Applegate said.

"Did you make that fine lace on the sheets?"

"I did. All of my sheets and pillowcases have lace like that. I learned to crochet when I was a young girl and have enjoyed it for most of my life.

Mary Margaret moved closer to her on the sofa as Mrs. Applegate took the yarn and expertly wrapped it around Mary Margaret's fingers instructing her how to hold the yarn. She placed the hook in Mary Margaret's other hand; and as she held Mary Margaret's hands in her own tiny ones, right before their eyes a chain of crochet stitches began to emerge just like magic. When they had completed a sufficient number of stitches in the chain, she showed Mary Margaret how to move the hook into the holes of the chained stitches to pick up the yarn from the ball and begin another row of stitches attached to the first chain. Magically, in a matter of a few minutes the stitches had formed a small rectangular piece of crocheted material. Mary Margaret was fascinated. It was decided that they would make a placemat. Mrs. Applegate began to work with her crochet hook and the pink yarn she had chosen as she watched Mary Margaret turn her blue yarn into a larger rectangle.

At first the conversation was only about the stitches, but soon Mary Margaret was handling her yarn very well. Mrs. Applegate took this opportunity to ask about her life in New York.

She learned about Charlene and Darlene. She was told about the apartment building where she lived and about Alice, her soul mate and best friend, who lived in the same building on the floor above her. Harry is the doorman, and she rides in a taxi to St. Mark's Academy. Before the evening was over, Mrs. Applegate knew that Mary Margaret liked math, was learning about fractions, and was beginning a science project on Tuesday.

The evening passed quickly, and Mary Margaret's parents arrived at the apartment to find the two new friends on the sofa with yarn wrapped around their fingers. They were surprised at their daughter's good mood as she showed off her handiwork.

Mrs. Applegate left, and the family got ready for bed. As her mother tucked her into bed, Mary Margaret looked for the lace on the pillowcases and secretly vowed that her own sheets would someday have lace, too.

Sunday morning was another beautiful, warm day in South Carolina. The Smith family, along with Mrs. Applegate had planned to go into Charleston for a day of sightseeing. Mary Margaret was excited to get back to her crocheting, but was told that it would have to wait. They drove into the city, and she felt like she was in the pages of a book as they drove down the streets lined with beautiful antebellum homes each lovelier than the one before. They had lunch in a small restaurant that overlooked the ocean, and in the afternoon they went into the antique shops. While the day was warm in the sunshine, the breeze off the ocean was cool. The afternoon was topped off with a horse-drawn buggy ride. Mary Margaret had seen these in Central Park, but had never ridden one. It was so exciting to ride high in the buggy, in the open air, as the horse clip clopped along the cobblestone streets.

The ride back to Left Fork in the failing sunlight was quiet. The sightseers were tired.

"Thank you all for including me in this trip," Mrs. Applegate said.

"Thank you for being our expert guide," Mrs. Smith said. "Without you, we would have been totally lost."

Mrs. Applegate went into her home, and Mary Margaret and her parents went upstairs to their apartment.

While Mary Margaret sat down with her crochet yarn and hook, her parents began to prepare a light supper. Mrs. Applegate had left the soup from Saturday. That was heated, and the homemade bread and a salad soon filled their stomachs, and they felt comfortable in the apartment in Mrs. Applegate's house.

On Monday Starr O'Hara brought papers by for Mary Margaret's parents to sign. As the grownups discussed the business of purchasing the house, Mary Margaret went into her bedroom with the crochet yarn and again added rows to her ever-growing placemat. It soon became apparent to her that it was almost the right size, and she didn't know what to do when she was finished to keep the yarn from fraying. She went into the living room, "Excuse me," she politely interrupted. "May I go downstairs to ask Mrs. Applegate how to stop this? I'm going to have a rug instead of a placemat if I continue."

Her mother laughed and admonished, "You may go, but don't be a nuisance. Don't overstay your welcome."

Mary Margaret rang the doorbell, and the tiny lady with the infectious smile answered the door.

"Mrs. Applegate, I need some help to finish this placemat. Can you show me how?"

Mrs. Applegate was surprised that Mary Margaret had completed so many rows of stitches. "Child, you have done a wonderful job. It is so neat." Together they sat on the sofa to complete the project.

"This looks complicated, but it's not," promised Mrs. Applegate. You just take the yarn and cut it leaving what I call the tail. It should be 4 to 6 inches long. Then with your hook, you just stitch it back into the work you've already completed. It's sort of reverse crocheting. That will keep it from fraying." Within minutes the four tiny hands had completed the project, and Mrs. Applegate reached for her scissors on the end table and snipped the yarn. The placemat was finished.

"I have a surprise for you," Mrs. Applegate told Mary Margaret. She got up and left the room. She returned with her pink placemat and handed it to her.

"A placemat was my first project when I learned to crochet," Mrs. Applegate said. "I, like you, was 9 years old when my Aunt Edna took my hands in hers and wrapped the yarn around my fingers for the first time. I made a pink placemat then, and my Aunt Edna made a blue one."

From her basket she pulled out the two placemats, which had been made more than 60 years before, a pink one and a blue one. "I put them in my hope chest to use when I got married, but they were too dear to ever be used. My daughter never had an interest in learning to crochet, and they have remained in my cedar chest until you reminded me of myself when I met you on Saturday. Something about your wonderment at the camellias took me back to a time when I first noticed how beautiful they were. Then you took to crocheting, and it took me back to a wonderful time in my life. My aunt was dear to me and I learned a lot at her knee. I want you to have the placemats we made this weekend, and the ones my aunt and I made. I know that you will treasure not only the placemats, but our time together." She put them in a bag along with the two new ones they had made on Mary Margaret's first trip to Left Fork.

Mary Margaret hugged Mrs. Applegate. "I have to go back upstairs. My mother and I have to go to the airport. Anyway, I wasn't supposed to overstay my welcome and be a nuisance. Thank you so much." She hugged the little lady and kissed her quickly on the cheek.

Mrs. Applegate waved good-bye as Mary Margaret jumped off the porch steps and ran to the stairs on the side of the house. She ran up the stairs so that she could show her parents the wonderful gift from Mrs. Applegate. She hoped that they would allow her to keep the placemats, as she realized they were very, very special.

"Are you sure you want to do this?" Cindy questioned in a phone call to Mrs. Applegate after Mary Margaret's explanation of the contents in the bag.

"Absolutely," Mrs. Applegate confirmed. "Your child is so dear to me already. I know that we will have a wonderful friendship when y'all move here. I want this to just be the beginning of memories we both share."

They said their good-byes on the telephone, and Cindy allowed Mary Margaret to keep the exceptional gift, reminding her that a special thank-you note would be in order.

The trip to the airport was quiet as Mary Margaret and her parents digested in their minds the events of the weekend. Mary Margaret had learned a form of art that would be with her the rest of her life. With practice she would be able to create beautiful pieces. Her parents had taken the steps necessary to purchase their first home.

Cindy had always lived in an apartment, first with her parents, then with roommates at college, and now with Mary Margaret's father.

Mike had lived in a house with his parents while growing up, but had lived in an apartment since he left home to attend college, and now with his wife. Having their own home had been a dream that was now coming true. *Our life is so wonderful,* he thought. *My dreams are coming true. We've found a beautiful house, Mary Margaret seems happy, Cindy is excited, and I can finally feel that I am moving my family to a place where peace reigns. There are no threats here. Mary Margaret can go to school and play outside and she'll make new friends who'll make her feel welcome and a part of the community. I just know it!"* he daydreamed.

More importantly Mary Margaret had met a tiny little lady who had brightened what she had expected to be a terrible trip to Left Fork, South Carolina.

The plane ride home was not frightening to her as she was a seasoned flyer and knew what to expect. When they arrived in New York, and went outside the airport to hail a taxi, the cold wind brought them back to the reality that it was mid-January; and it was cold in New York City.

Mary Margaret and her mother arrived at their apartment just after dark. Harry opened the door and tipped his hat as they exited the taxi. He helped them upstairs with the suitcase and asked if their trip had been good. Mary Margaret surprised herself when she answered along with her mother that it had been.

Chapter 10

In the taxi ride to school the next day Alice was almost sullen. Mary Margaret was chatting about learning to crochet, about the horse and buggy ride and the new house with the porch swing and pond in the back yard. However, the quick trip soon ended and the girls struggled from their seats as they carried in the plants for their science project.

The next few weeks passed uneventfully. Time was devoted every day to make notes on the science project, and the teacher kept them busy. At home Charlene seemed to take extra time with Mary Margaret before her mother came home from work. Mary Margaret and her mother spent time together while she worked on her homework, and her mother made lists and arrangements in preparation for the move.

Presidents' Day was coming up and Cindy announced that they would be traveling back to Left Fork. Mary Margaret became excited to again see Mrs. Applegate and perhaps have another lesson in crocheting. The weekend arrived and Mary Margaret was undaunted by the flight.

After greeting her daddy, she inquired, "Is Mrs. Applegate at home?" She was disappointed to learn that she had gone to visit her daughter, Beverly, and her family in Georgia. Instantly, her spirits dropped. She wondered how she would fill her time.

After sleeping under the Dutch Girl quilt between the sheets trimmed with lace, Mary Margaret awoke on Saturday morning to hear rain attacking the roof. It sounded like nothing she had never heard before, and she was frightened. The smells from the kitchen told her that her parents were already up. She ran into the living room to find them reading the newspaper and sipping coffee.

"What is that racket?" she asked them.

Her father laughed and explained, "Mrs. Applegate's house has a metal roof, and the rain makes more noise when it strikes against metal than it does on regular shingles. The fact that we are upstairs makes us closer to the roof, and the sound is louder."

Mary Margaret was calmed by their explanation and wriggled between her parents on the couch. It felt good there.

The rain stopped by midmorning, and her parents decided they should go on a walk to get acquainted with the town. He said they could walk to the shopping district from Mrs. Applegate's house. In fact, he said you could walk to just about everything in Left Fork.

As they came down the stairs, the air smelled clean. It seemed as though Left Fork had just been bathed. In the yard next door forsythia, as it was identified by Mr. Smith, was the most beautiful yellow that Mary Margaret could remember seeing. They walked around the house and could see the tops of tulips and jonquils just poking through the mulch in Mrs. Applegate's garden where Mary Margaret and she had first met. While New York was still frozen in with winter, Left Fork, South Carolina was beginning to welcome spring.

The family walked the two blocks to the shopping area and was greeted with smiles and nods as they passed other people along the way. Their first stop was at the Left Fork Grocery. Mary Margaret laughed at the name. "Is everything named Left Fork?" she questioned. Her father insisted that they go inside. Mary Margaret and her mother wondered why, as they had seen grocery stores. However, they were entering a grocery store like none other they had seen before. The first thing they noticed was that the floors were wood. Mary Margaret had only seen grocery store floors that were covered with tile or were concrete. Cindy said that she felt as though she had gone back in time. There were no conveyor belts at the check-out lines. The groceries were placed on a counter, and the cashier pulled a board toward her. On the end of the board was another board which came across the counter; and as the cashier pulled it toward her, the cross piece pulled the groceries to her. There were no scanners. The price of each item was keyed into the cash register. The aisles were very narrow and Mary Margaret noticed that the grocery carts were smaller than usual, too. As they walked toward the rear of the store, they saw the butcher shop. Mary Margaret stopped in her tracks as she saw through the windows in the doors to the rear of the store the skinned carcass of part of a cow hanging there. She had only seen pieces of meat in the butcher shop in New York. She had never thought about it coming from a whole cow, and she didn't want to think about it now. Their butcher in New York took the pieces of meat they selected from the display case, wrapped them in white paper, and tied them with string. This seemed uncivilized to Mary Margaret. She wondered if Charlene knew about places like this.

As they walked on through the town they stopped at Rowell's Department Store. It, too, had wooden floors. It had two stories and a basement. The first floor had perfume, accessories, ladies and children's clothes, and the menswear and housewares were on the second floor. Furniture was sold in the basement. There was no escalator. The only way to the second floor and basement were stairs and an elevator, which was operated by a man who sat on a stool beside the door.

A small dress and hat shop was next door to Rowell's. The sign said Miss Dottie's Dresses and Hats.

The library was in a small building between Miss Dottie's and the barber shop. The police department was on the corner. They rounded the corner. On that side of the street was Jerry Lou's Beauty Shop. Through the window Mary Margaret could see a lady as she took curlers from a customer's hair. She presumed this was Jerry Lou.

The next building housed a bakery. Mary Margaret smelled it before she saw it. The smell of fresh-baked bread made her hungry. In the window was a 3-tiered wedding cake with a bride and groom on the top. Pink flowers cascaded down the side, and it looked like there were little pearls all over the cake. On either side of the wedding cake were trays of cupcakes and cookies. The hand-lettered sign in the window said that the special was cherry pie. A picture of George Washington had been glued to the sign, and Mary Margaret decided that she would like Pat-A-Cake Bakery.

Jennifer's Shoe Store was next to the bakery. In one window Easter baskets and bunnies were holding pastel colored shoes for women and girls. A baby mannequin displayed white baby shoes. On the other side of the door was a window where men's and boy's shoes were displayed.

The drugstore was next to the shoe store, and just past it was a store called Orville's Seed and Feed. In front of Orville's Seed and Feed were bales of hay, wheel barrows, bags of seed, and wash tubs as big as bathtubs which Mary Margaret's father explained were used on farms to water the livestock. The family made its way around the display in front of Orville's Seed and Feed and continued on around the square. The bank was next, then a jewelry store, a doctor's office, pharmacy, dentist's office, an auto parts store, a florist, and a restaurant called *Grammy's Country Kitchen* filled the last building.

Mary Margaret and her parents went inside and immediately were struck by the wonderful smells of chicken being fried, fresh vegetables steaming, and cakes made fresh that morning. They sat down and were immediately greeted by a large, beautiful woman. Her slacks and blouse were partially hidden by a red and white checked apron.

"Well, now, you must be Mary Margaret and Mrs. Smith. You can call me Grammy, everybody else does." She extended her hand to Mary Margaret and Mrs. Smith. "I am so glad to finally meet you all. Your husband and daddy has been keepin' company here for several days now, and it's about time we got acquainted," she said as she laughed at her own humor.

It seems that Mary Margaret's father had been eating at Grammy's Country Kitchen most of the time since he came to Left Fork. He had told Grammy all about Mary Margaret, her mother, and their move. Grammy brought them iced tea which was served in glass jars.

"Why are we drinking out of jars?" Mary Margaret whispered. "Are all the glasses dirty?"

"No, Honey, serving drinks this way is part of the *atmosphere* of Grammy's," he explained.

Whatever the atmosphere was, the tea was better. Mary Margaret had never tasted such sweet tea in her life. She drank it very slowly so that it would last through her entire meal.

"May I suggest the *special?*" Grammy asked.

Mike agreed, "That will be wonderful."

A few minutes later Grammy brought plates piled high with fried chicken, mashed potatoes and gravy, and what Grammy described as *fresh green beans*. A basket of hot rolls was placed on the table. She left to return almost immediately with a pitcher of tea, which she placed on the table for them after first refilling their glasses. Mary Margaret and her mother were amazed at the amount of food, and her father just smiled.

After the lunch dishes were cleared, Grammy brought each of them a piece of carrot cake with cream cheese frosting. "This here's carrot cake she said as she placed the first piece in front of Mary Margaret's mother. My sister, Sue Ellen, makes this and all our desserts fresh every day. Well, as a matter of fact, all our food is made fresh every day. We get here at 5:30 every morning, and we start to cookin'. We cook the whole day through, and close about 7:00 o'clock. We get some help along about 11:00 for the lunch and dinner crowd. We leave about 3:00 but everything is ready for the help to get it out to the tables with very little preparation. If you ever need anything special cooked for you, you just let us know. We do caterin' and have take out, too."

The cake was as good as the meal had been, and Mary Margaret and her parents vowed that they would probably never have to eat again.

On the walk back to Mrs. Applegate's house, the family went by the school, which Mary Margaret would be attending. Left Fork School housed grades 1 through 8. In grade 9, the students were bused to the consolidated high school out in the county. The school was a brick, two-story building. A dirt playground was in front and on the side were swings and a slide. A black, decorative, 10-foot high wrought iron fence surrounded the campus. The school looked sad on that Saturday when no students were there. In the windows, Mary Margaret could see cut-out snowflakes, which looked out of place on this balmy February day in South Carolina. Other windows had hearts, which were left over from Valentine's Day. A cut-out of George Washington's head filled nearly one whole window on the second floor. Mary Margaret wondered which of the windows was in her soon-to-be classroom.

Back at Mrs. Applegate's Mary Margaret went into her bedroom and lay on the Dutch Girl quilt. She put her hands under the quilt and felt the lace on the edge of the sheet. She was disappointed that Mrs. Applegate wasn't home. She felt lonely even though her parents were in the next room.

Chapter 11

Mary Margaret had fallen asleep and woke up just as somebody knocked on the door to their apartment. Her father answered the door, and she could hear introductions being made. She went into the living room to find a man and a boy standing there with her parents. Her father saw her and introduced her to Gerry Gilbert, the Production Manager at the mill, and his son, Philip. Mary Margaret said "Hello" and went over to sit on the sofa. Her parents asked their guests to have a seat; and as they sat in the chairs, one parent sat on each side of her on the sofa.

The conversation between the grown-ups was about the trip from New York, and the activities of earlier in the day. Gerry agreed that Grammy cooked about the best food anywhere, but laughingly asked them not to tell his wife that he said that. Philip sat is his chair and tried not to look at Mary Margaret. Mary Margaret sat between her parents and sneaked glances in his direction. She figured that he was about 9 years old, too. He wore glasses, and black high-top tennis shoes. His jeans were neatly pressed, and his light-weight jacket said Atlanta Braves. The next glance told her that his eyes were blue, and his curly hair was brown. He never spoke a word, and seemed more interested in the carpet than the people in the room.

Before leaving they were invited to have dinner with Gerry and his family the next day at about 2:00 o'clock. Her parents readily accepted, and Mary Margaret silently groaned at the prospect of being with people she didn't even know.

After a supper of soup and homemade bread, which Mrs. Applegate had prepared for them before she left to visit her daughter, Mary Margaret and her parents played Monopoly. After a couple of hours, it was apparent that

Mike was winning. He had hotels on both Boardwalk and Park Place. He owned most of the other properties and had nearly all of the money. He was declared the winner, and the family turned in for the night.

Sunday morning was bright in Mary Margaret's room when she awoke. The birds were noisy. She heard church bells ringing in the distance. Her parents were again sipping coffee in the living room and reading the Charleston Sunday paper. It was nearly 10:30, and after teasing Mary Margaret about sleeping the day away, the family had a quick breakfast of pecan rolls. Mike said that he had gotten them at Pat-A-Cake Bakery. They were wonderful. Mary Margaret's mother had heated them slightly. The sticky rolls filled with sweetened cinnamon and nuts were topped with a confectioner's sugar frosting. Mary Margaret decided at that breakfast table in the apartment of Mrs. Applegate's house that Left Fork, South Carolina, was a good place to eat.

At 1:45 on Sunday afternoon the Smith family got into her father's rental car and drove out of town to the Gilberts. Mary Margaret had dressed in a skirt and sweater, but her father had suggested that she change into slacks. This was strange because in New York, when they visited friends for dinner, she was always told to wear a dress. Mary Margaret had hurriedly changed into a pair of slacks and put on loafers instead of her dress shoes.

When she felt that the car was slowing down, she leaned forward in her seat to see where they were. Her father was turning the car into a driveway which ran between white fences. Inside the fence to the left of the driveway were black and white cows. Inside the fence on the right of the driveway were beautiful chestnut and black horses. The fence had x's between the upper and lower rails and seemed to stretch as far as Mary Margaret could see. She gasped as she saw the horses. Their hair glistened in the sunlight and their manes blew gently in the breeze. There were two groups of horses. One group had three horses and a colt, and in the other group were two huge horses. The horses must have been startled by the car because in unison they turned and ran. Mary Margaret could hardly breathe. It was so exciting watching them run.

"Daddy, Daddy, you didn't tell me they had horses," she gushed.

"You didn't ask me, and I didn't know it mattered," her father responded. "Should we not stay? Should we turn around and go back home?" he jokingly asked.

"No, no, you know I love horses. I want to stay," Mary Margaret said emphatically.

The car pulled in front of the house, and two dogs ran to greet Mary Margaret and her parents. A Collie and a Dalmatian circled the car and barked a friendly greeting. Their tails were wagging, and while they didn't appear threatening, to a family from New York City, it seemed better to wait in the car until someone came from the house. Almost immediately Philip ran out the front door and jumped off the porch. He called and whistled to the dogs, which ran to him and sat down.

Mary Margaret and her parents got out of the car and walked toward Philip just as Gerry came out of the house. He smiled and said, "It appears that you have just met Goldie and Freckles." They all laughed and Gerry motioned for them to come inside.

Inside the house the front hall was dark. They all went into the living room to the right and sat down. Philip was the last one through the front door into the house, and he battled with Goldie and Freckles to keep them out while he closed the door. Embarrassed by the commotion of the dogs, Philip's face was flushed as he crossed the room and sat on the hearth. A lady entered the living room through the dining room and extended her hand to Cindy. "I'm Sylvia Gilbert, and I'm so glad to finally meet you. I'm sorry we didn't meet on your last trip, but I knew you were busy looking at houses." It was obvious that she had already met Mike, and she greeted him warmly. She looked at Mary Margaret and said, "What a pretty girl you are, Mary Margaret."

Mary Margaret blushed, smiled, and said, "Thank you." A quick glance at Philip showed Mary Margaret that he was again embarrassed as he, too, blushed and looked away.

The parents talked for a few minutes and Sylvia excused herself to get dinner on the table. Gerry followed her and instructed Philip to entertain their guests. Philip blushed again and looked as though he wished there was a hole for him to crawl into.

Mike sensed the uneasiness and calmed it by asking Philip about the horses. He said they had three mares, two stallions and a colt. "Another mare will be foaling any day now," he explained. With these words, he again blushed.

Mr. Smith asked Philip if he rode the horses.

"I compete in dressage," he answered.

"Does your family own the cows?"

"No, sir, a farmer rents the land and barn space. He feeds them and takes full care of them. They just live here." They all laughed at that explanation, and again, Philip blushed.

Sylvia and Gerry reappeared and invited their guests to join them in the dining room. The table was set with beautiful china which Sylvia explained had been her grandmother's when Cindy asked about it. The crystal glasses sparkled, and the ornate silverware was heavy in Mary Margaret's hands. As she unfolded her napkin into her lap, she noticed the letter G embroidered in the corner.

Dinner was another filling meal of rump roast, with potatoes and carrots. Sweet corn casserole was passed around the table along with a sweet and tangy cole slaw. A basket of homemade rolls topped off the wonderful Sunday meal. Mary Margaret could not remember ever eating so much delicious food in such a short period of time; and as she thought that, her parents echoed her thoughts in words. Mary Margaret's next thought was that she had better not say that to Charlene lest it hurt her feelings.

After dessert of pecan pie, Gerry suggested that Philip take Mary Margaret to see the horses. Philip looked as though he'd rather walk bare foot on razor blades, but instead he looked at Mary Margaret and asked her if she wanted to go. Of course, she jumped at the chance. Boy or no boy, she was not going to miss a chance to be up close and personal with a horse.

Mary Margaret and Philip put on their jackets; and as they went out the front door, they were immediately greeted by Goldie and Freckles. This time, however, the dogs refrained from barking and just slightly nudged the two young people as they crossed the yard to stand by the long, white fence. While Mary Margaret and Philip waited for the horses to amble over after Philip called them, Goldie lay down, but Freckles kept circling and nudging until Mary Margaret leaned down to pet her. When Goldie saw the extra attention that Freckles was getting, she got in on the action, too. Both dogs knocked into Mary Margaret in their excitement, and to her absolute embarrassment, she fell down, right at Philip's feet. He laughed and reached down to help her up.

Just as she was getting up, she felt a shadow pass over her, and it momentarily appeared as though the sun had gone down. She looked up into the face of a horse as it extended its huge head across the fence and looked down at her. The body of the horse had blocked the sun from her line of vision, and Mary Margaret gasped. Again, Philip laughed, but pulled her to her feet. In a standing position the horse didn't seem as large, and Mary Margaret laughed, too.

Philip told her that the horse was named Honey. The colt ran up; and as he blushed Philip explained that this was Honey's baby. He reached into his jacket pocket and pulled out a bunch of carrots. Honey immediately nuzzled his arm until he put a carrot within her reach. She munched it and came back for more. The other horses kept their distance and wouldn't come close to the fence. Mary Margaret decided that Honey was her favorite horse anyway. Philip shared the carrots with her and together they fed the bunch to the big chestnut horse.

"What grade are you in?" Mary Margaret asked Philip as they stood by the fence.

"Fourth grade."

"Who is your teacher?"

"Mrs. Stancil. She is the only 4th grade teacher."

Well, at least I'll know one person in my class, Mary Margaret thought.

Their conversation was cut short as the parents appeared on the porch and called to them. They turned to walk back toward the house and Goldie and Freckles were up and away, too. It was hard to walk with the dogs blocking their paths at every step. By the time they reached the front porch, all the adults and the children were laughing. It was a sight to watch them being *herded* by the dogs.

Mary Margaret thanked Mr. and Mrs. Gilbert for the lovely dinner, and she and her parents got into the car for the trip back to the apartment. The sun was setting in the clear blue February sky, and she realized she was tired after being out in the afternoon air. The day had turned out better than she had anticipated. She concluded that Philip was not too bad, for a boy.

Chapter 12

Mary Margaret and her mother returned to New York the next day. She would not be going back to Left Fork until the move, but her mother was going back in March. Mary Margaret would be staying in New York, and Charlene was spending the weekend at the apartment with her.

A heavy snowfall blanketed the City when Mary Margaret awoke the next morning. It seemed silent outside as she lay in bed. The snow muffled the sounds of what few cars were on the street. Her mother came in to wake her up and announced that school had been closed for the day. Charlene would be there, but Darlene could not make it. Alice was coming down to spend the day at their apartment.

Mary Margaret got up and dressed in her jeans and heavy sweater. Her mother had prepared two bowls of oatmeal with raisin faces, and Alice knocked on the door just as she went into the kitchen. As Mary Margaret opened the door, Alice almost jumped into her arms. She was so glad to see her after the separation over the long weekend. The girls ate their breakfast and had just finished when Charlene arrived. She reiterated what the weatherman had reported that the roads were nearly impassable. However, Charlene lived near the subway and was able to ride over to Mary Margaret's apartment. Darlene relied on a bus, and the snow was too deep for her to get to the bus stop.

The girls spent most of the morning in Mary Margaret's room. Alice experimented with new hair dos for Mary Margaret. Darlene's influence was making Alice more aware of her appearance and that of others. When they tired of that, Charlene fixed lunch, and the three of them played Rook for most of the afternoon. They laughed as each had winning hands. The grand winner for the day was Alice with more than 5,000 points. It was difficult for the girls to maintain their composure when they received the bird and Charlene was a good sport at her own expense. It was an unexpected grand day for the girls and Charlene. They all realized that these times would soon be ending, but nothing was said about the move except when Mary Margaret told Alice and Charlene about being knocked down by Goldie and Freckles. They all laughed until they nearly cried as they imagined the sight and the embarrassment that she felt.

Alice had dinner with Mary Margaret and her parents. Her mother phoned to tell her to come home shortly before 8:00 p.m. The day ended with a hug as Mary Margaret walked Alice to the elevator.

The bad weather subsided, but it took weeks for the snow banks alongside the streets to melt. When Mary Margaret went outside the next morning, the snow bank adjacent to her apartment building was nearly as tall as she. Breaks had been cut into the snow to allow travel from the sidewalks onto the street. She could never remember this much snow.

Things became routine again for Mary Margaret until in early March when the school play try-outs were announced. They would be presenting an original play, and there would be parts for 8 girls and 6 boys. She was excited as her teacher made the announcement. That is, she was excited until the date of the play was announced—May 28. Mary Margaret realized that she would not be able to be in the play, and her eyes began to sting. She sat in her seat and tried to look anywhere but into the eyes of another person. She didn't want anybody to see her cry, but apparently her teacher noticed. When it was time for the class to go to lunch, she asked Mary Margaret to stay behind. She couldn't imagine why she had been asked to stay. She hadn't done anything wrong, but she was relieved when her teacher told her that she had seen she was uncomfortable earlier that morning and wondered if she could help. Mary Margaret again felt the burning in the back of her eyes and nose. Oh, no, this time the tears were going to come up big time she thought; and they did. As she blubbered through the words that her family was moving before the play; and she was upset about moving to another part of the country where she didn't know anybody; and she would be leaving Alice, and her nanny, Charlene; and the school where she felt comfortable, her teacher kept providing her with tissues to wipe away the tears. When she appeared to have reached the end of her list of reasons for being upset, her teacher told her that she understood.

Into Addie's Arms

"When I was a young girl, my father was in the military. He was transferred about every other year. It was difficult to move, but with each move I gained new friends and relationships around the world. Some of these have lasted my whole lifetime," her teacher explained.

This opportunity to express her fears freely seemed to calm her down and soon the two were on their way to lunch

Mrs. Smith left on Friday afternoon to fly to Charleston. It was mid-March, and the weather was beginning to show definite signs of spring. Mary Margaret and Charlene rode down on the elevator and waved as she entered the taxi Harry had hailed. Then they walked down the street to the Italian diner to pick up the pizza. Alice was coming over for another Rook tournament and pizza. Mary Margaret almost felt like skipping as they walked back to the apartment. It was a beautiful afternoon.

Mary Margaret won the tournament, and Alice spent the night. On Saturday, Mary Margaret, Alice and Charlene went to the library to see an exhibit of African artwork being shown by one of the tenants in their building. They went shopping at Bloomingdale's and had lunch at a tea room. The school in Left Fork did not require uniforms so Mary Margaret's mother had made a list of clothing she would need. They returned about 5:00 o'clock, and Alice went on up in the elevator when Mary Margaret and Charlene got off on the second floor. On Sunday, Charlene and Mary Margaret went for one of their long walks around the neighborhood. They returned to the apartment just as Cindy was arriving from the airport. The three of them had baked chicken and stuffing that Charlene had prepared. For dessert, she had warm chocolate pudding. Mary Margaret was very tired as her mother tucked her into bed.

The announcement was made on Monday morning of the people who had gotten parts for the upcoming play. Alice had tried out and had gotten a small but important part.

"All the parts are important," the teacher explained. "The play will be incomplete without any one of the performers."

Mary Margaret felt the burning, but knew that no tears would appear. She had overcome her disappointment by this time, and was very happy for Alice.

The science project was making great progress. The plant being given 16 hours of light was growing and blooming. The one under the box was yellowing and had no new blooms. Even the buds that were on it when they got it were shriveled, and some had fallen off. Mary Margaret and Alice wished they could remove the box and give it some light, but Billy and Jimmy indignantly reminded them that they had to keep it covered. Of course, they knew that, but they didn't want it to die. The teacher was giving the groups time to work on their project presentation. Each group had to present their idea, show the progress and the conclusion. It was a nice diversion from regular classroom work, and the four of them worked well together.

As April arrived, so did spring. The air was warm in the afternoons. Mary Margaret and Alice rode the taxi home and as soon as they changed their clothes, they went up on the roof of the apartment building. A terrace had been built up there, and it was like a small park, 6 stories above the street. There were swings and a permanent hop-scotch was marked. There were not many other children in the apartment building, so they usually had the space all to themselves. The little children had been there earlier in the day, and they and their mothers had already gone home. It was good to be able to be outside for a short while after school. It got dark very early, but the hour after school was wonderful up on the roof.

"I'll really miss you when you move," Alice told Mary Margaret on one of the occasions.

Mary Margaret was shocked when Alice brought up the subject as it had hardly been mentioned since the first days after the announcement.

"I promise that I'll write you letters," said Mary Margaret.

"I'll write you too," promised Alice.

"My parents say that I can call," said Mary Margaret. "They even said that maybe you can come for a visit when school is out. Charlene may come, too," she said as she continued to swing.

With each passing assurance, the girls became more excited. They made plans to stay in touch and remain friends for the rest of their lives.

Chapter 13

The day of the science fair arrived, and the girls were excited as they met downstairs to catch the taxi. Darlene had French braided Alice's hair, and Mary Margaret thought that Alice may be wearing a touch of lipstick. Her lips looked brighter than usual. They giggled as they made their final ride to school together. This was Mary Margaret's last day of school before she moved, and she knew she should be sad, but somehow she felt excited. She was glad that the science fair had coincided with her last day. The exhibition had been set up the afternoon before, and the judging was done after school. The girls wondered if their exhibit would be worthy of a ribbon, and nearly ran into the school to see. They entered the room and quickly walked to their exhibit. Billy and Jimmy were already there, and they were smiling. Four blue ribbons had been placed on their exhibit, and the critique attached to it said that the work had been thorough and well scripted. They had won first place in their class. The four of them hugged each other and jumped up and down. Their teacher came over to congratulate and compliment them on their work. It was a wonderful start to the day. The parents were invited to attend an open house that evening and Mary Margaret's mother and father would be there. She could hardly wait for them to see the ribbons.

The teacher recognized that it would be difficult to maintain strict discipline on the last day before Easter break, and the day that the science fair winners were announced, so the activities of the day were less structured.

Near the end of the day, she asked the students to put away their work. "We have one more bit of business to complete." She began talking to the students. "You have reached a point in your life when you are becoming more aware of changes around you. Nothing will ever stay the same, and sometimes it is difficult to make these changes," she explained. "I challenge you to always look for something good in everything you do."

With that, she pulled out a handmade book from her desk and asked Mary Margaret to come to the front of the room.

"Mary Margaret, this is a book that your classmates and I have made for you. I sent notes home with each student advising them that you would be moving. I asked that they each write you a note, either telling what your friendship has meant to them, or that they share an experience in their life that involved change. I put all their letters in this beautiful book and want to present it to you to make your transition easier." She hugged Mary Margaret. "Good things will come to you. You only have to look."

Mary Margaret was so shocked by this that she didn't feel the sting in the back of her eyes and nose as the tears flowed down her cheeks. She was overcome with emotion and ignored the tears as she thanked her teacher and her classmates.

The ride home in the taxi with Alice was quiet. Mary Margaret was anxious to be alone and look at the book. She felt that this was the nicest thing anyone had ever done for her. She told Alice that she wouldn't be going up on the roof, and that she would see her at the school open house.

She rushed into the apartment and the words gushed from her mouth to Charlene about the book. Together they sat down to look at it, and had just settled in when Mary Margaret's mother and father came in together. As this was her last day at work, Cindy had left early to be sure to get to the open house on time, and Mike had flown in early. They met each other on the sidewalk and had come up together on the elevator. Again, Mary Margaret explained about the book, and the four of them sat down to listen as Mary Margaret read the letters.

The first one was from Alice. It read:

"Dear Mary Margaret:

We have been more like sisters than friends as we have known each other since we were babies. You have always been there for me, and I will be sad knowing that you are not just a few steps away, but I will be happy for you as you make new friends in Left Fork.

You have taught me to share and love. We are soul mates. You are my first best friend, and I know that there will be others, but never another first. I will love you forever!

Love,

Alice"

Mary Margaret realized that her voice was cracking as she finished the letter. She looked up, and her mother and Charlene were wiping tears. She heard her father clear his throat. She was sad and happy at the same time.

The family, along with Charlene realized that they needed to hurry to get ready to go to school. In the excitement of the book nobody had asked about the science fair, and Mary Margaret decided to keep the blue ribbons a secret.

When they arrived at the school, the teacher greeted Mary Margaret, her parents and Charlene. Mary Margaret's mother and father thanked her over and over again for the wonderful keepsake book she and the students had made for their daughter. They told her that they couldn't wait to read all of the wonderful things the students had written.

Alice and her parents arrived. The girls exchanged knowing glances and each knew that the other had not told her parents that their exhibit had won the blue ribbon. The families eventually came together just as they approached the winning exhibit. The girls were so excited and Billy and Jimmy were already standing near it with their parents. Nobody said anything until Mary Margaret's father said, "Oh, this is the winning exhibit." Cindy knew instantly that it was the one the girls had prepared as she had seen the Peace Lilies when they bought them. There was a round of hugs and introductions as the four families became acquainted while standing around the exhibit. The discussion eventually led to the fact that Mary Margaret and her parents were moving. Everyone wished them well in their new location, and the teacher announced that refreshments were being served in the lunchroom.

As the evening wound down and the exhibits were being taken apart, Mary Margaret asked for the plant which had been under the box. She wanted to give it an opportunity to grow and thrive.

After they arrived back at the apartment Alice and her parents came in for coffee. It was a bittersweet time for all of them. They had been friends for many years, and this would be the last time they would spend an evening together as neighbors. However, the evening was exciting as the girls were honored for all their hard work. They reminisced about their friendship, and it was decided that Alice would come to South Carolina for a visit in July. Charlene and Darlene would be coming at the same time, and she would travel with them.

The final good-byes were said that night as Alice and her family were leaving very early the next morning to go visit Alice's grandparents. The girls cried and again promised to write every day. The parents assured each other that they would each allow the girls telephone privileges within reason. The final hugs were exchanged, and as the door closed, Mary Margaret knew that her life as she had known it for more than 9 years would never be the same. Charlene spent the night in the den on the sofa bed as tomorrow was a big day and she was needed there early.

The Discoveries

Chapter 14

The movers arrived very early on Friday morning to begin packing. Charlene was there to oversee and give directions. She would remain until all the belongings had been packed and were safely on the moving van. She gave directions like a drill instructor, and the movers dutifully followed them.

Mary Margaret and her parents left in the early afternoon to catch their flight to Charleston. They had lunch at JFK International Airport. The flight was delayed in New York, and they arrived in time for dinner. They had dinner at a lovely seafood restaurant and drove to the apartment.

"Mary Margaret, you will be happy to know that Mrs. Applegate is home," her father told her.

Mary Margaret's spirits lifted slightly. It was dark when they finally arrived at the apartment, so she knew that she would have to wait until Saturday to see her friend. She was tired and went straight to bed. As she lay there, she imagined being able to create that beautiful lace. She imagined that she would make something and send it to Alice. She planned to ask Mrs. Applegate to help her.

"We need to go to the house to meet with some contractors who have been working there," Cindy said early the next morning.

She was disappointed that she couldn't see Mrs. Applegate, but at the same time she was anxious to see where she would be living.

Spring had definitely come to the South. Mary Margaret almost gasped at the site of wisteria in the trees. The tall pine trees were wrapped with the beautiful lavender cascading flowers as the vines climbed the trees. The air was alive with the delightful fragrance. She had never seen anything so beautiful in her life.

The flower beds were filled with tulips. Everywhere she looked there were flowers. She felt as though she may have been painted in a Monet.

When they arrived at their new house, the contractors were just putting their ladders on their trucks. Mike and Cindy had made most of the decisions when he came to New York on the weekends. Hardwood flooring had been installed, and the whole house had been painted or wallpapered.

The house was beautiful, and Mary Margaret especially liked her room. It had been painted a very pale blue. She looked out the window at the pond below and was shocked to see a fish jump and splash back down in the water. She shouted for her father to come and see; but, of course, the fish didn't jump again as they waited and watched. He assured her that he would see it another time, and promised that they would get some fishing equipment.

Her parents finished their meeting with the contractors. It was lunchtime, and they decided that Grammy's was the place to go. When they entered, Grammy yelled a greeting of hello and welcome to Left Fork. They all laughed as she brought them glass jars of wonderfully sweet tea, along with a pitcher for the table. Grammy said that the special of the day was ham, but the family decided that fried chicken was more to their liking. She rushed into the kitchen and in a few minutes brought back plates heaping with fried chicken, mashed potatoes and gravy and those *home grown green beans*. The homemade rolls were placed in the center of the table, and the family devoured their lunch. They decided that they would not have dessert, but Grammy insisted that they take some carrot cake with them.

They went to the Left Fork Grocery to pick up some fresh milk and bread before going back to the apartment. The cashier immediately recognized them as strangers, and Mary Margaret was shocked as she pointed that out to them. She wanted to know all about them, where they were from, who were they visiting, and was pleased when she learned that they were moving there and Mary Margaret's father was the new President of the mill. Mary Margaret had never seen a person so interested in strangers. In New York nobody knew if you belonged there or not, and nobody seemed to care. She wasn't sure if she liked this attitude. It seemed a little nosey to her.

When they finally got back to the apartment, Mrs. Applegate was in the yard. Mary Margaret knew that she had been waiting for them. She hugged her in a way that until now she had only experienced with her grandparents. Mrs. Applegate asked Mary Margaret's parents if she could borrow her for a while as she had a surprise for her. "Of course," they agreed, and instructed Mary Margaret to not be a bother.

As her parents went upstairs, Mary Margaret and Mrs. Applegate went into the house. A large box was on the dining room table, and Mrs. Applegate immediately walked over to it. She folded back the top, and Mary Margaret could see an array of beautiful fabric. She told Mary Margaret that she had been saving the fabric for years. It was left over from projects she had worked on. One piece was from a suit she had made for her daughter, another was a piece from her daughter's graduation dress. She could remember what each piece had originally been used for, and she told Mary Margaret that she would like to help her make a quilt for her new room. Mary Margaret told her how much she admired the Little Dutch Girl quilts on the beds upstairs. Mrs. Applegate told her that she could choose that pattern or maybe she would like another one better.

The two of them went into Mrs. Applegate's bedroom, and she opened her cedar chest. Inside Mary Margaret could see neatly folded quilts, and as Mrs. Applegate brought them out one after the other, Mary Margaret would squeal with delight. Mrs. Applegate described the Wedding Ring quilt, the Flower Garden quilt, the Log Cabin, and the list went on and on until the bedroom was filled with beautiful artwork covering a rainbow of colors and a lifetime of history all stitched together. Mrs. Applegate explained that she had begun quilting at a very young age.

"My mother was in a quilting circle, and I sat at her knee and learned. Initially, I was only allowed to embroider words on a patch. As years went by and my talent and interest grew, I was allowed to do more and more. I have made quilts for my children and grandchildren, and many others as well. I feel it's a way of passing along history."

After looking at all the beautiful quilts, Mary Margaret still wanted to make the Little Dutch Girl quilt. It was agreed that she and Mrs. Applegate would begin working on it that very week as she did not have to go to school and her parents would be working. She would be spending her days with Mrs. Applegate. They would not be moving into their new home for a week. The movers would arrive with their furniture on Wednesday, and it would take a couple of days for them to unpack and set up the furniture. Mrs. Applegate told her that they could get a lot done in a week.

Cindy knocked on the door. Mary Margaret saw her mother through the screen door and rushed to open it. She then realized that it wasn't her home, and apologized to Mrs. Applegate for being so forward.

"Darlin' I am delighted that you feel that comfortable," said Mrs. Applegate.

Mary Margaret gushed with enthusiasm as she told her mother that she and Mrs. Applegate would be making a Little Dutch Girl quilt for her bedroom. Of course, her mother told Mrs. Applegate that it was too much for her to undertake. Mrs. Applegate insisted, and it was agreed that it would indeed be a very special gift.

Mary Margaret and her mother said good-bye to Mrs. Applegate and went outside just as Mike was coming down the stairs. As they all got in the car, Mike and Cindy explained that they were going out to visit with the Gilberts. Mary Margaret could feel her heart quicken as she remembered the horses. She dreamed of being able to ride one of them someday.

When they arrived, they were greeted by Goldie and Freckles, and on this visit they knew the barks were friendly. Gerry and Sylvia came around the side of their house, and motioned that they should come over there. They walked around and could see the doors of the barn were opened and Philip was there stroking a colt. It had just been born, and the mother was very nervous as the strangers approached. She was comfortable with Philip and his parents, but the Smiths were unknown to her. She began to whinny and circle her baby. It was obvious she was agitated. They stopped walking, stood their ground, and waited until she calmed down. She soon realized that it was all right to let them come near. They began to approach. She watched carefully, but allowed them to walk up. When Gerry said it was all right, Mary Margaret began to stroke its mane. She had never experienced anything more wonderful than to feel the new life under her hands. She could feel the burning in the back of her eyes and throat and knew that tears were close at hand, but she kept swallowing until the feeling passed. She knew her eyes had probably given away her emotions, but at least the tears never rolled down her cheeks.

The parents decided that it would not be good for the children to stay with the colt without them, so they all went into the house. Mary Margaret was disappointed at having to leave the barn and the colt. It had been so warm under her hand, and she could feel its rapidly beating heart as she hugged it. At that very moment she would gladly have moved into the barn. She was shocked at this feeling. She had always admired the horses she saw in Central Park, but had never experienced an emotional attachment to one. The only time she had ridden a pony was on vacation to the shore, and it was an old pony with a polka dotted bow around its neck. Its hair had been dull and it was scratchy on her legs. This newborn colt had aroused feelings in her that she never knew existed. She felt maternal and wanted to protect it.

She and Philip sat in the den watching television. Mary Margaret was bored, and she thought Philip looked as though he was trapped. Neither of them enjoyed being inside, and they were at a loss for conversation. Their mothers were in the kitchen and their lively conversation filtered into the den. Their fathers had gone to the mill to check on a new loom that was being assembled.

"Do you want to play checkers?" Philip finally asked.

This is about as exciting as watching paint dry, Mary Margaret thought, but her good rearing kept her tongue in check, and Philip brought out the checker board. He was equally as bored, and she caught him gazing toward the barn. They wanted to be there, but because she was unaccustomed to being around horses, they were both stuck inside.

Just as the fathers returned, the mothers began setting the table, and it was apparent to Mary Margaret and Philip that they were eating dinner together. Philip was kind enough to not verbally express his dissatisfaction with this situation, but it was obvious that he was not happy. He hardly said a word during the meal, and his silence was equaled by Mary Margaret's. As soon as dinner was over, Gerry announced that it was time to go check on the colt as soon as the table was cleared. The children jumped to their feet and began carrying dishes into the kitchen. The adults laughed at their enthusiasm.

When the table had been cleared, Philip and his parents led the way for the Smiths. They were escorted by Goldie and Freckles as they opened the gate and went inside the fence. The colt was sleeping as they approached and struggled to its feet on wobbly legs. Its mother was nudging it, and soon it galloped a few steps and looked back as if to say, "Did you see that?" They all laughed in unison. The attitude between Philip and Mary Margaret changed as they chatted about the colt and how beautiful it was. They suddenly seemed longtime friends with everything to talk about.

The evening ended with homemade ice cream on the back porch. Philip's father cranked as Philip and Mary Margaret took turns putting ice and salt into the bucket around the churn. Mary Margaret had never had ice cream that didn't come from a cardboard carton or yogurt from a machine. She was fascinated with the prospect of actually making your own ice cream. Mrs. Gilbert had mixed up strawberry ice cream, and when it came from the churn, it was bright pink with chunks of strawberry mixed throughout. As the dishes were filled, Mary Margaret and Philip served the adults until it was their turn to eat. Mary Margaret took several bites in quick succession and was struck with a pain in her head that caused her to moan. Everyone laughed and told her that she had experienced *brain freeze* and that she should eat more slowly, so it would not happen again. She began to savor the sweet flavor of that wonderful strawberry ice cream on the back porch at Philip's house. The air was filled with the aroma of wisteria, and as Mary Margaret and her parents got into their car to go back to the apartment, Mary Margaret thought she heard the colt whinny good-bye to her.

Sunday was spent at the new house. Mr. and Mrs. Smith each had chores that they wanted to complete before the furniture arrived on Wednesday, and before they went to work on Monday. Mary Margaret was left to explore the surroundings, but also was cautioned to be careful and not go near the pond. She soon found that a house with no furniture is boring. She sat on the floor in the kitchen as her mother lined cabinets and drawers with shelf paper. She sat on the porch steps and watched her father as he mowed the grass. She finally sat on the porch swing, and the gentle swinging lulled her to sleep.

As she slept, she dreamed of the colt. She dreamed that it was hers, and her father had built a barn near the pond. It was a warm day, and Mary Margaret and the colt were in the shade of a weeping willow tree. She was lying in a hammock. Dragonflies were darting about, frogs were croaking, and a big fish jumped in the pond. Mary Margaret felt the water from the splash. This dream was too real. She woke up to find that it had started to storm and the croaking frogs was really thunder, and the splash of the fish was rain being blown onto the porch by the wind.

She felt a big disappointment when she realized she had only been dreaming. She knew then that she really wanted the colt to be hers. She ran into the house just as her mother reached the front door to call for her. They nearly collided in the doorway. Mary Margaret's father came running in from the outbuilding where he had stored the lawnmower. It was getting late, and the family decided to go to a nearby seafood restaurant for dinner.

The restaurant was loud and crowded. They were told that there would be a wait of about 30 minutes. Mary Margaret watched the people as they sat near the front door waiting. Most of the people seemed to know each other. They all seemed to be able to greet another person as soon as they arrived. She was fascinated with this. Even stranger to her was that so many people hugged each other. She had never seen so much hugging. Even the hostess hugged the customers. Such familiarity was certainly not what she had seen in New York.

Finally, the family was seated and they all ordered iced tea. Glasses that were big enough to hold a quart were served, along with a pitcher filled to the brim with the second best iced tea Mary Margaret had ever tasted. When their dinners arrived, the plates were heaped with seafood. The cole slaw was tangy and sweet at the same time, and the baked potatoes were huge, with butter and sour cream dripping down the edges. This restaurant served hush puppies and corn fritters, which had been sprinkled with powdered sugar.

"I have never seen so much food served at one time to three people," Mike said as he reached for more hush puppies. They laughed as they continued to indulge. It was hard to decide what they liked best, but Mary Margaret decided that the crispy corn fritters with powdered sugar were her favorite.

They arrived at the apartment at dusk. Mrs. Applegate was getting out of her car when they pulled in. They all went up the walk together, and she invited the family in for dessert. They declined dessert, but agreed to a short visit.

"I have a friend, Addie, who is interested in the position as housekeeper," Mrs. Applegate told Mary Margaret's mother. "I would highly recommend her, and hope that you will consider her." It was agreed that they would all meet Addie on Monday evening at 7:00 o'clock.

As Mary Margaret and her parents went up to their apartment, Mary Margaret began to feel uneasy in her stomach. She wasn't sure if she had eaten too much or was just upset at the thoughts of meeting Addie. Charlene had always been her nanny and the only one who ever took care of her. Addie was somebody she had never met. There were too many new things happening, and Mary Margaret was beginning to feel as though her world was coming undone. As they reached the top of the steps Mary Margaret knew that she was not feeling well. Just as she had on the morning of the announcement, she ran into the bathroom and was sick.

"You probably just ate too much," Mrs. Smith said, but Mary Margaret knew it was more than that. She didn't want to meet Addie. She didn't want to be here. She wanted to be back in New York with Alice and Charlene. Her parents were both going off to work in the morning, and the only salvation to all of this was that Mrs. Applegate would be spending the day with her.

She dressed for bed and as her mother tucked her in, she felt the burning in her throat and eyes, and this time the tears rolled down her cheeks. She was tired of being brave for her mother and father. She had supported them and had done all that they had asked, but now that they were together as a family again, she felt that she needed to let out her feelings. Her father had asked for her support while he was away. He wasn't away anymore. All of the sadness and anxiety of the move struck Mary Margaret in that very moment. She felt that she might smother if she didn't cry.

Mrs. Smith was shocked as Mary Margaret began to cry. It wasn't silent tears rolling down her cheeks any more, Mary Margaret was sobbing. Her mother wiped her cheeks and provided tissues. She kept asking her if she hurt anywhere and what was the matter. Mary Margaret was crying so hard that she couldn't talk. She finally was gasping for air.

Her father heard the commotion and came into the bedroom. He, too, asked her if she hurt anywhere and what was the matter. Again, she just sobbed. Finally the sobs became hiccups, and she was able to say that she didn't hurt. Between hiccups the words gushed out that she was nervous about being there. "I am nervous about being with somebody other than Charlene. The new school frightens me. I have no friends. I miss Alice." The words continued until finally she calmed down enough for them all to talk.

"We're sorry we hadn't recognized your concerns earlier," her parents said. "Since you hadn't mentioned them, we assumed that you felt good about the move."

"I've been trying to be supportive, but inside I'm feeling confused," she explained.

"I miss Charlene, too, and we will not choose Addie to be our housekeeper without discussing it with you. You do know somebody. You know Philip, and he'll be in your class," they continued.

"He's a boy, and we have nothing to talk about," she argued.

"It will be different to be with all new people, but you will soon make new friends." her mother said. "I have anxieties about working with all new people at the hospital, too. Daddy was anxious when he first came to Left Fork. Now in a little over 3 months he feels like he belongs here."

She knew that she belonged in New York, and right now that's where she wished she was. Her parents explained if she was in New York right now, she would be in an empty apartment as all of their furniture was on a truck somewhere on an interstate highway between New York and South Carolina. At least here she had Mrs. Applegate's comfortable bed to sleep in, and tomorrow she and Mrs. Applegate would work on her new quilt. Mary Margaret finally settled down; and as she stroked the lace on the pillowcase, she went to sleep.

Chapter 15

When Mary Margaret awoke the next morning, it was clearly daylight. She looked at the clock and was surprised to see that it was nearly 10:00 a.m. She jumped out of bed and ran into the living room. Mrs. Applegate was snoozing on the sofa, and she smiled at Mary Margaret as she heard her enter the room. She sat up and said that they both were sleepy heads. They laughed. Mrs. Applegate told her to get dressed, and she would warm up an egg casserole she had made for her family this morning. As Mary Margaret dressed, she smelled the aroma of something wonderful coming from the kitchen.

When she returned for breakfast, Mrs. Applegate had set the table with lovely flowers. There were two places set, and Mary Margaret assumed that Mrs. Applegate would be eating with her. She was not wrong in that assumption. Each plate looked like a picture. A large rectangle of egg casserole was on the plate along with slices of cantaloupe, strawberries, and grapes. Raisin toast was cut on the diagonal and was perfectly placed on the bread and butter plate. Orange juice was just above the knife and spoon on the right side of the plate.

"I've never had egg casserole before," Mary Margaret explained. Mrs. Applegate said that it was one of her family's favorite things for breakfast, and it was always served on Christmas morning. She explained that it has sausage and cheese in it, and bread has been torn into pieces and soaked with the eggs, cheese, milk and sausage overnight. After hearing this description Mary Margaret was not sure that it would taste very good, but one bite told her she was wrong. It was wonderful. She and Mrs. Applegate chatted about their plans for the day as they ate their breakfast.

Into Addie's Arms

It was determined that they needed to go to the library, and while they were there, Mary Margaret could apply for her own library card. They needed to go by the grocery store, and then they could come home and start cutting the blocks for the quilt.

After cleaning up the kitchen they walked the two blocks into town and stopped by the library. Along the way Mrs. Applegate spoke to every person that they passed and stopped to introduce Mary Margaret to each of them. Mary Margaret knew that she would never remember all of their names.

At the library, the Librarian took the information for Mary Margaret's card. She was embarrassed when she realized that she didn't know her address or phone number, but Mrs. Applegate was prepared.

Mrs. Applegate checked out two books, and Mary Margaret said that she would wait until they moved into their new house to check out any books. The Librarian told her about one of her favorite books, *National Velvet*, that was on the return desk. When Mary Margaret saw the horse on the cover, she agreed that maybe she needed a book after all.

Then they went to the Left Fork Grocery, where Mrs. Applegate got a head of lettuce, some tomatoes, and milk. Mary Margaret avoided looking into the rear of the butcher shop just in case a carcass was there. They made their purchases and started home, and along the way as in the grocery store, Mrs. Applegate spoke to all who passed and introduced them to Mary Margaret. She was so confused by all the new faces and names that she had clearly forgotten each of them. When she confessed this to Mrs. Applegate, she just laughed and told her that she would soon know all of them too, and would be able to call each of them by name. She said that Left Fork was such a friendly town. It would be easy to make friends.

Upon arrival at Mrs. Applegate's house, it was clear that she was set up for quilt making. Her dining room table had been covered with a large cutting board that was marked with one-inch squares. Mrs. Applegate had fabric neatly folded on the dining room chairs, and there were scissors and something that looked like a small pizza cutter. She explained to Mary Margaret that this was a rotary cutter, and would make cutting the blocks for the squares so much easier and faster. She cautioned her that it was very sharp, and she was not to touch it without permission and never without Mrs. Applegate being there to help her.

When the books and groceries were put away, they started the quilt. Mrs. Applegate explained that each Dutch Girl was placed on a block, and that the blocks would be cut out first. She showed Mary Margaret how to stack the fabric on the cutting board and how to align it with the markings. Then she took a smaller cutting board straight edge and placed it on top of the fabric. She picked up the rotary cutter, and like magic, cut through all the layers of fabric. She moved the straight edge and realigned it, and with the cutter again sliced through the layers of fabric. Within minutes the white fabric was all cut into squares for Mary Margaret's quilt. Then Mrs. Applegate took the pale blue fabric, and once it was aligned, she held Mary Margaret's hands in hers, and together they made the cuts through all the fabric. Almost as quickly as before, the blue material was neatly stacked into squares.

Mrs. Applegate explained that when she learned to quilt, each square was cut by hand with scissors. It took a lot of time, and she recalled how tired her hands would get. She said that it took many days to cut all the squares that were needed for a quilt. She said that usually she would cut only a few squares at a time and then appliqué the pieces to form the Dutch Girl. Then she would cut more squares and so on until the quilt had enough squares to be sewn together. They concluded that this way was much easier and a lot faster.

Mary Margaret's tummy growled and Mrs. Applegate realized that it was nearly 2:00 o'clock. She announced that it was time to eat and went into the kitchen and began scurrying around. She asked Mary Margaret to set the table and instructed her as she continued preparing the meal. Mary Margaret had never set the table before. Her mother or Charlene had always done it. She realized that she had just taken it for granted, and rather enjoyed placing the silverware in the proper places. Mrs. Applegate told her that the knife blade went toward the plate. The glass went above the knife and spoon, and although they weren't using one, the bread or salad plate would go above the forks, which were placed to the left of the plate.

Mary Margaret recognized the smell of bacon, and Mrs. Applegate said they were having bacon, lettuce and tomato sandwiches. The smell was heavenly, and Mary Margaret was not disappointed when she saw that Mrs. Applegate had made triple-decker sandwiches. She had cut them in triangles and secured each piece with a toothpick. A long sliver of what Mrs. Applegate called bread and butter pickle was on each plate. Mary Margaret was hungry. This smelled and looked wonderful. Mrs. Applegate made chocolate milk for Mary Margaret, and the liquid chocolate clung to the inside of the glass.

When Mrs. Applegate sat down, Mary Margaret could wait no longer. She took a big bite of the sandwich. Mrs. Applegate laughed.

Mary Margaret was suddenly embarrassed as she remembered she should have waited for the hostess to begin eating before she started. "Oh, I'm sorry. I should have waited," she exclaimed.

"No, Child. You have just done my heart good to see you begin to eat. You reminded me of my daughter. This is her favorite lunch, and she could never wait to begin. I'm truly enjoying having you share this time with me," Mrs. Applegate assured her new friend.

The two chatted through the meal and Mrs. Applegate said that they had made such good progress with the quilt squares that they would not go any further with that today. This afternoon they would work outside in the garden and plant tomato plants.

"Mrs. Applegate, you can grow tomato plants at your house?" Mary Margaret asked.

"Yes, dear, I have grown tomato plants for my family for all of my life. We have always grown enough plants to be able to can tomatoes for winter. It is one of the greatest pleasures of summer," she assured her.

"I thought tomatoes only grew on farms. I never knew anybody who grew their own plants," the little girl continued.

"Well, you do now, and we'll grow pepper plants, cucumbers, squash and maybe some green beans. I've already planted lettuce and green onions," she explained.

Mary Margaret was anxious to get outside and see how this was done, so they hurriedly cleaned up from lunch and Mrs. Applegate put a roast in the oven to cook for dinner. She told Mary Margaret that she and her parents would be eating with her that evening.

When they went out back, Mary Margaret saw several squares of ground that had no grass and looked all broken up.

"Orville from the feed and seed store came by and worked up the ground. He brought the plants and the fertilizer," Mrs. Applegate explained.

She showed Mary Margaret how to dig the hole and put some fertilizer in the bottom. Then she put dirt over the fertilizer.

"This will protect the roots of the plant from being burned by the fertilizer," she explained.

She took the tomato plant from its container and placed it in the hole. She had a deep hole and planted it until only the top few leaves were above the ground.

"With most plants you only plant as deeply as the roots are in the potting container, but with tomatoes, you can plant them very deeply, and they will grow much better." She removed the lower leaves as she placed the plant in the hole. She watered the first plant, and they moved on to dig the next hole. They filled one square with tomato plants, and watered them all.

As they worked, Mrs. Applegate explained, "I garden in what is called the square foot method. My squares are four feet square, and I can reach any part of the square from the paths which separate them. The reason for this is to keep the soil from being compacted by walking on it." Mary Margaret was fascinated with the knowledge that Mrs. Applegate had about everything.

When they finished with the tomatoes and put away the tools, they went inside and washed up. Mrs. Applegate asked Mary Margaret to peel some potatoes for dinner.

"I have never peeled potatoes before," she was embarrassed to admit.

"I allow it's high time you learned how," Mrs. Applegate said. She got out a high stool and put it next to her kitchen counter. She placed some newspaper on the counter and gave Mary Margaret a potato peeler.

They laughed together at her first attempts at peeling, which seemed as though she was peeling air instead of potatoes. Finally, the cutter took away a piece of skin, and she was on her way. It took her several minutes to peel the 5 potatoes, and her hands were cramping when she finished. She had never realized how much work was involved in this.

Her cooking instructor peeled carrots and together they put them into the steaming pot with the roast. Mrs. Applegate grated cabbage and instructed Mary Margaret about slaw dressing. She said that she made her own dressing. She measured the mayonnaise, vinegar and sugar and added a dash of salt and pepper. She got out a beautiful crystal bowl and after adding a few grated carrots to the slaw, poured the finished product into the bowl and asked Mary Margaret to put it in the refrigerator. Mary Margaret got off the stool, and Mrs. Applegate handed her the heavy bowl. She was not prepared for the weight, and nearly dropped it. Mrs. Applegate had her hand under the bowl and helped her recover from the near disaster. Together they put the bowl in the refrigerator.

Mrs. Smith arrived around 4 o'clock. She stopped by Mrs. Applegate's to see how the day had gone. Mary Margaret was setting the table and Mrs. Applegate was putting a pecan pie in the oven. Mary Margaret rushed to show her mother the blocks she and Mrs. Applegate had cut out and told her that she had peeled the potatoes for dinner. Cindy smiled to see the difference in her mood from the night before.

They discussed dinner plans and the time that Addie would be arriving.

"I thought we'd eat about 5:30, and Addie will be here around 7 o'clock. We'll save dessert and share it with her if that's all right with you, Cindy," Mrs. Applegate finished.

The entire day had passed and Mrs. Applegate had not mentioned Addie to Mary Margaret. Cindy went upstairs to freshen up and Mrs. Applegate and Mary Margaret sat down in the living room. As they sat there Mrs. Applegate began talking about Addie.

"We have been friends for many years. Addie's husband worked at the mill, but he died at a young age from brown lung. That's a disease which has been linked to working in the textile industry," she explained.

Addie has 4 children, 2 girls and 2 boys. Of course, they are all grown now, and the boys live in Atlanta, and the girls live in Charleston. Addie has worked as a cook for a restaurant, but now the work is too hard for her. She has had a hard life and has never been able to live without working," she continued.

So what, thought Mary Margaret, but she kept this to herself. *Everybody she knew worked. Her mother worked. Alice's mother worked. Charlene and Darlene worked. Nobody she knew had a mother who stayed home. Her grandmother even worked two days a week.*

Mrs. Applegate could tell by Mary Margaret's reaction that she did not understand what it meant to work out of absolute need instead of desire.

"I hope you'll give Addie a chance before passing negative judgment on her," Mrs. Applegate implored. She knew that Addie came across with a gruff manner, but she also knew that Addie could teach Mary Margaret so much that she so badly needed to learn.

Dinner was wonderful. "We'll just plan on eating all of our meals with you even after we move," Mike joked. They all laughed, and Mrs. Applegate said, "I would enjoy the company."

Chapter 16

As they were wiping off the kitchen table, the doorbell rang. "Mary Margaret will you please answer the door and ask Addie to have a seat in the living room? We'll join y'all in a few minutes."

Mary Margaret opened the door to see a very large, square looking woman standing there. She was wearing a white uniform dress. Her hair had been put up at sometime earlier in the day, but was now falling down and had begun to curl from the sweat Mary Margaret could see on her face. Addie opened the screen door and walked on in. She hardly acknowledged Mary Margaret and came into the house yelling for Sharon.

"Hi, Addie. Just have a seat and we'll be out in a few minutes," the old friend yelled back.

Addie looked around and picked up a magazine. She turned on a lamp, sat down beside it, and began thumbing through the pages. Mary Margaret just stood by the front door staring at the guest. She had never seen anybody come into another person's home and act like this. *She acts as though she lives here*, thought Mary Margaret.

When Addie noticed Mary Margaret standing there, she yelled to her, "Hey, girl, are you going to stand there all night?" Mary Margaret was shocked to hear her speak and didn't know how to respond. She never said a word; she just sat down. Addie just laughed and went back to the magazine.

After what seemed an eternity to Mary Margaret, Mrs. Applegate and her parents came into the living room and introductions were made. Mary Margaret was the last person introduced.

"She sure is a quiet girl," Addie said embarrassing Mary Margaret.

By this time Mary Margaret was glad when she remembered she would have some input in this decision. Her input would be that Addie would *not* be their housekeeper. She was bold and brazen. Mary Margaret could imagine her as a bull in a china shop. She could probably single-handedly destroy their home.

She remained quiet and watched with amazement as her parents, Mrs. Applegate and Addie talked. Her parents asked questions, Addie answered. Addie asked questions, her parents answered. Her parents were smiling, Addie was smiling, and Mrs. Applegate was smiling. Mary Margaret wondered why she didn't feel the corners of her lips turning up. As the time passed, she felt herself sinking lower and lower into the chair. She didn't feel this was going well. Her parents seemed to like this woman. She knew that Mrs. Applegate liked her. When was she going to get her vote, she wondered. Her vote was *NO*!

Mrs. Applegate was suddenly saying her name, and Mary Margaret was shocked back into reality. When she looked up, Mrs. Applegate was asking her to come and help her serve dessert. She felt like a robot as she followed her into the kitchen. The dessert plates were on the table. Mrs. Applegate asked Mary Margaret to get the whipped cream from the refrigerator. She opened the door, and looked for the red and white container that always brought forth whipped cream at their house. When she couldn't find anything that looked like that, she told Mrs. Applegate she couldn't find the can. Mrs. Applegate laughed, and told her it was in the bowl on the bottom shelf.

Puzzled as to why Mrs. Applegate would empty the whipped cream into the bowl instead of squirting it directly onto the pie, she asked her. Mrs. Applegate explained that she had actually whipped cream.

"You can buy whipping cream in a container much like milk. If you whip it long enough and hard enough it becomes whipped cream. You beat it with a whisk and incorporate air into it. I add a little sugar, and voila, whipped cream."

After so many discoveries from Mrs. Applegate today, Mary Margaret was beginning to feel that she didn't know much, but she was sure Mrs. Applegate knew a lot.

She carried the dessert into the living room and Mrs. Applegate brought the coffee. Her parents and Addie seemed to be getting along really well. Mary Margaret was beginning to get that uneasy feeling in her stomach again, but had to eat some of the pecan pie. It had smelled so good as it baked, and the whipped cream had gotten on her finger as she carried the dessert plates into the living room. She had licked it off, and it was better than she could have ever imagined.

Just as Mary Margaret had the fork to her mouth to take her first bite of pie, she heard her name being called.

"Mary Margaret," Addie called as though she was calling an animal.

Mary Margaret jumped and the piece of pie with whipped cream fell into her lap. She was so embarrassed. Addie laughed, and Mary Margaret pleadingly looked at her mother. Her mother smiled an apologetic smile as Mary Margaret and Mrs. Applegate cleaned the mess from her slacks.

Addie went on as though nothing had happened and asked, "What are your hobbies?"

Mary Margaret stuttered, "I like to read, and Charlene and I take long walks in the City and study architecture." She looked up as she finished her sentence and could see a disapproving look on Addie's face.

With dessert finished, Addie left after explaining. "I need to turn in early. I'm working the breakfast shift, and 4:30 sure does come early." Mrs. Applegate walked outside with her friend, and Mary Margaret and her mother carried the dessert dishes into the kitchen.

"What do you think about her?" Mary Margaret asked her mother.

"I think she is a delightful woman. She presents herself differently from most of the people we know, but she appears to be a hard-working, honest woman," Cindy replied.

Mary Margaret silently agreed that she presented herself differently from most of the people they knew. She probably was different from everybody else in the world.

Mrs. Applegate came in and was chatting about how much Addie liked them. She told Mary Margaret's mother that she hoped this worked out between them as Addie really needed a change in her work. "Addie is getting up in years, and it's hard on her to work restaurant hours any longer," she added.

Mary Margaret and her parents thanked Mrs. Applegate for the wonderful meal, and for taking care of Mary Margaret. They went upstairs and Mary Margaret knew that there would be a family meeting. She had already made up her mind no matter what they said. She didn't want Addie as their housekeeper. She was not like them. She was gruff, and Mary Margaret was sure that she didn't know all the things that Charlene had known. *Addie is not the housekeeper or nanny for our family*, Mary Margaret thought.

She was right about the meeting. Her father asked her to come back into the living room as she started into the bedroom. He used his business voice now, and she knew he would control the conversation. He started by asking Cindy what she thought about Addie.

"Well, on the surface, she comes across as hard, but as I spoke with her I realized what a wonderfully wise woman she is. She has not had a lot of opportunities in her life, but she has utilized her wisdom to raise 4 productive children. Her children are all working and completing additional education. Two of her children are teachers, and one son is completing his Masters degree. One son is an accountant, and her youngest daughter is still attending the College of Art and Design in Charleston and works full time. I think this speaks highly of their upbringing. What Addie lacks in finesse, she more than makes up for it with hard work, and a kind heart."

Mike agreed with her opinion. He added, "With her having worked in restaurants for so many years I feel sure that she is a wonderful cook as well."

As her parents laughed, Mary Margaret felt that uneasy feeling again.

Her father turned to her and asked, "Mary Margaret how do you feel about Addie?"

"I don't like her. She is rude and bold. She just walked into Mrs. Applegate's house, turned on the lights and picked up a magazine without even asking. I think she is loud, too."

Her parents again laughed and began to explain to Mary Margaret that in the South things were done differently than in New York. They said that Mrs. Applegate and Addie had been friends for more than 60 years. Her mother said that Mrs. Applegate would probably have acted the same way in Addie's home. She said she was surprised that Addie had even rung the doorbell. She figured she would normally have just walked right on in.

Mary Margaret was confused by this. She and Alice had been friends all of their lives, but it would never have occurred to either of them to not knock when visiting the other. Her parents went on to explain that in small towns in the South, people visit without an invitation. Her mother said that Addie understood that Mrs. Applegate was busy when she arrived, and instead of bothering her with formalities, she made herself comfortable and looked at the magazine until it was convenient for Mrs. Applegate and them to join her.

Mike went on to explain that Addie had told them that she had a hearing problem from working around machinery as a younger woman. Since she didn't hear well, she tended to speak louder than other people felt necessary. He said that maybe a hearing aid would help her with this problem.

Mary Margaret knew by this time that she had lost in the final count. Her opinion had been solicited, but her parents' two votes to her one meant that Addie was going to be the housekeeper and her nanny. To add insult to injury, they talked about the possibility of Addie moving into the house with them. They said they could finish the bonus room above the garage into a small apartment for her. Mary Margaret felt that she must have missed something. She did not like this woman at all, but her parents were already making room for her to live in their home. Now the uneasiness in her stomach spread to the burning in her eyes and throat. She asked if she could be excused, before one or the other overflowed.

Tuesday passed quickly as Mary Margaret and Mrs. Applegate worked on the quilt for a while. They worked in the garden and went shopping in town. Again, Mary Margaret was introduced to all the people they passed on the street, and those who worked in the shops. There were so many people, and Mrs. Applegate knew them all. Mary Margaret was able to set each place setting without asking for help, and she carefully took Mrs. Applegate's *wedding china* as she called it from the cabinet and the heavy silver knives, forks and spoons from the drawer and set the table. She even attempted to cut up an onion. The onion had not worked so well. Her eyes burned, and she finally gave up in total embarrassment as Mrs. Applegate laughingly took over the task and agreed that maybe she was a little young for onions.

Chapter 17

Mary Margaret and her parents went to their new house on Wednesday morning to wait for the moving van. It was to arrive at 9 o'clock. Her mother and father took the day off from work, and they were excited. Mary Margaret was caught up in the excitement until she saw Addie sitting in the swing on the porch. Her mood immediately changed. She sulked as she got out of the car, and Addie yelled her greeting to them. She could not understand what her parents liked about this woman, but they greeted her enthusiastically, and for a moment Mary Margaret was afraid that her mother was actually going to hug Addie. The adults all went inside leaving Mary Margaret on the porch wondering why she was even there. She followed them in and could hear her mother and Addie in the kitchen. Addie was saying what a beautiful kitchen it was. She was opening and closing cabinet doors just as though it was her own house. Mary Margaret thought that Addie and her mother looked more like friends than an employer and employee. She remembered that her mother and Charlene had been friends, but Charlene knew her place. Mary Margaret was shocked when she heard Addie ask her mother how much money would she be given a week to buy groceries. Mary Margaret had never heard money discussed with Charlene. When she needed groceries, she went to the neighborhood market, and the groceries were charged to the family's account. Then they were delivered. Sometimes Charlene just phoned the market, and they delivered the groceries. The same with the laundry. Charlene knew better than to ask questions like that. Her parents took care of everything, and she just got what they needed. The thing that Mary Margaret found so odd was that her mother was not fazed by the fact that Addie was prying into their business.

The moving van arrived right on time, and as the furniture was unloaded Addie stood at the door and directed the men. Each box had a number which corresponded to a number on a map of the house that Addie was reading. The living room was number 1, the dining room number 2, the kitchen 3, the den number 4, and each of the bedrooms had a number. Some of the boxes just said garage or outbuilding. Addie would see the numbers almost before the boxes were out of the truck, and she was pointing the way as the men came through the door. As the furniture was unloaded, Cindy was there with Addie, and she directed the men to the proper rooms. Within a few hours, the truck was unloaded, and the house was full of boxes and furniture. As the men carried in the furniture and were directed to the proper rooms, Addie followed them and told them where to place each piece.

Mary Margaret walked around the house and she could see that in all of the chaos, there was order. The furniture placement did seem to work, and the boxes were neatly stacked in each room so that they were not in the way. Addie had seen that the beds were assembled as they were brought into each bedroom, and when Mary Margaret walked by her parents' room, Addie was putting sheets on the bed.

Addie saw her and called, "Mary Margaret, come in here and help me make this bed."

Mary Margaret was in shock as she walked around the bed. She didn't know how to make a bed. Charlene had always done it. As she stood beside the bed Addie asked her, "What's wrong? Why aren't you helping?"

"I don't know what to do," she responded.

"Grab hold of the end of the sheet and wrap it around the corner of the mattress," Addie instructed.

She pulled and tugged and finally got it somewhat over the corner of the mattress. By this time Addie was at the opposite corner of the bed and pulled off the corner that Mary Margaret had just put on. Addie snorted as she looked at her in disbelief.

"Try it again," Addie ordered, and she folded her arms and waited. Eventually, the two of them wrestled the bottom sheet on the bed. Addie picked up the top sheet and snapped it as she unfolded it across the bed. Mary Margaret jumped when she heard the sheet snap. She had seen Charlene make beds in her apartment in New York, but she had never heard the sheets snap. Addie instructed Mary Margaret how to fold the corners at the bottom of the bed, and together they folded down the top sheet. "That's enough for this room," Addie announced. "You go get the sheets for your bed and make it."

This was more than Mary Margaret could take, and instead of going to her room, she ran to find her mother. By the time she found her in the den, tears were streaming down her face, and she could hardly get the words out. Her mother finally understood that Addie had told to make her own bed, and to Mary Margaret's shock, Cindy said, "That's a wonderful idea. The sheets are in the box in your room marked linens. You can choose whatever set you want."

Mary Margaret started to protest, but her father walked in and asked her mother to come outside and give him her opinion on something. Mary Margaret knew it was a losing battle at that point and went back upstairs to make her bed.

She found the linens box in her room and after removing the tape, she looked in and saw beautiful new white eyelet sheets. There was a note attached from Charlene. It read . . .

"Dear Mary Margaret:

I wanted to give you something that would give you comfort in your new surroundings. These sheets don't have crocheted lace like the ones at Mrs. Applegate's, but they are close. As you sleep on these, please know that I am thinking about you, and am looking forward to visiting with you in July.

I love you! Charlene."

Mary Margaret unfolded the sheet and wrapped it around her. She knew she could smell Charlene. There was a faint hint of perfume, and it made her happy and sad at the same time. As she was caressing the sheet, Addie walked by and told her not to dawdle as there was lots of work to be done. The spell was broken, and Mary Margaret began to make her bed. As she completed the final corner of the bottom sheet, she looked across the smooth mattress and thought she had done a pretty good job. She got the top sheet and carefully unfolded it on the bed. She didn't snap it. It was too fine for that. She tucked in the bottom of the sheet and carefully folded down the top so that the eyelet was evenly placed across the bed. She found her pillows and put the cases on them and was standing there admiring the bed when Addie walked by again.

"Start unpacking your clothes and put them in the dresser drawers," was her command on this pass. Mary Margaret had never even put away laundry before. She looked at the boxes and the empty drawers, and she knew that she could never do it all. She opened a box and found another note from Charlene. This one said, *"Mary Margaret, this box has all of your underwear in it. Please put it in the underwear drawer."* Mary Margaret looked at her dresser; she knew exactly what Charlene meant. The top left drawer of the dresser was her underwear drawer. She took the box over and in a matter of minutes; she had emptied the contents of the box into the drawer. She opened another box, and it contained her socks. Charlene had written another note, "These all go in your sock drawer." Immediately, Mary Margaret went to the top right drawer of the dresser and put her socks in the sock drawer. As she opened each box, Charlene had written her a note and reminded her where each thing went. In no time at all, the boxes were emptied, and Mary Margaret's clothes were all put away. Her mother came up as she was finishing and was amazed to find the room so well organized. Mary Margaret showed her the sheets and the notes that Charlene had written. The burning was in her eyes and throat again, but this time it was because she had been so loved, and she was so proud at her accomplishments.

Addie came by as they looked at the notes, and called in to Mary Margaret, "If you're finished, there's more to be done in the bathroom closet." Cindy hugged her daughter and said that she would help. Together they went to the bathroom closet; and as Mary Margaret handed towels to her mother, she placed them on the shelves. When they had finished, her mother suggested that she go to the mailbox and get the mail.

At Mary Margaret's apartment in New York, the mail was delivered to boxes in the lobby. Each tenant had their own box and key. Her father always brought up the mail when he came home from work. Mary Margaret had not seen a mailbox on this house and asked, "Where is the mailbox?"

"You'll have to walk to the end of the driveway, and it's on a post next to the road. Don't get into the road," her mother cautioned.

Mary Margaret had never walked to the end of the driveway before. In fact, as she thought about it, she had never been allowed outside by herself before coming here. Somebody always was with her in New York.

The driveway curved and part of it was hidden from the house. She rounded the curve and looked back. She could not see the house. She felt panicky, stopped, took a couple of steps back, saw the house, and went forward to the road. A pickup truck went by as she reached the end of the driveway, and the driver honked and waved. Following her mother's instructions, she stood beside the box, opened the door, and to her surprise, there was mail. She wondered who knew they lived there. She carried the mail back up the driveway and took it into the house. Her mother was waiting to see how the trip had gone.

Cindy put the mail on the desk and announced, "We have done enough for today. Let's go back to the apartment." She gave Addie a key and told her to leave when she felt like it.

Mary Margaret and her parents went back to the apartment and cleaned up for dinner with Mrs. Applegate.

Mary Margaret went downstairs to see if Mrs. Applegate needed help setting the table. She was delighted to see her and said, "I have saved that job for you." Mary Margaret got down the wedding china, got out the silver and set about creating proper place settings. Mrs. Applegate watched from the corner of her eye and smiled as Mary Margaret hummed and went about her task. She seemed to take such pride in creating a beautiful table setting.

Dinner was baked chicken, and Mrs. Applegate told Mary Margaret that she had made dressing. Mary Margaret was not sure what dressing was, but didn't want to ask. She figured she would find out soon enough. Her parents came down in a few minutes, and her father said it smelled like Thanksgiving. Mrs. Applegate laughed and said it almost was.

Mary Margaret learned that dressing was what her family referred to as stuffing they put inside a turkey, not in a casserole. It sure was good like this, and Mary Margaret realized that she was really hungry. She had a chicken leg, dressing, mashed potatoes and gravy, and corn. Mrs. Applegate had made dinner rolls, and Mary Margaret ate two of those. Her parents joked that if she kept eating like that, her new clothes wouldn't fit for long.

That comment reminded Mary Margaret that she would be going to a new school in a few days; and she got that anxious, uneasy feeling again. It didn't last long because her father said they were going out to visit with the Gilberts for a little while this evening and asked Mrs. Applegate to join them. She said that she would love to go, and after they hurriedly cleaned up the kitchen, they all got in the car and headed out.

As they pulled into the driveway, Mary Margaret searched the area beside the fence for the horse and her foal. Over in the far corner of the pasture, she saw them and was surprised to see how much larger in only a few days the foal had gotten. The mare heard the car and looked in their direction. She moved around in front of the foal as if to protect it. When they got to the house, Goldie and Freckles ran up to greet them. They got out, and Mike took Mrs. Applegate's arm. The dogs were walking between them and around their legs, and their tails were beating into them as they passed. It was hard to walk, but the sheer joy the dogs displayed at seeing them was contagious and they all laughed as they made their way to the porch.

Gerry Gilbert came out and called to the dogs, but by that time they were on the porch, and the dogs had begun to settle down. Goldie was already lying down, but Freckles was still circling Mary Margaret. She bent down to pet her, and Freckles literally flopped onto her back for Mary Margaret to rub her belly. She sat on the porch and petted Freckles. Goldie got up and moved over closer so that Mary Margaret could pet her, too. Philip came out and sat down beside Goldie. He started petting her, and Mary Margaret asked him how the foal was doing. He said she was great and asked her if she wanted to go see for herself. Of course, Mary Margaret jumped up and was already down the steps before Philip could get up. Freckles was again running circles around her and barking. This continued until they reached the fence.

The horses all moved in their direction, and Philip reached into a sack he was carrying across his shoulder and pulled out a bunch of carrots and gave them to Mary Margaret. He reminded her to hold her hand flat as she gave them to the horses; and as she did, she giggled as the horse's lips gently touched the palm of her hand. She said it tickled, and Philip agreed that it did. Honey and her colt were the last to arrive. The mother stood back and watched Mary Margaret carefully. When she felt comfortable, she walked up to the fence, reached her big head over and gently nudged Mary Margaret's arm. She gave her a carrot and thought that Honey's lips were the softest of all. The colt galloped over and kicked its hind legs. Mary Margaret and Philip laughed. It finally settled down next to its mother, and Mary Margaret slowly reached between the slats of the fence to pet it. The mane felt like silk. Mary Margaret was filled with such emotion, that she thought she was going to cry. It occurred to her that she was having this feeling a lot lately, and she didn't like it. She felt like crying when she was happy and when she was sad. It made no sense to her. Thankfully, she was able to stifle the tears, and continued to stroke the silky mane. Philip sat on the top rail of the fence and fed the horses carrots until it was dark and then he said they should go inside.

Sylvia was setting out dessert. She served lemon bars. The navy blue plates had been dusted with powdered sugar after the bars had been placed on them, and they looked beautiful. Mary Margaret enjoyed the sweet and sour flavor along with the crunch of the crust. She remembered what her parents had said at dinner about her new school clothes, but decided that it was a small dessert, and she ate all of it.

When she got into bed that night, Mary Margaret went right to sleep. Moving day had been very tiring for her, but at the same time, she felt proud of her accomplishments. She had made her own bed, and unpacked and put away all of her clothes. She thought of Charlene as she drifted off to sleep, and knew that she would be proud of her.

Chapter 18

Mary Margaret awoke the next morning and heard rain pounding on the metal roof. She recognized the sound and wasn't afraid. It still looked dark outside, but her clock said it was nearly 9. She went into the living room, and Addie was there. She was shocked to see her because she was expecting to see Mrs. Applegate. Mary Margaret asked, "Where is Mrs. Applegate?"

"She had a doctor's appointment and asked me to come by. I'll make you pancakes. You go on and get dressed."

Mary Margaret could hear Addie in the kitchen, and was surprised when she came out and saw her name, *MARY*, spelled out in pancakes across her plate. Addie had her back turned, but looked out of the corner of her to eye to see Mary Margaret's reaction. She was not disappointed. In spite of her determination to not like Addie, the corners of Mary Margaret's mouth turned up when she saw her plate. She thanked Addie for the pancakes, but ate her meal in silence.

Addie busied herself at the sink and added nothing to the already wordless conversation. When Mary Margaret had finished, Addie cleared the table, and Mary Margaret got up to go into her room. Addie stopped her chores long enough to tell her to make her bed. She looked back at her, but the large framed woman was bent over the sink scouring the already white bowl with bleach smelling cleanser. Mary Margaret decided against protesting and went into the room and began straightening the covers on the bed. Addie appeared at the door and said, "We're going out to the new house when you are finished."

Mary Margaret took her time. The last thing she wanted to do was spend the entire day at the new house with Addie. She had planned on spending the day with Mrs. Applegate working on her quilt. Maybe if she took long enough, Mrs. Applegate would come home before they left.

As fate would have it, Addie announced that she was ready to leave before Mrs. Applegate returned.

"I'll just wait on Mrs. Applegate," Mary Margaret told Addie.

"She has gone into Charleston and may not return until late this afternoon

Mary Margaret knew that she would not be able to protest anymore and resigned herself to probably the worst day in her life. It was still raining, and that meant that she would be stuck inside with nothing to do.

Together they went downstairs, and Mary Margaret was looking for Addie's car. All she saw was an old pickup truck; and when Addie walked around the rear of it, she knew that was their transportation. On the way out of town Addie pulled into the Left Fork Grocery.

"We need to do some grocery shopping," she announced.

Mary Margaret was relieved to be going into the grocery store. She did not like being alone with Addie. When they got in the store, Addie gave Mary Margaret a list.

"You get yourself a cart and help gather up some of the food," Addie said. The burning in her eyes and throat started again, but she was not going to let the tears spill out onto her cheeks. She had never gathered up groceries before, but she was going to show Addie that she could do it. Her list consisted of cereal, oatmeal, grits, whatever that was, bread, crackers, peanut butter, paper towels, cracker meal, bologna and toilet paper. As Mary Margaret looked over the list, she counted 10 items. She knew what most of them were, but grits were foreign to her and toilet paper was embarrassing. She was determined, however, to complete the list by herself.

Mary Margaret first went to the cereal aisle. She could complete that part of the list first. She got the cereal and oatmeal. As she picked up the oatmeal, her eye caught a glimpse of a box which said grits. She chose a box and felt pretty proud of herself. The bread, crackers, cracker meal, peanut butter and paper towels went into her cart next. She saw the toilet paper, but a man was in the same aisle, so she decided to come back there later. She went to the cold-cut section and picked up a package of bologna. She still needed toilet paper, and hoped that nobody would be in the aisle when she returned. Mary Margaret slowly went up and down each aisle attempting to sneak up on the paper goods. She nonchalantly rounded the corner and bumped into Addie. "How are you doing, girl," she inquired.

"Fine," responded Mary Margaret.

"Well, I'm about finished. You get whatever else you need and I'll meet you up front, toots sweet."

"Toots sweet," thought Mary Margaret. "What does that mean?" Somehow she sensed it meant soon, and she swooped up a 4-pack of toilet tissue as she passed by, without stopping. Now she needed to find Addie. She went to the front of the store, and Addie scanned the cart.

"Well, you did just fine, but we'll be needin' more toilet paper than that. You need to go back and get one of those big 12-packs. This little thing isn't enough to put a roll in each bathroom." Addie was holding up the 4-pack, and the customers waiting in check-out were watching the exchange with amused glances.

"Come on, I'll go with you," she said, sensing Mary Margaret's embarrassment. They returned the 4-pack, and Addie tossed the large 12-pack into her cart.

Together the two mismatched people approached the checkout stand. Addie's large frame was covered with a shiny pink raincoat from the bottom of which hung trousers that were too short. They met white athletic socks, which went into walking shoes. Her hair was in its usual state of disarray, with wisps around her face and down her neck. The sleeves on the coat were short and exposed large wrists attached to man-like hands. There was nothing feminine about Addie when you looked at the picture as a whole. However, when you took individual features, she had shockingly blue eyes, which were framed by long lashes. Her skin was smooth and clear with a healthy glow. Her nose was large, but fit her face perfectly, and her lips were full and seemed to smile easily to everybody except Mary Margaret.

Into Addie's Arms

Mary Margaret was willowy. Her navy jacket coordinated beautifully with her hunter green slacks. Her slacks gently folded as they touched the top of her loafers. Her hands were tiny, with delicate, beautifully manicured nails. Mary Margaret's hair was slightly curled under, and it bounced as she walked. Her face was nicely proportioned. Her dark brown eyes sparkled behind her long lashes. Her skin was dewy fresh. Her nose was straight and angular, but matched her sharp jaw line. Her mouth was rather plain, but completed the tailored picture.

Addie told Mary Margaret to place her items on the counter first, and as she did, the cashier pulled them forward. When she had finished with those items, she pushed the board back, and Addie began loading her groceries. When they had finished checking out, they had 15 bags of groceries. Mary Margaret had never seen so many groceries at one time, and suddenly realized that they would be taking them all to her new house. There was no delivery service here. Fortunately, there was a carry-out boy, who helped take all the groceries to the truck. It had stopped raining, so he placed them in the bed. Mary Margaret just stood there and watched. This was all new to her. When the groceries were all in the truck, Addie told Mary Margaret, "Get in, we are goin' home."

On the way home, Addie asked Mary Margaret if she could cook anything.

"I can make a peanut butter sandwich if I have to."

Addie laughed to herself, and they drove on in silence.

When they arrived at the house, Addie went to the bed of the truck and started getting out the bags. Mary Margaret started to go up to the porch, but was stopped by Addie. "Mary Margaret, come back here and get some of these bags."

When Mary Margaret turned around, there stood Addie holding out two bags to her. She went back and took the bags. While she felt put upon, she didn't realize that Addie had given her bags which held light items such as bread, toilet tissue, and paper towels.

They carried in the first load, and Addie announced that there was plenty more in the truck. Mary Margaret reluctantly went back out and was handed two more bags. This continued until all the groceries had been carried into the kitchen.

Mary Margaret went to her room and took off her jacket. Addie missed her and called, "Mary Margaret, come back to the kitchen. I need your help." Mary Margaret stomped down the stairs, and Addie recognized the sound of disgusted little feet. However, she felt that this child was a part of this family and needed to learn to participate in the responsibilities. Addie had come to realize that Mary Margaret had never been expected to share any household responsibilities.

Addie's children had been given responsibilities as soon as they were able to walk. Even the youngest child was expected to pick up toys when finished playing, and once they were out of the high chair, each child took their dishes to the sink after meals. Once they got older, they shared in the cooking and cleaning. Addie knew that they were better adults for this training, and she felt that Mary Margaret would benefit from this.

"Don't you have any clothes that aren't so nice?" Addie asked as Mary Margaret entered the kitchen. Mary Margaret looked down and wondered what she meant. She was wearing her everyday clothes. Her old clothes were given to charity when she no longer wore them.

"These are my everyday clothes," she said. Addie sighed and knew that she would have to talk with Mrs. Smith about getting Mary Margaret some clothes for everyday in the South.

Addie asked Mary Margaret to hand her the groceries and together they set up the cabinets so that she could easily find what she needed when it was time to cook. As they did this, Addie began to hum, and soon she was singing. At first she sang choruses of religious songs, and this led into full-fledged patriotic songs. Mary Margaret was surprised at the beauty of Addie's voice. It was strong and the tunes filled the house. When Mary Margaret recognized one of the songs, she found herself humming and then singing along, too. Addie was pleased when she heard the accompaniment of Mary Margaret's voice. It was soft and at first almost inaudible, but as they worked and sang, the timid voice became stronger, and one song led to another until they had put away the groceries, and Addie asked Mary Margaret what she would like for lunch.

She decided that a grilled cheese sandwich would be good and Addie agreed. She asked Mary Margaret to get them each a glass of milk and to set the table. Mary Margaret's spirits were lifted by the singing, and her good mood carried over into getting ready for lunch. Addie made them each a sandwich and cut them into quarters. She placed a pickle spear on each plate and added a few potato chips. They ate their lunch together, but neither could spearhead a conversation.

After lunch Addie told Mary Margaret that she needed to unpack some boxes and told her that she could go outside if she wanted to. Mary Margaret asked her if she could go to check the mail, and Addie decided that was a good idea.

Chapter 19

As she walked down the driveway she was more observant than she had been the day before. She looked into the trees lining the driveway and could hear noises in their branches. It was quiet at her house, not at all like it was when she went outside in New York. When she and Charlene went into Central Park, they could never have heard anything in the trees because of the noise around them. People were calling to each other, horns were honking, airplanes were flying overhead, and the sounds of nature were unheard. Here Mary Margaret realized that the birds were flying all around. As she stopped to watch, she saw a robin with a piece of straw in its mouth. She realized that it must be building a nest. She saw something flash along the ground and was thrilled to see a chipmunk hide inside a fallen log. The squirrels were playing up and down the trees. She was excited by all of this activity and almost forgot that her mission was to get the mail. She walked on, rounding the curve in the driveway, just in time to see the mailman as he stopped beside the mailbox. He waved to her and waited for her to come on down the drive. He said that his name was Warren, and he welcomed her to Left Fork. He handed her some envelopes which had been forwarded from New York, and a couple of magazines. She thanked him, took the mail, and started back. As she turned around at the edge of the driveway she saw something that made her stop in her tracks. Two deer were standing there. They appeared to be statues, but Mary Margaret had never seen them before so she knew they were alive. She began to move, and they remained in place making almost imperceptible moves with their heads as she approached. When she was about 10 feet away, almost on command, they both turned to their left and darted into the trees. Their white tails were held high, and they seemed to bound through the woods. She looked, but could see no trace of them. She finally started back toward the house just as Addie had come out on the porch to call for her.

When she reached the porch, she began to tell Addie about the deer. Addie told her that deer were often seen around here, and that while they were beautiful, she was to be careful about going near them. She explained that they were wild animals as were all the other creatures Mary Margaret would encounter.

Addie took the mail and put it on Mike's desk and asked Mary Margaret if she would like to help her clean windows. Mary Margaret had only seen windows cleaned by people riding up and down the outside of buildings on scaffolding in New York. She was not sure how this would be done in her house, but she agreed to help. Addie mixed up some vinegar and water in a bucket and filled squirt bottles with it. She gave one to Mary Margaret, and she took one. She explained that she would clean the top part of the windows and Mary Margaret could clean the bottom. Addie gathered up some newspapers, and they went into the living room. Addie directed Mary Margaret to watch her as she cleaned the first one. She squirted the smelly vinegar and water mixture onto the glass and rubbed the wet window with wadded-up newspaper. Much to the amazement of her young apprentice, the glass began to shine. Addie explained that they couldn't work on the same window at the same time, so she continued with the window she had started, and Mary Margaret started cleaning a window on the other wall. Mary Margaret soon realized that it was not as easy as Addie had made it look. She sprayed the mixture and it quickly ran down onto the next pane of glass. She took her wadded-up newspaper and began to rub. Soon, her pane began to shine. She continued until she had completed the 6 small panes of glass on her window.

Addie had completed the first window and moved on to a different one. Mary Margaret moved to the window where Addie had begun. Her arms began to ache. This was a lot like work, but when she completed the bottom 6 panes in the window where Addie had begun, the window sparkled, and she was proud of her accomplishment. She moved on to the third window and Addie was completing the one where Mary Margaret had begun.

When all three windows were shining on the inside, Addie said. "We now need to go outside and clean; and we will have one room finished."

Mary Margaret sighed. Addie realized that this was new to her. "Let's have some lemonade in the swing before moving on."

"That's a great idea," Mary Margaret agreed, together they went into the kitchen to prepare their drinks.

The two went outside and sat on the swing. A cool breeze was blowing, and the smell of freshly mowed grass was in the air. Addie broke the silence. "Mary Margaret your teacher, Mrs. Stancil, is a nice lady. We go to church together, and I'm sure that you will feel comfortable in her class."

Just the mention of school made Mary Margaret feel uneasy. She had been able to push it from her mind for a while and now resented Addie's bringing it up. Her mood changed, and Addie immediately sensed it.

They finished their lemonade, and Addie decided that they should get back to work. "I want to finish these three windows today. My goal is to clean the windows in one room each day, and that way they will all be cleaned in a couple of weeks; and I'll still have plenty of time to continue getting the house in order.

Mary Margaret cleaned the bottom parts of the two windows which were accessible from the porch, and Addie cleaned the tops. When those were finished, Addie asked Mary Margaret to come into the yard. "I need you there while I climb on the ladder to clean the last one. I want you there in case I fall."

This stunned Mary Margaret because she figured Addie thought she could do anything and everything single-handedly. It never occurred to her that this was just a common precaution whenever anybody climbed on a ladder—that they at least tell somebody that they are doing it, or better still have a bystander or somebody to hold the ladder.

Mary Margaret stayed close by as Addie climbed the ladder juggling her newspapers and squirt bottle. She reached the top of the ladder and squirted the windows. She put the spray bottle under her arm and balanced herself as she wadded the newspapers and began wiping the glass. Mary Margaret heard Addie begin to hum. As she worked her way down the window, her humming became a song, and she was again in full voice as she completed her task. Mary Margaret had never known anybody who sang like Addie. She only remembered hearing people singing at school, or in a group. While this was strange to Mary Margaret, she thought it was nice and was amazed at Addie's beautiful voice.

When the chores were finished and the ladder put away, Addie said it was time to go back to Mrs. Applegate's. She and Mary Margaret got in the pickup truck and started down the driveway. Addie suddenly stopped. Mary Margaret looked up to see the two deer. They were beautiful, and she wondered why Addie had told her to be careful of them. They seemed so gentle and not at all wild. They slowly walked off the driveway and watched as the truck went by.

Addie and Mary Margaret reached Mrs. Applegate's house just as Cindy was arriving from work. She hugged Mary Margaret and asked Addie how the house was coming. Addie gave her the details of the day's work, and they both seemed pleased.

"Addie, is there anything you need for the house?" Cindy asked.

"No," she replied. "When do you actually plan to start staying there?"

"We'll spend our first night there on Saturday," Mrs. Smith said smiling. She was very anxious to be in her own home, and wanted everything to be ready when she got there. "We're going out to the house tonight. I am so glad to have you helping us and taking care of Mary Margaret. It's reassuring knowing you're there."

Addie blushed. Cindy thought that Addie was unaccustomed to receiving compliments.

Mary Margaret and her parents took Mrs. Applegate to dinner at Grammy's. As usual, the aroma in the restaurant was welcoming, and Grammy was there to welcome them. After dinner, they drove out to the new house and Mrs. Applegate was given the tour. She said that she thought the house suited them perfectly. She admired the kitchen and said that her kitchen could use some remodeling. She thought maybe seeing this would inspire her to begin the renovation. They all laughed. Cindy remarked that the windows in the living room were so clean and the light reflected off them so beautifully. She thanked Mary Margaret for being such a good helper to Addie. Mary Margaret remarked that the vinegar water smelled awful. Cindy and Mrs. Applegate agreed that it probably did, but it was a wonderful window cleaner.

Mike was outside in the garage when he heard a noise behind him. He turned to see two deer standing in the driveway staring in his direction. He was stunned at their presence. He had seen deer in the woods, but never at this close range. He stood and watched them, and they watched him. He thought that they were checking out the people who had moved in on their property. He had to chuckle as they meandered back into the darkness of the trees and wondered if he had passed inspection or not.

He went to the front door and called to the ladies in the house to see if they were ready to go. They were, and as they got into the car, he told them about the deer. Mary Margaret told him about her two encounters with them earlier in the day. They all agreed that the deer were curious about the intruders on their property.

When Mary Margaret awoke on Friday morning, the birds were noisy outside her window. They seemed to be singing to the world that it was time to get up. She got up and went into the living room. Mrs. Applegate was there dozing on the sofa. She didn't hear Mary Margaret, so she went back into the bedroom and got dressed. She decided that she would fix herself a bowl of cereal, but when she went back into the living room, Mrs. Applegate was already in the kitchen making cinnamon toast in the oven. They sat at the table drinking hot chocolate and eating cinnamon toast as they planned their day.

It was decided that the quilt needed a lot of work today, so they agreed that the entire rest of the morning would be dedicated to that. Mary Margaret made her bed, without being asked, and she and Mrs. Applegate went downstairs to work on the quilt. When the morning was finished, they had completed one entire Dutch Girl square. Mary Margaret had no idea that it would take so long for just one square and there were many more to complete before the quilt was finished. Mrs. Applegate told her to be patient. "We have a lot of time to get this completed," she reassured.

In the afternoon Mary Margaret and Mrs. Applegate worked in the garden. It was time to plant squash, okra and beans. Mary Margaret had seen squash, but didn't think she would like to eat it. She had never even heard of okra. Of course, she knew what beans were, but was surprised to see how beans were planted. The squash and okra were planted using small plants, which had been brought over by Orville from the Seed and Feed Store. Beans, however, were planted from seeds which were really the beans that were inside the green pods that Mary Margaret was used to eating. Mrs.

Into Addie's Arms

Applegate had several seed packets and explained that some beans were pole beans, and their vines needed poles or something to climb on, and some beans were bush beans and grew in a shape that resembled, what else, a bush. When they finished their planting, Mrs. Applegate looked at the tomatoes and found them to her liking. She said that when they got larger she would have to pick off the suckers. When she saw the puzzled look on Mary Margaret's face when she said suckers, she explained that unwanted limbs grow on tomato plants, and they have to be picked off. She said these were called suckers. Of course, when Mary Margaret heard her say suckers, she immediately envisioned lollipops and they both laughed when she shared this with her friend.

It was time to start planning for dinner. This was to be the last meal that Mary Margaret and her parents would be regularly eating with Mrs. Applegate, and she wanted it to be special. She had a pork loin that she was going to bake, so she and Mary Margaret went inside to get things ready. Mrs. Applegate got the roast from the refrigerator and washed it off. As Mary Margaret watched, she noticed that Mrs. Applegate was so clean. Every time she touched the raw meat she washed her hands before she touched any other item in the kitchen. When Mary Margaret mentioned this, Mrs. Applegate explained to her that bacteria from raw meat could be spread by touching other things, so it was very important that she have very clean hands. Mrs. Applegate spread out a large piece of aluminum foil, and placed the roast on it. She put kosher salt and freshly ground black pepper on the roast and then massaged this into the meat. After again washing her hands, she did something which seemed unthinkable to Mary Margaret. Mrs. Applegate poured vinegar over the meat. As she expressed her shock at this, Mrs. Applegate explained that it would not only flavor the meat, it would tenderize it as well. "Please keep an open mind about this. I don't think you'll be disappointed." She placed the meat which had been wrapped in the aluminum foil onto a baking sheet and placed it into the oven. She moved on to the preparation of scalloped potatoes.

Mary Margaret knew about scalloped potatoes and told Mrs. Applegate that Charlene prepared them for her family. Mrs. Applegate asked Mary Margaret to help her peel the potatoes. Together it took no time to peel the 6 potatoes that Mrs. Applegate felt they would need. She took out her baking dish and asked Mary Margaret to spray it with non-stick spray. She did as she was asked, even though this was her first time. She watched as the spray coated the dish, and when it seemed entirely coated, she handed it back to Mrs. Applegate. Mrs. Applegate had been rummaging in her cabinet and exclaimed when she finally found what she was looking for. She brought out a wedge-shaped piece of equipment and explained to Mary Margaret as she was placing it on the counter that the blade was very sharp. She said it was called a mandolin slicer, and that they were going to slice the potatoes on it. Charlene had always sliced potatoes for their scalloped potatoes with a knife, Mary Margaret told Mrs. Applegate. "I did mine that way for many years until I discovered this slicer," she concurred. She showed Mary Margaret how the potato was placed in a holder for safety and then it was moved across the blade. Mary Margaret saw slices of potatoes fall onto the paper towel Mrs. Applegate had placed under the slicer. "The nice thing about using this type of slicer is that all the slices are uniform," Mrs. Applegate explained. She said that when she used a knife to slice the potatoes, some slices were thick, and some were thin. Consequently, the casserole took longer to bake because of the thick slices. Mary Margaret understood and waited to see if Mrs. Applegate asked her to slice, too. She was not disappointed. When Mrs. Applegate felt that she had seen enough slicing to understand the importance of keeping her fingers and hands away from the blade, she asked her if she wanted to try it. Of course, Mary Margaret said yes, and tentatively slid the potato in its holder across the blade. A perfectly sliced piece of potato dropped onto the paper towel. Mary Margaret continued under the close guidance of Mrs. Applegate until only a small piece of potato remained in the holder. When Mrs. Applegate took that piece out of the holder, she placed it on the paper towel next to the one from the first potato she had sliced and salted the two pieces. She handed one to Mary Margaret, and she took the other. Mary Margaret was surprised when Mrs. Applegate took a bite of her slice of potato. She had never seen anybody eat raw potatoes before. Mrs. Applegate motioned with her hand that Mary Margaret was to do the same. Mary Margaret put the piece of potato into her mouth and immediately tasted the salt. Her teeth crunched into the potato, and she began chewing. At first she didn't like the texture of the raw potato, but as she chewed and it mixed with the salt, she discovered that this was not only good; it was fun to be sharing this experience. She felt like hugging the tiny woman, but her upbringing kept her from it. Instead, she just nodded her head and kept on chewing.

Once the potatoes were all sliced, Mrs. Applegate said that it was time to build the casserole. She placed a layer of potatoes in the baking dish. She asked Mary Margaret to cut off pieces of butter and place them on top of the potatoes. Mary Margaret sliced off small chunks of butter from the stick and placed them randomly over the potatoes. When she had about 6 small pieces, Mrs. Applegate told her that was enough. Then Mrs. Applegate salted and peppered the layer. She then asked Mary Margaret to sprinkle flour. Mrs. Applegate watched carefully as Mary Margaret sprinkled a thin layer of flour. When this was completed, Mrs. Applegate and Mary Margaret continued the layering of potatoes, salt and pepper, butter, and flour until two more layers were in the dish. Mrs. Applegate then asked Mary Margaret to get the milk from the refrigerator. She poured the milk into the baking dish until it almost covered the layers of potatoes. She told Mary Margaret that it was important not to put in so much milk that it came to the top of the dish as it surely would bubble over in the oven and make a mess. She told Mary Margaret that as hard as she tried, she almost always had a mess in the oven when she made scalloped potatoes, but that they were so good, it was worth the time it took to clean it up. They both laughed as Mrs. Applegate placed the baking dish filled with potatoes and milk into the oven.

Mrs. Applegate then began making cole slaw. Mary Margaret was pleased with this. She remembered Mrs. Applegate's cole slaw from the meal she had prepared on Monday. When it came time for the dressing to be put on the grated cabbage and one grated carrot, which Mrs. Applegate said was added for color, she asked Mary Margaret to get the ingredients. She got out the mayonnaise, sugar and vinegar, and this time measured under Mrs. Applegate's direction. The creamy dressing was completed with a pinch of salt and a dash of pepper. She poured the thick mixture over the cabbage and somehow knew when to stop pouring. Mary Margaret could smell the cabbage and the dressing as the sweet and tart aroma was being stirred up with the spoon, and she was embarrassed when she realized that she was almost salivating. When this was placed in the refrigerator, Mrs. Applegate withdrew a bag of green beans.

They went out onto the front porch. Mrs. Applegate sat on a glider and Mary Margaret followed her there. The glider was turquoise and white and had cut outs in the back and seat. When Mary Margaret sat down, the glider moved beneath her; and soon she and Mrs. Applegate were gently moving back and forth. Between them was a colander which Mary Margaret had seen Mrs. Applegate use before when she washed off vegetables. Now she was using the colander to hold the beans as she and Mary Margaret strung them. Mrs. Applegate showed Mary Margaret how to snap off the ends of the beans and pull the end down and magically a string came with it. After each bean was strung, it was snapped into segments. Mary Margaret did her beans one at a time, first stringing and then snapping, but Mrs. Applegate would string several beans, hold them in her hand, and then snap them. It was amazing to watch her manage stringing and snapping. Soon the colander was nearly full, and the bean bag was empty. Mrs. Applegate said they were in no hurry to cook the beans, so they stayed on the porch and watched the neighbors pass by. Mary Margaret saw five girls riding their bicycles. They looked to be about her age, and she wondered if she would meet them at school. Oh, no, there was that feeling again. Her stomach felt uneasy, and she burned behind her eyes and down her throat. The good mood of the day with Mrs. Applegate had vanished with just the thought of going to the new school.

As they sat on the porch, Mary Margaret wondered what Alice was doing. Her Easter vacation was nearly over, and she would be going back to New York tomorrow. Mary Margaret thought that she would ask permission to call Alice on Sunday. She knew that Charlene was probably preparing her dinner or maybe she and Darlene were going to a movie together and out to eat. She suddenly was very homesick for New York.

Mrs. Applegate sensed that Mary Margaret had become quiet. She didn't want to ask her what was wrong, but rather decided to see if she could restore the energy they had shared throughout the day. She asked Mary Margaret to set the table and instead of using her wedding china, tonight she told Mary Margaret they would use her good china. She opened her china cabinet and together they got out the pieces of fine china that Mrs. Applegate had displayed almost as art. The pieces though, of course, hard, felt almost soft and delicate in Mary Margaret's hands. When they had chosen enough for 4 place settings, Mrs. Applegate closed the doors to the china cabinet and helped Mary Margaret arrange the beautiful dishes. Mrs. Applegate opened a drawer and pulled out a flat box, which she opened to reveal ornate silverware. Each piece of the silverware was monogrammed with the letter A in fancy script. Enough pieces were removed from the box for 4 place settings and these were added to the table. Mrs. Applegate opened a cabinet to reveal intricately cut crystal glasses. She explained they were Waterford crystal, and she and Mr. Applegate had purchased them on a trip to Ireland. Mary Margaret noticed a wistful look in Mrs. Applegate's eye as she obviously relived a moment or two of that trip.

When the table was set, Mrs. Applegate remembered that they needed to cook the green beans. She removed a large pot from her cabinet and after the beans were washed, they were placed in the pot, salt and pepper were added, and the lid was locked into place. Then Mrs. Applegate removed a round, metal piece from a drawer and placed it on the lid. Mary Margaret said that she had never seen a pot like that, and Mrs. Applegate explained that it was a pressure cooker. She said that pressure built up inside the pot, and the food cooked faster under pressure. She said the round metal piece was a pressure gauge, and it would jiggle when the pressure was built up inside the pot. Soon Margaret heard the pressure gauge begin to jiggle as the pressure inside the pot pressed against it through an opening in the lid. Mrs. Applegate lowered the heat under the pot and set her timer for 10 minutes. The jiggle slowed down to an occasional spew, and Mrs. Applegate removed a frozen apple pie from the freezer.

By this time the roast was nearly done cooking, and the house was filled with its aroma of meat mixed with the apple smell of the vinegar. Mary Margaret's stomach started growling, and she and Mrs. Applegate laughed. Mary Margaret heard a car door close and went to the front door to see her mother getting out of the car. She saw Mary Margaret, waved, and walked up on the porch.

She hugged her daughter as she came into Mrs. Applegate's house and was struck by the aroma of the roasting pork. Mrs. Smith told Mrs. Applegate that it was smelling up the whole neighborhood. She said she had smelled the aroma of her cooking when she turned the corner two blocks away. Of course, she was exaggerating, but the wonderful smell, the smile on Mary Margaret's face, the friendship of this lovely tiny lady, the warmth of Mrs. Applegate's home all combined to make Cindy Smith feel that she was home.

In New York, Cindy's life was very satisfying. Her work was fulfilling, her cultural opportunities were endless. Mary Margaret was satisfied with her station in life, Mr. Smith was a wonderful husband, but here in Left Fork South Carolina, something was different. It was better than all she had in New York. It was comfortable. Cindy found her new co-workers friendly and willing to help her as she adjusted to her new situation. She had worked with fine doctors in New York, and her fellow nurses were exceptional. Here she found the level of expertise to equal what she had in New York; and additionally, she found the people to be warm and generous. She silently decided that her first week in Left Fork, South Carolina, had been a great week.

By the time Mike arrived at Mrs. Applegate's home, the aromas had increased to include apple pie. When he walked into the home, he said he hoped dinner was ready because he had been smelling it for two blocks. They all laughed as his remarks had almost mimicked those of Cindy.

As they served dinner, Mrs. Applegate told Mike and Cindy what a great help Mary Margaret had been in preparing the meal. She said that she couldn't have done it all without her. Of course, they all knew that was not true, but Mary Margaret blushed with joy at the praise she was receiving. Cindy said that she hoped that Mary Margaret had paid close attention so that she could help her prepare these dishes sometime. Mike and Mary Margaret looked at each other and smiled because they knew that Mrs. Smith rarely cooked. Charlene had been with the family since Mary Margaret was born, and she had prepared all their evening meals on Monday through Friday. On the week-ends they often ate leftovers or ate out. Charlene always prepared casseroles and left them in the freezer, too. Cooking was going to be new to Mrs. Smith, and Mary Margaret thought it might be fun to cook with her mother.

After dinner the four of them sat on the front porch. The warm spring evening was all the Smith family needed after the week of moving to South Carolina from New York, and it was the beginning of a new chapter in the life of Mrs. Applegate. Tomorrow the Smiths would move into their new home permanently, but Mrs. Applegate knew that they would remain a part of her life.

Chapter 20

The five girls stopped and dropped their bicycles when they arrived at Allison Kincaid's house. They sat on the steps.

"Did you get a good look at her?" Allison asked. "She looked like a mouse. Her hair is brown and straight and she had big eyes."

"She wasn't so bad," Stephanie Scott said. "She just looked kind of sad."

"Yeah, I wish you hadn't told us not to wave. I bet we'll like her when we get to know her," Jane Ellis said.

"Yeah, I bet she's nice," said Linda Lively and Peggy Anderson agreed.

"What's the matter with y'all?" Allison said. "Don't you remember that we took an oath to shun her? She's not one of us. She's stuck up and thinks she's great because she went to a private school. Philip said she was nice, but he thinks everybody is nice. I know her type. She'll not fit in with us, and we are not going to have anything to do with her. In fact, I have an idea. Let's make fun of her so that she'll know up front that we aren't her friends."

Jane Ellis listened and knew she shouldn't be a part of this group, but it was exciting sometimes when the girls went into the drugstore for sodas to be a part of something. Allison had taken her bracelet at Christmas, but she had apologized and everything had been okay since then.

"Let's change the subject. I have something new for us to do. I have a book, and we're going to put people's names in it; and we can write what we think about them. Let me show you." She pulled out a beautiful journal from her back pack. The cover was a picture of pink, yellow and white roses. "It's called a slam book. I've already started it." She turned the pages to show that their names were the first ones in the book. The following pages held the names of their classmates. Allison had written comments on each page. She had been complimentary to the girls in the Cool Five. However, her comments were not as kind as the names continued. She had written that Philip Gilbert was cute and nice and that Davis was bashful and smart. However, she wrote that Nancy Miller was a brown nose to the teacher and couldn't be trusted.

"That's not true," said Stephanie as she read the page about Nancy Miller. "She has always been a good friend to me, and I do trust her."

"Well, if you want to stay in this club, she can't be your good friend any more. We're the only friends we need, and everybody else has to be left out. Do you understand?" Allison said looking directly into Stephanie's eyes.

"I don't know about that. I like Nancy, and . . ."

"I told you, you can't be friends with anyone who is not in this club." Allison said through clenched teeth. "We have to stick together or you can't be a part of us."

Stephanie sat there silently. She had never been a part of anything before, and it was fun having friends to call after school and people to eat lunch with. She had always felt left out of everything and for the first time in her life, she had friends. Somehow though she didn't realize that having friends would make her feel so bad at times.

The other three girls listened and knew that they didn't want Allison to speak to them in that tone. She seemed to cast a spell when she was with them. They no longer thought for themselves. They allowed her to make decisions they didn't always want to make, but then she would be nice and come up with fun things to do. Her mother allowed her to have sleepovers, and she made plans which included them every day. They rode their bicycles together. They went to the movies. Sometimes they had fun, but other times the girls felt uncomfortable as Allison would say cruel things about other people in their school. They especially disliked the way she spoke about the principal. Mrs. Calhoun was always fair, but Allison made it perfectly clear that she didn't like her, and had even written her name in the slam book and the comments were words none of the other girls had ever spoken or written before.

Allison pulled out a pen and handed the book to Stephanie. "Here, it's your turn, and you need to write what you feel about each person. Remember now, they are not one of us, and we don't really like them."

Stephanie took the pen and began with the girls in the Cool Five. It was easy to write something on those pages, but she found it difficult to continue. Philip's page was easy, and she wrote, "Good with horses." On the page for Davis she wrote, "Cute and very nice." The other girls agreed with the comments, but when she came to the page for Nancy Miller, she couldn't make her hand bring the pen to the page.

"I can't do it, Allison. I can't say anything bad about her. She's a nice girl." Stephanie's voice was trembling as tears were near the surface. She sensed that she was close to being outside the group if she didn't continue, but her heart said that was too wrong.

"Oh, okay, give it to Jane. She has some guts," Allison said exasperatedly.

Jane took the book and pen. She too filled in the first four pages with ease. The next 2 were easy as she wrote nice things about Philip and Davis. However, when it came to Mrs. Calhoun's page she hesitated. She remembered the time that Mrs. Calhoun had driven her home when she had the flu, and her mother couldn't come and get her. She remembered when Mrs. Calhoun had come to their home to bring her books and all the other times that she had watched her care for all the students in the school. This was a nice woman, and she couldn't write anything ugly about her.

"What's the matter with y'all? No guts, no glory. That's my new motto. We have to be the leaders in our school. We have to be in control or we'll be just like everybody else. We have to stick together and especially now with this girl from New York City comin' in. You just watch. All the teachers will think she's special because she's from New York. Her daddy thinks he's a big shot at the mill. Well, he'd better watch his back, or he might just find himself in trouble."

The other girls sat in silence as Allison spewed her words. This didn't feel like fun anymore. There had been other times when Allison made them feel uncomfortable, but those times were when she was admitting to being unkind to others. Now she was attempting to include them in her deeds and nobody felt good about it. However, the four girls liked being a part of something and one by one they came up with something to write in the book. When they had completed, Allison put the book back into her back pack and stood up.

"We need to renew our oath. Stand up!" she said.

The other girls stood up and waited.

"Raise your right hand," she demanded.

Allison was standing on the first step and the girls formed a semi-circle around her on the sidewalk.

"Repeat after me. I will not be a friend to the new girl from New York. I will do everything I can to ignore her. She will not be my friend, and she will be sorry that she ever came to our town."

Like sheep being led to slaughter, the girls repeated each phrase. When the last word was spoken Allison said, "Come on inside and let's get something to drink. I'm thirsty."

Stephanie and Linda started up the steps, but Jane said, "I can't. I have to be home for dinner."

"Yeah, so do I," said Peggy.

"Okay, but call me later. We need to make a plan for Monday," Allison said without turning around.

As the girls rode away, Allison said to Stephanie and Linda, "They better be careful or I'll make them sorry."

Stephanie and Linda exchanged glances, and each knew the other was afraid of their friend, Allison.

As Jane and Peggy rode away, Peggy asked, "Jane, does Allison scare you?"

"Yeah, sometimes she does. She scares me so much that I'm afraid not to be her friend."

Chapter 21

Saturday morning started early in the upstairs apartment of Mrs. Applegate's house. Cindy removed the sheets from the bed and began washing them while her husband began dusting and vacuuming. They were pleasantly surprised when they noticed that Mary Margaret had voluntarily begun to dust the living room. After the bathrooms and kitchen were cleaned, the sheets were ready to be put back on the bed. Mike and Cindy had packed their clothes and gathered up their personal belongings and placed them on the bed in their room. Mary Margaret had put her clothes in her suitcase, and all of her other things were in a box waiting for her father to take them to the car. They looked around the apartment and Cindy remarked that it had been a wonderful place to begin their lives here. It looked homey and ready for its next occupants, probably Mrs. Applegate's daughter, who would be here next month with her family.

When the luggage and boxes had been taken to the car, Mary Margaret and her parents rang Mrs. Applegate's doorbell. They were surprised when she didn't answer, and then they noticed that her car was not in the driveway out back. "She must have had an appointment that she forgot to tell us about," Mike said.

They all got in the car, and Mary Margaret had to squeeze in between some boxes as they started the drive to their new home. It was a time of bittersweet joy. They were sad at leaving Mrs. Applegate and her wonderful hospitality, but they were looking forward to living in their own home.

The quick drive bought the Smith family to their home to find that Addie's truck was already there along with Mrs. Applegate's car. They were surprised by this, but the whole family laughed as they saw the banner hung between two posts on their porch that said, Welcome, Y'All! Mrs. Applegate and Addie were nearly jumping up and down on the porch as they clapped their hands and shouted greetings. Cindy was so overwhelmed by this that she began to cry and simultaneously hug Mrs. Applegate and Addie. They reminded Mary Margaret of three teen-age girls going ga-ga over a rock star, and she was embarrassed to watch. Mike joined in on the hugging, and Mary Margaret was too overwhelmed by this and went inside. She felt left out. Her parents were ignoring her, and it was obvious that the welcome was intended for them. She went up to her room and lay on her bed. With her face turned toward her pillow, she smelled the perfume which reminded her of Charlene, and all the uneasiness in her stomach and the repressed burning in her eyes came alive, and she started crying and knew instantly that she was going to be sick.

Addie realized that Mary Margaret was gone. "Where's Mary Margaret?" she asked no one in particular. They quickly looked around, and Addie said, "I'll go in the house and look. I have a surprise for her."

She found Mary Margaret sitting on the bathroom floor. It was obvious that she had been sick, and Mary Margaret's tear-stained face told Addie that she had been crying. She wet a wash cloth and sat on the floor with the obviously upset child. She gently wiped Mary Margaret's face and almost cooed as she told her; "I understand that this move has been hard on you. I hope that someday you will come to realize that I only want to help you get through it. Please let me help you with your fears of being in a new place. I'll listen to anything you have to say, and welcome the opportunity to be your friend."

Mary Margaret was too surprised at Addie's nurturing attitude to even speak. She was mute as the one-sided conversation continued, but her mind raced with the thought that she didn't want Addie's help. She didn't want to be here. She liked her life in New York; she missed Alice, and she didn't want to go to the new school on Monday. She hated Left Fork, South Carolina, and would someday show them all. She would go back to New York.

Cindy was startled to hear Addie's voice coming from the bathroom as she walked toward Mary Margaret's room. She stopped and just listened as Addie continued her one-sided conversation.

Into Addie's Arms

"I know how you feel. When I was first married, and I was only 16 when I married, my husband couldn't find a job in Left Fork. We moved to Detroit, Michigan, where he had a job on the assembly line in one of the car plants. I was so lonely. I knew no one. I was frightened by all the activity in the big city. I didn't want to live there, but my husband needed to work, and this is where the work was. We lived there for 5 years. Over that five-year period I became friends with other people, some of whom have continued to be my friends after all these years. Once you start school you'll meet new people and make friends. It'll get better then," she concluded.

In her next breath, Addie said, "Mary Margaret, I have a surprise for you. I have arranged for you to go to school this afternoon, meet your teacher, see where you will be sitting, and have an opportunity to know a little of what's in store for you on Monday morning."

When Cindy heard this, she knew that she had made the right choice in selecting Addie as the nanny. Addie had just shown her that she had the compassion she needed to care for Mary Margaret. She also knew that Mary Margaret would soon adapt to her new surroundings with the help of Addie and Mrs. Applegate.

Cindy cleared her throat and walked to the bathroom door. Addie and Mary Margaret were getting up from the floor. She thought that Addie was extremely agile for a person of her stature. When they saw Cindy, Mary Margaret explained that she had been sick and that Addie had come in to help her and went on to explain that Addie had arranged for them to go to the school this afternoon and meet her teacher. Cindy said that she thought that was a wonderful idea, and winked at Addie as Mary Margaret turned to wash her face.

After lunch, which Addie and Mrs. Applegate had prepared, Mrs. Applegate left to run some errands and Addie and Mary Margaret got into the pickup truck to go to school. When they arrived, a tall woman was sitting on the steps. She was holding something in her arms, and Mary Margaret soon learned that it was a calico cat named Patches. As Addie and Mary Margaret approached the woman, she stood, and Mary Margaret could see that she was a tall, slender lady, with a warm, friendly smile. Her eyes sparkled as she greeted them, and Patches lay contentedly in her arms.

Mrs. Stancil reached out to hug Mary Margaret and said, "I am so glad to finally meet you. Addie has been telling me all about you."

Mary Margaret wondered what Addie had been saying. She had not really been nice to Addie, so how could she be saying nice things and blushed in embarrassment as she thought about this.

Let's go inside," said the teacher, and as they walked down the hall, Mrs. Stancil explained about where the principal's office was, the library, the cafeteria, and finally they reached what was to be Mary Margaret's classroom for the next 6 weeks.

They went inside and Mary Margaret immediately noticed that the room was decorated with cut outs of spring flowers. Daffodils, hyacinths, and tulips seemed to almost be growing on the bulletin board. Kites were flying above the flowers and a student's name was on each kite. As Mrs. Stancil noticed Mary Margaret looking at the kites, she pointed out one at the top of the others that had her name on it. It was a cheerful room. The desks were in a semi-circle around Mrs. Stancil's desk. There were three rows of 8 desks. They were old wooden desks with a right or left writing surface. There was an opening under each seat for books.

Mary Margaret had never seen desks like these. In her school, the desks were metal with writing surfaces that went entirely in front of you as you sat in the seat. She wondered how she would ever manage writing and holding a book or anything else in a desk like this. She began to feel uneasy and was glad that she had not eaten a big lunch.

"Mary Margaret, this will be your desk," said Mrs. Stancil as she put Patches down and indicated a place in the front row and to the right of own desk.

Patches stretched each of her hind legs and then began to walk from desk to desk until she was on Mrs. Stancil's desk. When she reached the teacher's place, she sat, and pulled one hind leg up and began bathing. The three onlookers laughed as she sat there methodically cleaning her body.

"Your books are already in your desk and here is a list of the items you'll need to make your first day go better," said the thoughtful teacher.

As Mary Margaret looked at the list, she noted that she already had everything. She walked to her desk and was relieved to see that the books were identical to the ones she had been using in New York.

You may choose a book from the library on Monday," said Mrs. Stancil. Mary Margaret remembered the book she had gotten from the public library; and when she told her, she replied, "That's a wonderful choice."

"It seems that you're all set for your first day at school. Have you met any other children since you have been in Left Fork?"

"I know Philip Gilbert," she responded.

Mrs. Stancil smiled and said, "He is a fine young man. Have you seen the new foal?"

Mary Margaret's heart jumped with joy at the thought of it. "I saw it immediately after it was born and one other time since."

"Do you have any questions?" asked Mrs. Stancil.

"I don't think so."

It appeared that the visit was winding down, and Addie took charge of leaving by asking Patches, "Are you ready to go home?" Patches looked up, yawned, and seemed totally unconcerned with whether she was at home or school. She was a very comfortable cat.

On the drive back home Addie began to hum, and as she had when she was working, the humming grew to singing. Mary Margaret noticed that Addie almost always sang gospel or patriotic songs. Whatever her choice, it was soothing and pleasant to hear her voice. Mary Margaret wondered how Addie knew so many songs. She would finish one song and go immediately into another.

Cindy and Mike were in the kitchen when Mary Margaret came in. Addie had dropped her off; explained that she had some errands to run; and said she would see her on Monday. Mary Margaret told her parents this when they asked her whereabouts, and Cindy quickly asked Mary Margaret, "Did you thank Addie for taking her time to introduce you to Mrs. Stancil, and did you thank Mrs. Stancil for taking her time to acquaint you with the school?"

Mary Margaret responded that she had, but as she remembered, she was not quite certain her thank you to Addie had been as heartfelt as it should have been.

Mike and Cindy asked Mary Margaret about the school, Mrs. Stancil, the classroom, and all the other things that parents seem to be interested in. Mary Margaret only wanted to tell them about Patches. Secretly, she wanted them to take her to see the foal, but she knew they had too much to do at the new house.

As her parents went back to their chores, she went outside and sat in the swing. She remembered her library book and went back into her room to get it. She came back out onto the front porch, sat in the swing and started reading National Velvet. She must have been tired because in just a few minutes Mary Margaret was swaying gently in the swing, the book was on her lap, and she was asleep. As she slept, she began to dream. Again, she was down by the pond, under the weeping willow tree. She was lying on a hammock, and the foal was standing nearby eating grass. She was having a wonderful time. The birds were singing, it was cool in the shade of the tree, and the blue sky was visible between the limbs. The pond was still, and the breeze gently moved the foal's mane like strands of silk. She wondered if anything could be more perfect. Mary Margaret felt as though she was falling from the hammock and her dream ended abruptly.

She awoke to find that she wasn't alone on the porch. Standing before her were two boys and each was holding a fishing pole. One appeared to be about her age, and the other a little younger. They were staring at her as though they had never seen a girl before. She wanted to yell at them to go away. She was angry that she was awake and was no longer in her perfect dream.

"Who are you?" she asked.

The younger one answered, "My name is Jordan Raver, and this is my brother, Davis. We live in the house next to yours."

Mary Margaret looked around for the car which had brought them, but instead she saw two bicycles which had been unceremoniously dropped in the yard.

Jordan seemed to be the spokesperson for the duo, and he continued the conversation by asking, "Are you Mary Margaret?"

Needless to say, she was surprised that he knew her name; and asked him, "How do you know my name?"

"Philip Gilbert told us about you," he responded. Davis still had not spoken. He continued to stare.

Mary Margaret could stand it no longer and she asked him, "What are you staring at?"

He blushed and said, "I wasn't staring. We just came over to fish in the pond," he concluded.

Mary Margaret had been nice about as long as she could. She was having a wonderful dream, which was interrupted by two boys who now announced that they were going to fish in her pond. She looked directly at Davis and asked him, "Who said you could fish here?"

"We always fish here," he replied.

"Well, you can't fish there anymore," the indignant little girl responded.

At about this time the front door opened and out stepped Mike and Cindy. They had heard the voices inside the house and had come to see what the yelling was about. It seems that as the conversation developed between Mary Margaret and Davis, their voices were getting louder and louder until they could be heard inside.

'We are Davis and Jordan Raver, and we live next door," Jordan said as he made the introductions.

'Those look like fine fishing poles," Mike said.

They grinned as he took the one from Davis to examine it. Jordan, still the spokesman said, "Our grandparents gave them to us for Christmas."

"Davis, what do you like to use for bait," Mike asked.

From his hip pocket he pulled an old Prince Albert tobacco can which was filled with dirt. He stuck his fingers into the can and pulled out a fat, wiggly worm.

Mike was immediately aware of the significance of the can and realized that there must be a story to accompany that but decided to save it for another day.

Mary Margaret couldn't help herself and she said, "Yuck-o" as he held the worm up for inspection. Mike took the worm and said that it was a fine specimen. He asked the boys if they had enough bait to share, and they figured they did. Davis said, "Anyway, we can always dig some more worms if we run out. The woods are full of them," he added enthusiastically.

"Do you mind if I dip my line in the water, too?" Mike asked, and the boys immediately said they didn't.

By this time Mary Margaret was thoroughly disgusted. Her father had allowed two boys whom she didn't even know to come onto their property and now they were going to fish. This was more than she could stand, so she marched across the porch, went into the house, and slammed the door. The boys thought it was funny and laughed, but Mike and Cindy were very unhappy at Mary Margaret's behavior, and Mike winked at Cindy as he left the porch to go into the garage and get one of his new fishing poles he had picked up just the day before.

The boys were already on their way to the pond and their voices were filled with excitement as a fish jumped. Mike followed Davis and Jordan, and they explained the best place to sit while fishing was in the shade of the weeping willow. "The fish like the cooler water in the shade," explained the ever helpful Jordan.

Cindy knew that Mary Margaret was unhappy with their situation, but she could not tolerate rudeness from her. Mary Margaret heard her mother coming down the hall toward her bedroom, and she was lying on her bed with her face in the pillow. She knew she had been rude, but she felt that the boys were rude first. They were the ones who had come on their property uninvited. Cindy walked into the room and in a voice that was stern and direct said, "Mary Margaret sit up, I want to talk with you."

Into Addie's Arms

Mary Margaret slowly rolled over, and her mother again told her to, "Sit up."

Mary Margaret being unaccustomed to this tone from her mother sat up and wondered what was going to happen next.

Cindy began, "Mary Margaret I have been terribly disappointed in your behavior at times during the past week. I feel that you were just next to being rude with every word you said to Addie, and your behavior on the porch with the boys is inexcusable."

Mary Margaret had never had her mother speak to her in this way, and she felt the tears burning in her eyes and immediately begin rolling down her cheeks.

She continued by saying, "I understand that you are unhappy, but the reason for our being in South Carolina has nothing to do with Addie or the two boys who came to visit."

Mary Margaret started to protest, but her mother cut her off by saying, "Addie has already proven herself to be your good friend, and I will not tolerate any behavior from you toward her that is anything but cordial. People who live in this part of the country have different social customs. It's not unusual for neighbors to drop by unannounced, and from this point forward, you are expected to treat them with respect," her mother concluded.

When Cindy finished her lecture, she told Mary Margaret to wash her face and put on some jeans and a t-shirt. Mary Margaret, being unnerved by her mother's stern manner, immediately went into the bathroom and washed her face. When she came out, her mother was sitting on her bed, and she held out her arms to hug Mary Margaret. Even though she was upset, she still walked over to be hugged. It felt good against her mother's cool body. Cindy released Mary Margaret from the hug and told her to hurry up and get changed that they were going outside.

When Mary Margaret came downstairs, she looked like a different person. She had put her hair up in a ponytail, had on a tie-dyed t-shirt she had won at a school carnival, and she was wearing jeans and running shoes. She looked like a little girl who was going out to play. At that moment Cindy was struck with the thought that Mary Margaret didn't know how to go outside and play. Her socialization had been mostly indoors, and it was never in a situation where she was outside by herself. She was saddened when she realized that until the day that Mary Margaret first asked to go across the street at Mrs. Applegate's to see the camellias; and then when she walked down the driveway to get the mail, she had never been outside without supervision. Anytime she went outside the apartment building, and most of the time while she was in the building, she was accompanied by an adult. She suddenly felt sorry for her and knew that while Mary Margaret was unhappy at this moment, she would grow to love Left Fork, South Carolina, the people who lived there, and the freedom that would come with being there.

Chapter 22

Mary Margaret and her mother went outside and she instantly saw that her father, Davis, and Jordan were under her weeping willow tree. She wanted to say it wasn't fair, but thought better of it in light of her mother's recent lecture. They walked down to where the fishermen were, and Davis held up a stringer of small fish to show off their catch. He explained that they were Bream, and his mother would fix them for supper. As they stood there looking at the fish, Jordan yelled that he, *"Had one!"* All their eyes turned in his direction to see his fishing pole bent toward the water. In that same instant a large fish jumped about 15 feet from the edge of the pond. The fishing pole went up with the fish and Mary Margaret thought that fish was going to pull the pole from Jordan's hands. However, Mike stepped up behind him, put his hands over Jordan's, and together they held the pole. The water began to swirl as the fish attempted to escape. Jordan was silent as his eyes focused on the pond, Davis was shouting to Jordan to, *"Hold On!"* Mike was intent on gently holding the hands that held the pole and silently hoping that this fish wouldn't get off the hook. Cindy and Mary Margaret were clapping their hands and jumping up and down. This continued for what seemed an eternity to Jordan, but in reality was about three minutes. With Mike's help, Jordan landed the fish, which he then explained was a big-mouth bass. After extracting the hook, and with Mike's help, he held it up for them all to see. It was a big fish. Mike estimated that it weighed about 4 pounds. Cindy ran to the house to get the camera, and Davis and Jordan were discussing whether they had known anybody who had caught a larger fish. Mary Margaret came down to the edge of the pond to get a closer look, and to her surprise, both Jordan and Davis were willing to freely share the experience with her. They included her in their conversation. They seemed genuinely glad that she was there. She began to wonder if she would like fishing.

After the pictures were taken, the boys decided it was getting late, and they wanted their mother to fry the fish for supper. They thanked Mr. and Mrs. Smith, got on their bicycles, and rode off down the driveway.

Mary Margaret felt lonely when they had gone. She thought about this and wondered why her emotions were changing so rapidly. She was unhappy when they arrived, but now she was sad when they left. She couldn't help but wonder why.

Mike told Mary Margaret that he wanted to speak with her and asked her to sit on the porch swing with him. Mary Margaret knew another lecture was probably on its way. She wasn't wrong in her assumption.

"Mary Margaret I was so proud of you while you and your mother were in New York, and I was in South Carolina. I appreciate the support you gave me while we were moving. However, I am upset with the way you treated Davis and Jordan earlier. Customs are different here in the South, and while I don't expect you to know all of them; I do expect you to treat people of all ages with respect, and I know you know how to do that."

Tears streamed down her cheeks. She knew she had been rude. Her mother had pointed that out to her as well. Now, her father was telling her. She was embarrassed and wondered if she was ever going to do anything right again. "I'm sorry," she sincerely told her father, and the two of them went into the house.

Addie had left a casserole for dinner, and the family ate in the dining room. Mary Margaret set the table and together they ate as a family alone for the first time in their new home. The discussion led naturally to the boys.

"They certainly were nice boys," Mike said to his wife.

"Yes, and I wonder if they are having their big fish for dinner."

A knock at the door interrupted, and Mike went to see who was there. He returned in a short time with a plate of fish, hushpuppies, and a dish of homemade tartar sauce.

"Mr. Raver brought this over and thanked me for helping Jordan land the "big one," he laughed.

"Did you invite him in?" inquired Cindy.

"Of course, but he said he needed to get back to his dinner. He seemed like a nice sort of guy. I'm looking forward to seeing more of him," Mike replied as he placed the gifts on the table and returned to his meal.

The fish was wonderful, and the hush puppies reminded Mary Margaret of the seafood restaurant where they had eaten when she had been visiting.

The family went to bed early, and Mary Margaret was immediately reminded of Charlene as she climbed in between the sheets and smelled the faint odor of her perfume. It made her feel comfortable, and she fell to sleep almost at once.

Chapter 23

Sunday started off as a rainy day, and the weather matched Mary Margaret's mood. Each passing hour meant that she was one hour closer to attending the new school. Even though Addie had introduced her to Mrs. Stancil and she knew where to go to find her classroom, she was apprehensive about her classmates. It was becoming more apparent to Mary Margaret that she was going to be different from all the other students, and she was feeling that she wouldn't know what to do. The other students knew the customs of the South, and she didn't. Would she do something that would offend them and not even know it? Mary Margaret was working herself into a frenzy when Mike suggested that they go to visit the Gilberts.

Cindy asked if they should call first, and Mike said that Gerry had told him to drop by on Sunday if it was convenient. Mary Margaret's spirits lifted at the prospect of seeing the horses and especially the foal. She hurried to get into her jeans and sneakers, so that if the opportunity to go outside presented itself, she would be ready. The ride over there was short, and as the car rounded the corner into the driveway, she saw Philip in the pasture riding one of the horses.

He sat erect in the saddle, and his high black boots looked smart against the side of the horse. His body seemed as one with the animal, and she was impressed as he went over jumps, which were set up in the pasture. When he finished his pattern, he turned and waved to them smiling. As they stopped at the end of the driveway, he was walking over holding the reins in his hand.

Of course, the dogs greeted them with what was known as their friendly greeting, and Mary Margaret squatted down to pet them. In their exuberance they once again knocked her over, but this time she fell into a puddle of water remaining from the rain earlier that day. She splashed as she hit bottom and was immediately soaked. The dogs thought it was part of the greeting and continued to nudge against her so that she couldn't get up. Her parents were laughing too hard to help, Mary Margaret was laughing, and it was Philip who finally held out a helping hand so that she could get to her feet. Gerry and Sylvia Gilbert came out just as she was swinging her hands to shake off the water. They joined in the laughter and at the same time scolded the dogs. Goldie and Freckles thought they were heroes—all this laughter and their names in the middle of it. They must have done something wonderful they thought.

Sylvia took Mary Margaret in to get her dried off and offered her a pair of Philip's jeans and a t-shirt so that she could get out of the wet clothes. She took Mary Margaret's clothes, clear down to her underwear, and put them in the washer. "You'll be good as new in an hour or so," she assured her. She gave her a pair of riding boots that Philip had outgrown, and they fit almost perfectly. When she was again presentable, they went back outside.

Philip was surprised to see Mary Margaret wearing his clothes, but didn't say anything about it. Gerry asked Mary Margaret if she was interested in riding a horse since she looked like an equestrian in those boots. She looked to her parents for an answer, but they only smiled and said nothing. Mary Margaret timidly responded, "I have never ridden a horse before, and I'm not sure I can ride."

"We'll put you on a gentle horse if it's something you really want to do," Mr. Gilbert promised.

"Oh, yes, more than anything, but I am frightened," she confessed.

"Well, why don't you ride with Philip first and get the feel. Then we'll put you on the horse by yourself," Mr. Gilbert suggested.

Philip silently cringed, but knew his father's actions were only to make Mary Margaret more comfortable about being on a horse for almost the first time in her life.

It was decided that was a good plan, and Philip went into the barn and came out with another saddled horse. He called this one Daisy, and he climbed onto the saddle. Mr. Gilbert stood beside Mary Margaret, helped her put her left foot in the stirrup, and told her how to swing her right leg across the horse's back; and soon she was behind Philip. The horse took a few tiny steps, and Mary Margaret held tightly. Once she was seated, and told them she was okay, Philip started slowly walking the horse around the pasture. Mary Margaret soon released her tight grip from around his waist. When he felt this release and realized that Mary Margaret was getting comfortable, he nudged the sides of the horse, and it increased its speed into a slow canter. Mary Margaret held tighter again, and soon released her grip, as she became comfortable at this speed. Once Philip had circled the pasture a few times, he went back to where the parents were watching.

"How did that feel?" Mr. Gilbert asked the new equestrian.

"It was wonderful."

"Do you want to keep riding?"

"*Forever*," she replied.

"Well, you just stay right where you are, and I'll hold the reins while Philip gets off."

Philip swung his right leg to the front and was able to jump from the horse. Mr. Gilbert continued to hold onto Mary Margaret as she slid forward in the saddle. He gave her a few instructions on holding the reins, and he walked with her and the horse around the perimeter of the fenced pasture. He gave her direction and soon realized that she was relaxing and feeling comfortable in the saddle. When he felt she was accomplished enough to stay on the horse by herself, he instructed Philip to ride alongside Mary Margaret. Philip mounted his horse, and he and Mary Margaret took a slow walk around the pasture. Mary Margaret was exhilarated as she felt the horse moving beneath her. It was so strong, but seemed to sense that she was unsure of herself. Once around, and Philip asked her if she wanted to try it by herself. She said she did, and as the two families watched, Mary Margaret rode the horse around the pasture; and when she returned, she knew that this was something she wanted to do again and again. She had never felt such freedom.

"May I canter now?" she tentatively questioned.

"If you feel you're ready," Gerry Gilbert said. "I do think you need to wear a hard hat. We feel it's best anytime you get on a horse, just for protection."

Mary Margaret put on the hat, adjusted her seating in the saddle, and nudged the sides of Daisy. Daisy seemed to comprehend the importance of this run, and gently cantered around the pasture. Mary Margaret smiled until her cheeks ached as she felt the air rushing past. When she came back around to the parents, she asked if she could do it again. Mr. Gilbert told her that she certainly could and told Philip he could ride again if he wanted. Philip asked her if she wanted to go out of this pasture into the field behind their house. She looked at Mr. Gilbert who nodded in agreement.

Mary Margaret and Philip headed in the direction of the gate at the opposite end of the pasture. The adults went to sit on the porch. Gerry went inside and came back with a tray of glasses and a pitcher of lemonade.

"I can't thank you enough for allowing Mary Margaret to ride," Cindy said. "She's been having a tough time adjusting, and this is certainly taking her mind off her troubles."

"I understand, and we're so glad y'all dropped by. I think that horses are good therapy for anything that ails you." The adults laughed and sipped their lemonade while the children rode in the adjacent pasture.

Mike said, "Maybe Mary Margaret should have her own horse."

Cindy looked alarmed when he mentioned the subject, but the Gilberts almost simultaneously gave their vote of approval to the idea.

"We feel that horses have been wonderful tools for teaching responsibility to Philip. He is responsible for feeding them, watering them, keeping the stalls clean, and the horses groomed. He gets up an hour early every morning to do his chores and does them again every afternoon after school. Of course, he sometimes has other obligations that make this impossible, and we cover for him, but it is chiefly his responsibility," they continued.

"Philip competes and does very well. Mary Margaret looks the part of a rider, and I'll bet she would enjoy that, too," Sylvia added.

It was agreed that it would be given some consideration, but that nothing would be said to Mary Margaret now. They would see how she reacted to the horses.

"I want to make certain that this is not a here today, gone tomorrow love," said her father.

Philip and Mary Margaret rode into the field, and he showed her how to negotiate the horse into a figure 8. In no time at all, she had accomplished this. Philip knew that Mary Margaret was not accomplished enough to try jumping, but he could see that she had a natural ability on a horse. He smiled as he watched her canter around the field.

Philip finally said, "We've probably been gone long enough."

Mary Margaret was disappointed, but agreed following him back to the barn.

When they reached their destination, Philip dismounted and came around to help Mary Margaret.

"I would like to do this myself, please," she politely responded remembering her lectures on respect of the day before. Though not as graceful as he had been, she soon had both feet on the ground.

"Now we have to groom the horses," Philip explained. Mary Margaret watched as he led his horse into the barn, and followed with Daisy. He gave her a brush, and she helped him with his horse. Then they groomed Daisy. Each horse shook its head, and its mane looked like silk. The horses seemed appreciative of the each brush stroke. Soon they both shone.

"I have to feed and water all the horses, do you want to help?" Philip asked his new friend.

"Oh, yes," she responded, and he instructed her on how to measure the feed and how to mix each horse's allotment.

"Horses don't know when to quit eating. They eat all they find until it's gone, so it's important not to put too much food into their feeder. Eating too much can make them very sick," Philip explained.

Mary Margaret was impressed with his knowledge and watched carefully each move he made. Together they measured the feed and mixed it. Soon all the horses had been fed and fresh water was put out for them.

"Does your father usually do this?" Mary Margaret asked.

"No, it's my responsibility to feed the horses. I don't feel that I can eat if I know the horses aren't fed first."

With the chores finished and the riding completed for the day, they left the barn. "You can keep the boots if they really fit you," Philip said.

"Oh, that would be great, but we better ask your mother first."

"I will, but I know it'll be okay."

When they reached the porch, Philip immediately asked his mother, "Can Mary Margaret keep the boots?"

Mary Margaret blushed at his directness and was pleased to hear the response, "Of course, if they truly fit her. That would be fine."

Mary Margaret excitedly answered, "Oh, yes, they are perfect," and wondered if this may be the best day in her life.

After they discussed the ride in the field and drank a glass of lemonade, Cindy said that they needed to get home as there was school tomorrow. Mary Margaret immediately felt like the props had been knocked from under her. Her good mood was instantly replaced with a feeling of dread.

Philip must have noticed the look in her eyes, and said, "I'll wait for you at the front door of the school, if you want me to."

Mary Margaret couldn't believe her ears as she heard him say the words. She, without looking at him for fear that he would see the tears building up in her eyes, told him, "That's fine, thanks."

Sylvia retrieved Mary Margaret's clothes from the dryer, and the families said good-bye. Mary Margaret started to get into the car and then ran back to Sylvia Gilbert. "Thank you so much for the boots, they are the greatest."

Without further thought she reached up and unaccustomedly hugged her benefactor before running back to leave with her parents.

"Philip, thank you for offering to meet Mary Margaret," his mother said.

"It was nothing. She seems okay for a *girl*," he said.

Gerry and Sylvia winked to each other as Philip opened the door to go inside.

Mary Margaret showered when she got home, and her mother fixed grilled cheese sandwiches and cups of tomato soup. The temperature had dropped this evening, and the soup felt good after being outdoors all afternoon.

After helping clear the table, Mary Margaret went into her room to arrange the things she would need the next morning. She took the list Mrs. Stancil had given her and got out the new book bag she and Charlene had purchased at Bloomingdale's. She put everything inside along with the library book and placed it beside the front door.

Next, she went into her closet and selected an outfit for tomorrow. Mary Margaret had never had to think about what to wear to school, but she wanted everything to be perfect. She wanted to fit in, but she wasn't sure what she wanted to fit in to. She only knew three boys who went to her school. She didn't know any girls. *Surely there are girls who go to school there*, she thought. Mary Margaret chose khaki slacks and a navy polo shirt. She polished her loafers. She placed her clothes on the chair in her bedroom, so that the morning wouldn't be too hectic.

She went into the family room where her parents were listening to the radio, and asked, "Mother will you help me write down our address and telephone number?"

Her mother was surprised that she hadn't already thought of this, but was pleased that her daughter had. *She has so much new information to digest*, her mother thought. Together they wrote out the information along with her mother's work telephone number, her father's work telephone number, Addie's name, and Mrs. Applegate's telephone number. Mary Margaret finally felt that she had everything to get started tomorrow.

Chapter 24

"Good night," she told her parents. She went into her bedroom, and slipped between the sweet smelling sheets which reminded her of Charlene and Alice.

Oh, no, she thought. *I haven't called Alice or written her a letter*, and silently promised herself that tomorrow after school she would call both Charlene and Alice. She drifted into a restless sleep. At some point Mary Margaret began dreaming. She was riding a horse, but it wasn't Daisy. It was a big, black stallion, and he was uncontrollable. No matter how hard she pulled on the reins, he would not respond. He was running faster and faster. There were trees up ahead. Mary Margaret began to duck so that the limbs would not hit her in the face. The horse swerved and jumped a log. She felt herself coming off the horse and falling, falling, falling! She was screaming! She awoke with a start just as she was ready to hit the ground in her dream. Her heart was beating very fast, and her breathing was quick.

It took her a few seconds to realize that she was not falling. She was safe in her bed. She didn't realize, however, that she had actually screamed. Her parents came rushing into her bedroom to find her lying safely in her bed.

"I had a bad dream," she explained. They assured her that everything was all right, and she went back to sleep.

A new dream began. This time she was in the subway. She needed to be somewhere at a specific time. She was alone, and people were shoving her. The train pulled in, but she was not able to make her way to the door before it closed, and the train whisked away. This occurred over and over again, and she was never able to reach the door, much less her destination. She finally awoke and realized that she had been dreaming. She looked at the clock, which glowed 4:00. Restlessly, she tossed and turned until the alarm rudely sounded at 6:00 a.m.

Mary Margaret lay in her bed trying to think about the upcoming day. *I know what I'm wearing, and I have my supplies by the door. Philip is meeting me at the front door, Mrs. Stancil has shown me where my seat is, and I know where my classroom is. I can do this*, she calmly thought.

Her anxiety settled, and she got up to get ready for school. Her mother knocked and stuck her head in. She was glad to see that Mary Margaret was already up.

"Breakfast will be ready in about 15 minutes," she cheerfully told her exhausted daughter.

When she came out for breakfast, she found her father, who was already dressed for work, at the table reading the Charleston newspaper; and her mother was putting her oatmeal on the table. The raisin happy face made her smile in spite of the day. She thanked her mother for thinking of it, and Cindy hugged her daughter. Mary Margaret was trying very hard to be in a good mood. She wanted to have a good start to this day.

Just as they were sitting down, Mary Margaret heard the key in the door and knew instantly that Addie had arrived. She came in and asked in her loud voice, "Mary Margaret, are you ready for the *big day*."

"Yes, ma'm, I'm as ready as I can be," she politely responded.

Her mother smiled across the table to Mary Margaret silently saying, *Thank you for being nice to Addie*.

Addie started a non-stop litany of words about what she had done on Sunday. Mary Margaret's parents seemed genuinely interested in hearing what she had to say, and joined in the conversation.

Mary Margaret was recalling her own Sunday and was lost in her thoughts as she remembered riding high atop Daisy and the wind blowing past her as they ran across the field. Suddenly, she realized that she was being brought into the conversation by Addie saying, "I saw you on that horse yesterday, and you looked wonderful." Mary Margaret blushed, not necessarily with embarrassment but with the pleasure she remembered from the experience. "Thank you, Addie, I appreciate the compliment," she politely responded.

With breakfast finished and Addie cleaning up the kitchen, Mike and Cindy kissed Mary Margaret good-bye and left for their jobs. They were discussing new cars as they went out the door. They were still driving a rental car, which was being shared; and it was obvious now that they were in their house they each needed a vehicle. Mary Margaret watched the tail lights as they disappeared around the curve in the driveway. She looked at her watch and it was almost 7:00. The bus would be coming at 7:15 according to what Mrs. Stancil had told her.

Mary Margaret went to her room and made her bed. Addie yelled just as she came out of the bedroom, "It's time to go catch the bus."

"I'm right here," she softly said coming down the stairs. She saw that Addie was putting on a jacket, and was relieved to know that she was going with her to wait on the bus. It was barely daylight, and Mary Margaret had wondered if Addie expected her to go out by herself. She picked up her book bag and together they walked down the driveway. The birds were awake and noisy. The sky was a beautiful shade of pink toward the east. Addie quoted, "Red skies in morning, sailors take warning; Red skies at night, sailors delight." Mary Margaret had never heard this before and asked, "Addie, what does that mean?"

"Well, child, it's from the Bible (Matthew 16:2-3) and means that if the sky looks red in the morning, there's a good chance for bad weather. However, if the sky is red at night, chances are that the next day we'll have nice weather. If it's raining after school, I'll meet you here with an umbrella."

"Thanks," Mary Margaret said softly. The bus was rounding the curve and she could see the red light flashing on the front. The burning immediately started behind her eyes, but she swallowed and took deep breaths. This was not a good time to cry. When the bus stopped, Mary Margaret told Addie, "Good-bye," and climbed up the steps.

She had ridden the bus in New York, but she was always with an adult, usually Charlene. They always sat together, and the other riders weren't important. However, today was different. Mary Margaret was on that bus alone; and as she walked toward the only empty seat, she was looking at the faces of strangers, whom she felt were looking at her like she was an alien. The only empty seat was on the right side of the bus, and as she sat down, she realized that Davis and Jordan were seated behind her. Jordan immediately said, "Hey," but Davis looked at his feet as though it was the first time he had ever seen them.

Mary Margaret returned the greeting to Jordan, and he came up to sit beside her. She had mixed feelings about this. She was glad to have the company, but wondered what everyone would think about her sitting with a boy who was younger than she. As it turned out, Jordan was such a chatterbox; Mary Margaret had little time to wonder much about anything. He talked so much about the fish he caught, his new sneakers, and his 4-H project that the time passed very quickly; and she realized that they were at the school when all the other students stood up to get off. She had to wait until everybody else had passed her seat before she and Jordan could stand, so they were the last ones off the bus. Jordan waved good-bye and ran to meet up with a friend.

Mary Margaret looked around, and got her bearings. She realized that the bus had stopped at the rear of the school. She walked to the front and standing on the bottom step was Philip, just as he promised. She smiled as she walked up, but Philip just said, "Hey," and started walking toward the door. Mary Margaret followed and remembered the foal following its mother. This gave her a passing good feeling, but she didn't like Philip's walking ahead of her. She was not a baby following anybody. They walked the length of the hall in silence as the other students hurried past. Some looked at her, but most were too busy with their friends to notice. She looked ahead and saw Mrs. Stancil standing beside her door. It was a relief to see somebody she recognized. Mrs. Stancil greeted her warmly and came inside the room with her. Philip had already taken his seat, and Mary Margaret noticed that it was beside where Mrs. Stancil showed her she would be sitting. Yesterday, she would have felt good about this, but today Philip's aloof attitude left her feeling angry toward him.

Mrs. Stancil showed her where to put her jacket, and she took her seat. The other students looked at her, and some nodded a greeting. Mary Margaret looked around the room and saw that Davis was sitting in the row behind her, and he still ignored her completely. Mary Margaret thought that the next time he came over to fish she would tell him to go home, but then she remembered her mother's lecture and knew that was impossible. She in that instant wondered if her mother had ever been 9 years old and had to deal with boys.

The bell rang, and everyone took their seats. Mrs. Stancil called the roll and the new student watched as the names were called, and her classmates responded. This time gave her an opportunity to look around the room, and she saw that there were an almost equal number of girls and boys. She was relieved to see that. When she finished taking roll, she asked Mary Margaret to stand, and she introduced her to the class.

"Class, this is Mary Margaret Smith. She has moved here from New York City, and I want you to make her feel welcome and a part of this class and this community." Mary Margaret blushed as she was talking, and she felt the burning in the back of her eyes and throat, but knew that she wouldn't cry. She kept swallowing and eventually Mrs. Stancil finished the introduction, and she, thankfully, was able to sit down.

Mrs. Stancil completed the morning activities and sold lunch tickets. Mary Margaret bought her tickets for the week. She noticed that most of the students didn't buy tickets, and she was surprised by this. Everybody at St. Mark's ate lunch in the school cafeteria, and the meals were included in the monthly tuition. She wondered where these students ate lunch.

Finally, it was time to begin the day's academics, and math was the first class of the day. When Mrs. Stancil announced the page to turn to, she saw that they were at almost the same place as her class in New York. She sighed with relief and took out her notebook to begin the day's work. The morning passed quickly, and when it was time for lunch Mary Margaret's stomach growled almost on cue. She looked around to see if anybody had heard her stomach, and Philip was smiling in her direction.

Chapter 25

"Jane Ellis, will you go with Mary Margaret to the cafeteria?" Mrs. Stancil asked.

"Of course," she answered.

Mary Margaret thought Jane didn't have a choice but to go with her. However, Jane seemed sincerely glad to show her the way. As they walked down the hall, Jane seemed to know most of the students they passed.

"What was it like to live in New York City?" Jane asked as they walked.

"Well, I lived there my whole life, and I think it's wonderful. I didn't want to move *here*!"

"I've lived here all my life, and I love it. I have 3 sisters and 2 brothers. My father teaches at the high school, and my mother is a secretary for a Judge in the County Seat. My family has lived here for 4 generations, and I can't imagine living any place else," she confidently concluded.

Mary Margaret wondered if she had offended Jane by telling her that she hadn't wanted to move here. She figured she probably had because she seemed to be offending everybody she had met since she came to Left Fork.

"Come and sit with me and my friends," Jane said once they went through the lunch line. She nodded her head in the direction of a table in the corner where 4 girls were already seated. As they walked toward them, Mary Margaret felt they were discussing her, and they were passing around a notebook. The book was pretty with pink, white and yellow roses on the cover. They were whispering and laughing, and their heads were nodding in her direction. The girls were all dressed in their Easter dresses, and Mary Margaret felt conspicuous in her slacks. They talked about their spring break and what they had done, and Mary Margaret felt like the outsider that she was. She had nothing to add, and that was good, because she was not asked to add anything to the conversation.

In fact, she soon realized that the girls were actually making fun of her. Allison was describing Mary Margaret's clothes and pointing her finger and laughing at her shoes, "It looks like she shops at the prison outlet store, and on the clearance rack at that," she hatefully said. "Look at her hair, it has no curl, and she probably smells like the garbage that's piled on the streets in New York City," she continued. The other girls giggled, and nobody came to her defense.

To Mary Margaret they were agreeing with her by not contradicting or trying to stop her nasty words. She hated this. She wished that she was in the cafeteria at St. Marks wearing a uniform just like everybody else and eating lunch with Alice and her other friends.

Lunch consisted of a piece of pizza, a peach half, salad, and milk. Mary Margaret was nearly in tears as she ate a bite of the pizza, two bites of the salad and all of the peach. She tasted the milk and decided that she had better not push her luck as her stomach was beginning to feel upset. The longer she sat there, and the more the girls insulted her, the more she knew it was not going to be good. Her throat and eyes were burning, her stomach was churning, and the girls had huddled to again write in their notebook. *Oh, no, please, not this*, she thought. She stood up, and before she could ask about the location of the restroom, Mary Margaret upchucked right in the middle of the cafeteria.

Of course, all eyes were on her as she stood there thoroughly humiliated. Nobody moved for an instant and then activity seemed everywhere. She was surprised to find Davis at her side holding her arm. The custodian was there and was cleaning up the mess. She just wanted to get out of there; and as she walked toward the door, Davis was at her side. She got into the hallway and started running toward the front door.

"Where are you going?" Davis asked.

"I'm going home," she responded.

"You can't do that," he countered.

"Yes, I can," she yelled as she ran out of the school. She found herself on the sidewalk in front of the building. She stopped and looked around. Luckily, she remembered that Mrs. Applegate lived nearby, and she started walking in that direction.

Davis stood on the school steps and watched her turn the corner. He realized that he should tell Mrs. Stancil what had happened, but she was in the teachers' lounge, and he had never been there before. He went down the hall and knocked on the door that said "Private—No Students Allowed." Another teacher answered the door, and he asked "May I speak with Mrs. Stancil, please?"

When she came to the door, he explained what had happened and that Mary Margaret had left. She thanked him and hurried to the front of the building and onto the sidewalk. Of course, by this time Mary Margaret was out of sight, and Mrs. Stancil realized that she must contact Addie.

She went into the office and placed the call; explained to her what had happened; and asked her to come look for Mary Margaret and let her know when she found her.

Addie got in her truck and started driving toward the school looking all along the way and was upset when she reached the building and had not seen her. She drove around town, and soon realized that she would have to go tell Mr. Smith. She drove to the mill and went in the main office. "I need to speak with Mr. Smith," she bluntly told the receptionist.

"I'm sorry, he's in a meeting, and you'll have to wait," she responded.

"His child is missing, and I don't think he'd want me to wait to tell him that," Addie replied.

The receptionist, who realized the urgency of the situation but equally realized her own danger if she postponed the message, told Addie, "I'll get him, just have a seat."

"I'll bet you will," the frightened nanny responded as she paced the floor. She immediately felt bad that she had come across so rudely. Tact had never been one of her finer qualities, and she always hated it when situations arose where that came to light. However, finding Mary Margaret was her main concern. She'd apologize later.

Mr. Smith came from the door the receptionist had entered, but she was noticeably absent. He listened to the explanation for Addie's being there, and he said that he would drive in one direction around town and asked Addie to drive in the opposite direction. They planned to meet back at the school in 20 minutes.

Chapter 26

Mary Margaret was crying as she walked along the street toward Mrs. Applegate's house. She was worried that she was in trouble for leaving school; she was embarrassed that she had been sick in front of the whole school; and now she was afraid that Mrs. Applegate would not be home. Her nose was running, and she had no tissues. She wiped her nose on her hand and then wiped her hand on her pants. Her face was red, her clothes were stained, and as she looked at her loafers, she saw that they were splattered. She was crying so hard and looking down at the sidewalk so that nobody could see her face, that she didn't notice the truck pulling in down the street nor the woman getting out. However, when she reached the place adjacent to where the truck was parked, Addie was standing on the sidewalk blocking her path.

She recognized the running shoes that Addie always wore. She looked up, and Addie was standing there, arms crossed, staring in her direction. Mary Margaret stopped walking and looked back at Addie. Addie's comment to her was, "I don't know whether to be mad at you, or to feel bad for you."

Mary Margaret sobbed, "Please don't be mad. I have had a terrible experience." Addie walked up to her and put her arm around Mary Margaret, leading her in the direction of the truck. Mary Margaret got in on the driver's side and scooted across. Addie explained that they had to go back to the school as her father was going to be there in a few minutes. She started crying again because she dreaded facing him.

They arrived at the school, and Mr. Smith's car was nowhere in sight. Addie said they had to wait, and she told Mary Margaret to stay in the truck so that she could go tell Mrs. Stancil that she had found her. Her stomach felt as though she had been kicked by a horse when Addie said she had to tell Mrs. Stancil. She knew that she was going to be angry that she had left without telling anyone. Addie went inside, leaving her alone in the truck.

Her father pulled up and walked over to the passenger side. Mary Margaret saw him and the tears flowed again. He opened the door and told her, "Mary Margaret I am so glad that you are all right. However, it is not all right for you to leave school like that no matter how bad things seem."

"But Daddy, you don't know. The girls were mean, and then I vomited, and . . ." she began.

"There is no excuse for your behavior. You don't have the right to upset people. I'm sorry you had a bad experience, but I am disappointed in the way you handled it," he concluded, his fear beginning to subside as his child was safely with him again.

Mary Margaret was sobbing by this time, and Mr. Smith knew that he had been firm in his words with her. He, however, also knew that she could not continue to behave like this and upset people who cared about her. He also knew that her safety was jeopardized as she wandered the unfamiliar streets alone.

Addie returned to find Mr. Smith standing by the truck and Mary Margaret sobbing. She looked at her employer and could tell by his look that he had scolded Mary Margaret for her behavior.

"I told Mrs. Stancil that we found her," Addie told Mr. Smith. She suggested that I take her home and allow her to get cleaned up and come back. They are starting a special project this afternoon, and she wants Mary Margaret to be a part of it."

"That sounds like a good idea," he said as he kissed his daughter good-bye. "Thank you for your help, Addie," he said as he smiled in her direction.

Mary Margaret thought it was a terrible idea. She didn't want to ever go back to that school. However, she knew that the decision was already made.

Chapter 27

When they arrived at home, Addie told Mary Margaret to hurry and wash up and change her clothes. Mary Margaret went into the bathroom and looked in the mirror. Her face was red, and her eyes were swollen. It would be obvious that she had been crying. She couldn't go to school looking like that. She cleaned up and changed her clothes. She went into the laundry room where she found Addie.

"Please don't make me go back," she pleaded as she handed over her soiled clothes.

"You have to go," she said as they headed for the truck to begin the short trip. In an attempt to change the subject, Addie said, "I'll pick you up after school, and we'll go to Orville's Seed and Feed and get some tomato plants."

Mary Margaret continued to sulk as she sat beside Addie. Addie continued her chatter and tried to lift Mary Margaret's spirits, but as she glanced across the seat, she could see tears streaming down her face.

"I'm sorry this happened to you, and I understand that you are embarrassed. Just think, the other kids are probably just glad it didn't happen to them, and they won't make a big deal out of it," Addie gently said.

"I think you're wrong," Mary Margaret politely said. "I have humiliated myself in front of the whole school. Some girls were already making fun of me, and I just got there. Now they have something to make fun of. One thing is for sure, though, at least everybody will know who I am," she concluded with a touch of humor.

"Maybe that isn't so bad. I'll go in with you," Addie said when they arrived at the school.

Mary Margaret was surprisingly glad to have Addie at her side. They went into the office, and the secretary told Mary Margaret that she was so sorry about her accident at lunch. She also said that the principal wanted to speak with them before Mary Margaret went to her classroom, and asked them to have a seat.

Within a few minutes, the principal, Mrs. Grace Calhoun, opened her door and invited them into her office. Mary Margaret was surprised. It looked more like a living room than a principal's office. There were rocking chairs, and Mrs. Calhoun didn't sit at her desk, but rather took a chair next to Mary Margaret. Addie and she were old friends and after the introductions were completed between Mrs. Calhoun and Mary Margaret, Mrs. Calhoun said, "Mary Margaret, I'm sorry your first day in my school was spoiled with a bad experience. I want my students to feel at home while they are here. You spend an equal number or more waking hours here as you do at home, and I feel it's important that you feel safe and comfortable. Just remember, child, you are not the first one to get sick here, and you surely will not be the last. During one flu epidemic we had more than 25 students in one day get sick and upchuck here. It's just unfortunate it happened to you on your first day. However, I think this day can be salvaged."

She told Addie that it was okay for her to leave. She said she wanted to walk with Mary Margaret to her classroom and sit in on the afternoon's activities. Addie told Mary Margaret that she would pick her up after school, and they'd get the tomato plants.

"One more thing, Mary Margaret, you cannot ever leave school again without permission. You jeopardized your safety, and broke one of our rules. If anything happens in the future and you need help, you just find Mrs. Stancil, me, or any of our other teachers. We'll help you with anything. We are going to overlook it this one time, but not a second, do you understand?" Mrs. Calhoun concluded.

"Yes, ma'm, it won't happen again," the frightened child said also remembering her father's lecture.

"Okay, now, let's go see what Mrs. Stancil has in store for your class this afternoon."

Mary Margaret wanted to spend the rest of the afternoon in Mrs. Calhoun's office, but followed her as she led the way.

Chapter 28

Mrs. Calhoun put her arm on Mary Margaret's shoulder as they walked down the hall; and when she opened the door to Mrs. Stancil's room, she walked in with Mary Margaret and took a seat in the back. Mary Margaret sat in her seat, and Mrs. Stancil winked at her and smiled. Philip looked over and raised his eyebrows in a gesture of understanding. Mary Margaret looked around the room. Nobody seemed at all interested in her, and they were concentrating on writing down spelling words which Mrs. Stancil had written on the board. Mary Margaret took out her notebook; and she, too, wrote the words.

Mrs. Stancil interrupted the students when a gentleman opened the door. This man was wearing bib overalls, a red plaid shirt, and was carrying a straw hat. Of course, Mary Margaret didn't know who he was, but Mrs. Stancil greeted him and introduced him as Mr. Clark. Mr. Clark came into the room and spoke quietly with the teacher. Then she asked the students to put their work away. They all cleared their desks, and Mrs. Stancil said they were going to go out to the back of the school. They all lined up and followed her, Mrs. Calhoun and Mr. Clark down the hall and out the back door. Mary Margaret never spoke to anybody as they walked, but the other students were quiet, too. When they got outside she was surprised to see a horse wearing a straw hat. Its ears poked through holes, and artificial daisies surrounded the brim. The horse was attached to a plow.

"We're going to do something different this term for our South Carolina History Project. We're going to plant a garden and grow vegetables and flowers much like it was done many years ago before tractors. Some of the vegetables will be ready for harvest before school is out, but it's my desire that some of you will stay involved and continue the project into the summer. The food we grow can be a part of a community project to help feed the needy," the teacher concluded.

A murmur went through the students; and Mary Margaret could tell that some were excited, while others were almost groaning. She was excited. She hoped that she could do something with the horse, and she wasn't disappointed. Mrs. Stancil asked Philip to come up first and with Mr. Clark's help, they started making furrows in the ground. When Philip had completed his turn, Mrs. Stancil told him to choose his successor, and he chose Mary Margaret. She blushed as she went up for her turn, and was so thankful that she was wearing slacks. She couldn't imagine doing this in one of her good dresses. When Mary Margaret had completed her area, she was asked to choose her successor, and she chose Davis. Since he was the only one she knew except Jane Ellis and her snooty friends, he was her likely choice. Anyway, he had come to her rescue when she got sick she thought. Oh, no, she didn't ever want to remember that again.

Mr. Clark and the horse continued with each student having an opportunity to plow. When they were finished, Mrs. Stancil told the students that they would be planting lettuce, radishes, squash, cucumbers, pole beans and tomatoes. Mary Margaret was relieved that she had helped Mrs. Applegate with her planting and felt comfortable when it was her turn to plant the tomato plants.

Mr. Clark was impressed that she knew about digging a deep hole for the tomatoes. He told her that most people weren't aware of this method of planting, but he sure felt it made for stronger plants. Mary Margaret smiled as she completed her 6 plants. Davis and Philip were tying string around stakes so that they made what appeared to be a t-pee. Mr. Clark had shown them the first one, and they were continuing down the row. These were for the beans to have support as they grew, Mr. Clark explained. Some of the students planted the cucumbers and squash plants while others raked the soil smooth to plant the seeds for radishes and lettuce. The afternoon sun was hot, and Mary Margaret was perspiring. Her hands were dirty, and she had wiped her face leaving smudges across her nose, but she was glad to have the opportunity to be outside. When they had finished, Mr. Clark said that he would water everything, but that the garden would need watering on a regular basis, and Mrs. Stancil said that she would set up a committee to see to this if it didn't rain.

Into Addie's Arms

The students went inside and Mrs. Stancil told them to go to the restroom to wash up before returning to the classroom to get ready to go home. When Mary Margaret went into the restroom, none of the girls talked to her, but they didn't laugh at her either. Everybody just seemed hot, tired, and ready for the school day to end. They went back into the classroom just as the bell rang.

"Don't forget your homework," Mrs. Stancil reminded them as they rushed to catch their buses.

Mary Margaret got her math book from her desk and the notebook in which she had written her spelling words. She started to leave and went to Mrs. Stancil's desk.

"Excuse me, Mrs. Stancil, do you have a moment, please?" she politely asked.

"Of, course, dear, what is it?" she responded.

"I just wanted to apologize for causing you to worry today. I shouldn't have left like that," she continued, her voice quivering.

Mrs. Stancil smiled, "You know what, if I had been in your shoes, I may have done the same thing. However, if you have any future problems, come to me, Mrs. Calhoun or any other teacher. We're here to help you not only with school work but with any adjustments you have to make."

Mary Margaret left and saw Addie's truck waiting behind the school busses. Her mood was much lighter than she had expected. She almost skipped to the truck and climbed in beside Addie.

Addie could see the lilt in Mary Margaret's step and was smiling when she opened the door. She immediately asked how things had gone, and Mary Margaret described the garden planting, never mentioning the cafeteria incident. Addie drove over to Orville's Seed and Feed and thought it best not to mention it, too.

Chapter 29

When they arrived at Orville's, Mary Margaret was surprised to see that Mr. Clark was Orville. He had tied up his horse in the front of the store, where it had made a *deposit* on the sidewalk. Addie and Mary Margaret walked carefully around the horse, its *deposit*, and all of the items that Orville had on display in front of his store. Today there were tillers, rakes, shovels, and some things that Mary Margaret had never seen before. She remarked to Addie that she was surprised that he would leave those things out there. Addie explained that there was almost no crime in Left Fork and to be caught stealing something from somebody in town would create a near shunning from the community. She said it just wasn't done.

Mr. Clark, Orville, greeted them warmly as they went inside the store, and he immediately told Addie that this little lady, of course, referring to Mary Margaret, was quite a farmer. He said she did the best job of planting tomato plants he had ever seen. Mary Margaret smiled and blushed. Addie was surprised to hear this and asked her if she had ever planted tomato plants before. She explained that she had helped Mrs. Applegate with her garden, and Addie and Orville simultaneously said "Oooh!"

Addie and Orville gathered up the supplies they would need for their planting. He selected what he called strong plants, got the fertilizer, stakes, and a shovel and hoe for *turning over the ground*. He helped Addie and Mary Margaret take their purchases and put them in the back of the truck.

"Do you like horses?" he asked Mary Margaret.

"Oh yes," she responded.

"Would you like to pet Martha?"

"I would love to," she said.

"Come on up here toward her head," he said, slapping Martha on the rump as he walked by.

Martha turned her head to see who was approaching. She apparently was satisfied with Mary Margaret, because she stood very still and patiently allowed herself to be petted. Mary Margaret was surprised at how soft Martha felt. She supposed that a work horse would have coarse hair. Mr. Clark reached in his pocket and withdrew some sugar cubes and handed them to her. He was pleased to see that she held her palm flat as she offered the sugar to Martha. Martha gently ate the sugar and nudged Mary Margaret for seconds. Mr. Clark, Addie and Mary Margaret laughed. Addie said they needed to be getting home, so they got in the truck and headed away from town.

When they drove in the driveway the two deer were standing just off to the right. Addie drove slowly past them, and they didn't move. Again, Addie gave Mary Margaret a reminder that while they were beautiful, she must remember that they are wild animals, and she must respect their territory. "Don't ever get them in a position where they have no escape except to run over you. They would most certainly do that if they felt trapped." Mary Margaret thought that Addie was exaggerating, but she knew that she would remember the warning.

As they rounded the curve in the driveway Mary Margaret could see that Davis and Jordan were fishing. Her immediate impulse was negative, but she remembered the lecture from both her mother and father, and decided to go inside the house. However, before she could reach the porch, Jordan was yelling for her to come down to the pond. Addie told her to go ahead, that she would take her books in for her.

Mary Margaret walked across the knoll to the lake. Davis was sitting on the ground and Jordan was sitting on a tree stump at the water's edge. Davis looked in her direction and asked, "Are you feeling better?"

Mary Margaret blushed and said, "Yes," not knowing what to expect. "Thank you for trying to help me."

"It was nothing," he said as he put a fresh worm on his hook.

"I threw up in my classroom earlier this winter. We had a flu epidemic that went through the school. It was awful," Jordan said.

"I know how you felt," Mary Margaret said. "It is awful."

"Yeah, Jordan, but when you puked, so did the rest of the school. It was no big deal," Davis countered.

"Yes, it was, too," Jordan said. "I puked more than anybody else. It was awesome!"

Mary Margaret felt better and sat on the grass in the shade of the weeping willow to watch.

"Mary Margaret, do you want to fish?" Davis asked.

"I don't have a pole," she said.

"We brought an extra one if you want to use it," Jordan interjected.

"I don't think I could put worms on the hook, Mary Margaret told him.

"I'll do it for you," Jordan offered.

She agreed and walked to the edge of the pond where Jordan was already digging into the can for a worm. Mary Margaret cringed as he threaded the worm on the hook all the while explaining his method was so that the worm would not fall off.

Jordan handed Mary Margaret the fishing pole, and she realized that she didn't know what to do with it. Davis immediately realized the dilemma and asked her to watch him cast. He reeled in his line, checked the worm, and cast into the pond. He explained to Mary Margaret how the reel worked as he cast his line. Then Mary Margaret attempted to cast, with the hook landing barely 3 feet from her. She was embarrassed, Davis and Jordan laughed, and she reeled in the line. Again, she tried, with slightly better results. Laughter again from the boys, and blushing from Mary Margaret. She reeled in the line and Davis came over to help her. He stood behind her with his hands on hers. Together they cast, and this time it was acceptable, with the hook landing about 20 feet from the water's edge.

Mary Margaret stood for a while, and then realized that this was not the way to fish. She backed up to a grassy spot and sat down. The line was equipped with a red and white bobber which Jordan explained that she had to watch. If it went under the water he explained, she had a fish on her line. Mary Margaret stared at the bobber until she thought her eyes went fuzzy. The sun was glistening, and she felt very relaxed and sleepy. Suddenly, the bobber went under the water, and her fishing pole was nearly pulled from her hands. She yelled and the boys jumped up and ran to her side. Together they shouted instructions to her, "Hold the line tight," yelled Davis. "Reel in the line," clamored Jordan. Mary Margaret tried to follow their instructions, but mostly just did what felt natural and reeled and pulled on the pole until the fish was dangling in mid-air in front of her face. The boys reached out, and Davis grabbed the fish. Jordan reached over and removed the hook from its mouth. It was an 8-inch Bream. The boys were excited, and Mary Margaret felt sorry for the fish. Davis put it on what he called a stringer and placed the stringer into the water. It was the first catch of the day, and Mary Margaret was the star of the moment.

Addie had been watching from the kitchen window and was pleased to see the activities taking place by the pond. She wanted to walk down and join in, but felt that Mary Margaret needed the time with Davis and Jordan to develop a friendship. She continued to watch and was not disappointed at what she saw. Another young person was seen running toward the pond. At first Addie was alarmed, but then realized that it was Philip Gilbert. She relaxed when she could tell that four children were having a good time by the pond on that beautiful sunny Monday afternoon.

Chapter 30

Philip yelled to Davis, Jordan and Mary Margaret as he got off his bicycle in the front yard. He carried his fishing pole, and ran toward the pond. Mary Margaret was surprised to see him, but Davis and Jordan acted as though they expected him.

"Mary Margaret, are you feeling better?" the new arrival asked.

"Yes, but I'd really rather not talk about it," she said.

"I understand. I threw up at school a few months ago when the flu epidemic struck. I'm sorry this happened to you though, and if anybody gives you any problems because of it, just let me know."

"Thank you," Mary Margaret said as she watched him get his can of worms from his back pocket. He pulled out a long worm and expertly threaded it onto his hook. He cast the line easily 20 feet into the pond. He sat down in the shade and lay back.

"How's the foal?" Mary Margaret asked.

"It's great," he said. He continued, "I would have been here earlier, but I had to feed the horses and muck out the stalls."

Mary Margaret again felt like Philip was expected at the pond that afternoon, but she wasn't aware of any plans for him to be there.

The bobber on Jordan's line went up and down, up and down, and finally down. Jordan jumped off the tree stump and pulled on the line. He continued to pull and reel until he had a Bream dangling from the end. Philip reached up and held it while Jordan removed the hook. The fish was placed on the stringer with Mary Margaret's and put back in the water.

There was little conversation during the next hour, and Mary Margaret was thinking about this and how conversation really wasn't necessary when Davis yelled. He jumped up and started reeling. A fish on the end of his line jumped from the water, and it was obvious that it was larger than the two previously caught. Everybody gathered around to encourage him as he reeled and pulled on his pole. He eventually brought in a bass which they estimated weighed about 2 pounds. Davis and Philip removed it from the hook, and it, too, was placed on the stringer, and the stringer was placed back in the water.

Philip was the next one to hook a fish, but this one got off before he could reel it in. He re-baited his hook and Mary Margaret was impressed with the ease with which he cast. His hook landed in what seemed like exactly the same spot, and almost instantly, the bobber went down. This time Philip landed a Bream which was about 8 inches long. It, too, was placed on the stringer.

Mary Margaret and Jordan each caught a Bream about 6 inches long. By this time Addie had joined in to watch. About the only time anybody said anything was when a fish was caught, and she was impressed how the other three encouraged the lucky angler.

At 5 o'clock the alarm on Philip's watch went off. "I have to go home," he said as he started gathering his fishing tackle.

"Get your fish," Mary Margaret said.

"I'm not going to take it. You keep it for your supper.

Davis and Jordan started gathering their tackle, too. "We're not keeping our fish either," Jordan said.

Addie just sat there and watched the three young boys share the bounty of their afternoon with their new friend. Mary Margaret looked at Addie, and she just winked at her.

"Our thanks to you young men for your fish. I'll clean them, and we'll have them for supper this very evening," Addie said.

"Yeah, thanks for the fish," Mary Margaret said after she recovered her manners.

They just waved it off, and the three of them got on their bicycles and pedaled down the driveway.

"Mary Margaret, would you please get the stringer from the water?" Addie asked.

The small girl was surprised at the weight as she struggled to pull the tethered fished out of the water. Unfortunately, they were still alive, and Mary Margaret wasn't sure about how to handle this. As she and Addie walked to the house, the fish flipped and flopped on the stringer.

"You go ahead and take your shower before your mother gets home," Addie suggested as she took the fish into the kitchen.

Chapter 31

Mary Margaret looked in the mirror when she went into the bathroom, and was appalled to see that her face was dirty, really dirty. She couldn't remember ever being dirty in her life. What must the boys have thought of her? She hurriedly showered and changed into clean clothes. She heard her mother's voice in the kitchen as she opened her bedroom door. Addie was filling her in on the day's happenings, and Mary Margaret could hear her mother's exclamations as Addie enumerated each incident—first the vomiting, then the leaving school, finding her, Mr. Smith's lecture, getting her cleaned up, going back to school, meeting with the principal, the horse, the trip to Orville's, and the fishing with the boys. Cindy was pleased to hear that it all had a happy ending, but she confided to Addie that it must have been a horrible situation for Mary Margaret to deal with on her first day in a new school. Addie agreed, but then told Mrs. Smith that she felt that Mary Margaret had gained favor with Philip, Davis and Jordan. Addie further confided that she felt they would be Mary Margaret's protectors if it became necessary. Mrs. Smith laughed and said she was thankful for those three little boys.

Mary Margaret decided she had listened enough and came into the kitchen. Her mother held out her arms and she walked into them for a hug. It felt good to be right there at that moment.

"It sounds liked you had an exciting day," her mother said.

"Well, it was pretty bad for a while, but it got better when Mr. Clark brought his horse to school."

"Mary Margaret, I'm sorry things went terribly wrong at lunch, but it is unacceptable for you to ever leave school or anywhere else without first advising an adult and getting permission or asking for help," her mother said.

"I know I was wrong, but at the time I didn't know what else to do. I was so humiliated," she concluded with tears near the surface.

"This time I understand your dilemma, but you have to promise never to scare anybody like that again."

"I promise," she softly said, holding up her right hand.

Addie had finished cleaning the fish, and they made quite a plateful. She was heating up oil and mixing up self-rising cornmeal, egg, milk, and onions for hushpuppies. She had a skillet filled with hot oil. After breading the fish, she carefully placed each piece in the skillet. Soon the raw fish was transformed into beautifully browned, cooked pieces. The aroma in the kitchen was wonderful and Mary Margaret's stomach growled. She realized that she really hadn't eaten since breakfast, and she was hungry. Addie took a bowl of cole slaw from the refrigerator and hurried to remove potatoes from the oven.

Mary Margaret offered to set the table; and after searching through many cabinets, she found everything she needed to set places for 4. It had already been agreed that Addie would stay and eat.

Mike Smith arrived just as Mary Margaret finished with the table. "It sure smells good in here," he remarked as he walked into the kitchen. An explanation was given for the bounty of the fish, and he beamed as he heard that Mary Margaret had not only fished, she had caught some of the fish, too.

"I know your fish will be the best," he said while Mary Margaret silently wondered how he would be able to tell hers from the others.

"How did the rest of your day go?"

"It was great," she responded.

Cindy and Addie smiled at each other as Mary Margaret described the garden planting and the horse.

"Why are you planting a garden at school?" her father wondered.

"It's part of our South Carolina History class. We're going to see how it was done before tractors, and then the produce will be shared with the needy," his daughter explained.

"I must say I'm really pleased with such an innovative teaching method," he said.

After dinner Addie and Mrs. Smith cleaned up the kitchen while Mary Margaret did her homework. Mike worked on some paperwork. While they were all busy with their activities the telephone rang. Mr. Smith called Mary Margaret to the phone, and she was surprised to hear Alice's voice on the other end. She was momentarily embarrassed that she had not been the one to call first, but Alice told her that she and her family had not gotten home until the night before, and she was sorry that she had not called Mary Margaret sooner. Mary Margaret asked her about her spring break vacation, and she described a wonderful trip to the shore to visit her grandparents, where the weather was cool; but she had a great time.

Alice asked Mary Margaret about her week in South Carolina, and Mary Margaret told her all that she could remember, riding the horse, fishing, working on her quilt, moving into their new house, and finally about throwing up in the cafeteria. Alice was so stunned at this that she didn't know how to respond. Mary Margaret finally broke the silence by laughing and saying how awful it was, but that she was over it now. They each promised to write the other every day, and after exchanges were made that each missed the other, they hung up. Mary Margaret related the conversation to her parents and went back to finish her homework.

Addie told Mr. and Mrs. Smith about the tomato plants she had gotten, and promised to plant them the next day. She said she had thought they would be a good diversion for Mary Margaret after school, but apparently the boys had decided to help, too. Addie said she realized their help would go further to allow Mary Margaret to forget the events in the cafeteria than planting a few tomato plants, and they all laughed as Mike walked with Addie to her truck. As she got in and he closed the door for her, he thanked her for being there for all of them and especially for Mary Margaret. She said that it was nothing. She enjoyed being a part of their family and knew that one day Mary Margaret would consider her a part, too.

Mike heard the deer snorting as he stood in the driveway watching Addie slowly leave. He glimpsed their white tails as they bounded into the woods as she passed.

Mary Margaret and her mother were going over her spelling words when he came inside, and he smiled as he thought of his family here under their own roof getting into a routine. He hugged them both, and they looked at him as if to question the reason for the hugs, and he just smiled. Mary Margaret started reading her library book and set a goal of 20 pages a day. She knew this was high, but she needed to finish it on time for the book report due at school. Cindy found her daughter sleeping with her book open to page 15 when she looked in a little later. She turned off the light and tiptoed out of the room.

Chapter 32

On Tuesday morning Mary Margaret awoke to the sound of thunder rolling through the house and lightening flashing in her windows. The alarm sounded just as she looked over to see 6:00 glowing in the darkness. She got up and dressed in jeans, a t-shirt and running shoes. She hoped that maybe they would work in the garden again, and she wanted to be prepared. Her parents were already in the kitchen when she got there, and her mother was making pancakes. Her father was packing his lunch.

"Daddy, will you fix lunch for me, too?" Mary Margaret asked.

"I'll be happy to," he said as he reached for the bread to make another peanut butter sandwich.

Addie was walking up on the porch just as she was putting her book bag by the front door, and Mary Margaret opened the door for her. Addie left her umbrella on the porch, and wiped her feet on the mat before coming in. She smiled as Mary Margaret waited for her

"If it's still raining when it's time to catch the bus, I'll take you to school," the nanny said.

Secretly Mary Margaret hoped it wasn't still raining because she wanted to ride the bus.

After breakfast Mike and Cindy left for work, and Addie cleaned up the kitchen. Mary Margaret read her library book until time for the bus. The storm had passed, and as she and Addie walked down the driveway, the water dripping from the trees sounded like it was still raining in the woods.

The birds were singing, and the sun was peeping between the clouds. The bus arrived within a minute of their arrival at the road, and Mary Margaret got on, again taking the only empty seat.

Davis and Jordan were in the seat behind her, and the three spoke. Jordan was enthusiastic in his greeting, but Davis was almost bashful. Jordan didn't come up to sit beside her, but instead leaned forward and asked, "Hey, what did your dad think about the fish?"

"Addie cleaned and fried them, and they were delicious. My mother and daddy both thought they were wonderful," she truthfully answered.

"Davis and I can't come over this afternoon. We have music lessons. I play the clarinet and Davis plays the drums. What do you play?" he asked talking seamlessly.

For a reason unknown to her, Mary Margaret was embarrassed as she said, "Nothing."

"You need to learn to play something. When you go to high school, it's a big deal to play in the band, and everybody around here plays something," he continued speaking in his most serious voice.

Mary Margaret had taken dancing lessons last year in New York, but had never thought about music lessons except maybe to take piano.

When the bus reached school, Mary Margaret was ready to get off with the rest of the students so that she didn't have to sit and wait until they had all passed her seat. She got off and quickly walked around the building to go in the front door. Mrs. Calhoun was standing by the door and waved to her as she walked by. Mary Margaret spoke and hurried on to her classroom. When she entered, Mrs. Stancil was not in the room, and Jane Ellis was standing by the door with her group of friends.

"Are you feeling better today?" Jane asked.

"I have never felt better," Mary Margaret responded.

The girls were wearing summer slacks outfits, and they looked Mary Margaret up and down as she walked to her seat. Mary Margaret could feel their eyes following each step she took, but she was determined to not be intimidated by them.

Philip was already there, and he was reading his library book. He looked up as she sat down and asked, "Did you eat the fish for supper?"

"Yes, and they were delicious," she replied.

"I have a riding lesson after school at 4:00. My mother wanted me to ask you if you would like to come and watch," he said with no embarrassment and without blushing.

"I would love to come, but I have to ask Addie first," she said almost breathlessly.

"You can have Addie call my mom if she has any questions. The instructor comes to my house, so Addie will have to bring you there," he said without hesitation.

Mary Margaret was surprised to hear about so many lessons. She knew her friends in New York took dancing and piano lessons, but she had never known anyone personally who played the drums or the clarinet.

Another girl in the room walked over. "Hi, my name is Nancy Miller. I was wondering if you would like to eat lunch with me today," she asked.

"I brought my lunch, but I would love to eat with you," Mary Margaret explained smiling at the pretty girl with blonde hair and blue eyes.

"That's okay. We can walk to the cafeteria together, and you can go ahead and sit down while I go through the lunch line."

Mary Margaret noticed that Nancy was wearing jeans, a t-shirt and running shoes, but something about her made her look special. Finally, Mary Margaret felt that people were being so friendly with her, and she began to relax.

Mrs. Stancil came in just as the warning bell rang. Jane Ellis and her friends took their seats, and Mrs. Stancil closed the door. Davis immediately opened the door and hurried in. Mary Margaret wondered where he had been as he had arrived when she did. Mrs. Stancil began their lessons, and the morning passed so fast that she was surprised when it was time for lunch. Nancy caught up with her, and they walked down the hall together.

Jane Ellis and her friends huddled as they walked and giggled with glances in the direction of Mary Margaret and Nancy.

"Just ignore those girls," Nancy advised Mary Margaret. "They formed a private club and anybody who's not in the club is their target. They keep some kind of a diary and a book that describes what they think of everybody in the class. They're really polite to the teachers, but are mean to everybody else when the teachers aren't around. I just avoid them as much as possible," Nancy concluded.

Mary Margaret decided that's what she would do, too.

When they went into the cafeteria Nancy showed Mary Margaret a table where she usually sat, and Mary Margaret went over. Nancy left her to go through the cafeteria line. Some other students came over and sat at the table, and Mary Margaret just smiled at them. Nancy soon came through the line and walked over to the table. She was sitting down just as Jane and her friends walked by. In a voice loud enough to be heard only by those at nearby tables, one of the girls said, "Watch out, you might get vomited on." The five girls laughed as they walked on, and Nancy sat down. She glanced over to the see the look in Mary Margaret's eyes and knew that tears were near the surface. She reached out and took Mary Margaret's hand. "Don't pay any attention to them."

Mrs. Calhoun walked behind the five girls and followed them to their table. Before they could sit down, she invited them to join her in her office. Mary Margaret, Nancy and the rest of the students watched as Mrs. Calhoun led Allison Kincaid and her friends out of the lunchroom.

Nancy smiled. "I hope Mrs. Calhoun heard what they said. They're always doing that to people, but are so sly that no adults ever hear their remarks."

Nancy got her wish as Mrs. Calhoun was watching and listening for something like this to happen. A student had gone to her office early that same morning and told her that he had been told that Allison Kincaid and her friends were going to do something to embarrass Mary Margaret at noon. Mrs. Calhoun has an open-door policy where any student may come in and discuss anything that's bothering them. She is completely discreet in her handling of such matters and confidentiality is upheld. She doesn't consider it *snitching* when something is being done in a mean-spirited way. She considers it as a way to keep peace in her school, and recognizes it as a responsibility of all her students. She realizes that sometimes she hears gossip and rumors, but she personally checks out information she is given and often is able to nip a problem in the bud. Today's information culminated an on-going investigation into what amounted to harassment of students by these five girls. Mrs. Calhoun had heard about it, but until today, she could not prove anything. Today she had personally heard the remark which of itself didn't amount to much, but when grouped with the other information she had gathered would probably result in the suspension of these students. At least it gave her a firm reason to bring them and their parents into the office for a conference. The girls didn't return to the class that afternoon and Mrs. Stancil made no comment of it.

After school Mary Margaret rode the bus home, and Addie was waiting at the end of the driveway.

"Addie, can I . . . Would you . . . Philip asked me to come to his house and watch his riding lesson at 4:00. Can we go? You have to drive me. I mean, would you please drive me?" She stammered and corrected herself.

"Child, slow down. It's all arranged Sylvia called me, and we'll go. First, though, you need a snack, and I need your help with some tomato plants."

Mary Margaret and Addie went into the house. Addie had cut an apple into quarters, and removed the seeds. She had spread each apple quarter with peanut butter. She took a cold glass of milk from the refrigerator.

After going to the bathroom and washing her hands, Mary Margaret gulped down her snack while Addie put a roast in the oven.

Then they went into the storage building to get the shovels. Addie had already dug up a place alongside the house, and the soil was ready for planting. Mary Margaret dug a deep hole, sprinkled in a little fertilizer, put in some soil and then put in the plant with just the few top leaves above the soil line.

"Sharon taught you well," Addie said as she watched the agile child bend close to the ground so easily. She remembered days gone by when she, too, had been able to bend at the waist to plant an entire garden. These days her large frame ached from years of hard work.

Mary Margaret smiled and moved on to the next plant. In short order they had completed all their planting and they put away the shovel and fertilizer. They stacked up the pots for Addie to take back to Mr. Clark. She said he recycled them and would use them for other plants.

With the planting completed, it was time to go to Philip's. Addie climbed in the truck and was backing up to turn around when three girls rode up the driveway on their bicycles. One was Jane Ellis and Mary Margaret recognized the others, but couldn't recall their names. Addie stopped the truck, and Jane rode up leading the other two.

"Hello, Ms. Addie, may I speak with Mary Margaret?" she asked politely through the open window.

Mary Margaret sank into the seat. She thought, *I don't have anything to say to these girls*, but Addie opened the door and stepped onto the driveway.

"Mary Margaret, you get out and see what these young ladies have to say," Addie said.

Mary Margaret walked around to the driver's side of the truck and stood beside Addie, who towered over the 4 girls like Mary Margaret's protector.

Grace Calhoun, a long-time friend of Addie had called her earlier in the afternoon. Addie recalled the conversation as she watched the event unfold on the driveway.

"Addie, I am so embarrassed about all of this in my school." She said after explaining the episode at today's lunch. "I had hoped that Mary Margaret's arrival would have been a pleasant experience for her, and these girls have gone out of their way to make her feel uncomfortable. I have required that each girl apologize to her before they will be allowed to return to school. I'm not certain yet what other punishment they'll receive for the slam book and other harassment I have heard about, but I witnessed this, and I am in a position to act quickly on it. The slam book was full of nasty things, and it shocks me that my students are involved in this kind of activity," the principal shared sounding very tired.

Into Addie's Arms

Addie had kept her confidence and hadn't mentioned the conversation to Mary Margaret. She was, however, pleased that these three girls were acting quickly on their punishment.

Jane Ellis began the conversation. "Mrs. Calhoun said we have to apologize to you. I'm sorry that I didn't make you feel welcome on your first day at school, and I'm ashamed of how my friends and I treated you at the lunch table. I know we were rude, and I am sorry," she said sincerely.

The other girls stepped forward and said similar words. Jane then said, "Allison Kincaid is always saying things to embarrass people. She told us not to be nice to you. We're not going to be a part of her club anymore because we don't like being mean to anybody. We really are sorry about this, Mary Margaret. We shouldn't have done what she said. We should have thought for ourselves, but sometimes she scared us and we were afraid not to do what she said. She is really mean."

The other girls, Peggy Anderson and Linda Lively, seemed to gain confidence as Jane talked.

"I hope you will forgive us," Peggy said.

"Yeah, and please give us another chance to be your friend. We really are nice girls. We just made a stupid mistake," Linda said.

Mary Margaret was surprised at their candidness, and agreed to forgive them. The girls had put down their bicycles while they were talking, and each one approached Mary Margaret and embraced her. Mary Margaret, still being unaccustomed to public displays of affection, was overwhelmed at this, and could feel the burning return to her eyes, but she knew this was a good thing.

Addie stood silently and was proud of all four girls. She had been appalled at the description of the near shunning Mary Margaret had received at the lunch table the day before, and then the remark today had disappointed her. Addie was acquainted with the families of all the girls and felt that their upbringing did not align itself with this type of behavior. Her faith had been restored with this sincere outpouring of contrition expressed by these young girls. She wondered, however, about the other two girls, who were conspicuously absent.

"Okay, girls, we appreciate your stopping by, but Mary Margaret and I are on our way to an appointment," the nanny said ushering Mary Margaret toward the door.

"Yes, ma'm, we know that you're on your way to Philip's riding lesson. We don't want to hold you up, but we wanted to apologize as soon as we could," Jane said.

Addie and Mary Margaret thanked them and said good-bye. The girls got on their bicycles and rode off down the driveway. They waved as they rounded the curve and went out of sight.

Mary Margaret and Addie got back in the truck, and Addie sat there for a moment before putting the key in the ignition. She looked at Mary Margaret and said, "I'm glad this is getting resolved."

"Me, too," Mary Margaret said. "My feelings have been hurt before, but never like this. One time I didn't get invited to a party, and it hurt my feelings, but nobody has ever said anything to embarrass me on purpose.

"Well, child, I hope you are sincere in accepting those apologies; and I hope you will give them another chance. I've always thought they were nice girls. I think they just made some bad choices," Addie said.

"I am, Addie, and today I met the nicest girl, Nancy Miller. She and I ate lunch together, and I think we will be good friends," Mary Margaret said as the truck rounded the curve in the driveway.

Chapter 33

When they arrived at Philip's, his lesson had already begun. Philip looked impressive as he sat on his horse. He approached each jump with confidence, and his body moved in unison with the horse as they glided over each one. The course was intricate and Philip led the horse from one jump to the next, over a water hazard, and the horse followed the commands of Philip's body, which were imperceptible to Mary Margaret. His instructor, who Mary Margaret was surprised to see was a woman, was beside the fence calling instructions to him, and he made corrections as she ordered. They went over and over the course until Mary Margaret wondered why she was having him do it so many times. Eventually, the instructor, who she later learned was Lois Sims, finally clapped for Philip and told him he had done a wonderful job.

Mary Margaret looked at her watch and realized that an hour had passed. It had seemed like just a few minutes as she was enthralled with each gallop the horse made. Philip rode the horse back to the gate and dismounted. Lois walked over to him and gave him some final instructions before she turned to leave.

"Ms. Lois, would you stay a minute and meet my friend?" he asked politely.

They walked over to where Mary Margaret and Addie had been standing, and Philip introduced Ms. Sims to Mary Margaret. She already knew Addie. She had been friends with Addie's children.

"Mary Margaret, have you been in Left Fork long enough to know if you like it or not?" the instructor asked.

"It's getting better every day," Mary Margaret said surprising Philip as he knew Mary Margaret had been upset at lunch again by the girls from the club known as the Cool Five. He had heard about their book they kept which rated the students at the school. He had been told that he was highly rated in the book, but he felt that it was wrong; and he didn't approve of their behavior. Since they liked him, they were always nice, but he had witnessed their sharp tongues with other students whom they considered to be beneath them. He had avoided them and was sorry that he hadn't warned Mary Margaret before the first day of school.

Addie complimented Philip on his riding and asked him how he was doing in competition. He told her that he was doing really well, and had another competition this coming Sunday in Charleston. Mary Margaret echoed Addie's compliment that he rode well. They both blushed, but he thanked her.

"Mary Margaret, would you like to ride?" he asked.

Uncertain if it would be possible, she looked to Addie for guidance.

Addie glanced at her watch. "Well, child, we need to be home in a few minutes so that I can finish getting dinner ready."

Sylvia Gilbert walked out just in time to hear this and said, "I'll bring Mary Margaret home after she and Philip ride a while if you think it will be all right."

Now Addie looked to Mary Margaret for guidance, and her eyes were open with anticipation, thankfully, Addie agreed. Addie said good-bye to everyone and left as Mary Margaret and Philip were heading for the barn to saddle Daisy.

Ms. Sims and Mrs. Gilbert stood beside the fence talking while Mary Margaret and Philip were in the barn. When they came out, Philip helped Mary Margaret mount Daisy, and he mounted his own horse. She tentatively rode around the fence until she felt more secure. Ms. Sims watched and was pleased to see that Mary Margaret adjusted quickly to the horse's pace and her movements melded into those of Daisy's.

"I wonder if she is interested in riding?" she asked Mrs. Gilbert.

"Well, in all confidentiality, her parents are considering getting her a horse, but they want to know that she has a sincere desire to ride and it's not a passing fancy."

"She looks like a natural to me, but they're right, she needs to have the desire."

"I'll pass along your comments to her parents. I'm sure they'll be interested in what you have to say," Mrs. Gilbert said as Ms. Sims turned to leave.

Mary Margaret and Philip rode into the pasture, and he gave her instructions as she gained confidence and speed. He felt that she was ready for a low jump, but he had misgivings about leading her in that direction, so they just rode through figure 8's and galloped in the field.

"At the first tone of the bell ringing Philip yelled to Mary Margaret, "We need to stop now."

He turned his horse and headed toward the barn. Mary Margaret followed his lead.

"It's time to groom the horses so that we can take Mary Margaret home," his mother explained.

"Okay, Mom, it'll take us about 30 minutes," he said without hesitation.

Mary Margaret dismounted Daisy without any assistance, and Philip clapped when he realized that she was on the ground. Mary Margaret curtsied before she realized what she was doing. She was embarrassed, but Philip just laughed. They led the horses into the barn, and together they groomed them. The stalls had been cleaned, but he said the horses needed to be fed and watered. Mary Margaret remembered from the last time she was there and helped him, so together they completed the grooming, feeding and watering.

"Thanks for your help," Philip said.

"Thanks for letting me ride," she returned.

They walked outside just as Mrs. Gilbert was coming from the house along with Goldie and Freckles. Mary Margaret realized at that moment that they had not been outside when she arrived, and when she asked about this, Philip said that when he has his lessons the dogs have to stay in the house. They are distracting to him and the horse, and his lessons just go better without them. As they lunged at Mary Margaret for her attention, she understood his rationale. Goldie waddled around and around, and Freckles, tried to walk between her legs. Mary Margaret was able to remain upright this time, but Philip finally had to hold the dogs by their collars so that she could walk to the car. Mrs. Gilbert, Mary Margaret, and Philip climbed in and they started down the driveway with the dogs barking their good-byes.

When they arrived at Mary Margaret's house, Mike and Cindy were standing on the front porch talking. They walked to the car and invited Sylvia and Philip in. Sylvia declined but said she would like a rain check. She said she had dinner in the oven and needed to get home. Mary Margaret thanked both Mrs. Gilbert and Philip for allowing her to ride and for bringing her home. Mrs. Gilbert said it was her pleasure, and Philip said it was nothing. Mike and Cindy were pleased to see that their daughter was smiling and her attitude seemed light and happy.

Chapter 34

Mrs. Gilbert left and Mary Margaret and her parents went inside. Addie was in the kitchen singing when they came in. She was not embarrassed that they had heard her, and their presence didn't interrupt her song. She continued in full voice as she stirred gravy in the roasting pan. When her song was finished, she asked Mary Margaret to please set the table for 5 after she had washed up.

Mary Margaret went into the bathroom and realized that Addie had said to set the table for 5 and wondered who the 5th person was. As she came from the bathroom, she saw her father going out the front door. She went into the kitchen and asked Addie who was coming to dinner, and she said it was a surprise. Mary Margaret continued to ask for an answer, but Addie playfully said she would have to wait and see. When the table was set and Addie was putting the food out, the front door opened, and her father came in behind Mrs. Applegate. He had gone to pick her up as she didn't like driving after dark. Mary Margaret rushed into the living room to greet her and hugged her before she realized what she was doing. She was genuinely glad to see her, and she allowed her feelings to surface in the hug. Mrs. Applegate hugged her back, and asked her how things were going. Of course, she was well aware of what had been happening. Nothing was a secret in this small town, and when something happened, everybody soon knew about it. Mary Margaret told her that the first day of school had started out badly, but that things were going better now. She told Mary Margaret to just be herself and it would all turn out just fine.

Cindy came into the living room and again hugs were exchanged. Addie yelled that supper was getting cold, and they all laughed as they went into the kitchen. Dinner conversation centered mostly on the happenings between the five friends gathered around the table.

Cindy said that her job was going well, and she was impressed with the professionalism of the hospital.

Mike said that the new equipment was being tested and would soon be operational. The new equipment would allow the mill to produce more product at less cost. He also said that 2 new cars were being delivered the next day, and he wouldn't be driving a company vehicle.

Mrs. Applegate said that her family was fine, and would be coming for a visit at Memorial Day. Addie said that she had been busy keeping Mary Margaret out of trouble, which caused Mary Margaret to be embarrassed and blush, but Addie's laughter and her patting Mary Margaret's hand as she said it, told the group that it was something she enjoyed doing.

When it was Mary Margaret's turn to speak, she said that she had discovered that things weren't always as they seemed to be. She told about the girls coming to apologize after school, and that she thought they were sincere. She told them about Nancy Miller and how nice she had been to her. She asked if she could have her over sometime to visit, and her parents said that would be wonderful. She finally got around to watching Philip have his riding lesson and how impressed she was with his ability, and then how wonderful it was to be able to ride Daisy again today. She said she had had a wonderful day, and the group around the table almost cheered.

Mrs. Applegate didn't stay long after dinner, and Addie took her home as she left.

Chapter 35

A couple of blocks off the town square a black SUV pulled into the driveway of a neatly kept house. The driver stretched his long legs as he got out, and he tossed his cell phone back into the console. He was agitated. His last call had been interrupted when the cell service was lost just outside of town. He mumbled, "This hick town has got to get into the swing of things."

From inside the house Allison Kincaid heard the door slam on her father's vehicle and locked the door to her room. His arrival marked the beginning of what she knew would be another evening of yelling and screaming, and she would be at the center of it all.

He walked into the house yelling her name, "Allison, Allison, come out here. Allison, get out here right now."

Allison remained in her room. She heard his footsteps take him into the kitchen where her mother was mopping the floor. She mopped the floor 6 times every day. This would be number 5. Number 6 would be right before she went to bed. He would walk on the wet floor, and her mother would begin to cry.

Like the script of a play, she heard her mother cry on cue, "You're walking on my clean floor. I work and slave to keep this place clean and you just walk in and make a mess."

"You don't keep this place clean. You keep this place sterile. You're obsessed with cleaning. Nobody mops their kitchen 6 times a day. Nobody cleans their toilets 8 times a day. Nobody vacuums 3 times a day. You're obsessed,

I'm telling you, obsessed. You make it impossible to live here. Nobody else in the whole world does what you do," he yelled.

"Hello, Daddy, welcome home," Allison whispered to herself, sarcastically. This had become a way of life for her. Her father worked and lived in Charleston, and she and her mother lived in Left Fork. He came home on Friday night or Saturday morning and left again on Sunday afternoon. She remembered when he drove to work every morning and came home at night. The nights were filled with chaos. Now only one or two nights each week were frightening.

"Where is she?" Larry Kincaid asked his wife.

"She's in her room," his wife replied.

"Get her out here now. I can't believe that I had to come back here today because she is in trouble again. I give her everything she could ever want, and this is the thanks I get—she rewards my hard work with trouble. If she keeps this up, I'm sending her away. She can't keep on like this," he said reaching into the refrigerator for a drink.

Allison knew her mother would be coming to find the door locked and would get the key to open it. She decided to climb out the window before this happened. Again, right on cue, her mother attempted to turn the door knob. When met with resistance, she said, "Allison, you open this door this minute. You know I have a key, but you don't want to make me go get it. I've had enough of you today. You open . . ."

Allison was gone before she heard the rest of her mother's sentence. She crouched around to the front of the house and cut through the yard across the street into the alley. She felt protected in the alley and continued to the corner. She turned left and in a few minutes was on the main road leading out of town. The evening traffic from Charleston was over and only a few cars passed her. Nobody took notice. She was jogging and looked older than her years. She could have easily passed for 12 and possibly 14 with just a glance.

She had no destination when she left, but as she continued, she realized that she was near Mary Margaret's house. She cut through the woods just before she reached the driveway. She followed the curvature of the drive and stopped at the edge of the woods to see that all was clear to pass through the open yard. Nobody was on the porch. The outbuilding door was closed. Nobody was by the pond. She bent over and ran from tree to tree until she reached the garage doors. She went around the rear of the house and was disappointed to find that the windows were too high for her to see in. She would have to go on the porch to see inside, and she knew that wasn't a smart thing to do.

Darkness had now taken over, and with nowhere else to go, she jogged back to town. She sat on a bench outside the Baptist church. Her small figure went unnoticed as joggers went by. The night air was chilly. Her stomach growled. Headlights flooded the area. They went off. A car door closed. Footsteps were coming in her direction, and she hunkered down to make her body as small as possible. The footsteps began to whistle. It was a happy tune, but she remained still and small. The footsteps passed her, and she sneezed, "Achoo!"

"Who is that?" "God bless you." "Is somebody there?" Reverend Ron Cross asked as he turned to look in the direction of the sneeze.

"Yes, sir, I'm here," Allison said.

"And, who is I'm," the friendly preacher asked.

"My name is Allison Kincaid," she answered still almost hidden in the dark.

"Well, Allison Kincaid, I'm Reverend Cross. I don't believe we know each other do we?" he asked.

"No, sir, we don't know each other," she answered in a small voice.

"Well, it's a pleasure to make your acquaintance, but may I ask what you are doing on my church bench this late at night. It's a school night, too. You should be at home doing your home work."

"Uh, uh, oh, I, I, uh . . ." she stammered.

"Did time just get away from you?" he asked hoping to calm her and keep her there so that he could help her.

"Uh, yes, sir. I was, uh, jogging, and I got tired and sat here to rest. I guess I was here longer than I thought. I'll go on home now," she said, standing.

"I'll tell you what. Why don't I call your daddy or your mama and have them come and pick you up. You can't be out on the streets after dark," he said.

"No, sir, it's okay. I don't live far away, and I don't want to bother my parents. They've had a busy day," she said.

"Well, Allison Kincaid, how about if I drive you home?" he asked.

"No, thank you, sir. I don't mean any disrespect, but I can't get in cars with strangers."

"I understand that. How about if you walk home, and I drive along in my car so that I can see you are safely there?" he asked.

Realizing that this man was not going to leave her alone, she gave in. "Okay, but you don't have to go in with me. I'm okay. I even can get there without you," she said.

"I'm sure you can, but I'd just feel better seeing you get there," he said.

"Okay, I live over on Oak Lane," she said knowing that she had met her match.

She started jogging, and Reverend Cross drove alongside until she reached her house on Oak Lane. She waved and rounded the corner, noticing that her father's vehicle was no longer in the driveway. The minister was surprised she didn't go in the front door. He stopped his car and got out. He walked and watched until he could see her open the window and climb back in.

"That is one troubled child," he said to himself. *I need to learn more about this family*, he thought as he drove the short distance back to the church.

Once inside Allison heard the hum of the vacuum cleaner as her mother continued her cleaning rituals. The child looked into the living room and saw her mother's tear-stained face. She knew her father was gone for the night, but not before he pushed her mother over the brink into misery. She closed the door and took off her shoes. She pulled back the sheets and slid in between the cool cotton, pulling the covers up to her chin. She made herself as small as possible and tears fell and circled the starched and ironed pillow case. Her stomach growled. Her body hungered, but her spirit's desire for peace overtook her hunger, and she soon slept still fully clothed.

Chapter 36

Mary Margaret got ready for bed, and did her homework. She asked her mother to go over her spelling words with her, and she spelled them all correctly the first time. When she went to bed, she lay there and suddenly remembered that she had not written to Alice or Charlene. She would do it tomorrow, she thought as she drifted off to sleep.

When Mary Margaret arrived at school on Wednesday, Mrs. Calhoun was standing by the front door. She asked her to come into her office. Mary Margaret's heart raced as they walked down the hall, but she couldn't imagine that she was in trouble for anything. Mrs. Calhoun took her into her office and offered her a seat in one of the rockers and she took a seat in another.

"Mary Margaret, I'm sorry you've had such a bad start at school here. How do you feel today?" she asked.

"I feel great," she said enthusiastically.

"That's great, Mary Margaret. I do want to explain some things to you, and want to reassure you that you are not in the least responsible for the actions of the girls in the lunch room," the experienced principal said. "These same girls have been under suspicion for some other activities, and you just happened to be involved when they got caught. You did nothing to create the problem, and you don't have to do anything to solve it, do you understand?"

"Yes, ma'm, I don't think I did anything wrong. I didn't even know them," the child responded.

"These girls must each apologize to you before they're allowed back in school. Additionally, Allison Kincaid has been suspended until Monday, and she may only return when and if she apologizes to you. I don't need to go into details with you about the extra punishment for her, but she did something and must be punished for it. Have any of the girls apologized yet?" she asked.

"Yes, ma'm, Jane Ellis, Linda Lively and Peggy Anderson came to my house yesterday after school. They were very nice and apologized and asked me to give them another chance to be my friend. They even hugged me," she finished.

Mrs. Calhoun was pleased with the speed of the first three apologizes, but was equally disappointed that Stephanie Scott was not included in that list, but she knew she was not the ringleader and would be contacting Mary Margaret soon. *Hopefully, before this day is over*, she thought. "If you have any further problems from these or any other students, please let me know. I want to know if anybody harasses you about any of this. Can you do that, Mary Margaret?"

"I don't want to be a tattle tale, but if anything bad happens, I'll let you know."

"That sounds good to me. Now, go on to class, and I hope you have a wonderful day," the principal said, standing.

"Yes, ma'm, I'll try," Mary Margaret said as she left the office. As she walked down the hall, she wondered if the other students would hold her responsible for their friends not being in class.

Mary Margaret walked into Mrs. Stancil's classroom just as the bell rang. Mrs. Stancil smiled and closed the door behind her as Mary Margaret took her seat. When she took roll, the names of Allison Kincaid and Stephanie Scott were called and no response was heard. Nobody said anything as they did when John Protzman's name was called and Davis answered that he was sick. Everybody knew why they were absent.

The morning passed quickly and Nancy Miller caught up with Mary Margaret on the way to the cafeteria. She asked her to save her a seat as she was going through the lunch line, and Mary Margaret said she was buying her lunch too. The girls chatted as they waited in line and moved their trays along. It was hot dog day, and Mary Margaret hoped she would have no trouble eating her lunch. When she and Nancy exited the line, Jane Ellis was waiting for them and asked them to sit with her and Linda and Peggy. Mary Margaret looked to Nancy for guidance, and she shrugged her shoulders and said, "Why not." The girls talked and giggled during lunch, and their behavior did not go unnoticed by both Mrs. Stancil and Mrs. Calhoun. After lunch as the class walked back to their room, Mrs. Stancil walked by Mary Margaret and patted her on the back as she continued to move down the hall.

In late afternoon Mrs. Stancil said that the garden needed a drink, and asked for volunteers to turn on the sprinklers. Several hands went up, and Mrs. Stancil chose Davis and Brett Mizerak. The rest of the class was given the time to read their library books. Mary Margaret was glad she had remembered to put her book in her book bag and wondered when it needed to be returned. She was relieved to see that she had another week before it was due back at the library.

The bus ride home was noisy and the talk was about Stephanie Scott and Allison Kincaid. Mary Margaret never entered into the conversation and was surprised to hear that nearly everybody was glad that they had finally been caught.

"One day Allison tripped me on purpose while I was walking from the bus stop," a small girl said.

"She always said ugly things to me and called me names," another girl confessed.

"Allison chased me and threatened to rip my shirt off in front of some boys," another student added. "I was able to outrun her, or she would have done it." The girl concluded. "Allison is the bad one. The other girls just did what she said. I think they were afraid not to."

The stories were rampant throughout the bus, and it seemed that all age groups were involved. Even the younger children had been harassed particularly by Allison. Mary Margaret thought in retrospect that what had happened to her had not been so bad compared to what the other students had endured.

Addie was not waiting for her at the end of the driveway when the bus stopped, but Mary Margaret was not upset. She jumped off the bus and ran around the curve coming face-to-face with the two deer. They were standing in the middle of the driveway, about 5 feet ahead of her. She stopped and waited for them to move, but they didn't seem to be in any hurry to get out of her way.

She started talking to them. "Pretty deer, I'm going to walk slowly past you. Don't be afraid. I won't hurt you," she reassured them.

She began to walk to the right of the driveway and stepped into the pine straw that covered the ground. The deer stood motionless with only an ear twitching occasionally to give away the fact that they were alive. Their large round eyes carefully watched Mary Margaret as she continued her slow broad walk around them, with Mary Margaret all the while remembering Addie's caution that no matter how beautiful they were, they were still wild. Mary Margaret was intently watching the deer and failed to notice a tree limb that was in her path. Her next step caught her foot on the limb, and she began to tumble forward. Her book bag propelled her even faster as she flailed her arms and tried to regain her balance before hitting the ground with a thud. The deer were startled and ran in her direction. She could see them approaching. She lay still while one of the deer jumped over her, and the other ran past her legs. Mary Margaret could feel the rush of air as the deer crossed over her head, and for whatever reason, she kept her head down. The deer ran into the trees, and Mary Margaret was catching her breath and getting up as Addie came running down the drive. She ran to Mary Margaret and helped her up, brushing off pine straw.

"Child, are you all right?"

"Yes, I'm okay, but one of the deer jumped over me. I kept my head down, but I was scared. Addie, I did what you said. I was careful. I walked away from them, but I tripped over that limb," she said all the while pointing to the now benign piece of wood.

Addie looked Mary Margaret over and realized that she had escaped serious injury. She carried the back pack up the driveway and Mary Margaret continued to brush pine straw off her clothes and out of her hair.

"I promise I'll always be at the bus stop from now on," Addie said.

"No, Addie, don't worry about it. It'll probably never happen again," Mary Margaret said.

After cleaning up and having a snack, Mary Margaret remembered that she needed to write letters to Alice and Charlene. She sat down at the desk in her room and wrote to Charlene first. She thanked her for her help with the notes in the boxes and explained that she had been able to unpack all of her things. She thanked her for the sheets, and admitted that the perfume made her happy and sad at the same time. She told her about the incident in the cafeteria, but went on to explain that things were working out better now. She told her that she had caught a fish and they had eaten it for dinner. She said that her other friends had caught fish, too, and had donated theirs. Hers would not have been big enough to feed one person let alone a whole family she explained. She tried to think of something to write about Addie, but couldn't decide how to put her feelings into words. She really wasn't sure what her feelings were. Addie was still loud and boisterous, but somehow it didn't seem to matter as much now. Her letter to Alice was pretty much the same about her daily activities. She told her that she was making friends, and she said that she loved to ride a horse named Daisy. She told her about Philip and how wonderful it was to watch him ride and how he competes in dressage. She mentioned Davis and Jordan, learning to fish, and the girls she had met from her class. She deliberately omitted the incident with the Cool 5, but did again mention that she vomited in the cafeteria on the first day of school. She knew that Alice would groan when she read that even though they had talked about it on the phone. After addressing the envelopes she went to her parents' desk to get stamps. Addie had placed the mail on the desk, and Mary Margaret recognized Charlene's handwriting on the envelope on top of the stack of mail. She wanted to read it, but it was addressed to Mr. and Mrs. Michael Smith and not to Mary Margaret, so she knew that she couldn't open it. She wondered what it would say and was anxious for her mother or father to come home to share Charlene's news.

Mary Margaret told Addie that she was going on the porch to read her library book and went to the big swing. She sat there and opened to her book to find herself lost in the fantasy of the horse world. Soon, she was daydreaming that it would be wonderful to have a horse of her own that she could ride whenever she wanted. She really wished that she could have Daisy, but she knew that Philip loved her; and if she ever got a horse, it would have to be a different one. As she daydreamed, she realized that she had no place to keep a horse. It couldn't stay in the garage, and the outbuilding was too small. She knew that her parents would never build a barn just so she could have a horse.

Her mood was changing to sadness when she heard voices. She looked around to see Davis and Jordan riding up the driveway on their bicycles. They were carrying fishing poles, and she knew without asking that they were here to fish. She was surprisingly glad to see them and jumped off the top porch step as they dropped their bicycles in the yard. Jordan as always was talking as they walked toward her. He was telling her about digging for worms and finding some humongous ones, all the while reaching into his back pocket for the can to pull one out to show her. The worm wriggled in his fingers, and he put it back in the can after Mary Margaret expressed his desired, "Yuck!"

"I brought an extra pole if you want to fish," Davis said.

"Thanks, but I'll probably just watch and maybe fish later," she said.

The three of them walked to the pond and just as they were settling in with Jordan on his usual tree stump, Davis on a patch of grass just under the weeping willow and Mary Margaret sitting between the two and further away from the pond, Philip rode up on his bicycle. He, too, had a fishing pole and Jordan offered him some worms. Philip pulled out his own can and began baiting his hook. He and Davis started talking about soccer practice, and soon Mary Margaret felt left out. The boys were involved in their conversation and fishing, and she was sitting there feeling like an outsider at her own home.

She finally mustered enough courage and said, "Davis, I think I'd like to fish now if it's okay."

He said, "Sure," and nodded his head in the direction of an extra fishing pole as it lay on the ground beside him. Mary Margaret picked up the pole and unhooked the hook from where it was inserted in the handle. She reeled the line tight to where the bobber was at the end of the pole. She just stood there with the bare hook hanging down when Jordan pointed to the can on the ground beside the tree stump and said, "You can get one of those worms."

She groaned and walked over to the can. As she looked down, all she could see was black dirt, and she knew that she would have to put her hands in there in order to get a worm. It was obvious that the boys were not inclined to helping her bait the hook, so she reached in and felt around with her fingertips. She felt the firm body of a worm, and withdrew her hand. She reached back in and this time pulled out a fat worm as it wriggled in her fingers. She looked at the worm and the sharp point of the hook and knew that she could not put that worm on that hook. She put the worm back in the can and started walking back up under the tree. The boys laughed, and Jordan hopped down to bait the hook for her.

"We did that on purpose," he confessed. "We wanted to see if you would bait your own hook," he laughed.

"If I have to bait my own hooks, I don't think I will ever fish," she said as she accepted the pole from Jordan.

Addie was watching the activities by the pond from the kitchen window. She realized that Mary Margaret was in good hands with the boys as she went back to preparing dinner.

Mary Margaret soon had her line in the pond, and her bobber lazily rested on top of the water. There were 4 bobbers gently bouncing up and down, and the four children alongside the pond were quiet. It seemed that nobody had anything else to talk about, even Jordan was especially quiet.

Finally, Philip broke the silence by asking, "Have Allison Kincaid and Stephanie Scott apologized to you yet?"

"I'm surprised that you know about that," Mary Margaret said.

"Everybody knows everything in Left Fork," he replied.

"No, they haven't, but Jane Ellis, Linda Lively and Peggy Anderson came by yesterday," she confided.

"I think that Allison is the bad one, and the others just followed her lead. I've known all of them, and they were nice girls until they started hanging around with her. She used to be nice, but she changed. I heard that Mrs. Calhoun took the slam book from her and showed it to her parents. It told about all the students in the school. Some of the things written in it are really bad, and her parents are furious with her," he concluded.

Mary Margaret was not pleased to have this brought up again as she felt somehow responsible even though she knew she wasn't.

"Do you think she'll come back to school again?" asked Davis.

"She can't until she apologizes to Mary Margaret," he replied.

Mary Margaret felt that uneasiness in her stomach, as she just wanted this to be all over and didn't want to have to deal with it again.

Philip's alarm on his watch sounded. "I need to go home he said all the while picking up his fishing tackle.

Chapter 37

A car pulled into the driveway. "That's Stephanie Scott's mother's car," Jordan whispered. Mary Margaret could feel her stomach tightening up as she saw a plump lady open the door on the driver's side and get out. The passenger door was away from Mary Margaret, but she could tell that the woman was talking to whomever was in the front passenger seat. Philip got on his bike and rode off yelling good-bye as he left. Davis and Jordan seemed in no hurry to leave, so Mary Margaret stayed put. Fishing was slow today. Nobody had caught anything, and there had only been a few nibbles.

Addie heard the car pull in the driveway and went to see who it was. She saw Ruth Scott, Stephanie's mother leaning in the car and from the body language; she could tell that it was not pleasant conversation between Mrs. Scott and Stephanie. Addie walked out onto the porch and yelled to Ruth, who stood up and waved.

"Hello, Ruth, won't you come in?" Addie yelled.

Ruth Scott walked to the porch. "Addie, I am so embarrassed about this situation with Stephanie and Mary Margaret. I brought Stephanie over here to apologize, but since Davis and Jordan are here, she won't get out of the car. She's too embarrassed," the harried mother said fanning her face with a handkerchief.

Realizing the difficulty Mrs. Scott was having she yelled down to Mary Margaret. "Mary Margaret, would you please come into the house for a few minutes?"

She asked Davis to watch her fishing pole, and slowly walked up to the porch. Addie explained the awkward situation to Mary Margaret and asked her if she would go over and invite Stephanie to come into the house. She really didn't want to, but she also wanted this whole thing over and done with, so she walked over to the car and asked Stephanie if she would like to come in. Stephanie had obviously been crying and would not look directly at her. She reluctantly, without comment, got out of the car and walked with her head down to the porch where Addie and her mother were still standing.

Addie led the way into the house and invited Mrs. Scott into the kitchen. "Mary Margaret why don't you take Stephanie into the den," she suggested. Mary Margaret led the way and Stephanie followed with her head down and her eyes fixed on the floor. When they got there, Mary Margaret sat down and offered Stephanie a seat. She sat in a small rocking chair and continued to look at the floor. Mary Margaret didn't know what else to say after that. She didn't feel it was appropriate to make small talk under the circumstances, so she just sat there.

Tears were falling onto Stephanie legs as her head was bowed over her lap. Dark blue circles formed on her jeans as the tears kept falling. Finally, sobs started, and between the sobs Stephanie croaked out the words, "I'm sorry."

Mary Margaret sat there wondering what she was supposed to say. She had never been in this position before to know what was appropriate. When the other girls had come by, they kept talking and finally asked her to forgive them. However, Stephanie just said she was sorry.

Mary Margaret just let her instincts take over, and she got up and walked across the room to where Stephanie was sitting. She stood beside her and put her hand on Stephanie's shoulder. Stephanie's body was heaving with each sob, and Mary Margaret was at a loss as to what she should do next.

Stephanie looked up, and as tears fell from her swollen eyes, across her red cheeks and dripped off her chin, she smiled at Mary Margaret and said again that she was sorry that she had been mean to her. She sobbed, "It was Allison's idea to shun you and pick on you in any way that we could. I'm not really that kind of person, and am sorry that I let myself be influenced by Allison. Will you please forgive me?"

Mary Margaret reached down and hugged her. "Of course, I will," she found herself saying willingly.

Stephanie sniffed and wiped her upper lip with her hand. Her hand was wet, and she had a string of snot connecting her hand with her face and was not sure what to do with it. Mary Margaret ran over to the desk, got some tissues and brought them back to her. She immediately wiped off her hand and face.

She was beginning to calm down and Mary Margaret went into the kitchen to get them some lemonade. When she returned, Stephanie was composed, but her face was swollen and still red. She took the glass from Mary Margaret and drank the whole thing without stopping. Then she unexpectedly belched an award-winning burp. As she tried to say, "Excuse me," she hiccupped. The two girls started giggling and could not stop. The hiccups continued and a sort of hysteria overtook them. The laughter and hiccups continued until Addie and Mrs. Scott came in to see what was going on. The girls were laughing too hard to explain what had happened, and as Stephanie hiccupped again, Addie and Mrs. Scott joined in the laughter.

Cindy opened the front door and yelled her usual, "Hello," and was met with laughter coming from the den. She walked over and saw Stephanie, Mrs. Scott, Addie and Mary Margaret all laughing too hard to speak.

Addie waved her in, and without knowing why, she was soon swept into the hysteria. Finally, composure overtook Mary Margaret enough that she began explaining in single words, "Stephanie, Mrs. Scott, apology, snot, burp and the hiccups." Amid the hysteria, she somehow understood that Stephanie and Mrs. Scott had come here for the apology, and there was something about snot, burping and hiccups. When they had all laughed until their sides ached, and they could laugh no more, proper introductions were made.

Mrs. Scott apologized for meeting Mrs. Smith and Mary Margaret under these circumstances. Stephanie looked as though she was about to cry when Mrs. Smith held out her hand to shake hands with her. She was unaccustomed to shaking hands and flinched as she saw the hand coming toward her. Mrs. Smith realized how upset she was and walked closer to put her hand on her shoulder.

"I'm very glad to meet you, Stephanie," she said.

"I'm glad to meet you, too, Mrs. Smith, and I'm embarrassed and sorry that I was mean to Mary Margaret," Stephanie said in a husky voice while attempting to retard more tears.

"I understand that sometimes things get out of hand and people are hurt, but I'm so glad you came to personally apologize and hope that you and Mary Margaret will grow to be friends," the kind mother said hoping silently that this was about to bring to an end the horrible beginning of Mary Margaret's introduction to Left Fork School.

Stephanie and her mother didn't stay long. When they left, Mary Margaret looked to the pond and saw that Davis and Jordan had gone home as well. Cindy asked about Mary Margaret's day, and Addie came in to be part of the telling of the deer incident. Mrs. Smith was upset that Mary Margaret had come so close to danger, and Addie assured her that she would always be at the end of the driveway when the bus arrived after this.

"Addie, I don't blame you for this. It could have happened with you watching her, but the presence of the deer concerns me," she finished.

Mike arrived while this story was being told, and he, too, was concerned about the deer being on their property when he realized the danger in which Mary Margaret had been placed.

Addie told them that dinner was about ready and that she would be leaving early to go to church. She said she had choir practice tonight and didn't want to miss that.

The family had dinner and discussed the Cool 5, their punishment and how the first 4 had handled the apologies.

"It will be very difficult for Allison to come and make her apology as she's in the most trouble and now probably considers Mary Margaret the cause of all her grief," Cindy said, not realizing the depth of truth in her statement.

They all worked together to clean up the kitchen, and Mary Margaret went into her room to do her homework when she heard her father announce, "We got a letter from Charlene." In all the excitement of the afternoon, Mary Margaret had completely forgotten about it. She ran into the den as her father opened the envelope and her mother came in from the kitchen.

Mike read Charlene's letter—

"Dear Ones—

It has been a long week since you left, and I trust that you are settling in nicely.

I wanted to thank you for the generous severance you gave to me. You treated me so nicely while I worked for you, and I never expected anything when it was over. The bank is taking care of depositing my payments monthly, and again, your generosity exceeded any and all expectations.

Darlene and I went to Atlantic City last week while Alice and her parents were away on vacation. We stayed at Trump Tower and had a fantastic time. We saw some shows and tried our luck at the slot machines.

It has been lonely without seeing you every day, but I am applying with some agencies to try to find a new position. There will never be another one like I had with you, as you became family to me.

Again, I do hope this finds you well, and hope to hear from you soon. Alice, Darlene and I are looking forward to our visit this summer.

Fondly,

Charlene"

Mike and Cindy thought that it was wonderful that Darlene and Charlene had gone to Atlantic City. Mary Margaret asked what severance was. Mr. Smith explained that since Charlene had worked for them for such a long time that they wanted to help her get through the transition from her position with them to a new position or until she was able to draw social security. Mary Margaret had never thought about Charlene's financial needs after they moved away, and she felt the burning in the back of her eyes when she thought about her parents taking care of her after she had taken care of them for so long. Cindy said that she was going to write Charlene a letter, and Mary Margaret was glad to say that she had written one that afternoon. Her parents were proud of her and said so.

Chapter 38

Thursday was spelling test day at school, and Mrs. Stancil gave the students a few minutes to go over the words before the test began.

Mary Margaret felt confident that she knew all the words, but a last-minute review built her confidence. She had never taken a test in Mrs. Stancil's class before, so she was not really sure what to expect. When the time for the test arrived, Mrs. Stancil told everybody to put away everything on their desk except their pencils.

She passed out paper with lines numbered 1 through 20. This puzzled Mary Margaret as there had only been 15 words to study for the week. Mrs. Stancil began calling out the words, "school," she said in her soft southern voice. "The boys and girls have gone to school."

Mary Margaret spelled out the word. Next she called out, "sling. The boy's arm is in a sling," she said. Mary Margaret had not studied this word, but wrote s-l-i-n-g on her paper. This continued and the next few words were the ones that she had prepared for in anticipation of today's test.

Number 10 was balloon. This was a new word, but Mary Margaret wrote *b-a-l-l-o-o-n* on her paper.

Numbers 11 and 12 were familiar from this week's list, but number 13 was transfer. Mrs. Stancil said, "We will transfer to another room." Mary Margaret was puzzled by this word and sounded it out in her mind and finally wrote *t-r-a-n-s-f-e-r*.

Numbers 14 and 15 were words she had studied, but number 16 and 17 were new. Number 16 was gasoline and number 17 was *remember*.

Mary Margaret could feel a little panic building up as she started to write g-a-s . . . and couldn't think whether the next letter should be an 'a' or an 'o.' She finally decided on an 'a' and completed the word, *g-a-s-a-l-i-n-e*. Once she looked at it, she knew it was wrong, but Mrs. Stancil had moved on to number 17, which was *remember*. Mary Margaret hurriedly wrote r-e-m-e-m-b-e-r and started to go back to number 16 to change it, but Mrs. Stancil was moving on to numbers 18, 19 and 20.

When she finished number 20 she asked that everybody put their pencils down on their desks. Mary Margaret wanted to go back and change gasoline, but felt that she would get in trouble.

Mrs. Stancil instructed the students to pass their papers to the person to their left. Philip took Mary Margaret's paper and Mary Margaret could feel the tears in the back of her eyes. She was embarrassed that she would be missing a spelling word. She had always gotten perfect marks in spelling, and this was the first time that she knew she would be missing a word.

"Philip," Mrs. Stancil said, "I want you to mark out the words numbered 2, 10, 13, 16 and 17 on Mary Margaret's paper. These words were not on the list given to her, and it would not be fair to test her on these," she explained.

"Mary Margaret, each week I take the 5 words which have been missed by more people the week before and place them on this week's test."

Mary Margaret was embarrassed at being singled out for this explanation, but secretly she appreciated what Mrs. Stancil was doing. When the tests were returned, Philip had marked through the 5 words as Mrs. Stancil instructed, and Mary Margaret had spelled the remaining 15 words correctly. She was pleased, and knew that she would always remember that gasoline was spelled with an "o" and not an "a."

Chapter 39

Math was the next class, and Mrs. Stancil was explaining subtraction of fractions when Mrs. Calhoun gently knocked on the door before opening it.

"Mrs. Stancil, I'm sorry to interrupt, but may I see Mary Margaret for a few minutes," she requested. Again, Mary Margaret was embarrassed for being singled out as Mrs. Stancil told her to go with Mrs. Calhoun.

When they got into the hall, Mrs. Calhoun explained, "Mary Margaret, Allison and her mother are in my office. She wants to apologize to you, and she didn't want to go to your home. Please come with me so that we may get this over with and be able to move forward."

When they entered, Allison was sitting on a love seat, and her mother was sitting beside her. Allison looked defiantly at Mary Margaret and stared as Mrs. Calhoun introduced Mary Margaret and Mrs. Kincaid. After the introductions were over, Mrs. Kincaid said, "Allison there is something you need to say to Mary Margaret."

Mary Margaret's stomach began to churn, and she was afraid that she was going to be sick. Her eyes and nose were burning. Was she going to cry, she thought? Why did she feel bad? She hadn't done anything. Still the defiant look from Allison was unnerving to her. Mary Margaret wanted to run out of the building as she had on the first day, but she knew that was impossible. Mrs. Calhoun had taken her seat behind her desk, and Mary Margaret was in one of the rockers. She thought that Mrs. Calhoun looked somehow different at her desk than she had when she sat beside her in the rocker.

Mrs. Kincaid again urged Allison to say something to Mary Margaret. Finally, through what seemed like clenched jaws the words, "I'm sorry" came from Allison. The words were not sincere, but they had been spoken. Mary Margaret sat silently, again not knowing what was expected of her. She felt awkward in this position. She didn't know if she was supposed to say something, but Mrs. Calhoun interrupted the silence by saying to Allison, "You said the words, 'I'm sorry', but I don't feel you were sincere. However, the punishment was for you to tell her that you were sorry, and you have done that." There was no question in the minds of anyone in that room that Mrs. Calhoun was not pleased with the event that had just taken place.

"Mrs. Kincaid," the principal continued, "Allison may return to school on Monday. However, if I ever hear of her ever again harassing any student, she will be suspended and other steps will have to be taken to fulfill her educational requirements. Is that clear?" she asked.

Mary Margaret was not sure what this meant, but she knew that she hoped Mrs. Calhoun never said anything like that to her. Her tone had become severe. Her soft southern drawl had become hard and firm. Mary Margaret was scared; and, apparently, Mrs. Calhoun sensed this as she excused her before she heard Mrs. Kincaid's reply.

Mary Margaret nearly ran back to Mrs. Stancil's room and was glad to return to her seat. The class was getting ready for lunch when she returned. They were excused to walk down the hall, and Mrs. Stancil told Mary Margaret that she would show her later in the afternoon what she had missed while she was out of the room.

Mary Margaret was unnerved by the experience with Allison. She had never had somebody stare at her with such defiance. She was afraid that Allison would somehow hurt her. Mary Margaret suddenly longed for Alice and the comfort of her old school in New York. She had never felt frightened there. She always felt safe, and here in Left Fork, she was beginning to realize that life was full of pitfalls. She had nearly been run over by a deer just the day before and now a girl her own age was making her uncomfortable just by looking at her.

Nancy Miller walked up beside her and noticed her sullen mood. "What's wrong," she asked.

"Nothing," Mary Margaret replied.

They walked on to the cafeteria, and Mary Margaret went over to a table to sit down. She had brought her lunch from home. Jane, Linda, and Peggy came over and asked if they could sit with her. Mary Margaret said it was okay, and they sat down, leaving an empty seat for Nancy, who soon came over with her lunch tray. Jane, Linda, Peggy and Nancy talked about their 4-H projects and Mary Margaret was feeling left out. Jane, Linda and Peggy each were raising sheep to be shown in the County Fair, and Nancy was doing a crewel embroidery sampler. In an effort to draw Mary Margaret into the conversation Jane asked, "Mary Margaret, would you like to come over to see my sheep?"

Absent-mindedly Mary Margaret answered, "Yes, I'd like to, but I don't know when I can do it."

As the lunch period continued, Mary Margaret became more withdrawn, and the other girls at the table wondered what was happening to her. It seemed as though her whole personality had changed, and she was a different person than they knew this morning.

Mary Margaret was continuing to be haunted by the look in Allison's eyes. Her imagination took over her reasoning, and she soon had convinced herself that Allison would come to her house and hurt her. When lunch was over, she hurried back to the classroom and only felt comfortable when Mrs. Stancil had closed the door to the room and the afternoon's lessons had begun. She was able to concentrate on science and history, but when it was time to get ready to go home, she again began to feel frightened.

The bus ride home seemed like a blur to her as she got off and was relieved to see Addie waiting for her beside the mailbox. Mary Margaret stepped off the bus and Addie could sense an agitation as she hurried up the driveway to the house. Addie tried to make conversation, but she was met with short answers and couldn't determine what was wrong.

Once inside Mary Margaret went into her room and started on her homework. After she finished that, she began reading her library book. She heard Addie calling her to say that Davis and Jordan were here to fish, and she just yelled out that she didn't want to fish today.

The boys went on down to the pond, and Mary Margaret could see them as they took their usual positions. Soon Philip joined them, but she still didn't want to go outside. She tried reading her library book, but couldn't concentrate. She would read a page and then re-read it. Finally, she put the book down and lay on the bed. Addie peeked in to see if she was all right, and she told her that she was.

When Cindy came home, Addie told her about the sullen mood. She knocked on Mary Margaret's door and entered.

"Hi, sweet thing," she said. Addie says you didn't want to fish with the boys. Is anything wrong?"

"I want to go back to New York. I'm afraid here," Mary Margaret cried.

Cindy was surprised that this fear was being expressed. She had never heard her say she was afraid of anything. She had expressed feeling anxious over things, but she had never used the word afraid. She was upset with this and asked, "Mary Margaret what happened to make you feel this way."

Between tears she explained, "Well, first the deer scared me."

"Well, you know what," her mother said, "I'm sure that would have scared me, too. But chances are that will never happen again.

Now the crying escalated without warning to hysteria.

Her mother continued the questioning. "Mary Margaret, did something happen at school today?"

Mary Margaret continued to cry, and the sobbing began.

Cindy held her as she cried, but her daughter seemed unable to explain what had happened. She attempted to take Mary Margaret through the entire day including the spelling test, math, lunch, the afternoon classes, and Mary Margaret could not find words to express what was wrong.

Mike arrived while they were still in the bedroom and after hearing Addie's explanation of Mary Margaret's attitude change this afternoon, he knocked on her door and went in to see what was going on.

Cindy was sitting on Mary Margaret's bed holding her like she was a baby. Mary Margaret seemed so fragile in her mother's arms. It was obvious to him that she had been crying, but at this moment the tears had stopped. He sat down beside them and asked, "Mary Margaret, what is wrong?"

"Daddy, I'm afraid here. I want to go back to New York."

"Tell me exactly what happened that frightened you," he continued.

She finally explained about the trip to Mrs. Calhoun's office and the apology from Allison Kincaid. Her parents were puzzled that she would be frightened when Allison had apologized, and again she couldn't put into words how Allison made her feel in the few moments they shared. The conversation continued a few moments longer and Addie yelled that dinner was ready.

"You wash your hands and face and come on to dinner. Everything will be all right. You're safe here with us," Mike said.

Mary Margaret did as she was told, but she knew that it was not all right, but she didn't really know how she knew that.

Finally it was Friday! Mary Margaret got ready for school and waited for Addie to walk with her to the bus stop. Until now she had begun to feel that she could make the trip by herself, but today she felt doubtful. She was uncomfortable, and couldn't figure out why. She thought about the incident with the deer, and knew it would never happen again. It was early morning, but it was daylight and she knew exactly when to leave the house to arrive at the end of the driveway almost at the same instant as the bus. Mary Margaret was confused about her feelings, and was becoming obsessed with thinking bad thoughts.

Chapter 40

At school Mary Margaret found out that the schedule was different on Friday. Her class went into another room for music, so the routine was different. She was uncomfortable not knowing what to expect as Mrs. Stancil went through what was routine to her and the rest of the class, but was new to Mary Margaret. She was beginning to feel that this day was worse than the first day had been. She was anxious about everything. At lunch she was sullen and hardly talked with the other girls who had now become lunch table regulars. Nancy Miller was going to visit her grandmother over the week-end in Charleston; and the other three each had plans, none of which included Mary Margaret.

After lunch Mary Margaret's mood darkened even more as the weather turned bad and a horrible spring storm struck the area. The tornado warnings sounded, and Mary Margaret was terrified as the other children got up and started into the hall. She followed the group, but when Mrs. Stancil shouted for them to *"Duck and cover"* and they all squatted down against the interior hall walls and ducked their heads under their arms, Mary Margaret was nearly hysterical. In New York, St. Mark's had periodic fire drills where all the students lined up and exited the building, but this was nothing she had ever experienced. The wind was blowing debris against the windows, and the rain was almost blowing sideways when they were in the classroom; but now in the hall she couldn't see what was happening outside except through the small windows in the doors at the end of the hall, and it appeared to be almost dark outside. The lights flickered several times and the hallway was darkened, but mercifully, the electricity came back on after just a few seconds each time.

Mary Margaret's anxiety grew until it overflowed as she quietly squatted with her arms over her head and cried. The noise from the storm and the muffled whispers in the hall hid any noise that she may have made. The tears dripped into the floor, and her nose ran until she had to take down one arm and wipe it across the back of her hand. She then wiped her hand on her slacks and put her arm back over her head. What seemed like an eternity was really about 15 minutes when the sirens were silenced. The teachers gathered their students and led them back into the classroom. Mary Margaret attempted to hide her face and wipe it at the same time so that no one would be aware that she had been crying, but Mrs. Stancil walked up beside her and quickly in an almost imperceptible motion handed her a tissue. Mary Margaret wanted to hug her, but wiped her nose instead.

Inside the classroom the students could see through the windows that limbs had been blown from trees. One tall pine tree had been uprooted and was leaning against the school. The limbs were brushing against the window, and the skies as suddenly as they had turned dark turned into brilliant blue with the sun shining brightly through the limbs. It was nearly time to go home, and Mrs. Stancil said that it would be a good idea to spend the rest of the day reading library books as book reports would be due the next Friday.

With this news Mary Margaret felt a jolt in her stomach. She had hardly begun to read *National Velvet*, and now she was faced with writing a book report. She wondered what was wrong with her. She had always loved to read and book reports were nothing new to her. She had written them all year long. Last year her class had given oral reports, but in the fourth grade, she had written a book report every two weeks. Why did she feel like things were slipping from her grasp? When the bell rang, she hurried out to be with the rest of the students. She didn't want to be the last one out and be by herself walking to the bus.

Addie was waiting for her at the end of the driveway, and it was apparent that the storm had been severe. On the bus ride home, Mary Margaret saw many trees which had been uprooted and others had limbs blown off. The road was passable, but there were limbs and tree branches all along the way. Other debris had been scattered about as trash cans had been overturned and anything loose had been picked up by the wind and carried away. When

Mary Margaret got off the bus Addie could see that her face was red, but she didn't ask her about it. As they walked up the driveway, they had to veer into the woods as a tree had fallen and blocked their path. When Mary Margaret stepped onto the pine straw it reminded her instantly of her brush with the deer, and she felt her heart begin to race. Once they were back on the concrete, she was relieved and was anxious to get inside the house. Once inside Addie asked her if the storm had been bad at school, and Mary Margaret told her about going into the hall and how dark it was outside. Addie explained that spring storms in the south come up quickly and usually pass quickly, but they can be violent.

Addie began to laugh.

"What's funny, Addie," Mary Margaret asked.

"Oh, I was just remembering a time when my daughter, Louise, was a little girl. For one reason or another, I can't remember why now, she was home alone except for our dog, Spooky. It was Tornado Awareness Day. She was watching television and saw a tornado warning. She didn't realize that it was a test. Then the warning sirens started. Instead of staying in the house and going to a safe place, she took Spooky and went to a neighbor's house. Unfortunately, this neighbor didn't allow dogs in her house and sent Louise back home. She was so embarrassed that she had done this," Addie laughed as she retold the story, but Mary Margaret silently empathized with the daughter's position. She knew that she would probably have done the same thing, and she didn't see the humor in Addie's story.

"I need to read my library book," Mary Margaret said as she went to her bedroom. She looked at the book and decided that she would try to finish it by Sunday night. She opened to her bookmark and read until she heard her mother's voice as she came through the door. Mary Margaret got off her bed and walked into the kitchen where Addie and Cindy were discussing the storm.

Cindy's voice was excited as she explained she had never seen such a horrible storm. She said that the hospital lost power intermittently, but the generators took over, and there was no real harm. She said that she had better call Mike and have him stop by Orville's Seed and Feed and get a chain saw on his way home.

Addie started to say that she knew one of the guys at work would loan him one, but then thought that they would probably need theirs, too, so she kept quiet.

Cindy waved at her daughter as she turned around while dialing the telephone. She noticed the sad look on her face, but wasn't certain if it was left over from the day before or new today. After her phone call, she walked over and hugged her asking her how she fared the storm. She explained duck and cover to her, but left out how frightened she had been.

Cindy went in to change her clothes and Mary Margaret retreated to her bedroom. She heard voices outside and opened her curtains to see Davis and Jordan at their usual fishing spot. She thought that they were presumptuous to come over every day without asking, but then remembered that her father had told them they could fish whenever they wanted. Her mood sank again as she thought that maybe she would like to go down to the pond by herself without them being there, but her father obviously hadn't thought about that.

The phone rang and Addie called to Mary Margaret that she had a phone call. She went into the kitchen and said, "Hello," but the person on the other end didn't speak. Mary Margaret repeated her greeting, but nobody said anything and finally she heard a click as the receiver on the other end was hung up. Addie turned around as she heard Mary Margaret repeatedly say, "Hello," and then saw the look on her face when she hung up the receiver. Addie saw fear in Mary Margaret's eyes.

"Who was it?" Addie asked.

"Nobody ever said anything," Mary Margaret said.

Addie laughingly said, "It was probably just somebody playing a trick. I remember catching my children calling people and asking if they had Prince Albert in a can. When they said 'Yes' the children would laugh and say, "You'd better let him out."

Mary Margaret just stared at Addie as this meant nothing to her. She wondered why anybody would put Prince Albert in a can, and who the heck was Prince Albert?

Addie realized that Mary Margaret was too young to know that there used to be a smoking tobacco called Prince Albert and it was sold in a can, so she explained all this to her, but again, she failed to see the humor in it. Addie tried again by telling her that they would call people and ask if their refrigerator was running, and when they said "Yes", they would say, "You'd better try to catch it." Again, the humor passed right by Mary Margaret, and Addie sighed deeply and returned to the cake she was mixing up.

Mary Margaret went back to her room and continued reading until her father came home. She heard the conversation and knew that something different was happening. She went out to see that her father had brought in a chain saw and put it on the kitchen table.

"Oh, Mike, don't you think the garage would be a better place for that?" Cindy asked.

"You're probably right, but after living in an apartment so long, I'm just used to bringing everything into the house."

As the adults laughed, Mary Margaret wished they were back in the apartment. She didn't have to worry about so many things when they lived there, and no one ever called her and hung up when she answered.

Her father hurriedly changed clothes, and they all went down the driveway to look at the tree situation. Mike decided that the important thing was to clear the driveway so that he and Cindy could get their cars in and Addie could get hers out. Orville had put some fuel in the saw and had given him a quick lesson, so he was ready to start. He pulled on the rope several times, and it finally roared to life amid a cloud of blue smoke. He put on his safety glasses that Orville insisted he buy and began cutting the tree into pieces that would be easy for him to handle.

The sound of the chain saw brought Davis and Jordan running up from the pond. They stood back and watched as the chips flew, and the blue smoke fouled the air. They were excited and Jordan was animated as he danced around from side to side to get a better view of the cutting.

"I helped my dad cut wood after an ice storm," he said.

Mr. Smith had no intention of allowing him to get any closer to the saw than he already was. As he thought about it, he realized that everyone was probably too close as the chips were flying in all directions. He decided that he would stop cutting and remove the already cut limbs from the driveway while he had his audience. He hoped that they would lose interest and go on back to the house without his having to insist that they stand back.

When he put down the saw and started pulling the limbs out of the way, to his surprise everyone joined in and in no time the driveway was clear enough so that the vehicles could get in and out. He decided that he would continue with his cutting in the morning when nobody was around to get hurt. So, he called it quits and everybody walked back toward the house.

Jordan asked, "Mary Margaret, why didn't you come out to fish?"

"I was reading my library book," she replied.

He was dumbfounded that anybody would be working on school work on Friday afternoon and said so.

Mary Margaret just ignored his comments and walked on ahead and went straight to her bedroom. Her parents and Addie went into the kitchen to finish getting dinner on the table and discussed her attitude. Addie quietly confided that Mary Margaret appeared to have been crying when she got off the bus, and she wondered if she had been frightened by the storm and the duck and cover situation at school. Cindy said that could be part of it, but felt that something had changed the day before, and she made a mental note to try to get to the bottom of it.

After dinner, Mary Margaret went back to her room to read some more. Mike and Cindy worked in the yard cleaning up small limbs and debris, which had been blown about by the storm. Davis and Jordan had gone home, and it was peaceful and quiet. When they finished cleaning up the yard and it was almost dark, they sat in the porch swing and listened to the frogs around the pond. They were very content. Mike discussed his week at work and how well things were moving along, and Cindy shared about a difficult surgical procedure in which the patient had done remarkably well. The new vehicles had been delivered, and they were both pleased. They were so happy to be on their front porch listening to the frogs and watching the sun set behind the tall South Carolina pines.

The telephone rang, and they assumed that Mary Margaret would answer it. Mary Margaret hesitated, but after the third ring she put down her book and ran into the kitchen. She picked up the receiver, said, "Hello," and the person on the other end said in a deep, obviously disguised voice, "I'll get you." Mary Margaret heard the click in the receiver as the last word was spoken and there was silence on the line. As the telephone had rung several times before Mary Margaret answered it, Mike and Cindy had come inside. They arrived just as Mary Margaret said, "Hello," and witnessed the fear as she heard the words. Of course, they didn't know what the person on the other end had said, but it was obvious that Mary Margaret was upset. She hung up the phone; and as she turned around, she was immediately crying. Mike and Cindy asked her what was wrong and between sobs, she told them about the earlier call where somebody had asked for her; and when she answered, they hung up after holding the line a few seconds. She told them about the threat of this call, and she ran to her room and flung herself onto her bed with her face smashed into her pillow.

Her parents followed, and they both tried to come up with reasons for the calls. Mike said it was just somebody playing a prank on the new girl in school. Mrs. Smith agreed.

"No, it's not a prank. Those calls were meant for me," she said emphatically.

"Do you know who it is that's making the calls?" her father asked.

Mary Margaret had always been taught never to accuse anybody of something unless you know for a fact that the accusation is true, but this time she felt sure she knew who it was even though she couldn't prove it.

"I think it's Allison Kincaid."

"What makes you think that?" her mother asked.

"It was just the way she looked at me in Mrs. Calhoun's office."

This seemed improbable to both parents, but as they discussed it later, they both agreed that Mary Margaret was not a person to jump to conclusions. Mike said that he would check with the telephone company on Monday to see what could be done to trace the calls.

"Come on, Mary Margaret, let's sit on the porch. It's a lovely evening, and you should be outside enjoying it," her father insisted.

Into Addie's Arms

Mary Margaret reluctantly went, but she was uncomfortable and jumped at any strange sound. The wind was picking up and tree limbs were falling in the woods. Mike said that they had probably been broken off in the earlier storm, but something caught them and kept them from falling. Now that the wind was blowing again, they were falling to the ground. The wind continued to blow, and soon it was obvious that another storm was brewing. Lightning was flashing off to the west and thunder could be heard in the distance.

Mary Margaret wanted to go in the house immediately after the first flash of lightning. Cindy agreed and in a few minutes rain was beating against the sides of the house. Mike and Cindy had gone into the kitchen and suggested that they play a game of Rook. Mary Margaret had a hard time concentrating because the large windows in the kitchen overlooking the pond showed the severity of the storm as the lightning illuminated the land surrounding the house. The closer the storm got, the louder the thunder clapped. Mike and Cindy kept the conversation focused on the card game, but Mary Margaret's heart was beating rapidly, and she played the game with one eye on the cards and the other on the windows.

The storm died down after about 30 minutes, and the card game continued for another hour. Cindy was declared the winner, with Mary Margaret coming in second. Her inattentiveness had kept her from winning what her parents had hoped would be a landslide victory for her. They gave her opportunities to make great plays and win points, but she was too preoccupied to notice.

They all decided to go to bed after the game, and Mary Margaret started down the hall to her room as the telephone rang again. Mr. Smith answered the phone this time, and when he said, "Hello" a girl's voice on the other end asked to speak with Mary Margaret. He politely asked who was calling, and Jane Ellis gave him her name. He called to Mary Margaret and told her that Jane Ellis was on the phone. Mary Margaret exhaled and realized that she had been holding her breath as her father answered the phone.

"Hello," Mary Margaret answered tentatively.

"Hi, Mary Margaret, this is Jane. What are you doing?"

"Oh, nothing. We were just playing cards." Mary Margaret replied.

"Well, I was calling to see if you would like to go with me tomorrow to my grandparents' farm. I need to bathe my sheep for a competition on Sunday. We'll have a great time, and my grandparents are lots of fun," she enthusiastically extended her invitation.

While Mary Margaret wanted to go, something told her that it might not be safe. "Thanks anyway, I can't go. But thanks again for asking," she managed to get out in spite of the lump in her throat.

"Are you really sure you can't go? It'll be lots of fun," Jane asked.

"Yes, I'm sure, maybe another time," she responded.

"Well, okay, then. I'll see you on Monday," Jane dejectedly said.

"Yeah, on Monday, good-bye."

Mike and Cindy had busied themselves in the kitchen to listen to this side of the conversation. When Mary Margaret hung up, her mother asked her what Jane had wanted. She explained about her 4-H project and the sheep. She said that Jane was going to her grandparents' home the next day to bathe the sheep.

Cindy was disappointed that Mary Margaret had not wanted to go. She wanted her to make friends and be involved in the community, even if she and Jane had gotten off to a bad start. She asked Mary Margaret if she wanted to reconsider and call Jane back, but Mary Margaret said she needed to read her library book the next day anyway.

Chapter 41

Larry Kincaid phoned his home. The telephone rang 10 times, and he snapped his cell phone closed. He looked at his watch. It was dark outside, and his daughter should have been at home. His wife should have been there, too, but he never expected her to answer. Until recently, however, Allison had been dependable enough to answer his evening call. Now, he wondered where she was. "Where is she?" he said to no one. "That girl is completely out of control, and her mother has lapsed back into her old habits. I can't deal with this right now," he continued talking to himself as he left his apartment to meet friends.

The ten rings echoed through the house as Mrs. Kincaid lay on the sofa and Allison had again climbed out her bedroom window and headed out the highway toward Charleston.

She watched from the tree line as the Smith family sat on the porch. She could hear the voices, but could not make out the words. She dared not go any closer, but she longed to be a part of the picture. The more she watched the closeness of this family as they sat on the swing, the more her heart ached. However, instead of softening the already hardening heart of this young girl, she became embittered. Her mind raced with destructive thoughts.

She thinks she's so good, sitting there with her parents. She won't feel so good when I get finished with her. I'll make everybody think she's bad. She doesn't stand a chance with me, she thought.

Allison moved along the tree line and tripped over a fallen tree limb. The family looked in her direction and exchanged words, but she was not detected.

Lightning flashed in the western sky illuminating the landscape. *Did they see me?* She wondered and squatted down.

Activity picked up on the porch and the family went inside. Allison knew from her earlier visit to the home that she couldn't see them unless she went on the porch. She wasn't ready for that, so she started jogging toward town.

The storm came in hard, and lightning flashed offering her opportunities to see her path and possibly keeping her from being injured as she ran along in the dark. The rain pelted her. The temperature dropped, and she was soon drenched. Her hair slapped against her face as she ran. Her slacks stuck to her legs, making it difficult for her to keep a steady pace. There was no place to take refuge, and no cars passed by as she ran the few minutes along the highway back into town and onto the sidewalks which would lead to her home.

She climbed back into her bedroom window and peeked out to see her mother was mopping the kitchen. *She probably didn't even know I was gone*, Allison thought as she stripped off her wet clothes and left them in a pile on the carpet. *This will give her something else to do. With this mess, she'll have an excuse to pull out the carpet shampooer. She'll love that*, the young girl thought sarcastically as she went into the bathroom to shower.

The water was hot—too hot. It burned her skin, but she enjoyed the pain. She shampooed her hair and remained in the shower until the water ran cold. She put on her pajamas which she found neatly folded in her drawer.

She looked around her room. Except for her book bag on the floor by the door and the pile of wet clothes, her room was immaculate. Her drawers were perfectly arranged. Her closet was organized by style and color. Her slacks were in one section, her blouses in another. Her shoes were matched and aligned on shelves. Her surroundings were in perfect order, but this little girl went to bed with her mind racing as she longed for something nobody seemed to be able to give her. She felt alone in her home with her mother not more than 40 feet away.

Chapter 42

Saturday morning was bright and clear. The storms seemed to have washed the area of Left Fork, South Carolina clean. The pine trees pollinate in the spring and everything gets a dusting of yellowish-green powder. The Smith family had never experienced anything like this, and it had just begun when they moved into their home. In fact, Addie had decided against cleaning the outside of the windows until it was over. The storms had washed away much of the pollen, but it was obvious that Mother Nature couldn't handle it all on her own. Cindy had decided to wash off the front porch and was pulling out the hose when Addie arrived. She stopped and waited until Addie walked up to the porch, and Addie said she thought today would be a good day to clean the outside of the windows. Cindy tried to protest, but Addie would have no part of it and went on into the house to get her paraphernalia to begin. Cindy started hosing off the porch.

Mike had gone to work to test the new loom while the plant was shut down for the week-end. Gerry Gilbert and a few key employees were there to help, and his excitement was high when he left.

Mary Margaret was surprised to hear Addie singing when she came out of her bedroom. She walked into the kitchen, and said good morning to her. Addie was so caught up in her song and gathering her cleaning supplies that she jumped when Mary Margaret spoke. They both laughed and Addie thought it was good to see Mary Margaret smile even if it was at her expense.

"I didn't expect to see you today," she said to Addie.

"After that rain the air just seemed so clean, and the pollen should be done, so I decided to come and do those outside windows. Do you think you can be my right-hand girl and help me for a while?" she asked the sleepy-eyed child.

"I can help for a while, but I need to read some more," Mary Margaret willingly replied. "I'll be out as soon as I eat something."

Mary Margaret fixed a bowl of cereal and went outside after putting her bowl and spoon in the dishwasher. Addie was climbing up the ladder to clean the second-floor bedroom windows. Cindy was hosing off the porch, and Mary Margaret nearly walked into the path of the spray as she opened the door. Again, there was laughter as she jumped back, and Cindy was glad to see the smile this early in the morning.

Mary Margaret walked around the house looking for Addie; and when she saw her up on the ladder, she wondered what she could do to help, but Addie furnished the answer before the question was asked.

"Mary Margaret, would you put your foot on the bottom rung and hold on to the uprights," she yelled from her high perch.

Mary Margaret placed her right foot on the bottom rung and extended her arms to help steady the ladder. She wondered if her being there was really of any benefit, but she stood there until Addie began to climb down. She stepped away.

"Not yet! Don't let go yet," she called, as she continued her descent.

When Addie's feet were level with Mary Margaret's hands, she stepped away, and Addie came down to the ground. They continued on around the house and Addie climbed up and down the ladder, cleaning the windows as they went. Mary Margaret followed and held the ladder at each stopping point.

When they had finished and Addie was putting the ladder in the out building, Mike drove up. He got out of the car and was carrying t-shirts over his arm. He was grinning as he held up the first shirts, which had been made with the new machinery that had been installed in the plant since he arrived in January. It had taken nearly five months, but the test this morning showed that everything was working as expected. He was so excited. His factory was now able to create the fabric and finish the shirts in one location. He had brought shirts for Mary Margaret, Cindy, and Addie even though he hadn't expected her to be there when he arrived. He showed them the seams and finish work on the shirts and explained the weave of the cotton fabric. Mary Margaret couldn't remember ever seeing her father so excited over something at work, and she noticed that her mother and Addie were caught up in the excitement. She said the right things, but in her heart, she wished they had never come here.

They went in for lunch, and the telephone rang just as Mary Margaret stepped into the kitchen. Addie rushed to answer it, and it was obvious from the conversation that it was a friend. It turned out to be Mrs. Applegate, and she asked to speak with Mary Margaret.

"Hello," the little girl said.

"Hi, Dear, I was wondering if you would like to come over this afternoon and work on your quilt?"

"I have to ask my parents, hold on."

Of course, they readily agreed and offered to take her there.

"They said it was okay, and they will bring me over," she spoke into the phone.

"That won't be necessary. I've got some errands to run, and I'll pick you up. I'll see you around 1:00. See you then."

Mary Margaret heard the phone click before she could acknowledge the comments. She relayed the message to her parents, and her afternoon was planned.

Addie and Cindy started fixing lunch, and Mike went into the den to make a call to New York to share the good news that the mill was up and running with all the new machinery.

Mary Margaret set the table, and as the four of them sat down to eat, the telephone rang again. Mike answered it, but whoever was on the other end hung up when they heard his voice. He said it was probably a wrong number and sat down, but Mary Margaret felt the jolt in her stomach and knew that it was intended for her.

Mrs. Applegate arrived a little after 1:00, and was in her usual good mood. She came into the house and said that they needed to run along if they were going to get anything accomplished. After a few pleasantries were exchanged, Mary Margaret got into Mrs. Applegate's car, and they drove off toward town.

"Tell me now, dear, how was the rest of your first week at school after that dreadful beginning?"

"It was all right," Mary Margaret quietly replied.

Mrs. Applegate sensed that it was not all right. She continued with the conversation and was finally able to extract from Mary Margaret that one of the girls involved in the incident at school had frightened her by just looking at her when Mrs. Calhoun made her apologize. Mrs. Applegate thought that on the surface that sounded petty, but she knew from experience what Mary Margaret was talking about. Her daughter, Beverly, had been a sensitive child; and when she was about the same age as Mary Margaret, a bully at school had made her life miserable. She could never be caught doing her deeds, but she was certainly doing them. When she learned that the girl harassing Mary Margaret was Allison Kincaid, she was not surprised. She did not know the family well, but she had heard rumors that Allison had been a troublemaker for a long time; and knew that Mary Margaret would be a prime target—being a new girl in town and being a sensitive type.

"You know, as I think about this, I remember that my daughter had a problem with a bully when she was about your age," Mrs. Applegate said.

"Really, how did she ever get through it?" Mary Margaret turned in her seat to ask.

"Well, it's been a long time ago, and I'll have to think about how it all ended," she responded as she parked the car in her driveway.

When they went inside the house, Mary Margaret immediately felt comfortable. She loved being here. The aroma was of something having recently been baked. The sunlight filtered through the sheer curtains, and the hues of color were comforting. The dining room table was all set up to work on the quilt, and Mrs. Applegate confessed that she had taken the liberty of doing some of the work on her own. She had pieced several girls together and had the pieces for many others arranged. Together she and

Mary Margaret worked on the quilt; and as the shadows indicated it was getting close to suppertime, they had three completed blocks.

"I didn't realize it would take so long to do this," Mary Margaret said as she sighed and placed a finished block on the pile.

"Yes, it will take a while, but it will be something that you will cherish for the rest of your life, and it will be time well spent," her mentor said.

Mary Margaret started to apologize because she was afraid that Mrs. Applegate had misunderstood and thought she didn't want to work on it, but that was not the case. Mrs. Applegate stopped the apology and said she understood that the statement was just that, a statement of fact that it would take some time to finish this.

"You know, I'm glad that it will take a long time because it's just that much more time we can spend together," she said as she hugged her.

Mary Margaret felt the now almost commonplace burn in her nose and behind her eyes, but no tears came. This time it was not a bad feeling. It was a good feeling of experiencing being loved by someone special.

The telephone interrupted their conversation; and as Mrs. Applegate went to answer it, Mary Margaret thought that at least she didn't have to worry about it being one of the bad calls she had been getting at home. When Mrs. Applegate called Mary Margaret to the phone, her heartbeat quickened. She was relieved to hear her mother's voice telling her that they had been invited to have dinner with Davis and Jordan's parents, and that they would pick her up in about 30 minutes.

Mary Margaret explained this to Mrs. Applegate and together they straightened up the pieces of fabric and stored them in a box on which Mrs. Applegate had written, *"Mary Margaret's Quilt."*

They had a few minutes to sit on the porch before her parents arrived, and Mrs. Applegate took that opportunity to tell Mary Margaret that she had to be strong in the face of the bully.

"Mary Margaret, I have been thinking about this bully at school, and I want you to be strong with her. Bullies usually pick victims whom they feel are weak. I remember telling this to Beverly many years ago. I know that things are different here and customs and expectations are different than in New York. However, if you watch for the good things you see people doing, you'll soon adapt to this new situation."

When Mike and Cindy arrived, Mrs. Applegate walked out to the car with Mary Margaret. They thanked her for sharing the afternoon with her, and Mrs. Applegate assured them that it had been her pleasure.

Chapter 43

As they drove away, Cindy explained that Mrs. Raver had come over just after Mary Margaret left to go to Mrs. Applegate's. She said that Jennifer was a very pretty woman, and she owned the shoe store in town. She had invited them over for a cook-out this evening. Jordan had come with his mother, but Davis was at soccer practice. Mary Margaret asked about Mr. Raver, and Mrs. Smith said he was an attorney, but she couldn't add anything else about him.

They arrived at the house, which sat back from the road as theirs did. The winding driveway curved through the woods and ended at the detached garage, which looked almost as big as the house. This garage had 4 doors, and there was another two-car garage attached to the house. Mike commented that somebody in this family must like cars. As if on cue, one of the garage doors opened and out came a handsome man wiping grease off his hands as he approached. Alan Raver apologized for not shaking hands, but explained that he had been changing oil in his Camaro. Mike recognized a 1969 Camaro, which he knew looked as good as it had on the showroom floor the day it was rolled off the truck. It glistened in the overhead fluorescent lights. To the right of it was a black, 1985 Honda CRX, which Mr. Raver explained was his first car and which had now been equipped for sport-track racing. A boat occupied the third bay, and a BMW filled the final place. Mike asked Mr. Raver, who then asked that he be called Alan, if he liked cars, and Alan laughed and said, "Just a little."

They walked toward the house and Alan and Mike were discussing cars, when Jennifer came out. Mary Margaret knew her mother was right when she said she was pretty. Mrs. Raver was tall and stately looking. She wore a beautiful ankle length broomstick skirt with a peasant blouse. The colors were brilliant; and when she smiled, her whole face lit up. Mary Margaret liked her instantly. Cindy introduced her to Mary Margaret, and Jennifer acknowledged her with a handshake. As Mary Margaret took her hand, she could feel the softness and noticed that her nails were immaculately manicured. Her dark brown hair was chin length, and turned under slightly. It bounced when she walked. Her dark brown eyes sparkled as she spoke. Mary Margaret thought she may be one of the most beautiful women she had ever met.

Jennifer spoke in a soft drawl that indicated that she had been raised in the South. Mary Margaret had noticed that most of the people she had met spoke in a manner that made you want to keep them talking just to listen to their voice and Jennifer, Mrs. Raver to Mary Margaret, was no exception. Her voice was soothing.

She led them into the house; and as they passed through, Mary Margaret could see that it was very casual. The family room was a mixture of earth tones and was anchored by a large stone fireplace with a log mantle. The kitchen was bright and cheerful with green granite countertops and wallpaper that looked like jeweled flowers, but they weren't really flowers. The colors reminded Mary Margaret of rubies and sapphires and emeralds when she looked into the room. Golden Sunflowers stood guard on the center island, and fresh vegetables had been carefully arranged on platters. French doors opened onto a screened porch, and Jordan and Davis were out there watching television. They both stood as the adults and Mary Margaret entered the room, and each said, "Hello." Mary Margaret knew her parents would be impressed with their manners, as they were always reminding her about hers.

Jordan turned off the television, and asked Mary Margaret if she would like to go outside. They went through the old-fashioned screen door into a yard that rivaled the beauty of most parks she had seen. The azaleas were in bloom, and the colors were magnificent. They were clumped in large bunches and were all shades of red and pink. The dogwood trees were still in color and Mary Margaret immediately thought of a Monet she had seen in a museum. She had never seen anything so beautiful in her life. She called to her mother to come and look, and Cindy was equally impressed with the landscaping. Jennifer followed them out, and Mary Margaret could see that she was proud of her yard, but was modest in accepting compliments on it. She explained that they had lived in their house for 5 years, and it was an on-going project to get it to this point. She said that Orville had been a big help, and her father had helped her do most of the planting when they first moved in. She said it had taken all this time for the plants to reach this maturity, and this was the first year that they had been so colorful. The ladies continued talking about the plants while Jordan led Mary Margaret to their play area.

On the backside of the lot, partially hidden from the house was a swing set that was like none that Mary Margaret had seen. It was made from timbers, and not only were there swings, there was a tree house, and overhead bars, a pole to slide down from the tree house, a ladder to get up to the tree house, 2 tire swings hung from an old oak tree, and a swimming pool was in the landscape and it looked like a pond with water tumbling down rocks into the pool, and plants completely surrounded the flagstone pool deck. Everything looked as though it had just grown there and nothing conflicted with the other. It all looked so natural. Jordan jumped to the overhead bars and started hand walking his way across. Mary Margaret got in one of the swings and as she swung back and forward, she saw that the edge of the property dropped off just beyond, and as she was swinging, she felt as though she were swinging into nothingness. It was an exciting and frightening feeling at the same time.

Davis came out and climbed into the tree house and looked into a telescope. When he seemed to have found what he was looking for, he softly called to Mary Margaret to come up and look. Mary Margaret climbed the ladder and was amazed at how high it seemed when she reached the platform. She walked around to where Davis was standing, and he motioned for her to look through the telescope. At first she wasn't sure what she was supposed to be seeing, but she soon saw a herd of deer down in the valley below their house. She counted 10 deer of varying sizes, but none were babies. Davis explained that they gather there about this time every evening to graze and drink from the stream. Mary Margaret could see them in great detail with the help of the telescope. Their eyes were blinking, and their ears were always twitching as if they were turning them to listen. When she said this to Davis, he explained that they were listening. He said their sense of smell was great, too. They seemed so peaceful down there that Mary Margaret never thought about her experience with probably two of them just a few days before. She was intent on watching them as they were in their habitat. Jordan was climbing on the swing set and yelled to them to come down. The deer tilted their heads in the direction from which the sound had come and listened intently. When they were satisfied that the sound was not close enough to bother them, they went back to grazing.

Mary Margaret and Davis came down from the tree house, Davis by way of the pole and Mary Margaret by the ladder. Jordan was hanging upside down and swinging with his knees bent over a rung on the overhead bars. Davis told him he looked like a monkey, and Jordan remarked that he took after his older brother. Davis went over and started tickling Jordan. As they horsed around, Jordan unlocked his knees from the bar and fell into Davis' arms. They fell to the ground with Jordan on top of Davis. They were both laughing so hard that Mary Margaret wasn't sure if they were laughing or crying. She was not accustomed to this type of rough play as she and Alice had never jumped on each other or rolled around in the dirt. Eventually, they rolled apart and lay in the pine bark chips under the swing set. Both were breathing hard and were attempting to catch their breath.

Davis was finally able to speak as Mary Margaret just stood there looking at them.

"Did Allison Kincaid apologize to you yet?" he questioned.

"Yes, that's why I had to go to Mrs. Calhoun's office. She didn't want to, but she did," Mary Margaret explained.

"You be careful of Allison. She's mean. She has caused all kinds of problems for people, and she has actually beaten people up before," he sincerely cautioned. "I'm glad she finally got caught. Maybe she won't be so mean now."

"Somebody is calling our house now. Mostly they just hang up, but one of the calls threatened me," she continued.

"I'll bet it's Allison, you be careful," Davis warned.

Jennifer called the three children to come back to the house. The boys ran, and then remembered the instructions their mother had given them to be good hosts to Mary Margaret. They stopped and waited for her to catch up and walked with her along the path between the azaleas.

The table was set with dishes of various colors. Mary Margaret thought it looked tropical to her. The tablecloth was covered with various geometric shapes—circles, triangles, rectangles, and squiggly lines in all the colors of the tableware. She thought it looked like something from a magazine. The center of the table was filled with a bowl of fresh fruit.

Jennifer asked the children to wash up, and the boys led Mary Margaret to a powder room just off the den. While she washed up in there, she heard the boys running up the steps to another bathroom. They shouted as they ran, and they were soon back running through the French doors into the screened porch. Mary Margaret noticed that there were handprints on the back of Jordan's khaki slacks, as he had used them as a towel.

Mike and Alan were coming in from the outside patio and Alan was carrying a platter of wonderfully smelling meat. Mary Margaret's stomach growled as the aroma reached in and awakened her appetite.

Jennifer instructed everybody where to sit, and she had put Mary Margaret between her parents. Jennifer sat across from Cindy, and Alan sat across from Mike. Davis sat beside his mother, and Jordan was between his mother and his father. Jennifer had prepared fried okra, squash casserole, and brown rice casserole. The meat was barbecued ribs, chicken, and pork chops. The barbecue sauce was crisp but not burned.

As the platter was passed, Mary Margaret had a hard time deciding what to eat, but finally decided on ribs. Her mother put a spoonful of each casserole on her plate as it was passed, and the fried okra rolled into the barbecue sauce when it was put on the plate. This array of food was unlike anything Mary Margaret had seen before. However, as she tasted everything, she found it all to be wonderful. The squash casserole almost reminded her of stuffing at Thanksgiving. The rice casserole was salty, had the flavor of onions, and was warm and comforting. The okra was crispy on the outside and flavorful.

The ribs, however, may not have been a good choice. Mary Margaret realized that they were messy as she attempted to remove the meat from the bones. She was embarrassed as her mother intervened and cut them apart for her until she saw that Jennifer and Alan were doing the same for Davis and Jordan. Mary Margaret attempted to eat hers without getting the sauce all over her, but Jordan made no attempt at neatness. His face, hands and shirt were covered with sauce when he finished eating. Davis had done a little better, but some sauce had escaped his napkin and was up near his ear. He was completely embarrassed as his mother took the corner of her napkin, stuck it in her water glass and began to wipe his face. She realized what she was doing as he pulled away, and she suggested that the boys go back upstairs and wash up after dinner.

When they left the room, Jennifer said more to Cindy than anyone that she was having a hard time realizing that they were growing up, and she couldn't do things like that anymore. Cindy agreed as she looked at Mary Margaret and asked her if she wanted to go wash her hands.

Mary Margaret was coming out of the powder room when Davis and Jordan were coming down the steps. They nearly knocked her down as they ran past the door. Mary Margaret bumped into the wall, and both boys immediately stopped running and apologized after asking if she was all right. She was more embarrassed than hurt, and they all went back to the screened porch as Jennifer was serving dessert.

The peach cobbler and vanilla bean ice cream was heavenly. Jennifer had used a touch of nutmeg and cinnamon to flavor the peaches and Mary Margaret forced herself to eat her entire serving. Now she wished she hadn't been so greedy. Her stomach was hurting, and she felt like she might be sick. This time, however, she knew that it wasn't because she was upset. She knew she had overeaten. Maybe if she sat very still everything would be all right. Davis and Jordan, however, had other ideas. As soon as dessert was finished, they were ready to go back into the yard to play. Mary Margaret's mother encouraged her to go with them, but she felt it was safer to sit quietly for a while. The boys bolted out the door when given permission, and their shouts could be heard from the swing set in the corner of the yard.

Mary Margaret soon blended in with the adults as they chatted, and they talked around her. The men were discussing work, golf and planning a fishing trip. The ladies were discussing good shopping places, recipes and the children. The small talk soon lulled Mary Margaret to sleep. She was embarrassed when she awoke as her mother got up, and they were leaving. She apologized and Jennifer assured her that it was quite all right, and she was glad that Mary Margaret felt comfortable enough in their home to sleep. Mary Margaret was still embarrassed and wondered what Davis and Jordan would have to say about it at school.

They arrived home to hear the telephone ringing. Mr. Smith answered it, and the party on the other end said nothing. He hung up the receiver, and Mary Margaret could see the anger in his eyes, but he said that maybe it was a wrong number. As they got ready for bed, the phone kept ringing, and when it was answered nobody would say anything. This continued until about midnight when Mr. Smith left the phone off the hook. Mary Margaret heard her father say that he would take care of the matter first thing Monday morning. She wondered what he meant by that.

Chapter 44

Sunday morning was beautiful. The sun was rising in the clear, blue sky. The birds were busy feeding their babies and were noisy about it, too. Mike and Cindy were on the front porch reading the paper when Mary Margaret got up. She looked around the house and was momentarily frightened when she realized they weren't inside with her. She then guessed that they might be on the porch and was relieved to find them there. Their cheerful greeting lifted her spirits, and her father handed her the comics. When she was younger, he would read them to her on Sunday morning, but now she could read them herself. She missed that special time as she remembered it this bright spring day.

The phone rang as they sat on the porch and Cindy went in to answer it. Her voice was not pleasant as she said, "Hello." She was not expecting to hear a voice on the other end of the line and was totally surprised when Charlene said, "Cindy, is that you?" She explained the reason for her intolerant voice and Charlene was concerned about the situation. Cindy assured her that they would take care of it the first thing Monday morning. They chatted for a few minutes and Cindy soon yelled out to Mary Margaret that she needed to come to the phone. Mary Margaret wondered who would be calling her so early on Sunday morning and was ecstatic when she realized it was Charlene. They talked and Charlene told her that she was doing well. She said that Darlene had been ill and that she had been staying with Alice while she was unable to work. She said that Alice was lonely and wondered why Mary Margaret had not been writing and calling, and Mary Margaret felt terribly guilty with those words. She promised Charlene that she would do better and made a mental note to call Alice later that day. They hung up with Charlene telling Mary Margaret how anxious they were to come and visit them.

Cindy had been preparing breakfast while Mary Margaret talked. The family sat down to pancakes; there were chocolate chips in Mary Margaret's pancake so that it looked like a happy face. She smiled as she sat down and saw the smiling face on her plate. Mary Margaret picked out the chocolate chips and ate them before putting on the butter and syrup. She pinched the dough as she removed the chips so she still had a smiling face, but now it was because pieces of the browned pancake had been pinched out. The syrup pooled in these spots, and Mary Margaret enjoyed her soggy breakfast.

As they were finishing, the telephone rang again, and Mary Margaret jumped up to answer it before either parent had a chance. When she said, "Hello," the voice on the other end said, "I'll get even with you." The caller hung up, and Mary Margaret stared into the handset as though expecting to be able to see the face of the caller. Her parents sat at the table and knew that she was frightened. When she explained what was said, Mr. Smith said that he didn't know if he could wait until tomorrow to do something about this. He said that he wanted to get this stopped today. Mrs. Smith reminded him that they weren't certain who was making the calls and until the phone company changed their service, they couldn't be certain. He agreed, but restated that he would do something about it.

Mike and Cindy decided that it would be a good day to go exploring. Mary Margaret protested that she needed to work on her book report, which would be due in a few days. Her mother assured her that she had plenty of time to finish her book and write the report. They dressed and drove into Charleston.

Mary Margaret remembered their first trip to Charleston with Mrs. Applegate and the ride in the carriage. It had been very cool that day compared to the heat of this early May day. They took a walking tour of the historic district; and while Mary Margaret loved looking at the beautifully maintained homes, she soon tired in the heat and was glad for the rest when they went to a seafood restaurant near the ocean for an early dinner. They sat on the screened porch and laughed as the seagulls sought out people carrying bread, which they threw into the air for them. The gulls seemed to recognize the bread bags and were following those who were carrying them. Mary Margaret and her parents were totally relaxed as they enjoyed the spring day on the shady porch of the restaurant while the soft breezes cooled them.

The people on the beach were mostly sunbathers. A few ventured into the water, but most were staying dry. A few people had kites and the kite lines extended out over the ocean until only a speck could be seen in the sky. They discussed that the winds normally came from the west to the east and that's why the kites went out over the Atlantic Ocean. Mary Margaret silently wondered if the kites on the west coast flew inland. She made a mental note to someday check out that theory if she ever got to California.

After finishing their meal they stopped by a few antique shops before getting back in the car to go home. It had been a wonderful, carefree day that the entire family had enjoyed. As they drove home, Mary Margaret fell asleep and had a dream that she was flying a kite on the beach, and she became entangled in the kite string. The more she attempted to free herself, the more she was caught up until she could not take a step. As she flailed her body, she attracted the sea gulls, which must have thought she was throwing bread to them. They dove toward her with their mouths open, and she could not move. Just as they were about to fly into her face, she awoke with a jerk and screamed.

Mike and Cindy had been lulled into total serenity in the front seat and were not aware that Mary Margaret had been sleeping. Her scream startled them, and Mike maintained control of the car while Cindy tried to calm down their daughter, who by now was crying hysterically, and they didn't know why.

Mike pulled over to the side of the road, and Cindy got in the back seat to console her daughter so that she could tell them what was wrong. Once she was calm enough to talk and had explained her dream, they were able to get back on the road home. However, Cindy realized that Mary Margaret was under too much stress and decided that she would have to take steps to help her through this ordeal.

They arrived home as Jordan and Davis were riding their bikes down the driveway. They stopped and showed them their stringer of fish, which was admirable by any standards. They had three bass, which Davis said probably weighed 2 to 3 pounds each and there were several Bream. Mike congratulated the boys on their good luck and fishing abilities. As he started up the driveway, a deer bounded across. He slammed on the brakes, and the deer grazed the front of the car as it ran off into the woods. He got out and looked. He said there was deer hair in the grille, but he didn't see any blood. He looked around for the deer, but it seemed to be gone. He hoped that the deer had not been seriously injured by the impact. After finally parking the car in the garage, the family was exhausted from their chaotic ride home.

The phone was ringing as they went inside, and Mike was in no mood for more of this telephone harassment. He shouted, "*HELLO*" into the phone and smiled as he heard Gerry Gilbert's voice on the other end. Gerry asked him, "Who put you in such a good mood," and Mike explained about the harassing phone calls. Gerry said he was sorry they were having that problem, but he felt sure the phone company would be able to help. He went on to say that they were having a late supper as Philip had just returned from a riding competition in Charleston and wondered if the Smith family would like to join them. Mike answered without asking the rest of the family that they would love to join them.

When her father told her and her mother that they were going to the Gilberts, Mary Margaret began to feel a panic that once again she had been put off about doing her book report. She began to cry and tried to explain that she just had to stay home and finish it. Her parents were totally perplexed at her outburst and realized that Mary Margaret was completely stressed out. Cindy explained to her that she had plenty of time to finish the book report and told her that she would speak with Mrs. Stancil if there was some problem at school.

Mary Margaret was so completely overcome with anxiety that she couldn't control her tears and Mike and Cindy found themselves looking at the body of their little girl, but the emotions being shown by this body were foreign to them. They had never experienced such anxiety from her and were at a loss as to how best deal with it.

Mike called Gerry back and explained that he hadn't thought there would be a problem with their coming over for dinner, but that he had discovered that they couldn't make it after all. Cindy had taken Mary Margaret out onto the porch and was swinging with her in an effort to calm her down. Mary Margaret was sobbing between hiccups as she tried to regain her control. Mike came outside and sat on the steps. The three of them sat there for nearly an hour in the peace of their 10 acres. The birds were noisily feeding their offspring. The breeze was softly whispering through the tall pines. Mary Margaret and her parents were only hearing the hiccups and sobs as they slowly decreased and finally stopped.

Once Mary Margaret had regained her composure Mike was the first to speak. He asked Mary Margaret if she knew what was causing her such anguish. She held her head down and hiccupped instead of speaking the first few words. Finally, she told her parents, "I am afraid."

"What are you afraid of?" her anxious parents asked simultaneously.

"I'm afraid of failing in the new school," she replied.

"I assure you that is not going to happen," her father responded. "You will do as well or better than you did at St. Marks."

"You don't understand," she continued with anxiety obviously building and her voice rising. "Everything is different. I don't seem to be able to focus on what needs to be done."

"It's just an adjustment period," her mother retorted. "I'll tell you what. We'll work with you so that you can devote a certain time to do your homework. It's obvious you have more distractions here. We'll work with you."

"Is anything else bothering you?" her father asked.

"I don't know how to explain it. I can't tell you how I felt in Mrs. Calhoun's office when Allison Kincaid glared at me. She's mean, Daddy. Davis told me that last night, and I can feel it in my heart. She is just mean," she completed with tears welling in the corners of her eyes.

"I will take care of the matter with Allison Kincaid. I'll do everything I possibly can to keep her away from you," her father promised.

"She'll be back at school tomorrow, and I'm afraid of her," Mary Margaret whispered.

"I'll take you to school, and have a talk with Mrs. Calhoun," her father said.

Mary Margaret began to cry again, and her parents looked at her and then at each other not knowing how to react.

"Why are you crying now?" her mother asked.

"I don't want Mrs. Calhoun to think I'm a troublemaker," she sputtered.

"I will handle it so that Mrs. Calhoun won't feel like that. Anyway, she knows you're not the troublemaker," he said.

Into Addie's Arms

Mary Margaret was crying uncontrollably. Again, her parents were confused as to how to react. What could be happening to their daughter who had gone from a happy 9 year old to a very unhappy 9 year old in a matter of a few days?

The telephone rang as they sat on the porch, and Mrs. Smith went in to answer it. When she said, "Hello," she heard noises in the phone that made her think the call was coming from a pay telephone. The person on the other end said nothing, and Mrs. Smith shouted that she would put a stop to this and hung up the telephone.

Mary Margaret and her father had followed her inside. They stood there as she turned around and said that she thought the call was from a pay telephone. Mary Margaret had stopped crying and was just snubbing. Mr. Smith said if the calls were coming from a pay phone it may be difficult to determine who was making them, but he would see if they could be blocked from receiving them.

Cindy suggested that they go down to the pond to fish, and Mike agreed that it would be a great idea. Mary Margaret reluctantly went along, all the while protesting that she should be working on her book report. At the edge of the pond Mike helped Cindy with a fishing pole, and Mary Margaret took care of her own. Her father had put artificial lures on the line, so there were no worms involved and Mary Margaret thought this was a much better way to fish. She cast her line out into the pond and walked backwards into the shade of the weeping willow. Her parents were still settling in, and she wished that nothing would ever change from this moment. Mary Margaret was suddenly filled with a sense of contentment and peace that she had not felt for several days. She felt safe here with her parents and was glad that nobody else was around. She knew that the telephone was not going to interrupt their time and that Davis and Jordan would probably not be back. She liked this time alone with her parents with no distractions.

Her parents each found a place to sit and soon the three of them were quietly staring at the pond. Her mother was the least settled of the three as she had never fished before. She would move and readjust her body. Her line in the water was constantly moving as she did this. She was really not paying attention to the bobber which had been bouncing on the gentle waves. Abruptly, the bobber went under the water, and the fishing pole came out of her mother's hands. As it dropped to the ground, they all three looked as it was being pulled toward the water's edge. Mike reached to pick it up, and it was again jerked closer to the edge of the pond. Mary Margaret was running in their direction. It was jerked from her grasp just as she reached it. Cindy was recovering from her shock and, too, was reaching for it. Just as the pole was pulled into the water, she grabbed the reel and was able to keep it from being pulled completely out of reach. Mike was at her side and asked her to hold his pole, and they exchanged his for hers. She stood there with her feet in the water while he attempted to regain control of the rod and reel. As he pulled for tension in the line, he felt the fish get loose from the hook. He saw the bobber pop back up to the top of the water and knew that some giant of a fish had been on that line and was now gone. He was disappointed, but told Mary Margaret and her mother that it would just give them all an opportunity to catch it again.

In the excitement of the moment, Cindy hadn't realized that she was in the water with her shoes on. They all laughed when they realized what had happened, and she said that she would go change her shoes and be back. Mary Margaret recast her line and was watching her mother walk toward the house. Her father was settling back in after recasting his line. Peace was again filling their little corner of the world. The birds were busy. The clouds were lazily passing through the clear blue sky. The sun was dropping into the western sky, but it was not yet dusk. It was a wonderful time of the day Mary Margaret thought. Her mother went around the house and was out of sight.

Mary Margaret and her father were quietly sitting there when he started talking to her about how sorry he was that he had been responsible for their having to move and make all the adjustments. He went on to explain that he had hoped all of his life that he would be in the position that he is today. He loved his new job. He had always wanted to live in a small southern town, and he told Mary Margaret that he felt that someday she would see the benefits of their move. He again apologized that the adjustments seemed to be more on her part than anybody else's. He promised her that he would do whatever was necessary to stop the harassment and to make her transition as easy as possible. He told her that he had known she would have to make adjustments, but he had not counted on the initial problem with the other girls and the bad feelings that would leave for Mary Margaret. He said that he would, if necessary, go and speak with the parents of this girl and work out some amicable solution.

Mary Margaret could feel the anxiety building as he talked, but she knew that it wasn't going to get out of control this time. It was just the burning behind her eyes and the flip of her stomach that made her aware of it. She began to take deep breaths, and her father was aware that she was uncomfortable again. He put down his fishing pole and walked over to where she was sitting Indian-style under the willow tree. He sat down beside her and put his arm around her. He suddenly thought that he had put a lot on these tiny shoulders, and he hoped that they would bear up under it. Mary Margaret didn't say anything for fear of really crying again, but she knew that he was attempting to comfort her, and it was working.

She loved her father and admired his honesty in his conversations with her. He hadn't talked down to her and he hadn't told her to just shape up as he could have. He had tried to explain why it was important to him to be here, and that he hoped it would someday be important to her that they were where they were. Right now she had a hard time seeing the importance, but nonetheless she was in South Carolina, and she had to make the most of it. She knew that in her heart, and she had attempted to make it happen. It just seemed as though each time she started feeling good about it something happened, and she was frightened all over again. Mary Margaret had never truly been frightened before. This was a whole new experience for her, and one she could get along without, she thought.

Mike could feel her breathing become more regular and easy. He knew that she was calming down. It occurred to him that his wife had been gone longer than she should have been to change her shoes. He looked in the direction of the house and saw that she wasn't on her way back.

"I think I'll go get something to drink, what would you like?" he asked his daughter rather than to mention the length of time that her mother had been gone.

Mary Margaret said, "I don't care for anything, but don't you think that mother has been gone a long time?"

He laughed at her insight and said he would check on her while he was at the house.

"I'm finished fishing anyway. I want to work on my book report," Mary Margaret announced.

He agreed he was finished, too, and got up to pick up the fishing poles. Mary Margaret reeled in her line and together they started walking back to the house. At the edge of the woods they heard a rustle and looked to see the pair of deer retreating. They wondered how long they had been there waiting for them to leave. Mike told Mary Margaret that he had seen them there several times drinking in the early evening.

As they put the fishing gear in the garage, Cindy walked by the garage door and jumped when she saw them standing there. She let out a yell and admitted that she must be a little jumpy and wasn't expecting them to be there. They all laughed, and Mike said they decided to call it quits. They were concerned about her, and that Mary Margaret wanted to work on her book report.

Cindy said that she had answered the phone when she came back to the house and it was Addie asking how things had gone over the week-end with the telephone. She said that she had explained the goings on and told her that they were taking steps the next day to trace the calls and block them. "She agreed that it sounded like a good idea to her," Cindy told them. They walked up on the porch as the phone was again ringing, but they decided not to answer it any more that night. It rang for 10 times, and they all stood still while waiting for the ringing to stop.

Mary Margaret went to her room and sat at her desk to begin her book report. She had worked on it for about an hour and was finally feeling a sense of peace when she heard the phone ring again. Nobody answered it, and it continued to ring for 10 times. She became tense with the first ring, and that tenseness increased with each one. When it finally stopped, she walked into the kitchen to get a glass of milk and found her parents sitting at the kitchen table each working on paperwork. It was peaceful in there, and Mary Margaret got her milk and went back to her room. After another 30 minutes, she had finished her report, and breathed a sigh of relief when she put it in her book bag. She could smell something good cooking in the kitchen and went to see what it was.

Cindy was baking a frozen pizza and the aroma enveloped the house. Her stomach growled, and she realized that she was very hungry. Her father was setting the table, and her mother was making a salad. They sat down to eat and the phone immediately began to ring. They just continued eating and acted as though the only sounds in the kitchen were their voices. Mary Margaret silently counted the rings, and it stopped ringing after 10. She realized that a pattern was forming now. The calls were coming about every hour and each time the phone would ring 10 times. The pizza tasted very good and her family enjoyed it at their kitchen table as the daylight changed from dusk to dark. It was really staying light longer now. It was 8:30 and just getting dark. It would soon be daylight until 9:00.

After cleaning up the kitchen the family each went their own way to prepare for the next day at work and school. Mary Margaret got her book bag ready and put it by the door. She was so much more relaxed now that the book report was finished. She wondered if she could turn it in tomorrow or if Mrs. Stancil would want her to wait until Friday. She would have to ask about that.

Her parents came into her room to tell her good night and the telephone started ringing. A glance at the clock showed that it had been almost an hour since the last call, and predictably it rang 10 times. Nobody even mentioned that the phone was ringing. It could have been a clock chiming the hour for all the attention it was given.

Mary Margaret quickly drifted off to sleep and was awakened to hear the phone ringing again. She looked at the clock and saw that it was 10:37, and she counted 10 rings. If the phone rang again in the night, she was not aware of it.

Chapter 45

Mary Margaret awoke to the sound of her alarm clock the next morning and to the aroma of bacon frying. She got up and dressed before going into the kitchen. Addie was already there and welcomed her with a hearty, *"Good morning."* Mary Margaret felt rejuvenated and surprisingly relaxed. She greeted Addie, with a *"Good morning to you, too"*, and Addie could feel the lift of Mary Margaret's spirits. She was surprised by this as Cindy had explained the bad episodes that Mary Margaret had the day before. She wondered what the reason was for this, but didn't dare remark about it.

Mike and Cindy left for work, and Addie cleaned up the kitchen all the while talking with Mary Margaret. The phone began to ring at 6:50, and Mary Margaret immediately told Addie to ignore it. It rang 10 times and stopped. Addie stopped what she was doing and just looked at the telephone as if that would show her who was on the other end. Cindy had told her that they were not answering the phone so she wasn't surprised by Mary Margaret's statement. She secretly hoped that Mike would be able to do something about it as she knew it was disrupting this wonderful family's peace. When it was time, she and Mary Margaret walked to the bus stop. They were surprised that Davis and Jordan were waiting at the end of the driveway. They said they had some extra time and just walked down the road to get on the bus with Mary Margaret. Addie smiled when she heard this. She knew that they were there to protect Mary Margaret from getting on the bus alone. She thought these were probably two of the nicest boys she had ever known.

The bus arrived, and Mary Margaret got on followed by Davis and then Jordan. As they walked down the aisle, the bus was totally silent. All eyes were focused on them and the girl in the aisle seat of row 5. It was Allison

Kincaid. She stared into Mary Margaret's eyes with boldness that sent a chill down her spine. As Mary Margaret passed her, she looked toward the rear of the bus and saw an empty seat. She focused on that empty seat, refusing to give in to Allison's stare. When she took the first empty seat, Davis and Jordan clamored into the seat directly behind her. There was a definite hush on the bus this morning that lasted until they arrived at the school.

When the bus stopped, the students stood up, and Mary Margaret joined them. She was unable to see that Allison had not stood up until she was almost at her seat. Just as she passed, Allison stood and bumped into her causing her book bag to drop to the floor. There were several hands helping her pick up the contents and Mary Margaret hurriedly shoved everything into the bag and was almost the last one off the bus. She was embarrassed and angry, but was convinced that the best way to handle the situation was to ignore it. She was determined to not let Allison know that she was getting to her.

When Mary Margaret got off the bus, Davis and Jordan were directly behind her. They helped her regain her composure and walked inside the building with her. Mrs. Calhoun was standing at the door and smiled as they entered, but no conversation took place. As Mary Margaret glanced past Mrs. Calhoun, she saw Allison standing a few feet away looking to see if she had a conversation with the principal. When it was apparent that she was not going to say anything, Allison hurried along and Mary Margaret lost sight of her in the crowded hallway.

When Mary Margaret and Davis came in, Mrs. Stancil greeted them as she did all her students with an enthusiastic, "Good morning." Mary Margaret looked toward Allison's seat and was surprised to find it empty. However, she saw from the corner of her eye that Allison was rushing in behind her.

The day began with the usual roll calling and Pledge of Allegiance to the Flag. All the students were present, and Mrs. Stancil seemed extremely happy about this fact.

The day progressed without incident, and it seemed like just a short time had passed when the bell rang for lunch. Jane Ellis and Nancy Miller were waiting by the door as Mary Margaret got there, and the girls all went into the lunch room together. Addie had packed Mary Margaret's lunch, and Jane had brought hers as well. Nancy was going through the lunch line. The two girls were looking for an empty place that would accommodate them and

Nancy, and the only place was at a table where Allison Kincaid was already seated. Jane looked over her shoulder at Mary Margaret with pleading eyes asking, "What do we do now?" Mary Margaret didn't respond verbally, but headed in the direction of the table. Allison was sitting alone, and it was obvious that she was not interested in sharing her table with them. However, she noticed that the lunchroom duty teachers were all watching to see how this situation unfolded. Mary Margaret sat down at the opposite end of the table from Allison. Jane sat to her left, and Nancy filled in on the right. There were two more empty chairs at the table, and as if on command Davis and Philip slipped into them, almost from nowhere.

Jane was ready to share her experiences of being at her grandparents' home and with the 4-H project. She had won a blue ribbon with her sheep, and she searched in her purse to show it around the table.

Nancy listened patiently as Jane told about her weekend, and then she shared her experiences of being in Charleston. She told how she loved staying in the tower room of her grandmother's home. She said that it had stormed there on Friday night, and in her room, which had windows all the way around, she could see lightning from every direction. She said that when she was a little girl she was scared to stay up there, but now she felt like a princess.

Davis and Philip tried not to laugh at her, but it was impossible. They couldn't imagine how anyone could feel like royalty just because they were in a tower room. *"Girls,"* they said simultaneously.

The conversation died down and everyone finished their lunch. Allison did not enter into any of the conversations. The boys talked quietly, and the three other girls seemed to be at a loss for words.

Immediately after lunch Mrs. Stancil gave instructions to those in charge of caring for the garden that day. They were excused, and the rest of the class was instructed to read their library books as the reports were due on Friday.

Mary Margaret had not given a thought until now to her report, which was safely tucked into her book bag. She picked up the bag and took out the library book. The remainder of the contents of the bag was in disarray, as she had not had time to straighten it up after she dropped it on the bus. She dumped everything on her desk just as Ms. Stancil walked by.

She paused at Mary Margaret's desk and asked her what she was doing. She explained that she had dropped her bag on the bus, and she needed to find her report and straighten up the rest of her papers. Ms. Stancil stood there as Mary Margaret shuffled through the pages, and it was soon obvious that there was no book report among the papers she had pulled from the bag.

Mary Margaret went through the papers again, and this time Ms. Stancil held them for her. There was still no book report. Mary Margaret could feel the burning and the embarrassment building up in her. She knew the report had been there when she left home. Now it was gone, but where could it be.

Ms. Stancil sensed the uneasiness and suggested to Mary Margaret that she had probably left it at home. Mary Margaret told her she knew it was in her bag when she left home. However, Ms. Stancil suggested that she go the office and call Addie to see if she would look for it on her desk. Mary Margaret explained that she knew it wasn't there. She had put it in her bag. Where could it be now?

Ms. Stancil told Mary Margaret that she could begin writing another book report, or she could study her spelling words if she wanted to wait until she could check at home for the report before starting over. Mary Margaret was on the verge of tears, and her ears seemed to be screeching.

Davis saw what was happening and remembered that the bag had been dropped on the bus floor. He suggested that Ms. Stancil could have the driver look to see if it was on the bus. She thought that was a wonderful idea and excused herself from the classroom to go have the call made. She was back in a few minutes with the news that no book report had been found

Ms. Stancil asked every student who had been on that bus to check their book bags to see if they had accidentally picked up the report, but no one found it in their bags.

All the while Allison Kincaid was sitting with her eyes averted, never focusing on anyone involved in this conversation. Ms. Stancil went over and stood next to Allison as she went through the contents of her book bag, and she saw that no report was there.

The afternoon finally was over, and the dismissal bell rang. Allison Kincaid hurried out of the classroom, and this did not go unnoticed by Ms. Stancil.

She followed her and saw that she was going into the girls' restroom. After just a moment Allison came out of the restroom and went directly to the bus. Ms. Stancil went into the restroom and looked around. Nothing seemed out of order; and as she was leaving, she noticed the corner of a piece of paper beside the trash can. She picked it up and recognized it as Mary Margaret's handwriting, and while there were only a few words on that corner, it was obviously part of the book report.

Ms. Stancil went to the custodian and told her that she needed some gloves so that she could go through the trash in the girls' restroom. While this was the first time a teacher had asked for gloves for that purpose, she went to the store room and soon returned with surgical type gloves. Ms. Stancil and the custodian went into the rest room and as the custodian held an empty bag, the teacher filled it with the contents of the can. Piece by piece she inspected the things she found in the trash, and all she found were used tissues, paper towels, candy wrappers, and a couple of notes. This was a true mystery to her.

When Mary Margaret arrived home Addie was waiting at the bus stop and she immediately started gushing about not having her book report when she knew she had put it in her book bag. Addie had to slow her down to understand the situation, but after a few attempts at telling her story, Mary Margaret finally made her understand that this was the most important thing in her life right now, and all she could think about doing was rewriting the report.

Addie went into the kitchen to get the snack she had already prepared for her. Mary Margaret went straight to her desk in her bedroom and was in the writing position when Addie came in. She placed the peanut buttered apple slices on the desk, along with a glass of milk. Mary Margaret managed to say, "Thank you," but she was intent on once again writing her report.

Addie left the bedroom and went into the kitchen. The telephone rang one time, and the panic jumped into Mary Margaret and Addie. When the ringing stopped, neither said anything and they both continued their tasks.

Addie was setting the table and decided that a special dessert was in order for this evening. She got out an old iron skillet she had brought over from her own home. Into it she put a stick of butter. When the butter had melted, she put in brown sugar. When that had melted into the butter, she placed pineapple rings on top of the sugar. Into each ring she placed a maraschino cherry. She mixed together some sugar and butter until they looked like a pale yellow cream. Then she sifted together flour, salt, and baking soda. She mixed together eggs and milk. She alternately added the flour mixture and the milk mixture with the butter. When this was all mixed, she added vanilla. The kitchen smelled heavenly. The caramel smell of the warm brown sugar mixture, and the vanilla aroma gave Addie such a good feeling that she burst into song. The words to *Amazing Grace* were filling the space when there was a knock on the front door.

To Addie's surprise, she saw a small girl about Mary Margaret's age standing there holding a bag. When she got to the door, she recognized the child as Allison Kincaid. She recognized the car in the driveway, but the driver had not gotten out.

She opened the door and said, "Yes?" Allison asked if Mary Margaret was home, and Addie answered that she was. Allison asked, "May I talk with her?"

Addie was so shocked by this that she just opened the door further and the girl walked in. Addie yelled, "Mary Margaret, there's someone here to see you."

Reluctantly, Mary Margaret got up from her desk, and as she came down the steps into the living room, she was so shocked to see Allison Kincaid standing there, that she didn't know what to say, so she said nothing.

The three of them, Allison, Addie and Mary Margaret, were as pillars until Allison broke the spell. She held out the bag and offered it to Mary Margaret. As she walked toward her with the offering, tears started streaming down her face. Steps could be heard on the porch, and front door silently opened. In stepped Ms. Stancil. Allison kept on walking, and no one turned to see who had entered. When she reached Mary Margaret, Allison started to speak. The words were barely discernible because of the sobs that accompanied them. A word here and there could be understood. "Sorry, sorry, sorry, telephone, book report, not nice, sorry" again, sob, sniff . . . Soon only wails could be heard.

At this point Ms. Stancil asked if they could all sit down. "Of course," Addie said, and led them into the family room, picking up some tissues from the kitchen on the way.

After they were seated, and Allison was somewhat in control of her crying, Ms. Stancil began to speak. She explained that she had found a piece of Mary Margaret's book report in the girls' restroom after school after Allison left there. This caused her to wonder if Allison had hidden the report in the bathroom earlier in the day and had retrieved it after school, so she went to Allison's house to confront the situation with Allison and her mother.

When she got to Allison's house and explained the situation to her mother, a search of her book bag turned up Mary Margaret's book report with the corner of the last page missing. When she held up the missing piece of the report, Allison confessed to having taken it in the melee on the bus that morning.

As Ms. Stancil was aware of the telephone situation with Mary Margaret's family, she also asked Allison if she was responsible for this. Allison admitted that she was. Her mother was so stricken that she nearly fainted and Allison's father had been called home from Charleston.

Ms. Stancil and Mr. and Mrs. Kincaid agreed that the situation needed to be dealt with swiftly. Ms. Stancil had offered to take Allison to apologize to Mary Margaret while Mr. Kincaid tended to his wife. With this agreed, they had ended up at Mary Margaret's.

Allison sat dejectedly on a leather chair. The tears were dried up, but the sniffing continued. She repeatedly blew her nose with a wad of tissues that was totally unmanageable and one by one they had fallen to the floor.

As Mary Margaret looked over at Allison, her heart suddenly felt light. She was no longer afraid. Her panic was gone. There sat the one person who had caused her such strife, and she felt sorry for her.

Mary Margaret picked up a small trash can by her father's desk and walked toward Allison. As she sat it beside her, Allison looked up with sad eyes. They were no longer defiant. Mary Margaret said, "Wow, I'm glad we found that report before I had to write another one," and she laughed.

Ms. Stancil and Addie exchanged knowing glances. They knew that Mary Margaret was a wonderful child. She had forgiven Allison and was attempting to make light of the subject, while they knew that the problem was deeper than either of them could handle and that Mr. and Mrs. Kincaid had a lot more to deal with.

Mary Margaret went back to her seat, and Ms. Stancil stood. As she did, so did Allison. Ms. Stancil said their farewells, and Allison sadly left with her. She never spoke, but Mary Margaret said good-bye to her. She and Addie stood on the porch and waved as Ms. Stancil's car turned around and disappeared around the curve of the driveway.

Addie hugged Mary Margaret so hard that she finally said she couldn't breathe, and Addie hugged her even tighter. Eventually she let go, and Mary Margaret feigned gasping for air. Their hearts were at the same time light and heavy. They knew without saying that Allison Kincaid would not be back to school the rest of the year, and that no part of her heart was light now nor had it been for a long time. They were sad for her.

They were heard before they were seen. Davis and Jordan rounded the curve in the driveway. They hurried up to the house to see why Ms. Stancil had been to Mary Margaret's house. When they asked this, Mary Margaret just said that she had found her book report and had returned it. Addie wanted to hug her all over again.

The boys asked what smelled so good, and Addie remembered her cake was in the oven. She ran inside and heard the boys asking Mary Margaret if she was going to fish with them. She said that she would as soon as she changed her clothes.

The front door slammed, and Addie removed the golden brown cake from the oven just in time. A few more minutes and the wonderful aroma of brown sugar caramel would have been an awful stench.

Mike and Cindy were both relieved and saddened when Addie and Mary Margaret brought them up to date on the day's happenings. Mike explained that it would have been a few more days before the telephone situation could have been covered with call blocking and tracing, and whatever else they were going to do. He said he was pleased that he had one more call to cancel all that nonsense.

Addie stayed for dinner and the dessert was a big hit. Mike said that he was going to have to buy a new wardrobe if he continued to eat like this. Cindy said that she loved the food, and she was going to start walking to help cut down on her weight gain.

Addie blushed. She loved working for these people. They were not at all what she had expected. She thought they would be stuck up and demanding. She had heard that all people from New York were like that. She had almost not even come to meet them when Mrs. Applegate suggested it. She was too old to deal with *cantankerous Yankees* she had told her. Mrs. Applegate assured her that they weren't like that, and by golly, she thought, she was right.

Chapter 46

The black SUV turned off the highway and stopped at the closed gate. A guard came out and checked the list for the correct name. Once it was verified that her name was on the list, Allison Kincaid and her father continued on through the now open gates and up the drive to the front door of the facility.

Nobody was outside. Mr. Kincaid got out and told Allison to do the same.

"Allison, I told you to get out," he continued as he held the back door open.

The girl, who looked very young, small and scared, refused to move from her position.

"Allison, don't make me pull you out of there. You created this situation, and I refuse to allow you to continue with this behavior. You are coming out of this car one way or the other, and I recommend that you come out on your own," Larry Kincaid said through clenched teeth.

His week had been one of upset as he searched for a place to put his daughter. She was out of control, and was not going to be permitted to attend school at Left Fork for an indefinite period of time. He knew he couldn't care for her, or didn't want to care for her. His wife was not able to take care of her, so his only choice was to place her in a facility for wayward children. He had enlisted the assistance of a psychologist in Charleston, and they had decided on this place.

The surroundings were beautiful. It resembled an antebellum home, with a large barn on the property. Horses were in the pasture, and flowers framed the entire house.

The front door opened and a man came down the steps. He spoke with Mr. Kincaid, and then to Allison.

"Hello, Allison, my name is Dr. Hanna, and I'd like to welcome you. We have a lovely place here, and I want to help you make your transition as easy as possible. Do you have a bag with you?"

Allison turned her head and looked in the opposite direction as he spoke.

He tried again. "Allison, please believe me when I say I am here to help you. Please don't make this any more difficult than it has to be. We have a room set up for you, and I think you'll find this quite pleasant once you get inside. Come on, now, hand me your bag and we'll get you settled in."

Allison continued her gaze in the opposite direction.

Filled with rage, Larry Kincaid began a tirade, "Allison, get yourself out of this car right now. I can't believe you're acting like this. What's wrong with you? I have given you everything you could ever want, and this is the thanks I get. Now, get out of there before I pull you out of there."

Dr. Hanna intervened. "Mr. Kincaid, you have some paperwork to complete inside. May I suggest that you go on in and get started with that? I'll stay here with Allison, and we'll see if we can't agree upon some common ground."

Mr. Kincaid was unaccustomed to being told what to do, but this time he took the suggestion and went inside, relieved that Dr. Hanna had assumed the responsibility for his daughter.

"Allison, I know this is not your choice. I understand that there have been some behavioral problems. You are being brought here to help you. We desire to help you work through whatever it is that's causing your unacceptable behavior and to give you tools to help you cope with life's influences. I'm going to ask you one more time to get out of the car, and if you decide that's not what you want to do, then more forcible means will be utilized.

However, you will be staying here today, and I do hope that you willingly walk inside."

He quit speaking and extended his hand to the little girl who now was looking in his direction. Her tear-stained face told a story he had seen too many times before. For various reasons, usually not the fault of the child, the lines of communication break down at home, and children are left floundering for boundaries and guidance. Without that they fall into traps of many descriptions which lead them down a path of destruction. He knew he could help this little girl, the youngest ever accepted into the program, but wondered if the parents would change their behavior to give her the foundation she needed. *Sometimes I wish the parents were here and not their children*, he thought.

Reluctantly, she scooted over to the passenger door, but she refused his hand. She got out and stood on the sidewalk.

"Allison, did you bring a bag?" he asked.

"Yes, sir, it's in the back," she said not looking him directly in the eyes.

"Do you think we can get the back open?" he asked.

"Yes, sir, I know how to do it."

She walked around to the rear and opened the door. Dr. Hanna reached inside for the bag. It was small and light. Her needs would be few. She was not going to be allowed to wear her own clothing until she had earned the right. The facility provided clothing. She only needed personal items, and they would be given to her only at specified times. She would earn the right to all privileges by good behavior.

Allison and Dr. Hanna walked inside the locked facility, and her father was anxiously waiting for them.

"Are we finished here?" he asked.

"Would you like to see Allison's room?" Dr. Hanna asked.

"No, I saw one of them yesterday when I was here, and I'm sure it'll be all right for her."

"Well, Mr. Kincaid, in that case if all the paperwork is completed you are free to leave."

Larry Kincaid looked at his daughter and kissed her on the top of the head. "Good-bye, Allie. You be a good girl, and you'll be out of here soon," he said as he hurried past her and out the front door.

Dr. Hanna looked into the face of this child and knew she would be a difficult case. "Allison, would you like to see your room?" he asked.

She didn't respond. He touched her shoulder, and she flinched away. "All right, Allison, I understand. Let's go down this hall and around the corner."

The two of them walked into a room which held only a bed and a desk and chair. There were no pictures on the walls. There was no decoration in the room. The closet had no doors. The bathroom had only a toilet, sink and small shower.

"Allison, this is your room. As you go through our program, you earn the right to receive privileges including television, radio, books, and your own clothing. You will wear our uniforms until that time. An assistant will be here in a few minutes to bring you the clothes for today. Every day you will be brought clean clothes. We will keep your personal items, and you will be given an opportunity to use them 2 times a day, at 7:00 a.m. and 7:00 p.m. Your stay here can be however you choose to make it. If you cooperate, you will earn privileges quickly. If, however, you choose to be uncooperative, you will find the stay most distasteful. The choice is yours, and it is my hope that you will cooperate and take advantage of this opportunity to turn your life around before you go too far with your self destruction. The staff and I are here to help you work through this difficult time in your life."

Allison still remained silent. A lady appeared, and she was carrying a white two-piece uniform. "Hello, Allison, my name is Ernestine, and I am your assistant today. Everybody else is at dinner, and I would like for you to change your clothes so that you may join them there. The kitchen closes promptly at 6:00 p.m., and if you don't eat this evening, you won't get another chance until 7:30 a.m. She handed Allison the clothing she brought along with slide-on shoes.

Allison took the clothing and went into the bathroom. A few minutes later she came from the bathroom wearing the 2-piece uniform and shoes.

Into Addie's Arms

"Where are your clothes and shoes?" Ernestine asked.

"I left them in the bathroom," Allison said.

"Please go get them and bring them to me. While you are here, you are expected to pick up after yourself. We are not here to accommodate you. We are here to assist you."

Allison brought the clothes from the bathroom. "Would you please use this marker to write your name on your clothes?" Ernestine asked.

Allison took the marker and fought the impulse to write her name in big, bold letters on her shirt. Instead, reason reigned and she wrote her name on the inside facing of her shirt and the inside waist band of her shorts. She wrote her name on the tongue of each shoe and the bottom of each sock.

"Thank you, Allison," Ernestine said. "When you earn the right to wear your own clothing, we will contact your parents and request that other things be brought to you. Until that time, however, you will be given a clean uniform each day, but we'll cover all that in orientation. Let's get you into the kitchen for dinner."

Ernestine led the way and soon they were in a kitchen not dissimilar from any family kitchen. Around the table were 9 other young people she guessed ranging in age from 14 to 17. She was by far the youngest, and felt vulnerable.

Ernestine introduced Allison to the group, but Allison had no interest in learning their names. Her mind was racing. Her eyes were sweeping the room, and she was already planning her escape.

I won't be here long enough to worry about names, she thought. *I'm out of here by tomorrow night. Mary Margaret Smith will pay for this. I am locked up in this insane asylum because of her. She'll be sorry she ever moved to Left Fork.*

Ernestine invited her to sit at the only empty place at the table. A plate of food was brought to her and ice water was provided. The food smelled good, and looked good, but her appetite was gone. Allison moved the food around on the plate, and took a couple of bites.

They can't make me eat. I'll starve and then they'll be sorry, she foolishly thought.

The time went quickly as she sat there, and her plate was removed.

"Allison, we act as a family here, and you will be assigned chores. Tonight, you are to wash dishes. Others will bring them to the sink, but your job is to actually wash the dishes and put them in the drainer to dry," Ernestine said.

"I don't know how to wash dishes. I've never done that before," she said almost whining now.

"Well, Allison, the dishes are your job tonight, and you may not leave the kitchen until they are clean. Do you understand?" Ernestine asked patiently.

"I'm not going to do that, and you can't make me," the now indignant child said.

"The choice is yours, my dear, but I am prepared to sit with you until the dishes are clean, even if it takes all night," Ernestine countered.

"I won't do it. I want you to call my mother," Allison now shouted, tears beginning to drip off her chin.

"I'm sorry, Allison, but you are not permitted to have phone calls or visitors at this time. You will earn that right," Ernestine said in a voice so even and soft, an outsider would have been shocked to realize she was in the midst of a confrontation.

"My daddy won't make me stay here when he hears how mean you are to me," she now shouted.

"Allison, it's time to do the dishes, and you need to be about getting that done," Ernestine said evenly.

"I won't do it, and you can't make me," she shouted as she attempted to leave the kitchen.

From what appeared to be thin air a security guard appeared and blocked the doorway. The young girl attempted to go around him, but he stood firm. She struck out, and he remained solid. She head butted him, and he remained steadfast.

She was crying so hard by this time, she finally gave up, gave in, and sat on the floor. Exhaustion overtook her. She wept uncontrollably. No words were said. Nobody consoled her. She was allowed to cry until there were no more tears. The scene continued for 20 minutes.

Resolutely, she arose and went to the sink. She turned on the water and began loading plates into the sink. One by one she washed them. The glasses were all washed, and the flatware was last. Eventually, all the dishes were draining in the rack at the side of the sink.

Her uniform was soaked from splashing water. It stuck to her body. She pulled it from her skin. "Can I have another uniform?" she asked.

"No, Allison, you are assigned one jumpsuit per day, and it's your responsibility to take care of it," Ernestine said without emotion.

Allison started to cry, but the tears never materialized. Almost like magic Allison changed her demeanor and asked, "May I go to my room now?"

"You have an opportunity after dinner to go out to the exercise area. Some of the other residents are still there. Would you like to go outside for 10 minutes?" Ernestine asked now expressing more compassion.

"Yes, I would, please," Allison said.

Ernestine led the way into an area that looked much like a school play yard. There were basketball hoops, and 4-square blocks had been painted. The other residents looked at her as she entered the area, but no one approached her. She didn't care. She had business to take care of. Her eyes darted from one area to another. She realized that this area was not fenced. A lone guard stood by the back door of the house.

This is a piece of cake, she thought. I'll be out of her by this time tomorrow.

Chapter 47

The school and work week went by without any major catastrophe. It seemed like the family was finally settling in. Mary Margaret taped the corner back on her book report, and she knew all the spelling words on the test. The weather was calm, and the deer had been strangely absent. Davis and Jordan fished a couple of times that week, and Philip had been busy preparing for a horse show, so he couldn't come over. Most afternoons it was just Mary Margaret and Addie.

Addie couldn't understand why Mary Margaret spent so much time in the house. She encouraged her to go outside, but the only place she wanted to go alone was on the porch to swing and read her library book. Addie was accustomed to children riding bicycles, fishing, and visiting other friends. She didn't know what to do with her.

Mary Margaret resented Addie's encouragement that she go outside all the time. She was not accustomed to being outside. She had spent her entire life in an apartment building, and she never went outside alone. She didn't know what to do. She was doing the only thing she knew how. Staying inside and reading. Her best friend Alice was not there, and Davis and Jordan just didn't take her place.

While things were peaceful, there was an undercurrent of uneasiness.

Saturday morning was glorious. Mike decided that he would mow the grass. He started up the mower. He was excited. The grass had really begun to grow, and each swipe with the new mower was instant gratification for him. The smell of fresh-cut grass filled his nostrils. The morning air was cool, and the world felt clean. After making several passes over his spacious lawn, he thought he saw somebody coming from out of the woods. He rode the mower in that direction and was surprised to see an elderly man standing just at the edge of the tall pines. As he approached, the man stepped out and extended his hand. Mike stopped the mower, got off, and walked toward him, all the while extending his hand as well.

"Good morning, sir, I'd like to introduce myself to you. My name is General Sherman Hood, and my friends call me Shag."

Mike Smith took the rough hand of this man whom he judged to be in his late seventies. "Mr. Hood, it's nice to meet you. I'm Mike Smith. Is your name a military title, or is your first name General?"

"Well, sir, the first name is General. My grandfather served under General William T. Sherman in the Civil War, and I was named in his honor. My father's name was Andrew Jackson Hood. It can be a might confusing at times," the older man confessed.

Mike took in this tall man with long dark brown, but graying hair, which had been pulled back. He was wearing jeans and a denim jacket. He wore a hat, not quite western, but almost. His demeanor was friendly; and a gentle, shy smile filled his face.

"Your mower seems to be doing a fine job," the older man said.

"Yes, it sure is, and I'm glad to have it. I've never done much yard work, and this makes it a lot easier."

Mr. Hood hemmed and hawed for a couple of minutes and finally said, "Mr. Smith I was passing through these parts a few months back and set up a camp in the woods a little ways from your house. Of course, it wasn't your house at the time. Nobody lived here, and I expected to move on when the house sold. I didn't reckon anybody would mind me being here for a spell since nobody was living in the house. When I noticed the activity picking up a few weeks ago, I wanted to move on, but I've been down in the back and walking has been hard for me, so I stayed on."

As he spoke, Mike decided he liked Mr. Hood. He was forthright and seemed honest. He was wondering how this conversation was going to go, however. Was Mr. Hood going to ask to stay on, or was he just telling him he was there? He soon got his answer.

"My back is still giving me some problems, and I don't think I could move on far. I was wondering if you could help me out by letting me do some odd jobs around your house. I could trim the shrubs and mow the grass."

As they talked, Mike learned that Mr. Hood had come from West Virginia, but had never stayed in one place very long. He had done various things for employment during his lifetime, and now that he was older he was looking to settle down in a warmer climate.

An idea was forming in the back of Mr. Smith's mind. The plant needed a night watchman. There had not been one before, but times had changed and people had been coming onto the property at night and it was probably just a matter of time until vandalism started to occur. He had thought that the presence of a person might deter such activity. He told Mr. Hood that he would see what he could do, and invited him to stay on in the woods for a while longer.

Mr. Hood thanked him and as he started to go back into the darkness of the tall trees, Mike asked him, "Is there anything you need?"

Mr. Hood turned around and said, "A job is all I need for now, but I'll let you know if anything comes up." He turned and disappeared into the tangled underbrush just as magically as he had appeared.

As Mike stood there he noticed that the trees were draped with vines and undergrowth that separated to almost form rooms. The sunlight dappled the woods, and the floor was covered with pine needles that looked as soft as a quilt, and they almost seemed knitted together where they had fallen.

He turned to return to the mower and noticed that Addie had arrived and was watching him. He wondered how long she had been there and if she had known Mr. Hood had taken up residence in his woods. He would ask her later, he thought.

He went back to his mowing; but as he reached the house, Addie was waiting on the steps. She immediately began questioning him about the man who had disappeared into the woods. He explained their conversation, and he couldn't quite read her feeling of the situation. He knew that he would know how she felt soon. With Addie you always know how she feels.

Finally, he finished mowing and put the mower back into the shed. He was so proud. The lawn looked like a striped blanket. He soon realized as he moved along that if he went in one direction, turned around and went back in the opposite direction directly beside his first swipe the grass would lay differently each time he went over it. He stood back and surveyed his work and decided that maybe he should be in the lawn maintenance business. He knew it had to be very satisfying.

As he walked into the house Cindy was hanging up the phone. She said she had been talking with Mrs. Applegate, and that Mary Margaret had been invited to go over there for the afternoon to work on their sewing project. She would be coming to pick her up, and she was having lunch with them.

Addie was already putting a chicken pot pie in the oven. The kitchen smelled wonderful with the savory spices Addie had obviously used. He wondered if there would be enough to take some to Mr. Hood, but decided not to mention that right now. He planned to investigate Mr. Hood's camp site later in the afternoon after he made a few phone calls.

He went into the family room and made a note from the phone book. He then took the cordless phone into the bedroom to have some privacy as he made his call. He called the Sheriff's office and after asking a few pointed questions he wasn't satisfied with the response he had gotten. He then called Orville Clark. He had come to trust Orville, and felt that he had his finger on the pulse of Left Fork. He again asked a few pointed questions and this time felt very satisfied with the results of his inquiries.

The house seemed so very quiet as he left the bedroom. He had become accustomed to Addie's voice and enjoyed the southern drawl as she talked and bustled throughout the house. However, today was different. She was too quiet. He started looking for his family and no one seemed to be around. Addie was not in her usual place in the kitchen either. Where could they all have gone? He looked out the back window toward the lake and no one was there, but it did look inviting as the mid-morning sun glistened off the lightly moving water. The willow tree branches moved gently, and a fish jumped almost as if on command. He felt glad to be right where he was.

He went to the front porch and even before going outside he knew he was headed in the right direction. The chain on the porch swing was creaking as it moved slowly back and forth, and muffled voices could be heard above the loud jawing of a mockingbird.

As he stepped outside the three females, Mrs. Smith, Addie, and Mary Margaret almost jumped with surprise. They all looked at him inquiringly. He didn't know what he was supposed to say, and none of them seemed to be willing to tell him. He just looked back. After a few seconds he asked them, "What's going on?" They looked at him, and Mrs. Smith said, "That's precisely what we want to know."

He realized that Addie had spread the word about the stranger from the woods, and now they wanted to know all about it. He explained to his wife and daughter just what he had said to Addie. He then went on to explain that he had checked with the Sheriff and Orville Clark to see if they knew anything about the stranger who had been in this town for probably a few months. They had both told him that they had seen him occasionally, and that he had not caused a minute's trouble. He had bought some kerosene from Orville, and the Sheriff said his men had seen him walking along the road, but had no reason to stop him or to suspect any wrongdoing on his part. He just appeared to have been passing through and decided to camp out on their property.

He explained that Mr. Hood had asked for a job, but said that his back was not good and that would limit him in what he could do. Mike said that he was thinking about giving him a job at the mill as the night watchman. He wouldn't expect much of him except to be a presence there to deter any possible vandalism. That would give him a little money, and he could get a better place to live.

Addie asked what the man had been eating, and Mr. Smith chuckled to himself as he explained that the conversation had not gotten that far. He said he was going to check out the camp site later in the afternoon. The females seemed more at ease with all of this explanation.

Mrs. Applegate arrived just as they all started into the house. They waited on the porch for her. After hugs were exchanged the tiny lady joined them as they went into the kitchen to prepare for lunch.

Mary Margaret set the table as Cindy made a salad. Addie put the finishing touches on a strawberry dessert she had been making. They all talked about Allison Kincaid and the sudden admission of wrongdoing she had made when she was confronted by Ms. Stancil. They admitted that they were glad it was over, but felt not only bad for Mr. and Mrs. Kincaid, but also

Allison. Rumor had it that she was going to a *facility* for young people with problems somewhere near Charleston.

After lunch Mary Margaret and Mrs. Applegate left to go work on the Dutch Girl quilt. They chatted about the weather, and Mary Margaret's new friends at school and how long it had been since they last worked on the quilt. They both said it seemed like an eternity, when they decided it had truly only been a few days. They arrived at the beautiful house and Mary Margaret was again taken with its charm. Every time she arrived it looked different. A different plant was blooming; the air smelled sweeter, the porch now was filled with potted plants for summer. She thought again of the paintings by Monet. Her heart suddenly started beating faster as she remembered this and her times with Charlene and her friend, Alice. She had not called or written to them for so long. *Would they be mad*, she wondered? She would call both of them tonight for sure. She knew her parents would allow it.

Mrs. Applegate had the materials they needed all ready. It was obvious that she had been working on this project without Mary Margaret. Several blocks were finished and were stacked neatly on the dining room table. Mary Margaret picked them up and examined the workmanship with which each had been completed. Each stitch was exact. Each piece met perfectly. She would never be able to do such fine work, but she was going to do her best, and that's all Mrs. Applegate would expect her to do. Even if they didn't work on the quilt, she loved being in this wonderful old home with the glow of time so enchantingly hanging in each room.

As the outside of the house always looked different, the inside of the house always looked delightfully the same. With the exception of the materials needed for their project nothing ever changed from each visit to the next. The furniture was never moved, the lamps were never moved, the pictures were always the same, and Mary Margaret found this as comforting as the softness inside a cocoon. When she was here, she never wanted to leave.

The one thing that was always the same and never, never changed was Mrs. Applegate. Her enthusiasm and genuine interest in others was something Mary Margaret loved, but still did not know how to deal with. She had come to recognize that people in South Carolina were more demonstrative of their feelings. She was not so shocked when people hugged each other as they passed on the street. Even the kissing, while she still didn't want all those people kissing her, was easier to watch. She wasn't embarrassed by it now.

But Mrs. Applegate was special. She truly cared about everybody. She only seemed to want the best for them. Mary Margaret was going to find out how true these thoughts were as time went by.

The two little ladies got into their work, and as Mrs. Applegate instructed, Mary Margaret cut and pieced. They were just about to finish one block when the telephone jolted them back into the 21st Century. They had been talking about women needing to make quilts for centuries to keep their families warm, not just for the pretty wall hangings of today. Mrs. Applegate explained to Mary Margaret that nothing went to waste. If an item of clothing was no longer useful for that purpose and nobody else was in line for wearing a part of it, the fabric would be saved and put into a quilt when the next one was made. She explained that many a quilt had been pieced with fabric from feed sacks, and that even dresses were made from those same sacks. Women would instruct their husbands to choose feed or grain in sacks of like fabric so as to have enough to make a dress or shirt.

The phone call was from Cindy saying that they would be over in about an hour to pick up Mary Margaret. They were going to the Gilberts' house for dinner. Mary Margaret asked Mrs. Applegate if she could speak to her mother. She asked her to please put her riding boots in the car. If she was invited to ride, she wanted to be prepared.

Mrs. Applegate fixed them some lemonade. They sat on the porch and waited for her parents. Mary Margaret asked about the garden, and they went around back to have a look. The tomatoes had begun to grow, and the entire area had been planted. Mrs. Applegate had marked each plant with copper tags. She was amazed to see that there was eggplant, zucchini, bell peppers, and a host of other plants all in such a small area. Mrs. Applegate explained that many of the plants would be staked to keep them off the ground or they would grow on vines, which would be lifted with string. Mary Margaret told her that she knew this from their South Carolina History Garden they were growing at school.

Mike and Cindy arrived and Mrs. Applegate walked out to the car with Mary Margaret. After some small talk was exchanged, the family drove off in the direction of Gerry and Sylvia Gilbert's home and the horses Mary Margaret had yearned for all week.

Chapter 48

As the car slowed down to turn into the driveway, Mary Margaret searched the paddock. She was not disappointed as some of the horses stood very near the road, but her gaze across the area did not show her exactly what she was looking for. Where was Daisy? She wasn't anywhere to be seen.

They turned into the driveway; and, as they drove between the fences on each side, Mary Margaret strained her neck to look around again, but Daisy was not in the paddock. Honey and her colt were under the tree next to the barn, and the other horses were standing as if they were painted in a picture with their heads bowed to the ground lazily eating grass. While it was impressive to see, it was not what Mary Margaret wanted to see. If Daisy wasn't there, she would not be able to ride, and if she couldn't ride, *what was the purpose of being there,* she thought.

The dogs announced the arrival of the Smith family. Gerry and Sylvia came out onto the porch and waved to them as the car came to its final resting place in the turnaround. The Smiths attempted to open the doors. They were greeted with tail wagging and barking in such an enthusiastic manner that it was almost impossible to get out. Gerry came down and held Freckles so that the exit could be made without anyone being knocked over.

Mary Margaret leaned down to pet Freckles, and true to her nature she jumped and knocked her flat on her bottom. This was not enough for Freckles; she stood over the embarrassed girl and licked her unrelentlessly on the face. Mary Margaret was sputtering and flailing her arms as she attempted to regain some composure, but this just excited Goldie as well; and she came over to join in the face washing.

Eventually, both dogs were subdued, and Mary Margaret was able to sit up, wipe off her face, and sputter out the *dog kisses*. Sylvia gave her a hand up and told her she could go into the bathroom and wash off if she liked.

Mary Margaret ran into the house and was momentarily disoriented as she came from the bright sun into the darkened foyer. Her eyes focused, and she could see that the dining room table was not set and the house was eerily quiet. She found the powder room and filled her hand with water, splashing her face several times. She spat the water away from her mouth and finally felt that she had adequately cleansed herself of all the dog slobber. Now she needed to go back out and face everybody. She had been embarrassed at the way she must have looked as she lay in the driveway with two huge animals slobbering all over her. She really didn't want to be here especially if she was not going to get to ride a horse.

She walked back to the front porch and nobody was there. She walked around the side of the house to the back yard and immediately smelled the wonderfully smoky aroma. It was like nothing she had ever smelled before. It was smoky, but it also had a flavor attached to it.

She found the ladies in wonderful old rocking chairs on a back deck, and off to the side was the source of the aroma. A large black container was sending out small billows of smoke. The front doors of the container were opened, and her father was holding a platter while Mr. Gilbert was removing large hunks of meat. Some of it was thick and others were thin and long. Mary Margaret recognized the long thin pieces as ribs, but she wasn't sure what the big pieces were. Whatever it was, it sure smelled good.

Her mother and Mrs. Gilbert called her over to them, and Mrs. Gilbert explained that Philip had gone to spend the day with Davis and Jordan, and he wouldn't be home for a while. Mary Margaret could feel the disappointment behind her eyes, but she knew it would be impolite to cry. She feigned indifference and sat down in one of the waiting chairs.

The cushion was a lovely floral print, and she was surprised at how soft it was. She sat there and gently rocked as the grownups chatted like long lost friends, and she suddenly missed her friends, Charlene, Darlene and Alice. She became sadder until suddenly she realized that a tear had run down her cheek. Unfortunately, her mother had seen the tear, too. She told Mary Margaret that she too was sorry that she wouldn't be riding the horse that night, but that there would be other times, and that there was no reason to cry. Mary Margaret attempted to tell her mother that the tear was not for the horse, but because she missed her friends. However, Mrs. Gilbert got up at that moment and said it was time for them to eat.

They moved to a large table, which was set on the deck beneath a green market umbrella. The plates were stacked up on one end of the table. They were plastic and had brightly colored yellow daisies on them. The thought of a daisy reminded her that she would not be riding, and again she wondered why she had to be here anyway. Mrs. Gilbert showed her which seat was hers, and she realized that she was being placed between Mr. and Mrs. Gilbert. That seemed strange to her. She didn't think she liked that either. *Who was going to help her cut her meat,* she wondered.

Just as she sat down, Gerry Gilbert placed a filled plate at her place, and she immediately knew that she did not need to cut her meat. Her plate was filled with ribs which had been separated from each other and huge pile of chopped up meat which had been covered in barbeque sauce. A small portion of baked beans and potato salad filled the space not covered with meat. Mary Margaret looked at this plate and then at her mother. Her eyes were seeking guidance, but the only guidance she got was a knowing smile and a slight head movement, sort of like a goose moving its neck, which meant to make the best of it and eat what she could.

After the blessing was said, the eating started. Mike and Cindy ate, licked their fingers, yummed, ate some more, licked some more, and yummed until they were nearly *busting* at the seams so they said. Mary Margaret attempted to eat her ribs without getting any sauce on her, and soon realized that it was okay to get sauce on your fingers. She looked at Gerry and Sylvia Gilbert and saw that they were licking their fingers, too. Well, she thought if they can do it, so can I, and for the first time that evening she started to enjoy what she was doing.

Gerry explained to her mother that the chopped meat was pork shoulder, and he told her how he had slowly smoked it, along with the ribs. He had used a dry rub on the meat, whatever that was, and that's what gave it the spicy flavor. He explained about a smoke ring in the meat, and talked on as Mary Margaret attempted to eat her share of this wonderful feast. She soon realized that she was never going to eat all he had put on her plate without being sick, and she was not going to let that happen.

She sat quietly as the adults finished their meal and went back to the comfortable rockers. The sun was barely visible on the horizon, and the sky was orange and purple. Mary Margaret remembered Addie's saying that "Red sky at night was a sailor's delight." The next thing she realized was that her father was waking her up. Philip was standing there along with Davis and Jordan. *Oh, no!* she thought, *will this embarrassing night never end?* She had fallen asleep again—just like at Davis and Jordan's house.

The boys were carrying mayonnaise jars, and Philip was holding another one out to her. She finally realized that inside the jars were bugs, and the bugs were lighting up. She could hear the words, "lightning bugs, come on, let's go," but she could not comprehend all the meaning. She just couldn't seem to wake up. Finally, it became clear that they wanted her to catch lightning bugs with them. She didn't like bugs, and catching them seemed like a nasty thing to do, but her mother and father were insisting that she join in the fun. Mary Margaret took the jar and walked off the deck. She sat down and watched as the boys yelled and screamed across the yard in search of the most bugs.

The lightning bugs finally lost out to a game of hide and seek. Mary Margaret was drafted to join in on this fun, and it was impossible to not take part without really seeming rude. It took a quick lesson on how the game was played, because Mary Margaret had never played hide and seek before. Of course, after one potato, two potato, she was It. She went to the base tree, hid her eyes, and started counting to 100. She could hear the footsteps as they ran off in different directions. It was hard to count out loud and think at the same time. Mary Margaret tried to remember where the sounds were coming from as the boys ran away. She also was thinking that she would rather be at home on her own front porch swing. No, she thought, she would rather be in New York where she could have spent the day with her parents in Central Park, or she and Alice could have played on the roof. *Anything she would have done in New York would have been better than what she had done this evening,* she thought.

She finally reached 100 and yelled as she had been instructed, *"Ready or not, here I come."* She opened her eyes and looked around. The adults were still in their comfortable rockers on the deck, and none of the boys could be seen. Mary Margaret walked away from the tree toward the house, and Jordan ran from her left to the base tree, touched it and yelled, "Safe." He laughed, jumped and danced all at the same time. Mary Margaret watched him disgustedly and continued in her quest for Philip and Davis. There were so many hiding places around, and it was dark. She didn't want to go past the glow of the light. From the back side of the smoker she could see the toe of a sneaker barely poking out. She smiled for probably the first time that evening because she recognized that sneaker to be one that Davis had been wearing. She walked around the back of the smoker and pretended to be passing it by, when she suddenly turned and was surprised to see that Davis had also turned and they were face to face. They both screamed and ran toward the base tree. Mary Margaret caught up with Davis just as he was about to touch the tree, and they somehow tangled their feet together and fell into a panting heap in the yard. Arms were thrashing and legs were kicking as they immediately jumped back up. Jordan was doubled over in laughter and off in the distance the footsteps of Philip running to home base could be heard. Thump-thump, thump-thump they went with each completed step he took. Mary Margaret decided quickly that she did not want to find herself on the ground again this night, so she stood back and let him run in undisturbed.

The adults on the porch had joined Jordan in his laughter, but Mary Margaret just couldn't see any humor in this.

It was decided that the Smiths needed to get ready to go home. Mary Margaret was really glad to hear this. This had been maybe the worst evening of her life, and she only wanted it to be over. Then she heard her mother saying to Sylvia that they were going to join Addie at church the next morning.

Church! Church! What were her parents doing to her, Mary Margaret wondered. They never asked her opinion on anything before they made plans, she thought. Her parents never went to church. Now they were making her go and they were going with Addie. *Will this day never end,* Mary Margaret asked herself silently.

She soon realized that it was not yet at an end. When they walked to the car, Davis and Jordan joined them. Jordan opened the door and got into the back seat and Davis followed. Mary Margaret stood there looking at her parents questioningly. Her father said, "Come on Mary Margaret, get in beside Davis. We are giving them a ride home."

The three children sat in the back seat, and Davis and Jordan chatted with Mr. and Mrs. Smith. Mary Margaret sulked in her corner and never added to the conversation. *What an awful day*, she thought.

Mother's Day—
May 13, 2001—
Our Life Is
Changing Forever

Chapter 49

Early Sunday morning Mary Margaret was awakened by the closing of a door. She looked toward the window and saw that it was barely daylight. *Who would be coming or going at this time on Sunday morning*, she wondered. She listened and didn't hear any more sounds. *Maybe I was dreaming*, she thought; and she dozed back to sleep.

She was awakened again by the sound of her father's voice as he cheerily yelled, "Good morning, sleepyhead," and knocked on her door. She looked toward the window and could tell by the light shining around the blind that the sun was up now. She sat up in bed and remembered that her family was going to church this morning.

Yuck, she thought. "I have to go to school five days a week and now I have to get up for church," she talked to herself.

She knew that she had just as well get ready, because when her parents made up their minds, they didn't change them easily, especially when they had promised somebody else, like Addie.

After her shower, she looked briefly in her closet and realized that her clothes may not be appropriate for church. In New York she only went to church on Wednesdays at school for chapel, and she wore her uniform. She had some party dresses, and school clothes, but she didn't know what to wear for church. Maybe she wouldn't have to go to church after all she thought. She couldn't be expected to go naked.

Mary Margaret opened her door and yelled for her mother. Cindy answered, and it was obvious from the direction of her voice that she was in her own bathroom. Mary Margaret asked, "What should I wear for church?"

Her mother stuck her head out the bedroom door. She had a puzzled look on her face, and said that she wasn't sure. They stared at each other's heads poking from the bedroom doors and finally Mrs. Smith said she would be there in a few minutes to help her decide.

Mary Margaret went back to her closet and pulled out a robe. She put it on and sat Indian-style on her bed. Her mother soon appeared, and she looked like springtime itself. She was wearing a lovely yellow suit with shoes that matched. Mary Margaret gasped when she saw her. She had never seen her mother like this except for some *special occasion.*

Cindy went into the closet and soon came out with a new skirt, a sweater set, and new white shoes. She was smiling as she held them up to Mary Margaret, and Mary Margaret was too stunned to speak. The skirt was made from a blue floral fabric, and the sweaters were pale blue. The shoes were some she had seen in Jennifer's Shoe Store window when they first came to town.

Finally, Cindy asked Mary Margaret, "What do you think?"

Mary Margaret asked, "Where did they come from?"

Her mother explained that she had done some shopping on Saturday afternoon while she was with Mrs. Applegate. She said she had hung them in the closet to see if Mary Margaret would notice, and obviously she had not. She told her to hurry and dress, so that they could have a bite of breakfast before they left for church.

Mike whistled when Mary Margaret came into the kitchen. She tried to not smile, but it was impossible. She knew the clothes were pretty, and she felt so grown up in them. They were unlike anything she had worn before. They weren't for a party with lots of frills, they weren't like her uniforms, and they weren't like her school clothes. *They were just special,* she thought.

They had toast and orange juice and hurried out the door. "Addie said she would meet us at the side door," Cindy told her husband. They drove into town and through the square, turning left onto Church Street. It was soon apparent why this street had that name. There were four churches just one block off the square. The Episcopal Church was on the right side of the street, then the Presbyterian Church. On the left side was the Methodist, and finally Eastside Baptist, the one they would be attending.

As they drove along Church Street many cars were pulling into the parking lots. Mary Margaret recognized Nancy Miller at the Methodist Church. She was getting out of a blue car. Another girl was getting out of the same car along with a man and a woman.

She started looking into the parking lot of Eastside Baptist as her father slowed down to turn in. A man in the parking lot was directing traffic, and he motioned for them to pull into the Visitor's Parking area. How did he know they were visitors Mary Margaret wondered? When she said this out loud, her father said that this man had probably attended this church all of his life and could recognize a visitor at 30 yards. Mike and Cindy laughed, but Mary Margaret didn't think it was funny.

They got out of the car and didn't have an opportunity to meet Addie at the side door of the church. She was standing beside the car when they stopped. She, too, looked so different than Mary Margaret had ever seen her. Her hair was nicely combed with just a few tendrils framing her face instead of the large pieces she usually kept pushing back. Her dress was soft peach, and her face glowed with joy. Her blue eyes sparkled. She wore lipstick in a shade identical to her dress. Her shoes were black patent pumps with gold buckles on the toes. She even was wearing hose. The entire family was shocked at the sight of her, but only said how lovely she looked.

Addie hustled them inside the building using the side door. She took Mike and Cindy to a room where a group of people were already seated. She introduced her parents to Lew Rowell, and it appeared that he was expecting them. His wife, Jerry, got up and came over to meet them as well. Addie said she knew they were in good hands, and off she went with Mary Margaret.

It was obvious that they left the adult part of the building and were in the children's hall by the balloons and flowers which had been cut out and taped on the walls. They passed by a few doors and Mary Margaret could see cribs in one room, and a gate covered the opening of another. Inside that room little children were playing on the floor. The next couple of rooms held children who could walk, and finally she turned into a room where 3 boys and 2 girls were already sitting in chairs. The teacher, Ms. Betty Tyler, turned around and smiled as Addie entered.

Ms. Betty as she asked to be called was a small lady with excitement and joy in her eyes. She was pretty and wore red lipstick. When Addie introduced Mary Margaret, Ms. Betty grabbed her and kissed her on the cheek before she knew what happened. The other children laughed, and Mary Margaret blushed. Again, Addie said that she knew she was in good hands, and she left.

Ms. Betty asked Mary Margaret to take a seat and as she looked toward the chairs, she saw Davis, Philip, and another boy from her class, but she didn't know his name. Jane Ellis was one of the girls and Peggy Anderson was the other. Mary Margaret sat next to Peggy.

After they chatted with Ms. Betty for a few minutes about their week, she asked for prayer requests. Davis asked for prayer for Allison Kincaid. Mary Margaret was so shocked that she turned around and looked right at him. He went on to explain that she was in a hospital somewhere and probably wouldn't be back at school this year. Everybody else was shaking their head, "Yes," in agreement with what he was saying. *How do these people know about this"* she wondered. She had not told anybody what had happened.

Philip asked for prayer for his Uncle Bobby, and the other boy asked for prayer for his daddy, that he might find a job. Peggy asked for prayer for her sister, Marilyn, who was going to have a baby, and Jane asked them to pray for her grandmother who was sick in Atlanta, not to be mistaken for the grandmother in Charleston.

Mary Margaret just sat there. She didn't know who she would pray for. In chapel at St. Mark's the prayers were recited by the Priest, and nobody asked for anything. This was all new to her. Ms. Betty seemed pleased that they had so many friends and family who needed praying for, and she asked them to bow their heads. She began praying . . .

"Our Father Who art in heaven, thank you for this beautiful mother's day."

Mother's Day" thought Mary Margaret. *Mother's Day! It's Mother's Day, and I don't have a card for my mother. Tears began to well up in her eyes as this thought kept crisscrossing her mind.*

Ms. Betty continued . . .

"Thank you for these beautiful children with pure hearts you have placed into my care this morning. Thank you for their families. Dear Lord, You have heard the special pleas from each of them, and You ask that we all come to You as children. You tell us that we shall ask and it will be given. You tell us to knock and the door will be opened. Dear Lord, I ask that You earnestly hear and answer the prayers put before you today. Be with Allison as she undergoes therapy to bring her to a place in her life that can give her peace. Be with Philip's Uncle Bobby and take care of his needs. Be with Peggy's sister, Marilyn, as she prepares to become a mother for the first time. Be with her and her husband as they go into this new part of their life. Dear God, be with Joey's father as he looks for work. You know the needs of this family and see that they are met as he travels outside Left Fork in search of gainful employment."

How did she know he was traveling outside Left Fork, Mary Margaret wondered. *He didn't say anything about that.*

She went on . . .

"Dear Lord, please be with Jane's Granny as she fights against her illness in Atlanta."

Mary Margaret heard a sniff and looked over to see that Jane Ellis was openly crying. Tears were streaming down her face, and Ms. Betty was silently handing her a tissue. She continued looking around and saw that Joey, the boy whose name she didn't know before today, was also crying. He already had a tissue at his eyes, and Philip had his hand on his shoulder.

What was happening here? Didn't these people understand that you don't cry in public?

Ms. Betty continued . . .

"Finally, Dear Lord, I want to thank you for Mary Margaret and the hand that you have played in bringing her into our group today. She has been through a lot in the few weeks since moving to Left Fork, and I pray that we can be an essential part of her feeling welcome in our wonderful community. We are thankful to have her here and are anxious to get to know her better.

"Dear Lord, please be with me as I bring today's message to these young people so that they can understand the meaning of love as we are told from Your word.

In Jesus' name I pray.

Amen."

The rest of the children said, "Amen."

Mary Margaret sat there in total disbelief. How could this woman who had never seen her before today know anything about the few weeks since she had been in Left Fork? *How did she know I was coming today,* she wondered? Then she remembered Addie had brought her, and the answers began to fill her head. Addie had told her everything. Mary Margaret wondered what else she might have told her. *Did she tell her about falling down and deer jumping over her? Did she tell her about the special sheets that Charlene had sent? Did she tell her about . . .?*

Her thoughts were interrupted as Ms. Betty asked the children to turn in their Bibles to Exodus 2:1-10. Mary Margaret immediately noticed that all the other children had their own Bibles with them. Well, she had one at home, too, but she never thought to bring it with her. Peggy and Jane had cases they unzipped and white Bibles were in them. The boys each had identical Bibles—small black ones, and she could see that Philip's had his name on it. Ms. Betty walked to a nearby table, picked up a Bible and handed it to Mary Margaret. She did this inconspicuously as the other children were finding the scripture. As she handed it to her, she stuck her thumb in where a book mark had been placed. Mary Margaret knew immediately that she had found the place for her and had mixed feelings. She knew how to find scripture. She did have religion classes at St. Mark's, but at the same time she was relieved that she didn't have to search for it, too.

Ms. Betty read the scripture and explained that at this time Pharaoh, the King of Egypt, had given an order that all boy babies would be thrown into the Nile and that only girl babies should live. This was done because of strife between Israel and Egypt. He gave these orders to midwives, the people who delivered babies at that time. However, the midwives feared God and didn't do what the King had ordered, she continued.

A boy child was born, she explained, and he was a fine baby. His mother hid him for 3 months. Finally, she couldn't hide him any longer so she made a basket for him and coated it with waterproof material. She placed the baby in it and put it in the reeds along the bank of the Nile River. His sister stood a distance away and watched to see what would happen to him.

Ms. Betty continued that Pharaoh's daughter came to the Nile to bathe and her attendants were walking along the river bank. She found the basket and sent her slave girl to get it. She opened it and saw the crying baby and felt sorry for him. She recognized him to be a Hebrew baby. The baby's sister who had been standing nearby asked if she should go get one of the Hebrew women to nurse the baby. Pharaoh's daughter told her to go, and she got the baby's mother. Pharaoh's daughter told the mother to take the baby and care for him, and she would pay her. The mother took the baby and cared for him. When he became older, she took him to the Pharaoh's daughter, and he became her son. She named him Moses.

Ms. Betty asked if anyone knew of things like this happening in the world today, and Peggy held up her hand. She said that in China girl babies would be killed, and that many people were trying to adopt the ones who were put into orphanages. Ms. Betty said that was correct. Philip said that Israel and Egypt still don't get along today. Ms. Betty said that was a wonderful insight.

Then Ms. Betty talked about the love that the baby's mother had for him. She said she risked her own life to keep him alive, and then was willing to give him up so that he might live. God seemed to reward her for this by allowing her to get the baby back and seeing that he had a chance to grow up. She said that this is the kind of love that most mothers have for their children and that on this special day and every day we should hold our mothers near and dear. She said that we should respect our mothers and our fathers.

She said, "This is the kind of Love that God has for us. He gave His son, Jesus, to die on the cross for our sins. He made a way for all of our sins to be forgiven. We only have to believe in Jesus, and ask that we be forgiven for our sins, and invite Jesus into our heart. When we believe that and take the proper action, we can, no, we will dwell in the house of the Lord forever."

Ms. Betty then thanked Mary Margaret for coming and told her that she hoped she would come back again. Then she closed the class with prayer.

"Dear Lord, thank you for giving me the opportunity to share Your word with these precious children. I have come to love them as my own. Please be with them and their families this week as they go out into the world. Protect them and keep them in Your care until we can be together in Your House next week.

Amen."

While Mary Margaret was in her class, Mike and Cindy were in their class with 16 other adults. Lew Rowell was the teacher, and he introduced them to each member, one by one. After their prayer request time, which was filled with heartfelt requests for family members, friends, acquaintances, the church, and the country, Mr. Rowell talked about Mother's Day.

He first read Proverbs 31:10-31

Mike listened as he heard this scripture for the first time. He heard of an excellent wife. One who is worth more than jewels. Her husband trusts her. He will gain much because of her. She will not do him evil, but good. She constantly looks for fine materials and does handwork with delight. She brings food to her family from afar. She rises early and gives food not only to her household, but to her maidens. She is wise in business and buys fields. She plants vineyards. She is strong. She doesn't go to bed early at night. She spins and reaches out to the poor and needy. She doesn't fear for her family because she has prepared for the bad weather. She dresses well and looks nice. Her husband is well considered. She makes and sells linen garments. She has strength and dignity. She looks forward to the future and speaks with wisdom. She speaks with kindness. She runs her household well and is not idle. Her children bless her. Her husband also blesses her and praises her saying that many women have done well, but she has done the best. She is a woman who fears the Lord and will be praised.

As he read this, Cindy could feel the tears welling up in the back of her eyes. It was the most beautiful thing she could remember hearing about a woman, and she knew instantly that she wanted to be looked upon like this woman was. She thought about the words and realized that this woman was looked upon by her husband with dignity. She cared for her husband, children and the people who worked for her and they rewarded her with blessings. She was a woman of valor.

Mike was moved as the reading ended, and he placed his arm on his wife's shoulders and hugged her gently toward him.

"I grew up in Birmingham, Alabama," Mr. Rowell said. "My sweet mama had five children. She had six if you count my daddy, and at times he needed to be counted. He was cantankerous, and my mama was loving. Our household was filled with uncertainty as we never knew the mood of my daddy, except to know that it would eventually be explosive. My daddy was taken to drink, and while my mama didn't like the way he acted, she always loved the man."

"My daddy never learned to drive, and my mama had to take him to work every day. He would never ride the bus. My daddy was a brilliant man, but he never felt that he had accomplished anything in his life. He was an artist, a historian, and father of five fine children, but he never felt completed."

"My mama didn't keep the neatest house in town, but the children were always clean, and she always saw to it that we were in church. My older brother was the first to cross the alley into the Baptist church. When I was 2, he carried my diaper bag and led me. When my next brother was 2, we carried his diaper bag, and the three of us went. Then my sister was 2, and several years later, my baby sister went as well. The point is, we were all in church. My grandparents also were instrumental in seeing to it that we had what we needed for church and for our being there."

He went on to tell some stories about his mama, some funny, and some sad, but he finally got to the story of the end of her life.

"For years I prayed for my mama's relationship with God. I probably prayed the same prayer for more than 30 years. One day my mama called me and said that she had renewed her relationship with Jesus Christ as her Savior. Never give up on a prayer. We prayed this morning, and many of the requests were not new. We have prayed for the same things for some people for a long time. Don't give up. There were times when I doubted that God heard my prayer, but each time I would reflect on His promise that we only have to ask and it shall be given unto us, and I would renew my faith."

"My mama had a stroke and lived for a week and was not able to communicate with us. I had peace in the knowledge that she was going to heaven. I didn't have to feel bad that she would not have the opportunity for a deathbed conversion. Her conversion had already taken place. One day I left her alone in the nursing home to have lunch and while I was gone, Jesus took her home. He had been with her. She was not alone when she died. Angels surrounded her, and she found herself in heaven at the right hand of God."

He cried as he told that story, and many of the other people in the class cried too. Some of them knew Mr. Rowell's mama, and some only knew the wonderful stories he had told them about her.

"My mama was a Proverbs 31 woman. I probably never told her that exactly, but I always told her I loved her. More than that, I showed her that I loved her. She raised me to be the man I am today, and I look forward to the day when we will be together again in heaven," he said.

He looked directly at his class members and charged them. "If you still have your mamas do not let the day go by without telling them that they are Proverbs 31 women, if you feel they are. If you don't feel that way, pray to God to cleanse your hearts of any ill feelings you might have against them. At the very least, each of you should lift your mamas up to God in prayer. Don't let this day end without calling your mama. I would love to be able to hear the voice of my sweet mama and hear her laugh."

He dismissed the class and spoke to Mike and Cindy as they prepared to leave, inviting them to come back again the next Sunday. Cindy was still wiping tears, and Mike shook his hand. They made no promises and left the room to find Addie.

They didn't have to look far because she was standing outside their door with Mary Margaret in tow. She whisked them away and up the stairs into the sanctuary. The room was filling quickly, and it seemed as though everyone knew everybody else. Addie herded them in the direction of a pew which held some other people, who were smiling and excitedly looking in their direction. Addie soon introduced them to one of her daughters who lived in Charleston and a son who had come from Atlanta. They hurriedly took their seats, and the organ began to play. Addie, however, did not sit down. She rushed out of the sanctuary, and they wondered where she was going. The choir started to fill up the loft, and Addie was one of the last to enter. She sat on the front row and smiled down at her brood. It seemed that her cheeks had to be hurting, her smile was so wide.

The music started and the choir director motioned for everyone to stand. It seemed that everyone except the Smith family knew what to do and what to sing. They were fumbling with the hymnal. Mary Margaret heard a hissing sound and looked up. Addie was holding up a church bulletin that a man had handed them when they came in. She was pointing to the inside page. Mary Margaret looked at her bulletin and saw something that said page 535 and showed it to her mother. Cindy turned to the page just as the singing started. She handed that hymnal to Mike and took another from the back of the pew. After turning to the correct page, she held it down for her and Mary Margaret to share. By this time the first verse was finished and it was hard to find their place, but at least they weren't still creating chaos, Mary Margaret thought.

The song was entitled *A Christian Home*, and Mary Margaret realized as she and her family sang the words that they live in a home where they love each other, but there is never any talk about the Savior, and that she has never been taught about His love. The burning in the back of her eyes began again, and before the song ended, a few tears are streaming down her cheeks.

There was a prayer. The man praying thanked God for the glorious morning and for the celebration of Mother's Day. Oh, no, there it was again. It was Mother's Day, and Mary Margaret was unprepared. How could this be happening? She and Charlene had always done something nice for her mother, and this day she had nothing. At the thought of this, the tears were about to flow from the edge of her eyes, when her mother put her arm on her shoulder and gave her a gentle hug. That was all it took and the tears started running down her face, and her nose started to run. Cindy was surprised when she heard Mary Margaret sniff. She looked down to see a red-faced little girl at her side, and immediately wondered what was wrong now. She handed her a tissue and the man finally finished his prayer. Neither Cindy nor Mary Margaret knew what else he prayed for, but Mary Margaret was glad he had finished.

The choir leader stood up and clearly said, "Please turn in your hymnals to page 534." As Mrs. Smith turned to the correct page Mary Margaret wondered why he hadn't done that with the first song instead of leaving them in the dark.

As the song, *She Will Be Called Blessed*, began, the choir director started speaking a verse, which Mary Margaret noticed from the hymnal was from

Proverbs chapter 31, verse 28. She had learned from her religion classes at St. Marks how to look up things in the Bible, and it said right on page 534, Prov. 31:28. Finally, she began to feel a little at ease about what was happening. However, the words of the song touched that spot in her body that turned on the tears, and again she was wet faced. The song sang of a woman with strength and dignity who excels in her works, and has compassion for the needy and gives of herself to others.

It went on to say that she will be called blessed by her sons and daughters and is precious to the Father. She will be held above every other. She gets up early in the morning to tend to her household and looks for joy in the future. She teaches her children to be kind and shares wisdom the world cannot destroy.

Mary Margaret realized this could be a song about her mother. She does all those things, except that Mary Margaret didn't know if her mother turned to God in praise. She also wondered about the part that said she was, "Precious to the Father." What does that mean, she wondered?

Another man prayed, but this time nothing was said that touched that spot that made Mary Margaret's eyes fill with tears. As the man prayed, some other men walked to the front of the church and they were holding gold colored dishes. He finished, and the men started passing them across the rows.

Singing started, and the voice was unmistakably clear and unmistakably Addie's. Unfortunately, the gold plate was being handed to Mary Margaret, and she was so surprised to hear Addie's voice that as she heard the voice and reached for the plate, she knocked it to the floor. Money flew and coins bounced. The man who had been passing it got down on his knees and retrieved it from under the pew. He again handed it to Mary Margaret, who by this time had tears streaming down her cheeks. The plate somehow was taken from her hand by her mother, and the man was busy picking up all the paper money, checks and coins that he could readily reach.

Addie sang the song, which by now was familiar to Mary Margaret, *Amazing Grace*. It seemed that hardly a day went by that Addie didn't sing that song at least once and usually more than once in the Smith household. Mary Margaret was surprised as she listened that she had learned many of the words from having heard Addie sing it so often before. However, this time it seemed different. It wasn't the singing of a peculiar old woman in their home. Now it seemed like a real song and something about it made Mary Margaret feel warm inside. Her mind went through each word as Addie sang, and this time it held some meaning for her. She wasn't sure what it all meant, but she knew that she liked the way it sounded, and for the first time she acknowledged to herself that she liked the lady singing it.

When Addie finished, the whole congregation stood up and applauded. Mary Margaret, Mike and Cindy, and Addie's son and daughter were the last to be seated and tears were streaming down all their faces. These, however, were tears of joy and pride. Addie had made them all proud to know her.

The minister stood and started his sermon, which he said would be taken from Luke 2:41-51.

Mary Margaret listened as the minister read. The story seemed to be about somebody who was 12 years old, and he and his parents had attended a Feast. When they were going home his mother and father discovered that he wasn't with them. His mother thought he had been with his father; and his father assumed he was with his mother. They had traveled for a day in a large group, the minister called a caravan. There were lots of relatives and acquaintances in this group, so the boy could have been anywhere, but after a search, it was determined that he had been left behind. His parents returned to Jerusalem and three days later found him in a temple sitting with teachers. They were listening to him, and he was asking questions of them. His parents were surprised when they saw this, and asked him why he had done this to them. They told him they had been looking for him. He was surprised that they were upset and asked them why they were looking for him. He said he had to be in his Father's house. His parents didn't understand this statement, and he went with them to Nazareth. He followed their rules and his mother treasured all these things in her heart.

The minister spoke about the customs and that at age 12 Jesus was almost considered an adult. He didn't spend a lot of time with his family. He explained that travel to and from the Feast was done in caravans for protection from robbers. He explained that it was customary for the women and children to travel in the front of the caravan with the men bringing up the rear. He said that Jesus could have been with either group, and Mary probably thought He was with Joseph, and Joseph thought He was with Mary. He explained that it is so different today as parents not only want to know the whereabouts of their children at all times they are considered derelict in their duties if they don't know the whereabouts and could be considered bad parents and the children could be removed from the home if the circumstances were serious enough.

As he spoke, Mary Margaret remembered the day she left school and how upset everybody had been when they didn't know where she was. She wondered what it must have been like for Mary and Joseph to not know where Jesus was for more than three days.

As she daydreamed, the minister said something and everybody laughed, but Mary Margaret had missed the joke.

He continued however that when His parents found Him He was sitting in the temple courts. Mary Margaret's first thought was that the temple had something like a tennis court, but the minister went on to explain that the temple courts were famous throughout Judea as a place of learning. He said at the time of Passover the greatest of Rabbis would assemble and teach great truths among themselves. He figured that the coming Messiah would have been a popular discussion topic as everyone was expecting Him soon. He said he was sure that Jesus asked probing questions, and the rabbis were astounded by the depth of His wisdom.

As he went on, he said that Mary had to let go of her child and let Him become a man, God's Son, the Messiah. Mary Margaret let this sink in and then began questioning herself. *Now wait a minute*, she thought. *First He was Joseph's son, and now this man is saying He is God's son. Which is right?* she wondered.

The minister explained that this is the first mention that Jesus is aware that He is God's son. However, Jesus did not reject His earthly parents and remained in their home and under their authority until He was 18. He asked the question, "If Jesus, the Son of God, obeyed his human parents, how much should we honor our family members?"

"As Mary had to let go of her child so that He could become all that God intended for Him, mothers today also have to allow their children to grow and become all that God wants them to be," he continued.

He finally concluded by saying, "If there is anyone here today who does not know God as their Father and Savior, now is the time to make Him first in your life. By reciting a simple prayer asking Him to dwell in your heart forever, and acknowledging that His son, Jesus, died on the cross and was raised from the dead for your sins, you can be assured that you will spend eternity in heaven. As the music starts, just make your way to the front, and we will pray with you as you make this life-changing decision."

The music started and the Choir Director said to turn to page 342. However, the singing had started before the page number was completely given. Most of the congregation knew the words to the song even before they turned to it. For the first time Mary Margaret heard the words to *Just As I Am*. She wasn't really sure what they meant, but she knew from the sound it must be terribly important, and she could hear sniffling from all around her. It seemed that for the first time today she wasn't crying, but others were.

Church was finally over and the Smith family turned to Addie's children, Carolyn and Jim. Mike and Cindy told them how much they loved having Addie as a part of their household, and Carolyn said that she had never known her mother to be happier with a job. She said that all she talks about is the Smith family, and she could almost be jealous of them. The adults all laughed as Addie made her way to their pew. After hugs were exchanged, which by this time were a way of life for Mary Margaret, and she was no longer embarrassed, a discussion ensued about what time they should all be getting together.

Mary Margaret's ears perked up because it seemed that plans had been made for them to spend some time with these people, and she didn't know anything about it. Maybe she didn't want to be with them, she thought. Maybe she just wanted it to be her mother and father and her today. She started to pout when she realized that she was being herded out of the pew and down the aisle to the doors at the back of the church. Standing there was the minister, and Addie had Mary Margaret in tow to be the first to be introduced. She reached around Mary Margaret to pull in Cindy, and Mike just stepped in naturally to complete the introductions.

The minister seemed nice enough, and he said that he had been meaning to come out to meet them, but was just giving them a little time to get settled in. He thanked them for coming to church and said he hoped they would be back again soon.

Mary Margaret's stomach growled, and she looked at her watch. It was 12:25. No wonder she was hungry. It had been hours since breakfast, and she couldn't even remember what she had eaten then.

As they walked to their car, Davis and Jordan yelled, and their parents waved and said they would be over as soon as they changed their clothes. The Gilberts were pulling out of the parking lot and stopped to say that they would be over in about an hour.

Mary Margaret wondered what was going on, but before she could ask Addie said that she would be out as soon as she picked up Mrs. Applegate. Finally, they were in the car and Mary Margaret asked, "Are we having a party at our house?" Mike and Cindy laughed, and said they guessed they were having a party. They were having a Mother's Day celebration and Addie and her children were coming, Mrs. Applegate was coming, along with the Gilberts and the Ravers. Mary Margaret slumped down into her seat and thought that she was always the last to know, and now she would be embarrassed that she didn't have anything for her mother for the celebration.

When the Smith family arrived at home and got out of their car, Mike told Cindy that he wanted her to come down to the pond before going into the house that he had a surprise for her from him and Mary Margaret. She started to protest, but he put his hands on her waist and headed her down the slope. As they passed some shrubs in the back yard the pond came into view and between two trees was stretched a beautiful and inviting hammock.

Cindy squealed with delight. "I have always dreamed about having one just like this," she said.

"I know that, and when we moved here, I learned about a place called Pawley's Island where they hand make hammocks. I ordered this one for you from Mary Margaret and me." He winked at Mary Margaret as he said this, and while it wasn't something she had made for her mother, at least her father had included her in the gift giving.

Cindy ran toward the hammock taking off her high-heeled shoes. She sat down and lay back smiling under the warm South Carolina sun, and she looked as radiant as a school girl.

"I may just stay here all day and demand that lemonades be brought to me hourly," she declared.

"That sounds like a good idea, but I don't know how the rest of our guests will take to your lollygagging around all afternoon." They both laughed until she nearly flipped out of the hammock. Mike caught the edge of it and helped her up. She reached up and kissed him.

Now this kind of kissing was too much for Mary Margaret. This was boy and girl kissing, and she didn't want any part of that. She was getting used to the cheek pecking kissing, but not this. No, no way!

As they walked back to the house Cindy asked Mike when he had put up the hammock. He said that he had gotten up very early this morning and sneaked out while she was still sleeping. At least Mary Margaret now knew why the door had opened and closed before she got up.

Cindy said that they needed to hurry and change their clothes because people would begin arriving at 1:30. Mary Margaret's stomach growled as she noticed that it was 12:45. Her toast and orange juice of 4 hours ago had worn off, and she was hungry. Her mother and father had already gone into their bedroom, so Mary Margaret went into the kitchen to see what she could find to eat. She opened the refrigerator and was shocked. She had never seen so much food in their refrigerator in her life. She couldn't tell what most of it was because it was all wrapped in aluminum foil, but there was no space left in the whole refrigerator. She immediately felt that today was going to be something different in the life of her family. *Why did they have so much food,* she wondered?

She closed the refrigerator door and looked in the pantry. It, too, was shocking to her. There were aluminum foil wrapped things in there. There were 2 round objects, and when she lifted the foil on one of them, it was a golden brown cake with some kind of sugary glaze on it. Mary Margaret knew that she had better not bother with that. It must be a special dessert. The second one was a dark brown, chocolate cake with a glaze that beckoned to be tasted. Mary Margaret broke off a small edge of the glaze that had found its way down to the plate on which it sat. As she tasted it, she was immediately taken to the shore and the wonderful copper kettle fudge that she remembered from their last trip. She at once felt homesick for the life they used to have, but that feeling was interrupted as Addie startled her.

"What's you doing, little one?" she asked, and Mary Margaret was jolted back to Left Fork, and turned to see Addie standing behind her. She was flanked by her smiling children and the tiny Mrs. Applegate. Mary Margaret felt as though she might have stolen a piece of the wonderful candy she was remembering and was not sure how to respond. A response really wasn't necessary, as Addie continued with the conversation and said, "Mary Margaret, I want you to properly meet my children. This is one of my sons, Jim, and my youngest daughter, Carolyn. They each stepped toward her and extended their hands. Mary Margaret instinctively extended hers, and they shook hands through the doorway to the pantry.

It suddenly seemed crowded in that tiny space and Addie told Mary Margaret to come on out of there, and she'd get something together so they could have a quick snack. As she usually did when Addie told her to do something, she obeyed and walked into the bright kitchen. Addie was totally in charge. She told her two children and Mrs. Applegate to have a seat at the table, and told Mary Margaret to go change her clothes.

Mary Margaret hugged Mrs. Applegate and started toward her bedroom. She realized she was still hungry, but she knew better than to go back into the kitchen.

After changing into her slacks and blouse, she returned to find that her parents were there and they both had on clothes she had never seen before. Her father had on khaki knee-length shorts and a pink golf shirt, and her mother was wearing new pale blue shorts and a sweater with flowers embroidered on the front of it. She had on sandals that matched her shorts. *Who are these people, and where did they get these clothes?* she wondered, but she never had time to ask. Addie was obviously in complete control and was loving every minute of it.

The table had been spread with a fruit tray that looked like a work of art. The containers on the tray were made up of a pineapple half, cantaloupe halves and a watermelon basket. These containers were filled with strawberries, melon balls, pineapple chunks, and apple slices. The watermelon basket had a saw-tooth edge, and was filled with balls of red-juicy watermelon. The cheese tray had chunks of yellow cheese, white cheese, cheese balls, and containers with cheese spreads. Each item had been labeled, and baskets of crackers and breads surrounded them. Addie was placing something on the table she had just taken from the oven. It smelled heavenly, and she said it was, "Cheese in crute." Everybody oohed and aahed as she announced it, and Mary Margaret had to admit it looked as pretty as it smelled good. It seemed to be some sort of crust that had been wrapped around what she assumed was some kind of cheese, but she didn't remember ever smelling any cheese that smelled like that before. Mike cut into the crust and melted cheese slowly oozed onto the plate. As he removed a piece and spread it on a cracker, the cheese continued to slowly melt and nuts and a kind of glaze were exposed. Addie was explaining that the cheese had pecans, brown sugar and bourbon baked on top of it. Mike handed the first piece to Carolyn, and he continued to serve first the ladies and then Jim and he had theirs.

Mary Margaret hesitantly placed the cracker into her mouth, and the aroma, while pungent, was very inviting. She was hungry enough to eat an elephant she thought, so she wasn't going to wait any longer for a second choice. The taste of the cheese was mellow, the pecans were sugary, and there was a slight taste of something she didn't recognize, and wasn't sure she would like on its own merit, but it blended well with all the other flavors.

As she chewed, the adults were all chatting away like old friends. Her parents seemed to like Addie's children as much as they liked her. Addie was glowing, not only from the heat that was building up in the kitchen, but from the joy she was experiencing.

Addie stood back and looked at the six people around her. She felt tears welling up in her eyes as she realized how blessed she was to have such a wonderful family. Mrs. Applegate and she had long since considered themselves family. Yes, she considered Mike and Cindy to be her family now, too. She had come into this situation not knowing what to expect from people from the north, *Yankees*, to some people's way of thinking, and they had turned out to be such a blessing to her. They had welcomed her and appreciated her. She turned around toward the stove and took a tissue from her apron pocket and quickly wiped her eyes. She didn't want to let her family see her cry, even though she knew they were tears of joy.

Just then, Mike said he wanted to make a toast before everybody else got there. He was pouring glasses of iced tea and as he passed them around, he held his glass high. The amber tone of the tea sparkled in the ice, and the condensation was forming on the outside of the glass.

The kitchen was heating up, and the aroma from the oven was almost overwhelming as a hickory smoked ham was warming. His eyes glistened. He hesitated, and then with a crack in his voice, he first turned to Cindy and thanked her for trusting him enough to make this move and for her unwavering support she had given him over the past few months and for being the kind of wife and mother that their Sunday School teacher had described this morning, "A Proverbs 31 woman." He said, "Each line of the scripture described you perfectly. You are everything I could ever imagine and more. You make me so very proud, and I hope that someday I can feel worthy of you." Cindy sniffed as she wiped away the tears that had sprung to her eyes.

He immediately turned his attention to Mary Margaret, and seemed almost at a loss for words, but he was really trying to find his voice. It seemed to have escaped him momentarily, caught somewhere between his tears and his mouth. Finally, his voice, suddenly sounding husky, found its way out, and he had tears streaming down his face. He thanked Mary Margaret for trusting and supporting him, and for being strong in situations that were not only strange to her, but that were frightening and new. He said that her support made it possible for him to come to this new place and not only make a life for his family, but hopefully to make life better for other families in the community.

He next turned to Mrs. Applegate. The warm smile on her face disclosed the affection she felt for this man she had allowed to live in her apartment, which had been saved solely for people in her family. He again hesitated, but finally explained that she had opened the door for him to move into this town and immediately feel like he belonged. She had shown him such immediate friendship that he felt at home the first day he was here, and she had welcomed his family into her life as easily and quickly as if they had been born into hers. "Mrs. Applegate," he continued, "God put you into my life and I thank him for the Proverbs 31 woman he shared with me in you." Her eyes twinkled and a tear dripped off her chin and quickly spread into a circle on her pink suit jacket.

He then turned to Addie, and by this time he was not trying to hold back the tears. They streamed down his face as quickly as the condensation was running off his glass. "Addie," he said, "I cannot adequately find the words to thank you for coming into our lives." He explained that when he was making the decision to move here, his main concern was not the work to be done at the plant, but the upset that would be caused in the life of his family. Their life in New York was wonderful, he explained. Charlene was there to take care of Mary Margaret. He had a good job. Cindy was happy in her work. Their life was simple in a world of chaos around them. He told her that his dream had always been to bring his family to a place where they could feel a real part of the community, and he could feel secure in knowing that his child could go outside alone, and his wife could go to work without fear, and they could all come home together to a place that was their own, and they could invite the world around them into that home. He continued as Addie sniffled and averted her eyes. "Addie," he said, "You have allowed me to make my dream come true. You came into our house, and you helped make it a home. You have taught us in the short time we have been together, not only how to love each other more, but how to love the world more. You have introduced us to a way of life of absolute honesty, and by inviting us into your church today, you have opened another door, a door on which I have been wanting to knock, but wasn't sure how. I have known that while we seemed to be accumulating all of our dreams something still was missing, and today I finally have to admit that the thing that has been missing in our home is God. Thank you Addie, for bringing God into our home. I promise He will never leave, and thank you, God, for bringing Addie to us."

By this time everybody was crying and nobody was trying to hide it, but Mike continued. He looked at Jim and Carolyn, and he said, "I hope that you and your brother and sister realize what a wonderful mother you have. She is a woman who has devoted her whole life to others. Her character speaks to the fact that she, too, is a Proverbs 31 woman. You are truly blessed to be her children."

He finally took a big gulp of his tea, along with the others in the room. Something in the Smith household had just changed, and everybody could feel it.

The Ravers and the Gilberts arrived at almost the same time. Suddenly, the house was filled with people. Mary Margaret was almost overwhelmed by all of the excitement. She had never seen so many people in her house before, and the food was being placed on the kitchen counters. *Who all is going to eat all this food?* she wondered.

Jennifer had brought deviled eggs and a congealed salad, and Sylvia brought fried chicken and potato salad.

Addie was taking the ham from the oven along with baked beans, and Cindy, Mrs. Applegate and Carolyn were heating up the green beans and setting out the paper plates and plastic silverware buffet style.

Mike was filling glasses with ice, and Jim was pouring tea. Alan and Gerry were setting up folding tables and chairs on the front porch, and Davis, Jordan and Philip were going behind their fathers putting on table cloths.

Mary Margaret wondered what she was supposed to be doing. She had never done anything like this before. She didn't have to wonder long before Addie yelled, "Mary Margaret, would you get the cakes and other desserts from the pantry and set them on the sideboard in the dining room, please?" *Finally*, she thought, *I know what I should be doing*."

She carefully took the cakes she had previously found in the pantry. She was surprised at how heavy each plate was as she carefully made her way through the kitchen and into the dining room. Each trip was a challenge as the women were carrying out their tasks in the kitchen. She went back to the pantry to get another plate, and peeked under the foil to find some kind of coconut cookies. On her next trip she carried in chocolate chip cookies, and the last plate covered with foil was a cherry pie. She finished and turned around to see the man whom her father had been talking to near the woods standing in their living room.

Mary Margaret gasped as the stranger stood in the middle of the room, holding his hat in his hand. Her father noticed him at the same time, and immediately walked in to greet him. He extended his hand and said, "Mr. Hood, we are so glad you could join us today." Mr. Hood took Mike's hand, and answered that he was honored to be invited. Mike took Mr. Hood outside to find Gerry, and the three men went out into the yard for just a few minutes before returning.

The food was all out, the tables were ready for eating, and it seemed that all the guests had arrived. Mike looked to Addie for a nod that all was in order, and upon getting that nod, he said, "I would like for everybody to form a circle, and hold hands. I want to say a blessing." The 15 people in the house joined hands, and the circle was formed. Mike began, "Dear God, I am new at this, and I hope you are listening to me. I want to thank you for bringing me and my friends to this place today. I'm not sure what I need to be saying, but my heart has never been so filled with joy, and I want to thank you for all that I have and for everybody in this circle. I want to thank you for the food we are about to eat. I want to thank you for Mother's Day. Thank you for hearing my prayer. In Jesus' name. Amen."

Addie immediately started the directions, "The food is in the kitchen, we have chicken and ham, potato salad, deviled eggs . . ." On and on she went until she named all of the food. She stood at the plates and handed them to each guest. The Gilbert family went first, followed by Mr. Hood. He nodded to Addie and introduced himself to her as he took his plate. She nodded and handed the next plate to Jennifer. Mr. Hood filled his plate and started out to the porch. Mike spoke his name, and said he wanted to introduce him to Cindy. After the introductions, he accompanied Mr. Hood to the porch and introduced him to Sylvia Gilbert and asked if it would be all right if Mr. Hood joined them at their table.

Mike returned to the house and was the last to fill his plate. He came outside to find his porch filled with his friends, and the joy that filled his soul again filled his eyes as tears stung them, and he wondered if he would be able to eat. He needn't have wondered. The first bite of food was so wonderful, that it led to the second and on and on until his plate was empty. His stomach was full. His friends were around him. *Will I ever again feel such joy*, he thought.

It was decided that everybody was too full for dessert right now. It would be served later. The tables were cleared, and the paper plates and plastic silverware were thrown away. The women laughed that this might be a new fad for everyday living. Throw-away dishes would make it easier to clean up after a meal. Mary Margaret knew this was not going to happen. It seemed that setting a proper table in the south was almost as important as taking a bath every day.

Mike, Gerry and Mr. Hood started walking across the yard and soon disappeared into the woods. Nobody noticed they were gone. Davis, Jordan, Alan, Philip, and Jim, started toward the pond to fish. Jordan yelled to Mary Margaret to see if she wanted to go. She decided that she might as well and ran to catch up with them.

The three men went a distance through the undergrowth that seemed to form rooms in the woods, and came upon Mr. Hood's encampment. It was immaculately clean. An area had been cleared, and small hole had been dug. The hole was surrounded by rocks. Scorched wood was in the hole. A tent was pitched under a large oak tree. A clothes line had been strung, and a shirt was drying. Mr. Hood invited the other men to have a seat on some large boulders. They all sat down, and they chatted for a couple of minutes. Mike began to ask Mr. Hood some pointed questions about his background. Mr. Hood admitted that he had been arrested a couple of times, but not for real crimes like stealing or robbery, but for vagrancy. He said that he had spent too much time in one place or another and had been found out. He had no serious criminal record, he said. He was from West Virginia. He had two sons; one was dead, and the other he hadn't seen for a while. He had worked jobs from time to time, but he had a wandering spirit, and it was hard for him to stay put, he explained. "I have hopped trains from New York to California and from California to Florida. I worked on a freighter for a while and went to Cuba, back years ago. I get by doing odd jobs and it doesn't take much for me to live. My needs are simple. I can cook as a short-order cook. I have washed dishes. I put together pipe for a piping company in Cleveland, Ohio. I have picked strawberries, tomatoes and lettuce. I milked cows on a dairy farm in New Jersey. I've done a lot of jobs, but I'm getting old, and it's harder and harder for me to travel these days. I stayed here longer than I expected, but like I told you yesterday, my back has been giving me some trouble."

Gerry was the next to speak. "Mr. Hood, we have an idea that might help you and us, too. Would you be interested in hearing it?"

Mr. Hood looked at him, and said, "It isn't dishonest is it?"

Gerry laughed. "No, we're thinking of hiring a night watchman at the mill, and we wondered if you would be interested."

Mike and Gerry had already discussed that they would meet with Mr. Hood; and if Gerry felt as good about him as Mike did, he would be the one to bring up the subject of the night watchman's job. By doing this, Mike knew that Gerry felt Mr. Hood was okay to be considered.

Mr. Hood jerked his head and shoulders back slightly. He was truly shocked at this. In his mind he figured they were going to feed him a good lunch and tell him he had to move on. He figured Mike had brought his friend along for support if there was a problem. Mr. Hood began to laugh.

Mike asked him what was so funny, and he explained what he had been thinking. They all laughed.

Gerry asked again, "Would you like to be considered?"

Mr. Hood replied, "I would be honored."

The two men explained that they would have to do a background check, and if it came back as he had said, they would give him the job. He would be making $1,000.00 a month, and they would provide him with a small house that was on the mill property. There were several that used to be used by company employees, but had long since been abandoned for that purpose. Now they were mostly used for storage. They said they would have it made habitable, and he could get out of the woods.

Mr. Hood said that he had never made $1,000.00 a month before. "I will be a rich man," he said. His dark eyes glistened, but tears didn't betray him. "I don't know how to thank you."

"Just make us proud, and that's thanks enough," Mike said and Gerry nodded in agreement.

With the business out of the way Mike stood. Gerry followed, and then Mr. Hood. As Mike started walking away he invited Mr. Hood to come back to the house for dessert. The old man declined saying he had eaten more already today than he usually eats in a week. This saddened the other two men, who realized that they took their plentiful lives for granted.

"If you change your mind later, come back over. I'm sure we'll have plenty."

The men shook hands, and started back toward the house. As they were beginning to see the light in the clearing something caught Gerry's eye. Something small was moving to his right. He stopped and Mike followed his lead. They stood still. Was it his imagination or had something moved. His eyes adjusted to the light and there at the edge of the woods was a fawn. It was standing on shaky legs. It was tiny. The camouflage of the spots on its soft brown fur hid it well, but it was unmistakably a newborn fawn. The two men didn't approach it any further. The mother had to be close by. They moved to their left and distanced themselves slowly from the fawn and came out into the lawn just right of where they had entered. A rustling behind them caught their attention and they turned to see the mother starting to walk in the direction of her baby, and to their surprise, she was accompanied by an identical wobbly-legged newborn. They both realized simultaneously that she had given birth to twins. They bridled their excitement and quietly left the mother to tend to her babies.

Back at the house, the men set up the croquet game Gerry had brought. The ladies were lounging on the porch and yelled directions to the men. Cindy was content. She was enjoying the entertaining being done in her home. She quickly thought to herself that she could not have done it alone, and was thankful Addie had been there to help.

The rest of the day was filled with games, food and fellowship. When everyone had left and the house was again quiet, Mike, Cindy and Mary Margaret all three sat on the porch swing. As it hummed with each movement, they sat there quietly, each thinking over the day's events. Mary Margaret was soon sleeping with her head leaning on her mother's shoulder and her feet in her daddy's lap. Her parents smiled at each other and silently conveyed to the other their love.

Chapter 50

Allison Kincaid watched as families joined together in the common room. Mothers cried, fathers fidgeted, siblings squabbled, and she sat alone in the corner. Her heart was heavy. It was Mother's Day, and she couldn't spend it with her mother. She was not permitted visitors. She was not permitted phone calls. She chose not to interact with the other residents. She sat in the shadows and allowed her mind to race and sometimes rant silently at the anger she felt. She hated being in this facility. She hated the lack of control she had over her life. Somebody else decided when she ate, slept, showered, studied, almost when she breathed.

"I will get out of here," she silently promised herself as she had many times in the previous week. "I will not spend any more time in here than I have to. They can't keep me here, and when I do get out, I will make that smarty Mary Margaret Smith sorry she did this to me. I will make her so miserable, she will be sorry she ever met me."

Dr. Hanna watched the activity in the common room. He had seen it every Sunday for years. Today was only slightly different since it was Mother's Day, but every Sunday was pretty much like the Sunday before. Today, however, he focused more on the tiny figure in the shadows. He could imagine the thought patterns she was having. Her behavior in the preceding week had been disturbing as she vented her anger at a classmate whom he knew to be innocent of her rantings. Allison had accepted no responsibility for her actions, and he was concerned. Usually, a child of this age could be led into more positive thinking, but she had not altered her stand from the moment she arrived. *She's a tough nut to crack*, he thought, and he silently prayed to God to give him the guidance to break through the hard shell that had been formed around the young heart of this girl. He could only imagine the torture she had experienced in her home, all the while pretending to live a normal life to the rest of the world.

Eventually, all the guests left, and the residents gathered in the kitchen for supper. Allison and another resident were given the duty to clear the tables of the plates and silverware. As the dishes were taken to the washing area, Allison slipped a steak knife into her waistband and pulled her shirt over it. Her plan of retaliation was beginning, and now she had only to watch for the opportunity.

Left Fork was only an hour away by car, and at the end of that hour was the person who had made her life miserable. Preparation would meet opportunity. She would be ready she silently vowed.

Chapter 51

The next week was uneventful. School was school. Spelling tests were aced. Math tests were struggled through. The garden was tended. The days were getting hotter and hotter, and it felt like summer was already here.

Mike had the background check done on Mr. Hood, and it was as he said. He was told he could begin work, and arrangements were already underway to repair the company building for his home.

Cindy continued to enjoy her work. She joined Mrs. Applegate and Addie in a Bible study on Thursday night.

Soon it was Sunday and they were back at church. This week, however, Addie didn't have to meet them. Mary Margaret remembered where to go and Mike and Cindy found their way to Lew Rowell's class.

Ms. Betty greeted Mary Margaret with her usual kiss and surely left a big red lip print on her cheek. All of her students wore this imprint almost as a badge of honor. The same people were there this week and Jordan was there, too. When it was time for prayer, Philip asked again for his Uncle Bobby, with no further explanation. Peggy said that her sister had a baby, a girl, and she was named Emma Jane. Joey asked that his father might find a job. Nobody else asked for anything.

As she did the week before, Ms. Betty prayed. She first thanked God for the privilege of being here with these precious children. Then she asked Him to answer these prayers for Philip's Uncle Bobby, and Joey's family as his father looks for work. She thanked Him for the birth of Emma Jane, and asked that He be with Peggy's sister and her husband as they began their role as parents. Then she asked for the Lord's blessing as she brought the message, and asked Him to prepare the hearts of the children to receive His word.

This week Ms. Betty taught about Noah. Now Mary Margaret knew that Noah was in the Bible and that he had built a boat, an ark, and that he had put two of each kind of animal on that boat. However, she had never heard the story quite like Ms. Betty told it. She seemed to bring the story to life.

Ms. Betty explained that the story of Noah is found in the Old Testament in the book of Genesis starting in Chapter 6 and she began reading. As she read she explained that God saw that men and women of the world were becoming wicked and He was not happy with them. He said that He would destroy them along with all the animals and birds.

However, Noah had found favor in the eyes of God, she explained. Ms. Betty read the scripture that said that Noah was a good man who walked with God.

God told Noah to build an ark of cypress wood. He told him to put rooms in it and coat it inside and out with pitch, which she explained is something that keeps water out. He told him to build it 450 feet long (1 1/2 times as long as a football field, she explained). He told him to make it 75 feet wide and 45 feet high. He told him to make a roof for it and to finish it to within 18 inches from the top. He wanted a door on the side and three decks, lower, upper and middle.

He told Noah that He was going to destroy the world by flood waters and it was up to Noah through a covenant or a promise with God to save his sons, his wife and the wives of his sons, and to bring two of each unclean animal, two of each bird, two of each creature that crawls on the ground, a male and female, onto the ark to be kept alive. He was also told to take 7 clean animals. These were animals used for sacrifice, and he took 7 pairs. He was to take and store food for his family and for the animals. Ms. Betty said that it was estimated that almost 45,000 animals could have fit in the ark.

Noah did as he was commanded.

The Lord told him to go onto the ark with his family and all the animals and that in 7 days it would begin to rain and it would not cease for 40 days and nights. After all were loaded onto the boat, the Lord shut them in.

Just as God had promised, the rains came. Noah was 600 years old and he had never seen such rains. The water covered the earth. Even the highest mountains were covered with water, and the boat rode above it all. Every living thing left on the earth perished except what Noah had placed in the ark.

The water stayed on the earth one hundred and fifty days.

Ms. Betty continued to read that God remembered Noah and the living things on the ark and sent a wind to dry up the water. After 40 days Noah started sending out a raven, a black bird, she explained, and it kept flying back and forth. The water kept receding and finally Noah started sending out a dove, but the dove couldn't find a dry spot to rest, so it flew back. Then the dove finally came back with a branch in its mouth and Noah knew that the water had receded. He waited 7 more days and sent the dove out again, but this time it didn't come home.

Noah then opened the ark and saw that the surface of the ground was dry. Finally God told Noah to come out of the ark with his family and all of the animals.

Then Noah built an alter and made a sacrificial offering to Him. When God smelled the pleasing aroma He said that he would never curse the ground because of man. He said that He would never again destroy all living things. (Gen. 7:20)

God promised that He would never destroy the earth again with rain and with every rainbow we will be reminded of that promise.

Ms. Betty asked the children how they would feel if God told them to build a boat as large as the one he told Noah to build.

Philip said, "I would tell God that I am too young, and I don't know how to build."

Davis said, "I would tell God that I don't have enough wood to build such a big boat."

Jordan said, I would tell God, "Are you nuts?"

They all laughed, including Ms. Betty. Ms. Betty said, "Many of Noah's friends asked him the same thing, 'Are you nuts?' Why are you building this? You're too old to do this. We're in the middle of a drought."

Then she asked, "What did Noah do?"

Mary Margaret's voice said, "He obeyed God."

Ms. Betty was so pleased that she had joined in. "That's absolutely right, Mary Margaret, he obeyed God."

Ms. Betty then asked, "What do you think you would do about the animals?"

Jordan said, "I would catch them all and bring them in by myself."

Davis shoved him, and said, "You would not, you're afraid of snakes, and God said to bring them, too."

Ms. Betty said, "Do you think that Noah was afraid of any of the animals, the lions, the tigers, or the snakes?"

Peggy said, "I'll bet he was afraid of them, but he trusted God to take care of him and his family."

"That's right," Ms. Betty said. "He trusted God."

Ms. Betty closed by saying. "Just like Noah, God tells us to do the right thing. We know it's the right thing, but we try to make excuses for not doing it. We're too busy. We're too little or too big. But deep down inside, we know when God is talking to us, and we have to trust and obey Him."

"Jordan, when you sat on your chair this morning, you did not think it would let you down and you would fall?"

"No," Jordan said.

"How about the rest of you. Did any of you think about sitting in those chairs this morning that they might not hold you up?"

Each child said, "No."

"That's the kind of trust you have to place in God, that He is the chair holding you up. He won't let you fall. Noah trusted God with that kind of faith and he didn't fall. In fact, he and his family were the only ones to survive," Ms. Betty said.

"Are there any other comments?"

Nobody responded. "Well," said Ms. Betty, "Let's go to the Lord in prayer.

Dear Lord, thank you for this day, and these precious children and the families they represent. Please lead these children to be like Noah, to be obedient, not only to their parents, but to You. Let them be the ones in whom God is pleased. In Jesus' name we pray. Amen."

"I hope you have a wonderful week," Ms. Betty said, and the children started to leave the room. She stopped Mary Margaret and told her she was so glad to have her in her class. She explained that she would like to get to know her family and that she would call to arrange a time for her to come and visit them.

"Okay," said Mary Margaret not knowing what else to say.

Mary Margaret walked out into the hall and realized she didn't know what to do. She and her parents hadn't discussed if she was to come to their room or if they were going to meet in the sanctuary. All of her friends had already gone, so she decided to make her own decision to go to the room where her parents' class met. She got there, and it was empty. Oh, no, she thought and just as she turned around her father was hurrying back down the hall. He grabbed her hand, and was saying, "I'm sorry, we didn't forget you, we just didn't know where you were." They hurried into the sanctuary just as the organ music was beginning.

While the choir was filing in Mary Margaret looked at the bulletin and knew that the first song was on page 493 and turned to that page and was ready to sing.

Addie was watching from the choir loft and smiled as she saw Mary Margaret and her new family. They had become so dear to her. Her life had become so much simpler and more complete. Addie no longer had to lift heavy pots in a hot kitchen or stand on her feet for hours on end cooking to fill the plates of restaurant customers who never showed any appreciation for what she did. Now she was surrounded by three people who daily made her feel appreciated and needed. Mary Margaret was coming around.

Addie realized that the move was harder on Mary Margaret than on Mike and Cindy. She had the least control over the outcome. Then the situation at school had made matters much worse. She silently thanked God for them as she stood in the choir loft and started to sing the words to the hymn on page 493 in the *The Hymnal for Worship & Celebration, It is Well with My Soul*. Addie knew that all was well with her soul that morning.

Mike sang the words and tears filled his eyes. His spirit was under attack that something was missing. His world was well, but his soul felt unsettled. He loved his new job. His family was content. He was glad he had moved to Left Fork, South Carolina, and still there was a nagging feeling that something was wrong. He had just begun to feel it last week. He kept remembering the minister's words, "If there is anyone here today, who does not know God as their Father and savior, now is the time to make Him first in your life." Mike knew that he did not know God as his Father and savior, but he wanted to, he thought.

As the song continued, he sang the words, and his mind wandered further. He was thinking about the lesson Mr. Rowell had presented to the class that morning. He had ended the class by saying, "You should live your life like it was an open Bible as it may be the only Bible some people ever 'read'."

Before he could become more lost in his thoughts Cindy nudged him to pass the collection plate to him. He had gone through the motions of singing, standing, sitting, praying, and his mind had been racing with his own thoughts. The minister stood to begin his message, and it seemed as though he made direct eye contact with him. Mike realized he must pay close attention because he knew he didn't want to miss a word of the message.

He listened to the words and followed along in his Bible as the minister read the scripture. He was beginning to feel as though he might explode. Finally, the minister got to the part about making a decision, and Mr. Smith looked over at Cindy. She was standing there looking as lovely as ever, but she was not showing any signs of moving toward the front of the sanctuary. He thought he could not do this on his own, so as the words to the hymn of invitation, on page 376, *I Have Decided to Follow Jesus* were sung, he stood in his place as two other people went forward to make a decision for Jesus Christ.

The congregation was dismissed, and the Smith family filed out with the rest of the people. The minister was at the back of the church and reached out to take Mike's hand. As he shook it, he told him he would like to meet with his family later in the week. Cindy answered that it would be wonderful and invited him out for Tuesday evening. The minister said he would check his calendar and let them know.

As they reached their car they saw that Mrs. Applegate was parked beside them. They waited until she reached her car and invited her to come out to their house for lunch. Mrs. Applegate thanked them, but said that she needed to take a rain check, as she already had plans. They hugged and got into their car for the short drive home.

Mary Margaret told her parents that Ms. Betty wanted to come and visit with them this week, and that she would call for a time. Cindy thought that was a good idea, and Mike was lost in his own thoughts and the upcoming visit with the minister. He had never spent any time with a minister, and never any time in his own home. He had met the minister who performed the marriage ceremony when he and Cindy married, and had never really had any contact with a man of the cloth in a one-on-one situation since then.

His mind was racing. What would it be like? Would the minister ask him to pray, he wondered? As the chaos in his mind was building Cindy said she thought it would be a good idea to invite the minister and his wife to dinner on Tuesday evening. That way they could get to know each other better. Mike thought that this was getting out of hand. It was one thing to have a minister come to his house, but to spend an evening with him and invite him to eat. He wasn't sure he was up to this. His head was spinning and his stomach was uneasy. He needed to get home and lie down. He didn't feel well.

As they drove down the driveway, the house came into view and Mr. Hood was sitting on the front steps. He stood as they approached and tipped his hat to Cindy and extended his hand to Mike. He got right to the point and told Mike that he needed to speak with him privately. Cindy excused herself to go get lunch ready and invited Mr. Hood to join them. He looked embarrassed and said he would leave that up to Mike after their conversation. Mary Margaret and her mother went inside, and Mary Margaret went to go change her clothes. She and her mother were both again wearing new outfits, which were more appropriate for church.

Mike invited Mr. Hood to have a seat on the porch, and as they settled in, Mr. Hood looked more and more uncomfortable. He hemmed and hawed, and seemed unsure as to how to begin the conversation. Finally he just said, "Well, Mike, I don't know any other way to say this than to just say it. Do you suppose I could do a few odd jobs around the house so that I could earn a little money until the job at the mill begins? I know it's to start in another week, but I could sure use a little money. I don't have many needs, but my kerosene for my heater has run out, and I'm getting low on my canned goods. I mostly eat beans and chili, and they're cheap, but I only have a few cans left."

Mike looked at Mr. Hood, and his heart began to melt for this gentle man standing before him. He was proud, honest and in need. He fought tears which he could feel forming in the back of his eyes. He felt shame—not for Mr. Hood, but for himself. His immediate thought was how he could have been so blind. He had a homeless person living on his property, and he had not given any thought to determining if he needed anything.

Before he knew what was happening, Mike was standing. As he stood, so did Mr. Hood. Mr. Hood wasn't sure what was happening. Was Mike going to tell him to leave, he wondered.

To his surprise, Mike embraced him. Mr. Hood's arms hung at his side. He didn't know what to do. Nobody had hugged him in so many years, and he had forgotten what it felt like.

Suddenly, Mr. Hood heard Mike sniff. Mr. Hood pulled back his head and looked directly into Mike Smith's face. They were only inches apart, and Mike was crying.

Mr. Hood responded by patting Mike on the back. The embrace only lasted a few seconds, but a bond was formed between those two men that would last for their lifetimes.

Into Addie's Arms

Mike took a step back and told Mr. Hood how sorry he was that he had not asked about his needs sooner, and that he had placed him in the position of having to ask for help.

"You asked me, and I said I'd let you know if I needed anything. I didn't mean to upset you." He tried to explain that he usually did odd jobs in whatever area he was staying so that he always had a little cash flow, but somehow this time he hadn't been able to find any work.

Mike stopped the explanation and said that not only did he have work to be done, but he knew that Gerry Gilbert needed some work done as well as Mrs. Applegate. He laughed and said he would have to be careful or there would be so much work to do that he wouldn't want to work at the mill.

Mr. Hood looked at him. "Mike," he said, "You don't have to worry about that. I will work for you as long as you need me. Nobody has ever been so generous in my life, and I will be happy to settle down in Left Fork, South Carolina and be your night watchman forever."

The two men shook hands, and Mike said, "Let's go in and see about lunch."

"Are you sure? I don't want to be a burden. I have a few cans left. I'm not out of food yet."

Mike opened the screen door for his new friend, and the two men walked in as Cindy was removing a casserole from the oven. Addie had made it and left it especially for Sunday lunch.

Mary Margaret already had the table set for 4, and Mike smiled when he saw the guest had been anticipated. His heart suddenly felt full. He wondered why he had felt so empty just an hour earlier. His life is full. His family is full, and today for lunch, his table is full. *Hallelujah! Life is so good*, he thought.

As they sat down, Mr. Hood took his napkin and placed in on his lap. He sat with his hands in his lap. Mike took notice and asked that they hold hands and pray. Mr. Hood was beside Mike and Cindy was on the other side of the table next to Mary Margaret. As they held hands and made a circle at that table in their kitchen, Mike and Cindy somehow knew that their life was changing. Somehow things were going to be different from this day forward, and it was a good feeling.

Mr. Hood had wonderful table manners, which did not go unnoticed by Cindy. She noticed that he never took a bite of food until Mike had taken his first bite. He rested his knife and fork on the edge of his plate, and when dessert was served he again waited for Mike to take his first bite before he had the four layer pudding that Mary Margaret had helped Addie prepare. The rich first layer was made up of butter, flour and finely chopped pecans. The second layer had cream cheese and confectioner's sugar. The third layer had coconut cream pudding, and the fourth layer was whipped topping. Everybody *oohed* and *aahed* as they took their first bite of this tremendous dessert. Mike and their guest had seconds, but Cindy and Mary Margaret were too full and almost moaned in misery.

When Cindy stood to clear the table, Mr. Hood was immediately on his feet and was helping. She tried to protest, but he insisted. He explained that he had worked around food a good part of his life. He was usually able to get a job washing dishes or helping prep food for a chef. He said that he had even waited tables on a cruise ship many years before. Mrs. Smith now knew the secret to his good manners. He had learned by watching those he served. She doubted that he had had many opportunities to be served in his life, but he had served many. She was really beginning to like Mr. Hood.

Mike gave Mr. Hood $50.00 and asked him if that was enough to get him through for a few days. Mr. Hood said it was more than enough and told him that he would do whatever chores he wanted done. Mike said he would leave him a list on the shed door in the morning, and he could get started when he wanted. Before he left, Mr. Smith told Mr. Hood to go get his kerosene can, and he would take him and get it filled. Mr. Hood practically ran toward the woods. Filling the kerosene can was always difficult. It was a 5 gallon can and each gallon of liquid weighed about 8 pounds. It was very difficult for him to carry a full can, so he usually only got a gallon or two, which meant he had to make more trips. The two mile trip to the station was not so bad, but the two mile trip back was becoming harder each time. Of course, there was another reason for only getting a gallon or two at a time. Usually he only had enough money for a gallon or two at a time.

When the two men returned with their full five gallon can of kerosene, Mr. Hood got it out of the trunk of the car, and Mike saw the pained looked in his eyes. He told Mr. Hood he had an idea and they walked to the shed. Mike got out the riding lawn mower which had a large box-like container on the back. The can of kerosene fit perfectly in the box, and after a few instructions, Mr. Hood was riding across the lawn toward the woods. Mike knew that the forest floor could create some problems, but he felt that Mr. Hood would be able to ride over any limbs he encountered and around any trees blocking his path. Mr. Hood turned around and took off his hat and waved it in the air before disappearing into the hidden rooms of the woods.

Cindy was sitting in the swing. As Mike turned toward her, he smiled and again felt the tears stinging the back of his eyes. He was so much in love with her. She had been so supportive of his wanting to take his family from the only place they had called home and coming to this place which was so foreign to them. She had never once complained and only found good in everything that had happened to them. *How could he be so lucky?* he wondered.

He walked up and sat down beside her. It was strangely quiet. Davis and Jordan had not come over to fish. Mary Margaret was in her room working on her book report he learned, and for the first time he and his wife were having a quiet Sunday afternoon on their front porch in this secluded area of the world. As he looked around, he could see no other people. Even the animals were away. The birds were strangely quiet. It seemed to him as though they were the only two people in the world. They didn't talk for a while, they just sat there swinging and holding hands. He wondered if he was dreaming and would soon awaken to hear the horns blowing and people yelling on the streets of New York City. No, he thought. *This is real. This is my dream. It has come true. I am a happy man.*

The peace was soon interrupted by the ringing of the telephone. Cindy went inside to answer it and returned to announce that the minister and his wife would be joining them for dinner on Tuesday evening. The jolt in his stomach caught him by surprise. He sat upright and thought he was going to be sick. Where was all this emotion coming from he wondered. He had been in tears 3 times today. He had become unglued about meeting with the minister. This was not the man who lived inside his body. This man had been unwavering in his strength. He had gotten through college on scholarships, grants, and hard work to pay what those things didn't cover. He had come up through the ranks in his company from beginning as an intern to now operating an entire branch of the company, which is being studied by the powers that be with an eye toward expansion. He had met with many high ranking corporate officials. Nothing had ever fazed him. Now, almost in the blink of eye, he had become what he would have considered soft in somebody else. He never considered himself to be tough, but he always felt he was strong. Now, who was he becoming, he wondered.

The telephone must have ignited the noise in the area because Mr. Hood soon returned with the mower, and Davis and Jordan arrived at almost the same time. Cindy gave Mr. Hood a bag of fruit and plate of leftovers for him to take back to his camp. He secretly hoped she had put in some of that dessert, but he, of course, did not ask. He didn't stay long and Mike joined Davis and Jordan at the lake after he changed his clothes.

The boys asked about Mary Margaret and both of them were dismayed that she was working on her book report. Jordan said he would never do that on a Sunday afternoon. He said, "Sunday night is plenty soon enough for me." They all laughed and continued fishing.

Cindy soon joined the guys at the lake and brought down lemonade in a frosty pitcher along with red plastic cups. They each filled their cups and returned to their fishing spots. Mike was sitting on the grass under the weeping willow. Davis was sitting on the tree stump, and Jordan was a few feet away near a few stacked boulders which hung out over the water.

Cindy got into the hammock and closed her eyes. She thought she had just closed them, but soon realized that she must have fallen asleep. Her first thought was to jump as she was awakened by a scream. As she surveyed the area, she saw Davis and Mike, and they were looking in the direction of Jordan, who was perched on one of the boulders. He was not moving. He was sitting with his bare feet dangling over the edge of the rock barely above the water. His fishing rod was in his hand, and a large water moccasin was swimming under his feet. Its head was erect. Mike was talking softly. "Jordan, stay calm. It's okay, Buddy. I want you to scoot slowly back on the rock. Don't try to pull back your legs. Just scoot slowly back, and your feet will be out of his reach. That's it Jordan, keep slowly scooting. Good boy, Jordan. You're doing it." As he spoke, Jordan listened and followed his direction. Soon his feet were high enough above the water that he was out of the reach of the snake. He then jumped up and stood on the top rock. Mike ran over to him and Jordan jumped into his arms, nearly knocking him down. Davis was right there, and before he realized what he was doing, he was hugging Jordan and asking him if he was all right. The boys were obviously overcome with emotion and tears were streaming down their faces. Cindy had run down, and she, too, was near tears.

They looked around and the snake had disappeared. Mike said there was probably too much noise for him, and maybe he wouldn't come back. He questioned Davis and Jordan if they had encountered snakes in the area before, and they both immediately responded that they had not, and they hoped they never did again. Mike silently hoped the same thing.

Mary Margaret had heard the scream and came to investigate the commotion. After the story was relayed, she said, "I don't think I ever want to come back here again."

"That's ridiculous," her father implored. "That snake is more afraid of us than we are of it."

"I'm not sure I believe that," his daughter said.

Cindy invited everyone to the house for something to eat. The boys said they had eaten lunch, so she suggested a little dessert. "I guess we have room for dessert," Davis answered.

As they all sat on the porch eating some of four-layer pudding dessert Mary Margaret and Addie had made, Phillip rode up on his bicycle. When Mary Margaret saw him, she wished he had been riding his horse. It had been such a long time since she had been able to ride. The last time they visited the Gilberts, Honey wasn't there, and that had been a week ago. She suddenly wished they were at Phillip's house instead of him being at hers.

He rode up to the porch, and agreed that he could eat some pudding when Cindy asked him if he would like some. She went inside to get it. Davis and Jordan started telling Phillip about the snake, and Mike was alongside them as they related the story.

Mary Margaret had not witnessed the incident, so she felt left out. Her mother soon returned with Phillip's dessert and saw Mary Margaret's face. She knew that she felt left out of the male conversation, so she suggested that she and Mary Margaret go shopping at a nearby megastore, Shop-Mart.

Mary Margaret thought this was a wonderful idea. She had not spent any time alone with her mother since they had moved, and she had never been to one of those stores. She had seen one on the trips they made from Charleston and wondered what it would be like to shop there, but nobody had suggested that they go there before now, so she had never questioned it. *This will be a whole new experience*, she thought.

When they arrived at the store, Mary Margaret's first thought was that everybody else had the same idea as her mother. The parking lot was filled with cars and pick-up trucks. Her mother drove up and down several aisles until she found an empty parking space. She pulled in and had to dodge a wayward shopping cart which had been left there. They got out of the car, and her mother started pushing the cart toward the building. It seemed that they were walking into a grocery store. Mary Margaret wasn't sure this was right, as she hadn't thought that Shop-Mart was a grocery store. Her mother explained that this was a super Shop-Mart, which had groceries and general merchandise as well. They went to the left, leaving the groceries behind. Her mother seemed to be on a different mission today.

Mary Margaret hurried to stay up with her. The store was crowded. The aisles were stacked high with merchandise. It reminded her of her favorite toy store in New York. At Christmas they had merchandise stacked high on the shelves. However, it was not as large as this Shop-Mart.

Cindy walked up and down the aisles, but didn't stop at anything for a long while. She seemed intent on finding just the right thing, but she didn't know where it was. They walked through the crowded aisles and had to dodge congregations of people who had stopped to hold what seemed like family reunions. Throughout the store groups of people were chatting as Cindy and Mary Margaret went on unnoticed. Finally, they arrived in the area which had towels and rugs for the bathroom. Cindy stopped and started smiling as she picked up the towels and sometimes rubbed them against her hand. She looked at every color and every style. Then she told Mary Margaret they were going home.

"Aren't you going to buy anything," she asked questioningly.

"No, I can't," said her mother.

'Why not?"

"We have to support the United States and the mills which still operate here. The towels I like were manufactured outside the United States, and I can't in good conscience buy them."

They made their way out of the store and back into the parking lot. "I think the car is over here," said her mother, and they found their car after traversing several wrong aisles.

"We'll do our shopping at Rowell's Department Store. I'm sure they understand the economics of buying American made."

"Will we ever go back to Shop-Mart?" Mary Margaret asked.

"Oh, I'm sure they have good things, they just didn't have what I wanted today."

The rest of the evening the family spent time getting ready for the upcoming week. Mary Margaret finished her report. Mike went through the previous week's mail and paid bills. He also took time to drop a note to Charlene. As he wrote he realized how easily he had made the transition from her caring for his family to Addie taking over the reins. He wasn't sure that he liked the feeling that he had. Naturally, he wanted his family to be cared for and Charlene had done such a wonderful job at that. He never dreamed that just a few weeks after the move his thoughts would not constantly be going back to the way Charlene did things. As he thought, he realized that Addie's style was so different; there was no way to compare the two women. Each was wonderful and each did a wonderful job at what they did. They both came to the same point, but the way in which they reached that point was diametrically opposed.

Charlene was very professional, almost clinical in her approach. Addie was very casual and more family-like in hers. *Which is right*, he wondered. Then he realized that both are correct. No two people do things the same way. It's the result that matters. He remembered that from a business management class, and it is a skill he utilizes every day at work. Sometimes he must tell people exactly how to do something, but he has found over the years that if he allows people to find their own solution, the outcome is usually far better.

He finished up his work and smelled the aroma of pizza coming from the kitchen. Cindy had prepared a frozen pizza, and was just taking it from the oven. Mary Margaret followed the aroma, too, and the family had pizza at their kitchen table overlooking the lake. The snake was on everybody's mind, but nobody mentioned it.

Chapter 52

Allison seemed uncharacteristically light hearted at dinner. She joined in with the conversation and was totally engaged with the other residents. Her task was to wipe off the tables when they had been cleared, and she hurriedly completed the assignment and was dismissed to go into the exercise area.

She could feel the knife against her skin as she attempted to make a few basketball hoops. She finally gave up the ball and slowly backed away from that group toward the edge of the property.

The guard noticed her movements, and he called to her to come back closer to the group.

She eagerly complied with his request and soon joined three girls who were playing 4 square. A few minutes later she again backed out of the group and tried a different strategy, this time moving toward the guard and the other edge of the property. She knew her window of opportunity was closing, and she needed to make a move quickly.

The guard continued to watch the entire group, with an eye on Allison. She moved closer to him and attempted to engage him in conversation. He looked away as the basketball players began shouting. He turned his back to her, and she struck in a very fluid movement.

She plunged the knife downward into the back part of his thigh, and could feel the resistance as the knife penetrated his flesh. She quickly withdrew the weapon and saw the look of pain on his face as he turned back toward her. Blood was pulsing as he attempted to reach for her, but he collapsed as she ran away.

The other residents ran to the aid of the guard, and Allison ran almost unnoticed to an area she had already chosen for her escape.

The high, black, wrought-iron fence along the front of the facility was primarily to stop vehicles on the driveway. It extended only a few feet past that area, and her escape was easy. She ran around the end of the fence and could hear the telephone at the guardhouse as she hunched down and ran onto the main highway.

Her next destination was not as easy, but she remembered a truck stop just down the road. She made her way there running among the trees that lined the highway. The parking lot was filled with vehicles as she knew it would be. She needed to find a pickup truck with a covered bed. She looked around, and the choice was wide. However, she wasn't sure how to know which direction the truck would be traveling when it left the lot.

Her pale pink uniform blended in with the other people and she watched as trucks pulled in and out. Her patience was soon rewarded as she saw a truck she recognized. It bore the name of a business located just a few miles from Left Fork, and appeared to be traveling toward that destination. The driver exited the vehicle and went inside the building. Allison watched a few seconds and ambled over to the truck, opened the tailgate, and saw that it was nearly filled with boxes. She quickly rolled up onto the tailgate and nudged her way in between the boxes, pulling the tailgate up as she went. She exhaled, beginning to breathe easily for the first time in nearly an hour since her escape.

She waited, and waited, and waited some more. Finally, the driver returned to his truck and started it. He drove just a short distance and stopped again. He opened and closed the driver's door, and Allison could tell by the outside sounds that he was refueling.

Voices could be heard. "Have you seen a little girl about ten years old?" she heard Dr. Hanna's voice ask.

"No. I've been here about 45 minutes, and I haven't seen anybody like that; is she lost?"

"Well, you might say that," Dr. Hanna said. "Thanks for your help."

The door again opened and closed, and the engine roared to life. The ride in the bed of the truck was not easy as the truck pulled quickly onto the highway and the driver maneuvered the curves leading from Charleston into the heart of South Carolina.

The next hour was filled with bumps and rolling as Allison lay undetected in the bed of the truck. Finally, the truck slowed and appeared to be turning into a driveway. Allison had pushed boxes to the tailgate side of the bed so that the driver wouldn't notice her when he began to remove his cargo. The truck came to a stop and again she could hear voices. This time the driver and the person with the other voice agreed that they would unload the truck the next day and Allison heard the door of a house close.

It was dark in her hiding place. The driver was gone, and she was inside with no way out. She wanted to scream. Her mind, however, sprang into action and she began kicking toward the cover and was relieved when the snaps alongside the edge of the bed began popping. She turned around and peeked out. Nothing looked familiar, and nobody appeared to be anywhere around.

Allison felt the knife in her waistband as she pushed her way out of the truck bed and ran toward the setting sun.

The road intersected with the highway she knew would lead her to Left Fork. She was tired, and needed to rest, but she also knew that darkness would soon be upon her. She continued her journey and saw a familiar road which she remembered would lead her to vacation cabins. Her father had taken her to one of these cabins before he moved to Charleston. Every time she passed this intersection after that, she longed to regain the joy they shared there those few days.

She ran up that road, and was not disappointed to find the cabins vacated. She went to the one she and her father had shared and found a rock to break a window. She went inside and got a bottle of water from the refrigerator. She looked in the cabinet and removed a can of tomato soup. She poured it in a cup and heated it in the microwave. It tasted remarkably good.

Allison lay on the sofa and turned on the television. She had not been permitted to watch TV since she left home.

Maybe I'll just stay here by myself, she fantasized. *No, I'll go take care of Mary Margaret and then I'll come back here,* she thought.

Within minutes sleep came upon the child as she relaxed for maybe the first time in more than a week.

Chapter 53

Addie arrived early Monday morning and she seemed quieter than usual. She walked with Mary Margaret to the end of the driveway, but her mind seemed to be somewhere else. She had seemed fine at church the day before, and Mary Margaret wondered what was wrong, but she didn't ask. The bus came and there were several empty seats. Mary Margaret thought this was strange, as she usually got the last empty one. Davis and Jordan each said, "Hey," but even Jordan was not talkative. Mary Margaret got off the bus and noticed that there were not nearly as many students in the school yard as usual. They seemed to be in small bunches talking instead of the usual running and playing. It certainly seemed different today, but Mary Margaret didn't know why.

When Phillip saw her, he told her he needed to talk with her. She thought this was strange because he was always friendly when their families were together, but he hardly acknowledged her existence at school. However, before they could begin their conversation Mrs. Calhoun approached them. Behind her was a policeman. She apologized for interrupting, but asked Phillip to go on to class and asked Mary Margaret to join her in her office.

Mary Margaret's heart started racing. She began to feel clammy. Her stomach was churning. *What is happening,* she wondered. *I haven't done anything wrong*, she thought. Before she could say anything, Mrs. Calhoun turned to her and said, "Don't be upset Mary Margaret. You are not in trouble. You haven't done anything wrong. We just need to speak with you."

The children on the playground stopped their conversations and turned toward Mrs. Calhoun, Mary Margaret, and the policeman. Even the birds stopped their singing. It was eerily quiet as the trio walked into the school and the short distance down the hall to Mrs. Calhoun's office.

When they got inside, Mary Margaret was surprised to see her father sitting in one of the rocking chairs. He stood up as they entered and held out his hand to Mary Margaret. Her thoughts were racing. "Has something happened to mother," she asked, with tears running down her cheeks.

Her father grabbed her and hugged her. "No, no, mother is fine. We just need to tell you something, and Mrs. Calhoun thought it would be better if I was here when you were told."

"Is Addie okay," she asked.

"Addie is fine," said Mrs. Calhoun. "Everybody is fine," she continued. "Just have a seat, and we'll bring you up to date on something that has happened with *Allison Kincaid*."

Allison Kincaid, thought Mary Margaret. "I thought she was out of my life," Mary Margaret said bluntly.

"She is," said Mr. Smith. "However," he continued, "She has run away from the facility where her parents took her, and it is felt that she is trying to get back to Left Fork."

The policeman finally spoke. His voice did not match his size. He was enormous to Mary Margaret. He towered over Mrs. Calhoun and her father. However his voice was kind and mellow. "Mary Margaret, I understand that you had some problems involving Allison when you first came to this school, is that right?"

"Yes, sort of," said Mary Margaret. "She didn't seem to like me and said some ugly things to me and about me, but she apparently had been doing that to other kids for a long time."

"I understand that, too," said the policeman. "However, it seems that since she got in trouble as a result of being mean to you, she feels you are responsible for her being put in the facility. In the short time she has been there, she had been concentrating on you, and last night she overpowered a worker by using a knife from the kitchen; and she has run away vowing to get even with you. For that reason, we feel that you will need a little extra protection until she is captured."

The tears have dried on Mary Margaret's face. Her father is standing with his hands on her shoulders. Mrs. Calhoun is facing them, and the policeman is standing by the door. Nobody seems to know what else to say.

Finally, Mr. Smith asks, "Do you feel that for the safety of the rest of the children that Mary Margaret should be kept at home?"

Mrs. Calhoun said, "We have thought about that, but after speaking with the Board of Education, we feel that we can provide adequate security for all our students at this facility. We will have a security person with Mary Margaret while she is here, and the State Police will have a sentry at the main gate to the school, and all other gates will be locked. The bus will have an escort, and a policeman will be on duty at your home. Nobody feels that this will continue for any length of time. How long can it take to capture a 10-year-old child in this area?"

Mr. Smith asked about the details of the escape, and Mrs. Calhoun explained that after dinner, at about 5:30 the day before, the residents at the facility were outside for their evening exercise. Allison had apparently kept a knife from dinner, and when Allison saw the guard was distracted, she attacked him and jabbed the knife in his leg. Naturally, the guard was surprised by the attack and fell to the ground. Allison took advantage of this and ran out through an open gate. Since this is not a criminal facility no police security is available on the grounds. A short search of the area was done by the employees, and then the police were called in. By this time, it was getting dark, and no sign of her could be found.

After further assurances that Mary Margaret would be safe at school, Mr. Smith kissed her good bye, and watched as the policeman walked her down the hall to Mrs. Stancil's classroom. He went on to work, but he did not feel good about this situation.

The school day was different. Instead of going outside, they stayed in and played board games after lunch and at recess. Nobody was permitted to tend the garden. Mary Margaret hated this. Once again the attention was on her, and she did not like that. She wanted to be back in New York where she felt safe and nothing like this ever happened to her or her friends.

Finally, the day was over, and the policeman walked with her to the bus. She got on, and he got in his car to follow the bus. Her stop was the last one in the morning and the first one in the afternoon. When she got off the bus, Addie was waiting by the mailbox. Mary Margaret knew by just looking at her that she was aware of the situation. The police car followed them as they walked up the driveway. Addie put her hand on Mary Margaret's shoulder. She knew that it was to be comforting, but she didn't want any part of it; and she shrugged it away and took a step to the side to get out of her reach. Mary Margaret's thoughts went immediately to Charlene. Nothing like this ever happened when Charlene took care of her. The tears started and by the time they reached the front porch, Mary Margaret was crying and ran into the house and up to her room. She pulled down the comforter on her bed and felt the sheets. She tried to find Charlene's scent on them, but of course, they had been washed many times since they were sent to her. She tried to remember Charlene's face. *How could she forget something like that so soon*, she wondered. Finally, she remembered. She remembered all the times they had walked around the city and the museums they had visited. Nothing ever happened to her. Charlene kept her safe, Mary Margaret thought.

Was that a knock, she wondered. Mary Margaret realized that she had been sleeping, and somebody was knocking on her door. "Who is it," she yelled.

"It's me." said Addie, "May I come in?" "No," said Mary Margaret. "I want to be alone." She heard Addie's footsteps retreating down the steps. Good, thought Mary Margaret. *Maybe now she'll quit working here, and we can go back to New York.*

However, an immediate second knock was heard, and as the knock was heard, the door opened. Cindy stepped inside, and she did not have a happy look on her face. "Mary Margaret Smith, I am ashamed of you," said her mother. "You have hurt Addie's feelings, and all she wanted to do was to help you."

Mary Margaret immediately began to cry. *I am the victim here*, she thought. *Why is my mother mad at me?* "Mother, do you know about Allison Kincaid?" asked Mary Margaret.

"Yes, but that gives you no excuse to be rude. Everybody in this town has gone out of their way to keep you safe and you respond with rudeness. That cannot and will not be tolerated. Do you understand?" she asked.

In absolute awe that her mother was speaking to her in that tone, Mary Margaret could not verbally respond, but shook her head up and down.

Very well. Now, you get up, wash your face, and come down and apologize to Addie." With that, she left the room.

Mary Margaret got up, washed her face, and started down the steps. The telephone rang.

The policeman said he would answer it. "Smith residence, Officer Oglethorpe here." All eyes were on him. He again said, "Smith residence, Officer Oglethorpe here." When there was obviously no response, he hung up. He looked around the room, and saw three pairs of eyes staring at him. "Nobody would talk," he said.

Addie, Mrs. Smith and Mary Margaret all started talking at once. "That's her," they all said. Mrs. Smith explained about the hang-up phone calls they had been getting before. He asked if they had put any services on their phone to trace the calls, and she said her husband had contacted the phone company, but Allison had been found out before they could be placed into service, and she didn't know if anything had continued. He immediately dialed 3 numbers, took his notebook from his pocket and wrote down a phone number. When he hung up he explained about *69 and how you could get the number of the last incoming call. He said that apparently it had been activated, and he knew the number from which the call had been placed.

Officer Oglethorpe asked if it was all right for him to use their phone, and of course, he was given permission. After several calls were made, he said that the call had been placed from a nearby area, and that police cars were on the way there now.

Mary Margaret, Addie and Mrs. Smith all took a deep breath and exhaled. Addie offered the policeman something to drink, and Cindy took Mary Margaret into the living room. They sat down, and Mary Margaret knew she was going to get a lecture. She had never been lectured before this year began, but now she was getting used to it and could anticipate when one was about to begin.

Her mother was no longer angry as she had been in the bedroom. Now she was disappointed. Mary Margaret secretly thought she might like anger more than disappointment, but tried to keep her mind on what her mother was saying. By the time she focused on her mother's words, she was startled to see tears streaming down her face. Mary Margaret really felt bad now. She had made her mother cry. Never in her life had she done anything bad enough to make her mother cry. She had cried good tears before, but Mary Margaret knew there was nothing good about these tears. They were sad and disappointed tears.

Mary Margaret interrupted her mother. "Oh, mother," she cried. "Please don't cry." Mary Margaret was out of her chair and was nearly in her mother's lap. She was hugging her and crying too. Their tears felt cold as their faces touched, but Mary Margaret didn't care. She didn't care about anything except making her mother happy. "Oh, mother, I am so sorry," she said. "Please forgive me. I was just upset and scared, and I missed Charlene so much. I always felt safe with Charlene, and I have always been afraid since we got Addie. I am sorry. Mother, please don't cry."

Addie heard the commotion and had stepped from the kitchen into the living room. She didn't mean to intrude, but was glad she had. As she listened, her thoughts were racing. She had only meant to help Mary Margaret, and she thought they were making great strides, but if she was causing such an upset in this wonderful household, she thought, then she would not stay another day longer than necessary. She would just leave. *Yes, she thought, as soon as I know that this child is safe, I'll give my notice.*

Cindy opened her eyes to reach for a tissue and saw Addie standing in the doorway. She held out her hand to her, and Addie hesitantly walked toward her. Mary Margaret sensed another presence in the room and turned around to see Addie. She knew by the stricken look on her face she had heard what she had just said to her mother. Mary Margaret jumped up and hugged Addie. "Oh, Addie, I am sorry. I've hurt you again," said Mary Margaret. "I don't mean to hurt your feelings. I know you are trying to help us. I guess I am just scared all the time, but I know it's not really your fault."

Addie just stood there looking more stunned than unforgiving. Working for this family was unlike any other job she had ever had. It was more like raising her own family. Well, she thought, *I guess I'd better face it. I'm stuck with this family. I love them, and when you love somebody you don't leave them because they hurt your feelings. It's probably only because they love you that they feel safe in lashing out. While it's not polite, in love it's safe.*

The policeman stepped around the corner. The ladies in the living room had not heard the phone ring. He had answered it and received the report that when they responded to the home from where the last call was placed; they found it to be a vacation cabin about 5 miles away. Nobody was there, but some empty soup cans had been found, so apparently Allison had been there and had gotten something to eat.

Cindy squeezed Addie's hand and she hugged Mary Margaret. Their hopes of an immediate conclusion had been dashed, and it was certain that Allison was nearby.

The policeman went on to say that the State Police were bringing in some K-9 units to search. He said they were very concerned for her safety as the area was known to have copperhead snakes and bears. Also, he said, the temperatures were expected to fall into the 40's and rain was on its way. "It will not be a comfortable night for a little girl in those woods," he said.

Cindy suggested that they go into the kitchen and get ready for dinner. Mike came in just as they were setting the table, and he shook hands with the policeman. Addie told Mary Margaret to set 5 places as she was staying the night with them. Mike and Cindy looked at her, and she said, "If that's all right with you . . ." They laughed and Mike said, "Of course, we'll feel better knowing you're here."

The policeman looked up, and Mrs. Smith said, "You'll be eating with us, too."

"Thank you, I'll be on duty until 8:00, and then we'll be switching. Hopefully, it'll be over before then."

Silently, they all wished him to be right.

After dinner Mary Margaret went to her room to do homework. Mike and Cindy discussed the day's activities, and when Mike heard that Mary Margaret was longing for Charlene, he suggested that they call her. He placed the call and Cindy went to get their daughter. When they returned to the kitchen, Mike and Charlene were already absorbed in a conversation about her upcoming trip to South Carolina. They could tell that she was looking forward to it.

"Surely, by July this will all be over," Mary Margaret whispered to her mother.

Her mother just laughed and said, "Hopefully it will be over before this night ends."

Mary Margaret finally got her turn to speak with Charlene. They talked about school, and Mary Margaret told her about Davis and Jordan. She told her about riding the horse at Philip's and her not too secret desire to have her own horse. For a few minutes Mary Margaret was again feeling joy. She wondered how she could have momentarily forgotten what Charlene looked like. As she heard her voice, she could see her sitting in her recliner in her small apartment. It was an efficiency apartment, and everything was neatly arranged. The TV was on a stand in one corner, a sofa was across the room, with a matching chair on the wall next to it. The coffee table had a big book on it about architecture. The tiny kitchen would be cleaned up by now, and everything would be put away for the night. Charlene might be having a cup of tea. She would have already had her shower and would be wearing a long night gown and a heavy robe. She would be wearing a frilly hairnet on her head. Her face would be glowing after she had scrubbed it clean. Mary Margaret had spent a few nights with her over the years, and she always loved the secure feeling she got when she stayed there. It was small, but it was safe and cozy.

The conversation continued and nothing was said about Allison. Mary Margaret wanted to tell Charlene how scared she gets in South Carolina, but something inside her told her not to. They only talked about good things. She said that Darlene and Alice were fine, but that Alice was a little upset that she didn't hear from her often. Mary Margaret felt bad and said she would go write her a little right now. They said their good-byes and it was Cindy's turn.

Mary Margaret went to her room and took out her stationery box. She put her homework in the floor and sat at her desk to write.

Dear Alice:

How are you? I am fine.

School is good. We will be getting out in a few days. I hope to be able to ride a horse more in the summer.

The boys next door, Davis and Jordan, are fine. They still fish in our pond, and a snake almost got Jordan. He's okay.

We have a man living in our woods. Mr. Hood is his name. He is nice.

I miss you. Write when you can.

Love, your soul mate!

She signed her name and addressed the envelope. That wasn't so hard, she thought. I need to do that more often.

She finished her homework and got ready for bed. She went to tell her parents good night and Addie was sitting in the kitchen with them. She had forgotten that she was staying. She went to Addie first and hugged her and said good-night—then to each of her parents.

The front door opened and a different policeman came inside. He introduced himself to her as Officer Levy and told her he would keep her safe through the night.

Her mother and father walked her to her bedroom and her mother tucked her in while her father stood at the door. Mary Margaret lay in the darkness and could hear conversation in the kitchen, but couldn't understand it. She knew they were talking about Allison, but she was glad she didn't have to hear it. She didn't want to be a part of any of this. She really just wanted to be safely back in New York City.

Chapter 54

Allison awoke with a start and realized that it was nearly 10:00 a.m. *Oh, no. I had hoped to be finished by now,* she thought, realizing that it was Monday morning and she had missed the opportunity for her planned Sunday night attack.

She went to the bathroom, got another bottle of water and spent the day watching television and plundering the cabinets for food. She ate several cans of soup and opened a can of sardines. The smell was gross she thought as she attempted to take a bite, and she dumped the rest of the container along with the bite she had on her fork into the trash can.

The crackers she found weren't too stale, and she coated them with peanut butter. Finally, her appetite was satisfied, and she dozed in the afternoon. When Oprah went off, she figured it was time to leave.

She opened the door and stepped out. She could smell rain in the air,

"Yuck," she said. "It's going to rain."

She went back inside and found a clear plastic poncho in the closet. She held it up, and while it was huge, she decided it was better than nothing. She took the last bottle of water from the refrigerator, made one phone call, and again stepped into the damp afternoon air.

The stillness was deafening. The birds seemed to have already settled in for the night. The air was still and heavy. Allison looked around and contemplated going back in. She removed the knife from her waistband, and ran her fingers over the blade.

Her journey began with a few steps, and then the adrenalin kicked in and she began to jog. Within minutes she was back to the main highway. The poncho was tied around her waist, and was cumbersome. She stopped and slid it over her head. The hem dragged on the ground. Each movement was a near tumble as she stepped on the plastic. Ten steps into this scenario, she stopped again and pulled the poncho back over her head. She squatted and with the knife, she began to remove the lower portion. Soon, she completed this task and again slipped it over her head. Finally, she was able to run unimpeded until the perspiration ran into her face. The temperature inside the plastic on the athletic body was rising with each stride. Finally, she stopped and again removed the poncho, this time leaving it alongside the road.

Allison knew she was about 5 miles from Left Fork. She figured she had come about a mile when she realized a car was pulling up alongside her. She kept jogging, and the car pulled in behind her driving on the shoulder of the road. The driver honked the horn, but Allison ignored the signal. She kept running, now wishing that she was back in the cabin. The car continued to trail her, and she kept looking back over her shoulder. Finally, she came to a bridge, and the road shoulder ended. Allison stepped onto the highway, and heard the brakes screech as she stepped directly into the path of an oncoming car. The driver was able to bring the vehicle to a stop as Allison continued running. The driver of the vehicle which had been following her pulled onto the highway and passed her as she stepped back onto the shoulder of the road on the other side of the bridge. Both vehicles disappeared from her view, and she slowed her pace.

The air was getting heavier, and the sky darker as a mountain of clouds moved in. Allison continued until she felt she could go no further. She stepped away from the road and sat on the ground at the tree line. She drank the bottle of water and rested. It was prematurely dark as the bad weather loomed. Traffic had picked up as commuters returned from the day in Charleston.

Allison waited among the trees until the rush hour traffic subsided, and she again began her trek. She jogged and walked. Cars passed by, but no one stopped. Things began to be very familiar, and she knew she was not far from her destination, but she was too early. She didn't want to make her attack until everyone was asleep.

I'll go Davis and Jordan's and hide in their tree house, she thought, remembering her visit for Davis' birthday two years earlier. When the driveway loomed before her, she again took to the trees and made her way to the swing set tree house at the back of their property.

Lights shone softly inside, and the aroma of something cooking filled the air as she made her way back to the tree house. She was none too soon, as rain began pelting her while she climbed the ladder. The temperature was dropping, and the rain chilled her to the bone. She quickly moved to the rear of the tree house, and was thankful for the shelter albeit limited. The wind roared as the rain continued. Limbs swayed, and mist was blown into the small space. The short sleeved pink shirt she wore provided little protection as the storm settled in.

Allison somehow dozed, and awoke to find the wind had died down but the rain continued. The lights in the distant Raver home were out.

I wish I had my watch, Allison thought. She waited, and saw a light come back on in the house. It was only on a few minutes, and the house was again dark.

Allison sat very still, rolled herself into the smallest ball possible and again dozed. This time she awoke to find that the rain had stopped, and she decided it was time to make her attack. She made her way back to the driveway, and was soon at the highway. After arriving at the Smith's driveway, she inched her way along the tree line until she saw the police car near the house.

This excited her. "They think they can stop me, but I know better," she said to no one. She ran into the woods and back up alongside the driveway at the Raver house. She reached the house and began running into the woods toward the Smith house. Her eyes adjusted to the darkness, but her pace was slow. She went deeper into the woods, and tripped over something. She began to get up, and looked to see what had stopped her when a tall man was standing beside her. He yelled, "What are you doing here?"

In one quick movement the small girl retrieved the knife from her waistband and slashed toward the man. The resistance she felt told her she had reached her mark. The man groaned, and dropped to his knees all the while reaching for her.

He shouted, "She's back here."

Allison ran, and he was unable to reach her before she disappeared in the darkness.

Mr. Hood assessed his injury, knew that he needed help as he felt the warm blood running down his leg, and he needed to alert the people at the house that Allison was on the property.

He walked and dragged his bleeding leg, all the while shouting. His calls were heard, and he was met at the tree line by the policeman. The officer made numerous calls on the radio attached to his lapel, and within minutes the area was bathed in light, and sirens filled the once-still air.

The girl appeared to have vanished.

Chapter 55

What time is it? she wondered. She knew she had been asleep. She knew it was still dark outside, but there were lights everywhere and she could hear people's voices. Loud voices. Excited voices. What was happening? Should she get out of bed? Should she just try to go back to sleep? All of these thoughts passed through her mind in a matter of seconds, and before she could take action on any of them, she heard her door open. The hallway was dark, but she knew that somebody was in her room. She heard the footsteps, and finally her mother asked, "Mary Margaret, are you awake?" Mary Margaret exhaled and realized that she had been holding her breath. She said, "Yes, mother, what's happening?"

"Mary Margaret, you're safe, but Allison is in the woods somewhere outside. She stumbled across Mr. Hood's camp, and she cut him with the knife she has, but he's okay. He has been taken to get a couple of stitches. Unfortunately, though, he wasn't able to stop her, and she is somewhere out there. The police are here, and they have brought dogs. They expect to find her soon. I just wanted you to know what is happening."

The tears were streaming down Mary Margaret's face. *Now I am responsible for hurting* Mr. Hood, she thought. *I hurt Addie feelings. Even Allison being out in the woods is my fault, too.*

Her mother hugged her and seemed to sense what she was thinking. "Now, Mary Margaret, none of this is your fault. Allison is a troubled child who was troubled before your paths ever crossed. She would eventually have been in the same situation. It's just unfortunate that you were the contact that created a situation that had to be dealt with."

The words made sense, but still the guilt remained. If they had never moved to Left Fork, South Carolina, none of this would be happening. She and her family would be safe in New York City.

The dogs were barking. Some were baying. The noise was almost deafening even inside the house. Mary Margaret and Cindy sat in the darkened room. There was activity in the rest of the house, and a light had been turned on downstairs, probably in the kitchen. A door opened, and voices could be heard.

Somebody was running up the steps, and Addie ran by the door and yelled, "They caught her." She ran past the room and opened the linen closet. As she ran back down the steps, it was obvious that she was carrying something. A few minutes later she came back into Mary Margaret's room and said that Allison was safe. They had found her in the outbuilding. She had been out in the rain all night, and she was cold and wet. She was scraped up from being in the brambles, but overall was fine. The policeman asked for towels and a blanket to put around her. "I saw that child and she was shivering and crying," Addie said shaking her head in pity.

They all hugged each other, and Addie suggested that they say a prayer. She began,

"Dear God, we want to thank You for bringing Allison's capture to a safe conclusion. She is a troubled child, God, but she is Your child, and I want to place her in Your arms to keep her from harm. You love her, and so we should love her, too. While it's not always easy to love some people, they are usually the ones who need the love the most. Thank you, too, God for keeping Mary Margaret and her family safe during this time. Please see that Mr. Hood is cared for properly and that he heals quickly. Also, Lord, be with the guard from the facility and give him a rapid recovery. Lord, please be with Allison's parents as they deal with this problem. I know that when your child hurts, you hurt, and their child is hurting terribly. They must be in agony. Give them the strength to do what is right and the love to carry them through. In Jesus' precious name we pray. Amen."

"Amen," said Mary Margaret and her mother simultaneously. Mike came up the steps and turned on the light in the hall. He announced that Allison had been taken to a hospital in Charleston to be checked out. He said that the police would be around the house for a while taking photos and completing their reports.

Addie said she would make some coffee, and Cindy said she'd get out something for them to eat.

Mary Margaret didn't know what to do. Should she get up or stay in bed. She looked at her clock and it was 3:17 a.m. She thought she would stay in her bed. The house felt cold, it was raining outside, and her bed felt so warm and . . .

Chapter 56

The alarm sounded at 6:30. The house was quiet. Mary Margaret felt so tired and momentarily forgot about the early morning events. Suddenly, the thoughts came rushing back, and she pulled the covers over her head. *Had this all been a dream?* she thought. *No, it was real. Allison had been captured in their outbuilding, and she had been taken away wrapped in one of their blankets.* How awful must that have been? Mary Margaret wondered. She remembered how bad she had felt when she hurt somebody's feelings. *How awful must it be to actually inflict an injury?*

Her door opened and her father stuck in his head. "How are you feeling this morning?"

"I'm tired, but okay."

"Do you feel like school today?"

"I guess so."

"Are you sure?"

"I never gave anything else a thought.

"Good girl. Take your time about getting ready though. You don't have to be ready to catch the bus. I think it'll be okay if you're late."

I think I could get used to this, Mary Margaret thought as she and her family took their time about leaving the house. Her mother left first, and her dad and she left shortly after. He was taking her to school. On the way, he told

Mary Margaret that he had heard about her hurting Addie's feelings, and that he knew she had apologized. "However," he persisted, "We cannot allow you to continue to lash out at Addie when things don't go your way. She is not the cause of any problem you may have. Addie has come into our family and is a part of the solution, not a part of the problem. You must remember that, do you understand?"

Mary Margaret knew her father was right, and she also knew how wrong she had been. She promised to never let it happen again. He assured her if it did that there would be serious consequences.

After checking Mary Margaret into school, Mike didn't go to work. Instead, he started to the hospital to see about Mr. Hood. As he was driving, he noticed someone walking along the opposite side of the road. He turned the car around and stopped beside the limping man. Mr. Hood had not looked up until he was beside the vehicle. He was intent on each step he took. He was overjoyed at the sudden prospect of not having to walk the rest of the way home.

Mr. Hood got into the car, and the extent of his injury was apparent to Mike. His trousers were saturated with dried blood, and they had been cut and were taped back together. As he settled himself in the passenger seat, the look of relief registered on his face. He sighed as he rested his body. His pain was apparent.

The two men drove in silence for a few minutes and finally Mr. Hood spoke. "I apologize for being so much trouble to you."

"That's nonsense. You're no trouble at all. I should be apologizing to you for allowing you to remain in the woods."

"I've lived that way for years, and I'm not your responsibility," countered Mr. Hood.

"While your life has been like that in the past, I'm going to see that it improves beginning today. You cannot return to the camp to live. You can gather your belongings and store them in the outbuilding, but you can't do that right away—not before your leg has begun to heal."

Mr. Hood started to protest again, but Mike told him, "You'll be staying in our home until the mill house is completed in a few days. Then you can

Into Addie's Arms

move there even before the job officially starts if the house is ready and you are able."

Again, Mr. Hood protested, but Mike stood firm. "Nothing is going to sway me."

When they pulled in the driveway, Addie was getting out of her truck. She was carrying groceries, and the two men went to help her. Mr. Hood hobbled toward her, and Mike swept the grocery bags from her arms. She was startled. She had not had anyone be so gallant in many years. She reached back into the truck to pick up some more bags, but Mike told her to go on into the house. He would bring in the groceries. Then he told Mr. Hood to go with her.

When Addie heard this, she glanced around at him, and the look did not go unnoticed by Mr. Hood. Mike explained that he would be staying with them for a few days until the mill house was habitable.

Addie started to speak her mind, but instead she glared at Mr. Hood and went directly into the kitchen. She began to put away the groceries as Mike carried in the bags. Mr. Hood came in along with the last grocery bags. Mike told him to sit at the table, and he began to prepare something for the old man to eat. He knew that it had been a long time since his last can of beans, and nobody was going hungry in his home.

Addie continued with the groceries and allowed Mike to continue with the food preparation. They kept bumping into each other as they attempted to share the same space, and while Mike kept apologizing, Addie never said a word. Her actions spoke her thoughts. She loudly closed cabinet doors; and when she threw the potato bag into the pantry with a thud, Mike knew that they needed to have a conversation, but it would have to wait. He would not allow further embarrassment to Mr. Hood over Addie's attitude about his being there.

After he ate, Mike took him to the upstairs office which had a pull out sofa. He opened the bed and got clean towels from the linen closet. He showed Mr. Hood around the bathroom and prepared everything he would need for a nice, hot shower—something he knew he had not experienced for a long time. Then he wondered how the old man had kept himself clean. He had never noticed an odor about him, and while his clothes were not stylish, they were clean and he always appeared neat.

When he left Mr. Hood, he went to find Addie. She was not hard to find, as she was waiting for him at the bottom of the steps. She announced, "We have got to talk." Mike agreed, and they went onto the front porch. He offered Addie a seat in the swing, and then he sat beside her. Nobody said anything for a few seconds, and then they began talking at the same time. Addie said, "He can't stay here." Mike simultaneously said, "He's going to stay here." They looked at each other, neither was smiling. Finally, he said, "Okay, Addie, you go first."

Addie was silent for a moment then said, "Mike, I respect you for what you are trying to do. This shows the kind of man that everybody should strive to be. But, this time, you have gone too far. You don't know enough about this man to bring him into your home. You have your wife and daughter to think about. He could be an axe murderer for all you know."

He tried not to laugh. He was thoughtful for a moment before he began. Then he said, "Addie, I admire you and all you have done for my family. I know you have made us your family, and I can't begin to tell you how much that means to me and to Cindy, too. I also want you to know that I would never bring a stranger into my home if I wasn't certain my wife, daughter, and you would be safe." He explained that he had done a background check on Mr. Hood and what it uncovered. He went on to explain, that there was something about this old man that touched his heart. He said that if this was his father he would hope that there would be somebody in the world who would see the good in him and help him at this stage of his life. He told Addie that Mr. Hood had chased Allison down in the woods during the night. He had heard her as she approached his camp, coming through the woods between their house and the Raver house. She knew there were policemen at our house, he explained, so she left the highway and went up the Raver's driveway into the woods, and cut through to come in the back way. She had not planned on anyone being in the woods, and when she came upon Mr. Hood's camp, she was surprised when he heard her. "Of course, I had told Mr. Hood about Allison's escape, and he tried to subdue her. However, she stabbed him in the leg and was able to escape his grasp. Mr. Hood made his way to the policeman outside, and that's how we knew she was in the area. He could have bled to death if the cut had been much deeper. As it is, I am thankful that he is okay and we are all safe."

Addie sat there for a few minutes, and finally said. "Well, he can stay here for a few days, but I'm not going to wait on him. He can eat when we eat, and he can do for himself."

Mike inwardly chuckled, and said, "I wouldn't want you to do anything more than that. You have your hands full, just taking care of me and my family, and we love you for what you do. I'll do what I can as well, to take some of the load off you."

Addie mumbled something, but Mr. Smith didn't ask her to repeat it. He knew that the obstacle was overcome, and that was the important thing. Now he prayed that his instincts about Mr. Hood were good, and he was not making a mistake.

Addie announced that she needed to go into the house as company was coming for dinner. Mike had forgotten that this was the night that the minister and his wife were coming over. His stomach started to churn. He hated to admit it, but he was scared about this. He had been as solid as a rock earlier in the morning when the police were at his house, and the dogs were searching the woods for someone who wanted to harm his daughter, but now at the prospect of the minister coming to dinner, he knew he was scared.

He went into the house to check on Mr. Hood's progress. He was still in the bathroom, and Mike could not hear any noise from there. He knocked on the door and asked, "Are you okay?"

"Yes, but I have a problem."

"What is it?"

"I don't have any clothes to put on, and I can't come out naked."

"That's right, don't come out without clothes. I'll find you something to wear," Mike assured him.

After a quick search through his drawers, Mike returned with underwear, pajamas, and a bathrobe. Mr. Hood partially opened the door and retrieved the clothes through the crack. When he looked at them, he laughed. He could not remember that he had ever worn pajamas before. However, when he put them on, he thought that he might have been missing out on one of life's simple pleasures. The fabric was soft next to his skin, and they smelled like the outdoors. They were warm. He had been cold ever since he was awakened. He had gotten wet, and the hospital was cold. The shower had helped warm him and these pajamas, though short in the arms and legs, were quite nice he thought. He put on the robe and opened the door.

Mike was amazed at the transformation. He had never seen Mr. Hood in anything except jeans and his denim jacket and one of his two plaid flannel shirts. He looked distinguished as he stepped into the hallway. He must have felt good too, as he attempted to twirl. The twirl almost turned into a tumble as his injured leg gave way under him. Mike caught him, and was shocked as he felt the bones of this old man's frame. He was so thin. Tears rushed to his eyes, and he prayed that they not betray him. His prayer was answered, as Mr. Hood was not looking at him, but was reaching for the wall to keep from falling. Mike steadied him and brushed the tears away.

The two men made it into the bedroom and Mr. Hood sat on the side of the opened sofa bed. He was unsure about what he should do. He was so tired. He hadn't gotten much sleep the night before, and the loss of blood and pain had drained him of what energy he had. He wanted to lie down, but he didn't know if it would be okay. It was after all the middle of the morning.

Mike sensed this and immediately began making moves to help him into bed. He pulled back the covers and asked if he needed his help. Mr. Hood said he could manage by himself, but his face gave away the pain he was experiencing. Once he was settled in, Mike asked him if the doctor had given him anything for pain. Mr. Hood said they had numbed his leg before stitching it up, and had given him a prescription, but admitted he didn't have enough money to have it filled at the hospital pharmacy.

"Where is the prescription?"

"In my pants pocket in the bathroom." His eyes showed his embarrassment as he remembered that he had left his dirty clothes in the bathroom. He attempted to sit up, but the pain was so severe, he just groaned. Mike gently settled him back and told him he would retrieve everything from the bathroom, and he could get the prescription from his pocket.

When this had been completed, Mike left the tired injured man to rest and went downstairs to tell Addie that he was safely tucked in bed, and would probably sleep for a while.

Addie muttered and mumbled as she went about preparing for this evening's dinner with the preacher.

"I need to go to the pharmacy to have a prescription filled. Will you be all right with Mr. Hood in the house?"

"I guess so, but I still hope he isn't an axe murderer."

Mike laughed as he went out the door, and prayed that Mr. Hood only used the axe he had seen at his camp to chop fire wood, and was not a serial killer disguised as a frail old man.

Addie went about her chores, with an eye trained toward the stairs and an ear open for any noise that Mr. Hood might be awake. She had gone upstairs a couple of times, and could hear gentle snoring coming from his room.

Mike returned with the prescription, but he, too, found Mr. Hood sleeping, so he left it with Addie. He knew that while Addie would complain, she would not allow his guest to suffer any further while he was in their home.

What time is it? he wondered. *Where am I?* Mr. Hood came from his deep sleep to confusion. He looked around, and he knew he was not in his tent. He wasn't in a hospital. He looked toward the window and could see light around the edge of the shade. It was daytime. Why was he sleeping in a strange place in the daytime? As he turned, the pain shot through his leg, and his memory was instantly restored. He remembered being stabbed. He remembered going to the hospital, and he knew he was in the Smiths' house. He, however, didn't know what time it was. He tried to locate a clock in the room, but he didn't see one. He listened, and the house was quiet. Was he alone? He finally negotiated his body until he was able to sit on the side of the sofa bed. He tried to stand, but the pain in his leg was so bad that he lost his balance, and this time he fell to the floor.

The unmistakable thud did not go unheard by Addie. She had been listening for sounds that the guest was awake, but this was not a sound she wanted to hear. She ran up the stairs and knocked on the door to the study. She heard him groaning as he was attempting to lift his body off the floor and back onto the bed. She didn't wait for an answer. She went in just as he was raising himself. She grabbed him under his arms. Together they were able to get him on the bed, but his pain was evident in his contorted face. She told him to stay right there as she went to get the pain medication. Her thoughts were racing. *This man is a skeleton*, she thought. She had been so shocked as she helped lift him. He was so light, and his bones were evident as she touched his rib cage. "He is nothing but skin and bones," she said out loud, "I'll have to fatten him up."

Addie got the pain medicine and antibiotics. She poured a glass of milk and picked up a yeast roll she had just taken from the oven. She had noticed that one of the prescriptions had said to take with food. *This will be a start,* she thought. She went back up the stairs and was out of breath. "I'm not used to moving this quickly," she realized.

Mr. Hood gratefully took the medication and the food. He drank the glass of milk without stopping. Addie wondered how long it had been since he had had a cold glass of milk. He broke off a piece of the roll and put it in his mouth. He had gotten into a position that was not as painful, and Addie could see that he had once been a very handsome man. The years had not been good to him, and his face was extremely thin. His skin reminded her of tanned leather. However, there was something in his eyes that made her feel comfortable. *He has kind eyes,* she thought.

Mr. Hood was in a dilemma. He needed to go to the bathroom, but he didn't want to say anything to Addie who seemed intent on staying in the room with him. Finally, he asked her if she could help him stand. She stood beside him and placed her arms around his back with a hand in each armpit. She lifted, and he pushed up with his hands, and together they stood him. He steadied himself, and started to walk. Addie kept holding him until she realized he was going to the bathroom, and he seemed to be able to make it on his own. She told him she was going to let go, and he was relieved. He appreciated her help, and he didn't want to offend her, but he also didn't want her to think she needed to go to the bathroom. Addie, too, was relieved that he could walk alone. She was not looking forward to going into the bathroom with him.

Addie went to the kitchen and fixed a bowl of cottage cheese and canned peaches. She placed a few crackers around the bowl. She took this back to Mr. Hood's room, and placed it along with a big glass of iced tea on the table beside the sofa bed. She straightened the sheets and fixed the covers so that he could get back in bed and pull them up if he got cold. As she left the room, she heard him unlock the bathroom door, so she hurried on down the stairs.

Mr. Hood was surprised to see the food on the table. He sat down on the bed and looked around the room. From this position, he could see more clearly and saw a clock which said it was 2:37. He picked up the bowl of cottage cheese and placed a piece of peach on the spoon. When he put it in his mouth, he just held it there. It tasted so good. He had not had a peach since last summer when he picked peaches in Georgia. The man he worked for was kind enough to allow him to stay through the season, even though his production was far below the other migrant workers. He was paid by the box, and was given a place to sleep. This canned peach was almost as sweet as a fresh warm peach right from the tree. The cold cottage cheese felt good as he swallowed it, and the sweet iced tea was almost like nectar.

Mr. Hood finally got the courage to lift his legs onto the bed. The pain shot through him, but this time he was braced for it. First his good leg, then his injured one. Now he was back in bed, and he scooted until his head was resting on the pillow. He wasn't sure what he was supposed to be doing, but this felt really good to him.

Addie listened from downstairs. She knew he had returned to the study, and now she heard nothing. She would wait a few minutes and go up to check on him. When she did, she heard the gentle snores, as Mr. Hood once again was sleeping.

The school bus was just pulling up when Addie rounded the curve in the driveway. She walked toward Mary Margaret, and could see that she looked very tired. *She should have stayed home today*, thought Addie. Mary Margaret walked toward her, and Addie reached out to take her book bag. Mary Margaret didn't argue as it was taken from her hand. Addie asked her about her day, and she said it had been okay. She said everybody wanted to know about Allison. Addie was not surprised. Mary Margaret said she just told them that Allison was safe, and that's all she knew. "I didn't want to talk about it," said Mary Margaret. "I just want it to go away," she said. "I just want my old life back, where nobody cared about what I did, and I never felt like I was in danger," she sobbed. As she said this, she looked at Addie. I'm sorry. I didn't mean to be rude." Addie reached down and put her arm around the tiny body, and told her she understood. She silently wished she was nine years old again. She might cry too.

Chapter 57

Mike and Cindy came home at 4:00. This was early for both of them, but Cindy wanted to help Addie finish up dinner, and Mike wanted to see if Mr. Hood needed anything.

The two women went about setting the table and putting the finishing touches on the meal preparation. Addie was serving savory chicken squares, a combination of white chicken meat, cream cheese, a little onion, a little mayonnaise, and a few other seasonings, which were all mixed together and placed in the center of a crescent roll rectangle and then the edges were pulled together to make a square. This was dipped in butter and then into crushed seasoned croutons and baked. It was one of Addie's favorite recipes, and it made an impressive presentation. She was making a brown rice casserole, and steaming fresh asparagus in a lemon butter sauce. She wanted *her family* to make a good impression on the preacher.

Addie knew that he was often served chicken when he visited the homes of his congregation, but she was certain he didn't get chicken fixed like this very often. Addie also knew that the preacher's wife did not eat pork. It seems that when they first came to Left Fork they were invited to visit someone in the congregation who raised pigs. On the first visit they were shown cute little pink piglets. On the second visit as they were eating pork loin, she asked about the cute little baby pigs and discovered they were eating one of them. From that day forward, she swore off pork of any kind.

When she took the German chocolate cake from the pantry, Cindy gasped. It was so beautiful. Addie had prepared it the day before so that the moisture from the coconut-pecan filling could penetrate the three cake layers. Addie knew that this was the minister's favorite dessert, and most of the other ladies in the church used boxed cake mix and canned frosting, but Addie would have no part of that. She continued to use the recipe on the baking chocolate package, and would only serve the *real thing* as she called it.

Mike went upstairs and didn't hear any noise coming from Mr. Hood's room, so he gently knocked. Mr. Hood said, "Come in," and Mike opened the door to find the old man propped up on the pillows looking at a magazine. He chuckled to himself at the sight. It could have been anybody's grandfather recuperating from an illness instead of a homeless person recuperating from a stab wound, which had been inflicted by a troubled little girl. *This could make a good book*, he thought. The two men exchanged greetings, and Mr. Hood attempted to sit up even straighter.

Mike sat on the side of the bed so that Mr. Hood would not feel that he had to get up. It was determined by their conversation that the patient felt rested, and the pain medication had taken effect. He seemed to be resting comfortably. Mr. Hood thanked Mike for getting the prescriptions filled, and offered to pay him back with his first wages. Mike said he would hear nothing further about that. He told Mr. Hood that he felt guilty that the injury had come about as he was trying to protect his family, and it was the least he could do to pay for the medication.

Mike explained that the company house was coming along nicely. All the materials which had been stored in there had been removed, and the painters were already making headway. The kitchen was in good shape, and it only needed some new appliances. The linoleum on the floor was worn, and he said that new flooring was ordered and would be put in when the painting was done.

Mr. Hood listened intently, and tears filled his eyes. He had not lived in a house for so many years, except to spend an occasional night in an abandoned one; and to be moving into one which was going to be his very own was more than he could fathom—especially one that was being fixed up just for him.

He attempted to speak, but words would not come out. Tears streamed down his face. Mike was shaken as he saw the emotion on his friend's face, and he, too, started to cry. Nobody said anything, but the two grown men sat in the shadowy room and cried. Mr. Hood found his voice first, and though it was more like a croak, he attempted to say, "Thank you."

Mike took his hand and held it. Between the sobs he told Mr. Hood that it was not necessary to thank him. He explained that Mr. Hood would be earning the house as part of his wages for working at the mill.

The old man knew that Mike was doing more than was necessary for him. He knew that he could have gotten a night watchman without providing him a place to live, but he was more grateful than he could begin to express.

The aroma from the kitchen had reached upstairs, and Mr. Hood said that something smelled good. Mike explained that the minister and his wife were coming to dinner and that Addie had prepared something special. "I'll bring you up a plate when everything is ready. In the meantime, is there anything you need? Would you like something else to drink?"

"I could use something to drink if it's not too much trouble."

Mike said it was no trouble and it was determined that a glass of milk would serve the need nicely.

As he came down the stairs, he was bowled over by the dining room table. It had been set with the best china, and crystal candle holders held tall, tapered, gold candles. The crystal stemware sparkled under the soft light of the new chandelier.

The chandelier was a sight to behold, as the cuts in the center crystal pineapple sparkled. The brass hardware shone, and Mike had never been more proud of his home than he was at that moment. He and Cindy had never had many opportunities to use the beautiful china and crystal they had gotten for wedding presents and they had continued to collect over the 15 years they had been married. Much of it had been stored in boxes in New York, but tonight it was beautifully displayed on their new dining room table, and he was rightfully proud. As he continued down the stairs he saw that Cindy was standing in the opposite corner of the room just taking in the table. He walked over to her and put his arm around her waist, drew her close, and kissed her on the top of her head. They both laughed as the slight embrace was over.

Addie hustled in with the butter dish and salt and pepper shakers. She said, "Don't you two have something better to do than admire your beautiful table?" They all laughed and were immediately drawn back to the moment.

Mike said he needed to get some milk for Mr. Hood, and asked Addie if she had thought of dinner for him. She looked at him. "Did you think I would let the man go hungry? Of course I thought of him, and his plate is already fixed if you want to go ahead and take it up."

Mike juggled the plate, silverware and glass of milk as he went up the stairs and knocked on the door.

"Come in."

Mike was attempting to reach the door knob when Mary Margaret came out of her room. She saw her father's predicament and went to help. "You know, Dad, a tray might have made this a little easier to handle."

"You're pretty smart for a little girl."

Mary Margaret took the milk and opened the door. She was not prepared for Mr. Hood's appearance in her father's pajamas, and she nearly gasped when she saw him. His arms and legs extended from the too small pajamas as he sat on the side of the bed. He was not expecting Mary Margaret to be with her father, and he immediately attempted to cover himself with a blanket. Mike tried to cover for the shock Mary Margaret had expressed and sat down the plate he was holding on the bedside table. He walked over to his desk and pulled a TV tray from beside it and with a swoop sat it up in front of Mr. Hood.

Mary Margaret put the milk on the tray and helped her father set the silverware beside the plate. The food looked wonderful. The savory chicken squares were golden brown and had a point on the top where the dough had been gathered and twisted together. The brown rice casserole smelled wonderful and the color on the asparagus was brilliant green. The lemon sauce had gotten on Mr. Smith's finger and as he licked it off, his stomach growled. He realized he had not eaten since early this morning, and he was hungry.

Mary Margaret was having a conversation with Mr. Hood, as everything was being put in its place. She asked about his injury, and he said it was nothing and he would be up and about by probably tomorrow. Mike told him not to rush anything. It was more important that he get well. Mr. Hood reminded Mike that he owed him $50.00 in work, and he intended to do it before he moved into the company house. Mike reminded him again that he had risked his life for his family, and that was worth more than any work he could ever do. Mr. Hood said he still had the list Mike had left for him on Monday, and he would get right to it in the next day or so.

Before he could protest further, the doorbell rang. His stomach churned, and he thought he might have to run to the bathroom before he went downstairs. He and Mary Margaret told Mr. Hood they would be back later to get the dishes, and that he should call for them if he needed anything. Mr. Hood said he would be just fine, and as they closed the door, he took the first bite of his chicken square. Mike heard just before the door closed, "Mmm, Mmm, Mmm." He smiled as he heard Cindy invite the minister and his wife into their home.

"Oh, no," he thought, his stomach was really hurting. He told Mary Margaret he needed to go to the bathroom and asked her to go downstairs and tell her mother that he would be there soon. Mike went into the master bedroom, and Mary Margaret went downstairs.

When Cindy saw that she was alone, she asked her to go get her father—that he was in the bedroom with Mr. Hood. Mary Margaret told her mother that her father had gone into their bedroom and that he would be down in a few minutes. Cindy was surprised and disappointed that he was not being a better host. *This is just not like him,* she thought.

Cindy, Mary Margaret and their guests went into the living room where Addie had placed a tray of vegetables and dip. The minister and his wife sat on the sofa and Mary Margaret and her mother each took a chair. A pitcher of tea was on the coffee table with the vegetables, and Cindy offered the preacher and his wife a drink. She stuttered, as she realized that most people think of a *drink* as being an alcoholic beverage, and she wanted to make certain that they didn't think she was offering them liquor. "I mean iced tea!" she blurted out. "I don't mind if I do, how about you, honey," said the minister as he reached for an ice filled glass and started pouring. Cindy was relieved that he had not taken offense. The minister continued pouring until all the glasses were filled, and he had passed them out. By this time, she was relaxing with her guests, but was becoming more agitated that Mike had not made an appearance. The minister passed around the vegetable plate, and assumed the role of host instead of guest with such ease that Cindy didn't realize it was happening.

Addie walked into the room and spoke to the minister and his wife. She looked around, and asked, "Where's Mike?"

"Mary Margaret said he was in the bedroom, but I can't imagine what's taking him so long."

"Mary Margaret, did your father know the preacher and his wife were here?" asked Addie.

"Yes," said Mary Margaret sheepishly. She didn't want to tell them he was in the bathroom, but if they kept on, she would have to say something, she thought.

Addie said, "I'll go up and get him."

Mary Margaret jumped up and before she could stop herself said, "Don't do that Addie, he's in the bathroom. He has an awful stomachache."

Cindy gasped and Addie said, "Well, child, why didn't you say that before. We all have to go to the bathroom, and I guess for him now's as good a time as any—especially after the day we've had."

The preacher chimed in, "I really expected that you would have cancelled dinner tonight after all the hoopla that went on here last night."

"Oh, no, we didn't want to cancel; we have so looked forward to this evening. I'm sure that everything will be all right in a few minutes," Cindy replied.

The conversation continued as Cindy told the minister and his wife about all that had happened, and she finished with the fact that Mr. Hood was recuperating upstairs.

The minister's wife, Nina Cross, asked, "Who exactly is this Mr. Hood?"

"Well, he's a homeless man who has been living in a tent on our property. He made himself known to us, and Mike and he hit it off immediately," Cindy explained.

Nina Cross, who was accustomed to her husband reaching out to anybody in need silently thought, *Cindy Smith must be one trusting soul to allow her* husband to bring a homeless man into their home to stay. "I just don't know if I could do that," she found herself saying.

Cindy explained that he had been thoroughly checked out by the police, and that he would be working as the night watchman at the mill in a few days. As the story unfolded it became more and more unbelievable.

As Addie listened from the kitchen, she thought, *if I was hearing all this for the first time, I'd think these Smith people were nuts instead of just the wonderful people that they are.* As she thought about it all, she wanted to go hug them all. Yes, she thought, *I was upset at first, but God knows this man needs our help, and we have to help him.*"

Ron Cross, the minister said, "Now let me get this straight. Mr. Hood is a drifter, a homeless person, who has been camping on your property. He just came out of the woods one day and announced his presence there. He's going to work as a night watchman at the mill and is going to live in one of the mill houses, and he got stabbed by Allison Kincaid when he attempted to stop her in the middle of the night after she ran away from the facility where her parents had her placed after she was suspended from school for bullying Mary Margaret and many of the other children, is that right?"

As Cindy heard him restate the situation, she almost laughed out loud. "As unbelievable as it sounds, that's the story. It seems that Mr. Hood has even won Addie over. She told me that she helped him get up, and she said he is nothing but skin and bones. She is now on a crusade to fatten the poor man up. Of course, that is a wonderful predicament to be in—to have Addie trying to fatten you up. It's happening to me, and I don't think she's even trying."

Nina Cross said, "I believe in helping him, but it seems to me that he should have stayed in the hospital or maybe in a motel—not right here in your house."

Ron Cross looked at his wife and reminded her that Jesus said, "'When I was hungry you fed me, and when I was naked you clothed me.' These people are living the right life. They are a fine example to our community. They are not talking the talk, they are walking the walk."

Cindy realized that 30 minutes had passed, and her husband had not yet made an appearance. She said she had better go check on him, and excused herself. As she went into the bedroom, she could hear her husband moaning. She went in to find him leaning on the bathroom counter. He was holding a wet wash cloth on his forehead. He was pale, and perspiration was running down his face. She asked him what his symptoms were, and he explained that his stomach hurt, and he had been vomiting. As a nurse, she knew that he was very sick. She took his temperature and it was 102. She got out her blood pressure cuff, and when she realized his blood pressure was 150/100, she said that she was taking him to the emergency room. Mike protested. "You can't do that, we have guests. What will they think?"

"They'll think I was negligent if we stay here and your appendix burst, which is what I think is about to happen, if it hasn't already."

Cindy called for Addie to come up, and she explained the situation to her and asked her to go ahead and feed Mary Margaret and their guests. She asked Addie if she could stay over if Mr. Smith needed the surgery she was expecting. Addie said it would be no trouble.

Addie and Cindy helped Mike down the stairs and Ron and Nina Cross were at the bottom along with Mary Margaret. The nursing personality had taken over and Cindy hurriedly explained the situation. Reverend Cross took the arm Addie had been holding and said he would go to the hospital with them. Cindy said that would not be necessary, that she would phone ahead and have a surgeon waiting in the ER. She insisted that the reverend and his wife stay and enjoy the wonderful dinner that Addie had prepared and suggested that maybe Reverend Cross could meet with Mr. Hood before he left.

As the tail lights of the Smith's car went out of sight around the curve in the driveway, Addie said they had better come on in and eat before the dinner was ruined.

Addie brought in the tray of chicken squares, which by this time had lost a little of their luster. The brown rice casserole was dry enough to begin to crack, and the asparagus was dirty green, instead of the bright green of an hour before. The dinner rolls were no longer warm, and the iced tea glasses on the table had to be emptied as the ice had already melted. Addie replaced the ice and sat down at the table. She had not planned on eating but now it seemed fitting that she join the guests.

Dinner did not go as Addie had earlier imagined it. The conversation was strained, and nobody complimented the food. Addie knew that it was not as good as it could have been. She really didn't even care that there were no compliments. She was worried about Mike, and it was evident that everyone else was too. Reverend Cross chatted with Mary Margaret in an effort to take her mind off her father, but as would be expected, it was to no avail.

Mary Margaret's emotions were stretched about as far as they could stretch. She was tired from losing sleep the night before, and there had been nothing but turmoil surrounding her since January 1. Now her father was sick. He had never been sick. Mary Margaret didn't remember that he had ever even had a cold. He was the healthiest man she knew. Now that he was sick, she was not certain that she could take much more.

Addie excused herself to go get the cake for dessert, but Reverend and Mrs. Cross said they were too full. Addie was again disappointed, but insisted that they take some home with them. They agreed and as they were about to leave, Reverend Cross remembered that Mr. Hood was upstairs. He asked Addie if she would check to see if it was all right that he come up for a moment.

Addie went upstairs and could hear Mr. Hood snoring. She came back and reported that he was asleep. Reverend Cross said he would stop by the next day to visit with him.

Again, they started out the door and the telephone rang. Addie quickly answered it and Mrs. Smith reported that her diagnosis was correct. Mike was being prepped for surgery for appendicitis, and thankfully, it had not ruptured. The surgery should be routine, but she didn't know when she would be home. Addie told her not to worry, that she would take care of everything on the home front.

Reverend and Mrs. Cross were brought up to date, and he said that he would drop off his wife and go stay with Mrs. Smith at the hospital until the surgery was over. Addie was relieved to hear that Cindy was not going to be alone, but she knew that the hospital staff would take good care of her as she was an employee there.

Addie went about clearing the table and Mary Margaret helped. The pots and pans had long since been washed and put away and Addie felt the china and crystal needed to be hand washed. As she filled the sink with hot sudsy water, she got Mary Margaret a linen towel and they silently washed and dried the beautiful dinnerware that Mike and Cindy had not been able to enjoy.

Addie heard footsteps overhead and knew that Mr. Hood was up. She went part way up the stairs and yelled to him to see if he needed any help. He told her that he was fine and was just going to the bathroom. Addie took this opportunity to take him a big piece of German Chocolate cake and a cold glass of milk. She also filled a pitcher with iced water and took up a clean glass. She juggled the tray and went into the room. Mr. Hood's plate had been cleaned. She wondered if he had licked it. There was not a sign of food left. She exchanged the dessert for the dirty dishes and straightened the sheets on Mr. Hood's bed. She was just about to leave when he came into the study.

"Addie, isn't it a little late for you to be here?"

She then realized that he didn't know that Mike had taken ill, so she explained everything to him. Mr. Hood was alarmed, but Addie assured him that Cindy had diagnosed him immediately, and her quick action had taken a serious situation and turned into a not so serious one. She told him to get a good night's sleep, and that she would be staying over if he needed anything. She reminded him that he needed to take his medication, and when he saw that she had brought him the cake, he told her that it was his favorite. His sister used to make it for him before she died, "God rest her soul," he said.

Addie left him to check on Mary Margaret who was already in her pajamas, and under the covers. She knew that she was exhausted and made a decision to keep her home from school tomorrow. *That child needs some rest*, thought Addie. *I'm in charge, and I say she stays home.*" Addie tucked Mary Margaret into bed and said she would like to pray with her.

Addie began, *"Dear Lord—I come to you at the end of another day, and I want to thank you for this one and everything in it. I ask that you be with Mike as he undergoes surgery, and be with Cindy. Be with the doctors and nurses who are tending to him. He is a fine man, Lord, and I know that you will bring him through this and restore him to his health. Be with me and Mary Margaret as we prepare to sleep, that we have the peace to be refreshed tomorrow. Be with Mr. Hood as he recuperates. And, finally, Lord, be with Allison Kincaid and her family as they continue to work through this situation. Give them peace and understanding, and touch Allison's heart that she may come to know you and your way of life. In Jesus' name I pray. Amen."*

Mary Margaret said, "Amen."

Addie tucked her in, turned out the light, and shut the door behind her as she went into the hall. The door to Mr. Hood's room was closed, and she tapped on it gently.

His crackled voice said, "Yes,"

"Is there anything you need?"

"I'm all settled in for the night, thank you."

Addie said, "Good night," and she went downstairs to turn out the lights. She was not ready to go to bed even though her body was feeling its age. Her mind was not ready to be quiet and rest just yet, so she went to sit a spell on the front porch swing. The night was dark and quiet. A soft breeze blew and the tall pines gently swayed and the branches rustled. There was no light anywhere and after Addie's eyes adjusted to the total darkness, she saw the mother deer and her twins. The moon came from behind a cloud and now the spots glowed almost iridescently in the bright light. The tails on the twins twitched, and the mother munched grass as they nursed. Tears sprang to Addie's eyes. *God is so good to me*, thought Addie. *This home, this place, it's such a wonderful place to be. I am blessed to be a part of all this*. She wiped away her tears, and got up to go inside. The mother deer was immediately aware of the movement, and quickly and quietly ushered her young ones into the safety of the dark woods.

Addie shut and locked the front door and went up to the guest room. She put on her nightgown she had worn the night before and got ready for bed. She decided, however, to sleep on the sofa in Mary Margaret's room. She didn't know why she made that decision, but she felt she needed to be near her. When she walked down the hall, she could hear Mr. Hood snoring. She opened the door to Mary Margaret's room and was overcome with love as she saw the child sleeping. Mary Margaret had gotten a photograph of her mother and father and she was hugging it as she slept. Tears streamed down Addie's face when she saw this. *This sweet child is so worried about her parents,* thought Addie. *God, give her a time of peace. She really needs to be a little girl and not to have so many big problems,* Addie silently prayed.

Addie picked up a chenille throw and got a pillow from the closet. She made herself a *nest* on the sofa. *This is surprisingly comfortable,* she thought, and the next thing she heard was a lawnmower outside the house.

Chapter 58

Addie sat up. It was barely daylight judging from the light peaking in around the blinds. *Who is mowing grass at this time of day?* she wondered, as she went to look out a window on the front side of the house. She couldn't see anything, but she knew the sound she heard was a lawnmower. She came back out into the hall and noticed that Mr. Hood's door was open. She peeked around and could clearly see that he was not there. The bathroom door was open, so she hoped he wasn't in there. "Surely, he's not mowing grass as this hour," which she had determined was not quite 7:00 a.m.

Addie went into the guest room and got ready for the day. She was so thankful that she had brought clothes there to keep for emergencies—although she had never really planned on this type of emergency. She went downstairs and on the kitchen table she found a note. It read, "Addie, I have gone to my camp to get me some clean clothes. I'll be back directly." It was signed, "Hood."

I'll bet he rode the lawnmower to his camp, thought Addie. *Pretty clever,* she allowed. She put the coffee in the pot and decided that this morning would be a good morning for a big breakfast. She started making pancakes and put the bacon on to fry. As she did all this, she set the table, and cleaned strawberries for the pancakes. When she heard the lawnmower again, she nearly had breakfast ready.

Mr. Hood rode up to the porch and painfully climbed off the big machine. He had attached his clothing on the back in the basket he had used to haul kerosene to his camp. He hobbled up the steps and was glad to see the front door was already open. He had wondered what he should do if he returned and nobody was up. Should he wait outside or just go on in. He wasn't sure of his place just yet.

However, Addie made it quite clear that he was to come in when she yelled through the opened door that breakfast was on the table. He came in and told her that he needed to put his clothes upstairs. She told him to just leave them in the laundry room, and she would wash them. He protested and said he would do it, but he soon realized that this was a battle he was not going to win and acquiesced.

She told him to sit down, and he followed her command. The kitchen smelled wonderful, and his stomach was growling. Mr. Hood attempted to hide the sound, but Addie heard it and told him to go ahead and eat. "We'll be eating in shifts around here this morning, and you're the first," she explained. As he filled his plate, Addie sat down and put some pancakes and bacon on her plate as well. She had just begun to eat when the telephone rang. She jumped to answer it for two reasons. One, she didn't want it to wake up Mary Margaret, and two, she almost knew it was Cindy reporting on Mike. She was right, it was Cindy.

The surgery had gone well, and he was out of recovery and into a room. He would have to stay in the hospital a day or two and then could come home. She said she was coming home to shower and then would return to work her shift. Addie tried to talk her out of returning to work, but she said she had gotten some sleep and would be just fine. Addie told her that she would have everything ready for her when she got there.

True to her word, Addie had everything prepared for her arrival. Her clothes for the day were laid out on her bed, and her toiletries were set up in the bathroom. She was amazed that Addie had thought of everything. After her shower and a good breakfast, she was back on the road to the hospital in record time. She was disappointed though that she had not seen Mary Margaret, but agreed that it was a good day to keep her home from school. She did peek in and was touched to see the photograph next to her. Addie explained that Mary Margaret had apparently gone to sleep hugging it, and Cindy was so moved that the burning started in the back of her eyes. She knew, however, that she could not cry. She had to stay focused in order to get through the day.

Addie stayed upstairs after she left and cleaned up the bathrooms and made Mr. Hood's bed. When she returned to the kitchen, she noticed that Mr.

Hood was no longer there. His whereabouts were soon discovered though when Addie heard the lawnmower start. She looked out to see him make his first swipe across the yard. "He's going to make a mess, mowing in this heavy dew," Addie said to no one, but she went into the kitchen and left him to his mowing.

She heard her scream, and then heard her run across the floor. *Mary Margaret is awake*, thought Addie. After a quick trip to the bathroom Mary Margaret yelled, "Is anyone up? I'm late for school." By this time Addie had come upstairs and was trying to explain that she wasn't going to school today, but Mary Margaret was not listening. She was reaching in her drawer for a t-shirt and was looking in the closet for a pair of shorts. Then reality struck her, and she stopped. "Addie, did my daddy die? Is that why I'm not going to school?" Addie saw the worried look on the tiny face surrounded by the brown hair, which she suddenly realized needed cutting.

"No, Honey. Your daddy is just fine. He came through the surgery just fine and will be home in a day or two. I just thought that you needed to rest. You have been through so much. Today is just for you to do nothing."

"But I can't do *nothing* today. Today is important for me. It's my day to work in the garden, and Mr. Clark is bringing Martha, the horse, so that I can plow with her. I have to go to school today. He's coming at 10:00 o'clock, and it's almost ten now. I hope that Mrs. Stancil hasn't given the job to somebody else. It's my job, and I have to do it," she implored.

"All right, child." Get your shoes and socks on, and I'll call the school. You can eat some toast in the car on the way." Addie went off to make her call and to fix some toast. "This child is going to get the best of me yet," she muttered to herself, and she went down the stairs.

They arrived just as Mr. Clark was unloading Martha from the trailer. Mary Margaret hurried in and took the note Addie had written for her. Addie spoke to Mr. Clark, and she quickly brought him up to date on the happenings around the Smith household. "I can't remember when we've ever had such excitement at Left Fork," he mused, and Addie had to agree. She left to go to see Sharon Applegate as he went around the building with Martha.

Mrs. Applegate was on her front porch stringing green beans and was surprised to see Addie's truck pull up to the curb. She lay aside the produce and waited while Addie made her way up. The two hugged, and when

Mrs. Applegate asked, "What brings you by here this morning?" Addie commenced to telling her about the preacher arriving and Mr. Smith getting sick, and brought her up to date with the report from Cindy earlier this morning. Mrs. Applegate was shocked.

"I don't remember when we've had so much excitement in Left Fork," said Mrs. Applegate, and Addie laughed as she said, "That's just what Orville Clark had to say."

The two old friends reminisced and got caught up on each other's children. They shared such a long friendship, that time was immaterial to them. If they saw each other daily it was wonderful, or if it was only in church on Sunday it was okay. They knew that the bond was everlasting, and they always enjoyed any time they had together. Addie stayed so long that they shared lunch. Then she remembered that Mr. Hood was at the house by himself. Addie was ashamed that she had forgotten all about him, but Mrs. Applegate assured her that he was a man who was accustomed to fending for himself, and he would be capable of taking care of himself for a few hours in such a fine house as he now found himself. Addie laughed, but insisted that she needed to get back just to make sure he had some lunch.

Mrs. Applegate laughed to herself as she remembered that Addie had just told her a day or so ago that he was probably an axe murderer, and here she was now rushing back to see that he had lunch.

Addie saw the car before she saw the person. She knew that Reverend Cross was at the Smith house. Has something gone wrong? I shouldn't have been gone so long, she thought as she pulled onto the parking pad. Her anxiety was short lived, however, as she saw Reverend Cross and Mr. Hood sharing lunch down by the pond. She walked down, and the two men stood. Mr. Hood was a little slower than Reverend Cross, but she noticed that his mobility was improving by the moment.

She immediately saw that they were enjoying leftovers from the night before. When Mr. Hood realized that she was looking at the food, he immediately started explaining that he didn't think she would mind. Addie said she was glad somebody was enjoying the food, because it had lost some of its glow the night before.

The telephone was ringing when Addie entered the house. She rushed over to answer it and was glad to hear Cindy's voice on the other end. She reported that Mike was doing so well that he would be coming home with her after work that evening. She explained that his surgery had been done laproscopically which would allow a shorter hospital stay and the recovery period would be much shorter.

When they hung up, Addie went upstairs to prepare the Smiths' bedroom for the patient. She snatched the sheets off the bed, and the clean sheets were snapped as she spread them across the mattress.

She went from room to room to be certain that everything was in order. She was surprised to find that Mr. Hood had closed up the sofa bed, and there were no signs of a sick person in that room. All the dishes had been removed, and it looked as though it had never been used.

Mary Margaret's room was cleaned up and the bed had been made. The photograph which she had held the night before now sat on her bedside table.

Addie heard voices downstairs and knew that Reverend Cross and Mr. Hood would be bringing in the dishes from lunch. She picked up the sheets and dirty towels she had gathered and started down the stairs. One of the sheets was hanging to the floor, and she stepped on it just as she reached the middle step. She felt it underfoot, and knew she was going to fall, but could not stop the situation. As she fell, she silently prayed, Dear God, don't let me break a hip. She tried not to scream and wasn't sure if she had or not, but the two men came running from the kitchen to find her at the bottom of the stairs in a heap of dirty laundry. She figured that she had made enough noise as she bumped down the stairs to alert the dead even if she didn't scream.

Reverend Cross reached her first and was picking away the dirty towels and washcloths. A sheet had become entwined with her legs, and he was attempting to delicately remove it so as to not injure her further and to keep her dignity intact. He reached down to help her up, but Addie couldn't move. She was laughing too hard to get up. She was nearly hysterical as she envisioned herself bumping down the stairs with dirty laundry flying about her.

Reverend Cross thought she was crying, and he knelt beside her and tried to console her saying, "Don't cry, Addie, dear, everything will be all right." The more he crooned comforting words to her, the more hysterical she

Into Addie's Arms

became. She knew she was not injured, except maybe her pride was a little hurt.

Mr. Hood was pacing in a semi circle around her as he said, "Oh, my, oh, my," over and over again. Tears were running down Addie's cheeks and were contributing to the theory that she was crying; and, therefore, she must be injured.

Reverend Cross finally stood up and said he was calling 911. With this Addie knew that she had to gain enough composure to stop this move. She shouted, "No!"

Reverend Cross stopped in his tracks and looked at her. She finally was able to mutter the words, "Okay, I'm okay."

He was relieved to hear her say this, but the tears were still rolling down her cheeks, and he wasn't totally convinced. He came back to her and said in a voice as serious as when he is giving an invitation at the end of his sermon, "Now, Addie, dear, I have to make certain that you are not seriously injured."

Addie looked at him and tried to regain some sort of composure, but the hysteria was on the verge of exploding again.

He held up three fingers and said, "Now, dear, how many fingers am I holding up?"

With this, she couldn't control herself any longer, and the laughter began anew. By this time, however, Reverend Cross assessed the situation a little closer and realized that the scene was indeed hysterical. Here the three of them were in the foyer of a home where none of them lived surrounded by dirty linens. One was totally entwined in the laundry, one was crouched down holding up three fingers, and the third was pacing in a semi circle around the other two. The best part of it all was that he realized that Addie was really okay, maybe a few bruises would appear on her body as well as her dignity, but she was going to be fine.

Mr. Hood on the other hand was not certain of the situation. He had taken a seat on the stairs. Reverend Cross looked up and realized how pale he had become. His attention immediately went from Addie to Mr. Hood, and when Addie followed his gaze, she, too, gained control and was untangling herself from the sheets to tend to him.

Reverend Cross took Mr. Hood's hand and it felt cold. He took his pulse and was relieved to determine that it was fine at 80 beats per minute.

Addie sat down beside Mr. Hood and tried to engage him in conversation, but he just sat there for a few seconds, and finally said, "Oh, Addie, I thought you had broken your hip."

With this, Addie began to giggle again, but quickly regained her composure when she realized how concerned he was about her.

He continued by saying, "A lot of *old* women die when they break their hips, Addie."

With this, she became indignant and said, "Why you old coot, who are you calling *old*?"

She got up and started gathering up the linens. Reverend Cross attempted to help, but she told him, "I put them there, I can pick them up, thank you." He stepped back as she reached to pick up a towel on which he was standing.

She left the two men in the foyer and mumbled something about, "Who was old around here" as she went through the kitchen to the laundry room.

Reverend Cross told Mr. Hood, "We should probably make ourselves scarce for a little while. I think you've insulted her. Did I hear her say something about an axe murderer?"

Mr. Hood realized that Reverend Cross was probably right, so he attempted to get up and with the help of the Reverend he stood, and they hurried out the front door.

Mary Margaret came around the curve in the driveway and was startled to see the car parked there. She knew it belonged to Reverend Cross, and she ran to see if anything was wrong. She saw the two men sitting on the porch swing and couldn't tell anything by that. She rushed up to the steps and knew her alarm was unwarranted when Reverend Cross was tying a fishing fly. They greeted her, and she went on in to find Addie.

Into Addie's Arms

Addie was beginning to fix dinner. She was cooking macaroni and had something in a skillet that smelled good and bad at the same time. It sort of smelled like bacon frying, but there was another odor that was strange to Mary Margaret. Addie didn't know she was there until she heard her say, "What is that strange smell?" Addie turned around to see Mary Margaret standing there as dirty as a little pig, with the tiny forefinger of her right hand under that perfectly shaped little nose.

Addie still stung from Mr. Hood's remark about old women, which she had taken very personally. She was beginning to ache in more places than she cared to count. That, combined with all the tension she had been carrying over Mike's illness and surgery and Mr. Hood's incident with Allison Kincaid caused her to unleash her frustration when she saw this little girl turn her nose up at wonderfully steamed cabbage.

Tears began to stream down Addie's face. She looked at Mary Margaret, who was totally unaware that she was the cause of Addie's pained expression. She ran to her and put her arms around Addie's waist. She said, "Addie, Addie, what's wrong? Did my daddy die?" With this, Addie sucked up all the fury she had been feeling and knelt down to her level. "No, no, child, your daddy is just fine. He'll be home in a few hours. You're just witnessing the emotions of a foolish old woman." They hugged each other and finally Addie asked Mary Margaret if she had left any dirt in the garden.

Mary Margaret beamed as she looked down at herself. "Oh, Addie, it was so wonderful. Martha is such a neat horse. I hope that someday I can have a horse of my very own. I would never ask for anything else if I could just have a horse."

Addie laughed with the child and told her that she should go get cleaned up and do her homework before her parents came home from the hospital. Mary Margaret started up the stairs and came back carrying a wash cloth saying she had found it on the stairs. Addie snatched it from her hands and went toward the laundry room.

Mike and Cindy arrived at about 5:00 p.m. Mr. Hood had gone upstairs to rest, and Reverend Cross had gone home. Mary Margaret had taken a shower, changed her clothes, and finished her homework when she heard the uproar of their arrival. Addie was ushering Mike into the house as Cindy was following. She looked tired, and this did not go unnoticed by Addie, who ordered her to go straight up and have a shower before dinner. Cindy protested that she had to help Mike get settled, but Addie assured her that she had everything under control and was nearly pushing them up the stairs as Mary Margaret was attempting to greet her parents.

When she hugged her father, tears streamed down her cheeks. All the fear and anxiety she had experienced surfaced as she reached around his waist, and he grimaced as she squeezed him a little too tightly. Cindy and Addie both recognized what was occurring and reached toward her. However, Mike held up a hand to them to let them know that he was all right, and it was important that he and Mary Margaret share this moment.

Finally, the entourage was able to move from the staircase and on into the master bedroom suite where Addie had prepared the bed for her patient, and the shower was all ready for its next occupant.

When he was settled, Addie asked Mary Margaret to come with her to set the table, both as a need she had and as a way to allow Mike to have his needed rest.

Mr. Hood could hear all the commotion, but he stayed in his room. He did not want to interfere with the homecoming. He knew he was welcome, but decided the family was best left alone right then.

As he lay in the dim room he thought of how his life had changed in just the past few weeks. He had spent so much of his life alone and often in near hiding as he pitched his tent in woods surrounding homes and along busy highways. He was always careful to find a place that was secluded, but attempted to stay away from others in his same situation. He remembered a place in Georgia near a mission where men had created a tent camp along a busy highway. They drank at night and begged money during the day. A few of them worked as day laborers, but for the most part they just lived off others. They ate their meals at the mission. The camp was littered, and the stench was bad in the summer heat. Mr. Hood felt he was different from that sort. He had chosen his lifestyle while the others had become victims of theirs. He especially felt bad for the homeless families he encountered—most of whom found themselves in that situation by a series of unfortunate circumstances. Now he was safe in this beautiful home and had hopes of his own home in just a few days along with a job which would be paying him $1,000.00 a month, more than he had ever dreamed of earning. He realized that God was blessing him.

Mary Margaret set the table, and Addie got all the food prepared. Cindy came down and looked a little more rested even though she had chosen to put on a nightgown and robe. She thanked Addie for taking over and handling the house and their homecoming so well. She hugged her, and both women were wiping away tears when they turned back toward Mary Margaret. The exhaustion was thick in the room.

Cindy prepared a plate for her husband and started back up the stairs with it. Addie asked her to knock on Mr. Hood's door and tell him that dinner was ready. However, he was coming down the stairs just as she started up. They exchanged greetings, and she told him that dinner was ready. He thanked her and started toward the kitchen.

Dinner was quiet. Mary Margaret did most of the talking as she told her mother about Martha and her experiences in the garden earlier in the day. She again expressed her desire for a horse, but it seemed to fall on deaf ears as her mother didn't comment one way or the other.

The dishes were cleared and Addie was getting ready to go home. A storm was brewing, and she was hoping to get home before it hit. However, the sound of the rain pelting against the windows told her she had missed her target. Now she had to decide whether to wait it out or go on in the storm. She was tired, and she really wanted to be at home. The family was settled in, and she decided to go ahead and drive the short distance in the rain. Mike and Cindy were already in their bedroom and Mary Margaret was reading in her room. Mr. Hood had gone back to his room as well.

Addie gathered up her purse and dashed to the truck. She left without saying good-bye. The large rain drops splashed on the ground and dirt splattered onto her pant legs. She had not used an umbrella, and her thick curly hair hid water which snaked its way to her scalp. She arrived at the truck, jumped in and wiped her face with her hands. She shivered as the cold rain seemed to chill her to the bone. The truck roared to life as she turned the key, and the wipers seemed to be keeping the same beat as Addie's heart. Swipe, swipe, thump, thump, swipe, swipe, thump, thump. They attempted to wipe away the pounding water. Soon the sounds of the pounding rain, the wiper blades, and her heart were taken over by the unmistakable sound of hail as it drummed against her truck. The small balls bounced off the hood. They accumulated on the edge of the windshield as they were pushed by the blades, and soon they were no longer little bouncing balls, but were as large as golf balls and then the size of baseballs.

She suddenly regretted her decision to go home when she had. She wished she was safely back in the Smith house surrounded by those who loved her. As she drove, she realized that she had not told them good-bye; and they would be worried, not only about the storm, but about her safety. She decided that it would be better to continue driving instead of pulling to the side of the road. She could see the large pines and oaks being twisted by the ever increasing winds. She knew that if she pulled to the side of the road, one of the trees could be uprooted and fall onto her truck. "A moving target is harder to hit," she heard herself say as she inched along the darkened road. She suddenly realized that the electricity to the area was out. "Why am I such an old fool woman?" she asked herself, and then laughed out loud. "I am not only an old fool woman, but I talk to myself," she went on to say. The one-sided conversation continued as she drove toward her apartment. It had never looked so good when she finally reached her destination. The hail had stopped and the rain and wind continued. The area was dark, and she was the only one on the streets. "Everybody else has better sense," she continued as she walked up the stairs and opened the door.

The telephone was ringing, and she rushed to answer it. Cindy was on the other end, and she was relieved when she heard Addie say, "Hello." The two spoke for just a moment and decided that it was best not to remain on the phone in the storm, and the call had only been made to see if Addie was safe. Both women felt better. Addie was glad to be home, and Cindy was glad that her friend was safely there.

Chapter 59

Addie awoke on Thursday morning with the sun shining brightly into her bedroom. *What time is it?* she wondered. It was almost always dark when she woke up. She looked at the clock and found that it was blinking 12:00. She then remembered the storm the night before and that she had gone to bed with no electricity. She got up and turned on the television. At least there was power, and after a few minutes she realized that it was 7:15. *Oh, no,* she thought. She was late for work. Addie hurriedly showered and dressed and arrived at the Smith home at 8:00. Her wet hair gave away the speed with which she had dressed. After parking her truck, she began to notice the dents all over it. She was circling the vehicle when Mike stepped onto the front porch and sang out a greeting. Addie half-heartedly waved to him as she surveyed the damage. Her truck, while it was old, was the best she had and could probably ever hope to have. It was dependable, and for all practical purposes not in bad shape. Now, however, it looked as though it had been beaten with a baseball bat. She was heart sick. She only carried liability insurance, and there was no way she could afford to have it repaired. *Oh, well, she thought, at least it still runs.*

Mike had come into the driveway and was equally upset as he surveyed the damage. He had never seen a vehicle that had been in a hail storm, and he had never even imagined the damage that could be done. He immediately looked toward the garage and was glad to see that no car was parked outside. He wondered if Cindy's new car had been outside in the storm. She had already gone to work, and he couldn't remember if she put it in the garage the night before or not. They had both gotten new vehicles the week before, and now he wondered if one of them was a near total.

He put his arm around Addie and they walked inside. She explained that she had overslept because the power had been off, and he laughed at her making excuses for being late. "Addie, my dear Addie, you don't ever have to explain your actions to us. We know that if you're not here, you have a good reason. Anyway, if I paid you for all the hours you are here, I would have to take a second job."

They went inside and Mr. Hood was coming down the stairs. He was dressed and told Mike that he would be taking the mower into the woods to start gathering up his belongings for his upcoming move. Mike said that was a good idea as he poured himself and Addie a cup of coffee and sat at the table. He offered Mr. Hood a cup for the road, but he declined saying he had already had his cup for the day.

Addie sat at the table with Mike, and the mower could be heard as it started up. She asked him how he was feeling, and he explained that he was feeling remarkably well. He apologized to Addie for ruining her dinner party, and she was shocked at his remark. "You couldn't help that. You were a very sick person."

He laughed as he explained that he had been feeling sick for a couple of weeks and thought it was just nerves at the idea of spending time with the preacher. He told Addie that he had never known a preacher before, and he truly was nervous about the evening.

Addie was shocked at his honesty. She had been raised in the church and had always been around preachers. She couldn't imagine a man like Mr. Smith being nervous about something like that. She looked him square in the eye, and she said, "Mike, you are one of the finest men I have ever known. You have a good heart. You love your family. You love your job, and you are a good provider. All of those things are wonderful. However, until you know that God gave us His son, Jesus, who died on the cross for our sins and you are willing to put your life in faith in His hands, you are never going to be the man that you could be. Something will always be missing in your life, and you will forever be searching for that something. Do you know that?"

Mike Smith sat there sipping his coffee, looking into the warm eyes of this woman and he answered, "Addie, I know a lot of things, but until I met you and your Jesus, I don't think I knew that something was missing in my life. However, you are such a fine Christian woman that it only takes a few minutes with you to know that you are set apart. You have a joy that spreads like sunshine on a July day. You have a peace that makes people want to be more like you, and your spirit fills the room when you lift your voice in song, even when you clean the toilets, but especially when you sing about His Amazing Grace, and your face is lifted to the heavens in front of the congregation. I always thought I was a good man," he continued, "and probably thought I would go to heaven because I was so good. However, since you invited me to church and I heard the plan of salvation, I now know that I could never be good enough to get to heaven. I have to accept that gift from God. You see, Addie, until Mother's Day, I had not heard about the Jesus you know and the way to get to spend eternity with Him."

By this time Addie had tears streaming down her face. She could not believe that a man his age and with his education had never heard the plan of salvation before. She had always assumed that everybody knew that. She couldn't remember a time when she didn't. "Mike, I'm sorry. I didn't realize that."

He handed her a napkin, and she wiped her eyes and then blew her nose. They stared at each other. She not knowing what to say next, and he not knowing what to do next. A few seconds passed, and the doorbell rang. They both stood, and Addie moved quickly to open to the door to find Reverend Cross standing there.

She knew that God had sent him at that pivotal moment in the life of Mike Smith. She *invited* him in, and the three of them returned to the kitchen. The two gentlemen were discussing Mike's health, and Addie brought the conversation back to the point of salvation.

"Reverend Cross, Mike and I were just discussing salvation, and he said he had never heard the plan of salvation until you explained it to him in church on Mother's day. Until that time he thought you got to heaven by being good. I told him that he had to know that Jesus died on the cross so that our sins could be forgiven."

Reverend Cross took over. "Yes, Addie, I know that. Mike and I had some time to spend together at the hospital. During that time we discussed salvation and eternity. He knows that he not only has to know these things, but he has to believe in them as well. He is thinking about them, and has been for nearly 2 weeks now."

"Well, what are you waiting for?" she asked.

Her honesty amused him, but he was touched by it. "Addie," he explained, "You grew up knowing about Jesus. You probably can't remember a day when you didn't know it. I have only known about it for a couple of weeks, and I'm still getting used to the idea. I need some more time."

"Mike, "Addie said, "If you had died on Tuesday night, where would you have spent eternity. Would you be in heaven or hell?"

"I suppose if what you're saying is correct, I would be in hell."

"Where do you want to spend eternity?"

"I would prefer to spend it in heaven."

"Then what's keeping you from making that decision?"

"I'm not really sure. Maybe it's foolish pride—sort of like teaching an old dog new tricks, or something like that."

"You're a smart man, and a good man, we've established that. It's sort of a win-win situation here. If what I'm, or we're, saying is right, you have nothing to lose. If you accept Jesus Christ as your savior and ask forgiveness of your sins, and know that He died on the cross to save you from those sins, you are going to heaven. If what I'm, or we're, saying is not right, you haven't lost anything, have you?"

Reverend Cross jumped in and took control of the conversation. "Mike, God is working on your heart and has been for longer than 2 weeks. You just didn't know exactly what was happening. When you're ready to make that decision, He will be ready to accept it. You have to be willing to freely give your heart and soul to God and accept the plan of salvation. When you're ready, nothing will hold you back. I do just caution. Don't wait too long. None of us know how many days we have on this earth, and it is a decision only you can make for yourself."

"Fair enough," he said.

Addie got up and excused herself to go upstairs to see to the housekeeping. "Foolishness, that's all it is, foolishness," she could be heard saying as she climbed the steps.

Reverend Cross looked Mike squarely in the eye, and said to him, "If she was in my pulpit, we may have more believers."

"You may be right," said Mike, as the lawnmower could be heard coming out of the woods.

The two men got up and went to the porch. Mr. Hood had his backpack on his back, and the container on the mower was filled with canned goods and bottled water. The three men unloaded the cargo, and Mr. Hood returned for another load. His next trip brought forth the nearly unused kerosene and the kerosene heater. The third trip brought his sleeping bag and a folding chair. Finally the tent came out on the final trip. These things were all stored in the outbuilding until they could be moved into the new house.

Mike suggested that they go to the mill to see how the new house was progressing and to show Mr. Hood where he would be working. He couldn't drive yet, and asked Reverend Cross to drive them. He yelled to Addie that they were going to the mill, and she was about to put a stop to that trip when she heard the car start up and speed away.

He knows better than to be out running around like that, she said to herself. *Maybe he isn't as smart as I thought he was. He's just full of foolishness, just plain foolishness*. With that she snapped the sheet across the bed she was making and continued on with her chores.

At the mill the three men stopped in to see the progress on the house being prepared for Mr. Hood. It was amazing to see the transformation that had occurred in just a few days. While small, it was cozy and the new appliances were being delivered when they arrived. A small refrigerator already stood watch in the corner of the kitchen. The white stove gleamed and a dishwasher was being installed where a portion of the kitchen cabinets had been removed.

Mr. Hood stopped in the living room and looked around. He could see into the kitchen and eating area from there, and he couldn't believe his eyes. He had never seen such a fine kitchen except in other people's houses. The old metal cabinets had been spray painted to a fine finish. The new appliances were in place, and to have a dishwasher was more than he could have ever dreamed. His first thought was that he didn't even have enough dishes to fill it up. All he had was his tin plate, a fork, knife and spoon, a cup, a pot and a skillet. He was so overwhelmed that he felt faint. He grasped his chest and leaned out to support himself on the wall. Reverend Cross was there in an instant to reach for him. Mike turned around just to see this happening and attempted to reach for him as well. However, his sudden move aggravated the recent surgery, and for a second he thought he might fall as a pain shot through his abdomen.

Reverend Cross eased Mr. Hood onto the floor where he sat almost speechless. He was trying to tell them he was just overcome with emotion and that he would be all right, but Reverend Cross diagnosed the situation as a possible stroke. Mr. Hood's broken speech, his loss of balance, and nearly falling spelled disaster to him. He immediately yelled to one of the workers to call 911. Mr. Hood could not allow that to happen. For the second time in two days the reverend was stopped from calling 911 when he shouted that he was all right. The deliveryman put away his phone, and Mr. Hood explained to Reverend Cross that he had just lost a lot of blood, and the doctor had explained that it would take a few days for him to regain his strength. "I'm getting to be an old man, preacher, and I haven't had this much excitement in my life for years. The old ticker isn't used to such goins' on. I'll be all right in a few days, but for now I guess I need to take it a little easier."

Reverend Cross looked up into the face of Mike Smith, whose pain was written across it. He was bent over, and he grimaced as he attempted to make his way to them. "What have I done?" Reverend Cross said. "I have taken two men barely out of the hospital, and I've put them in grave danger. Addie will have my hide when I take you back home." They all laughed, and knew he was right.

Mike insisted on going into the office since they were already there, but he promised not to stay more than a few minutes. Needless to say, their arrival at the office was unexpected, and Gerry Gilbert came out when he heard Mike's voice.

"What are you doing here," he asked. "More importantly, how did you ever get away from Addie. I figured she'd hold you hostage for at least a week."

"It wasn't easy. I caught her upstairs and yelled that I was leaving. Reverend Cross was already in the car, and by the time she realized what was happening, we were gone. She'll get me when we go home though."

They all laughed and knew he spoke the truth. Mike looked briefly at the mail and told Reverend Cross he was ready to go home, but needed to speak with Gerry privately before they left. Reverend Cross and Mr. Hood took seats in the reception area while Mike and Gerry went into Gerry's office and closed the door.

"Gerry, thanks for taking over so suddenly when I got sick. You're such a good friend and such a support to me here."

"It was nothing. That's what I'm supposed to do."

"Well. I just needed to say thanks. Another thing is I feel I need to get some furniture for Hood's house. How do you feel about that?"

He thought for a moment and then said, "I think we ought to go to one of those stores where you can buy rooms of furniture and get whatever he needs for the living room, bedroom and a kitchen table and chairs. How do you feel about that?" he asked.

"That's exactly what I had in mind. Do you think we could do it for about $1,500.00?"

"That's the amount that came to my mind, too."

"Very well, then, here's my personal check for $1,500.00 to cover it. Do you think one of the assistants could go into Charleston this afternoon and select something? I think it should be something neutral, and it must include some sort of comfortable chair."

Gerry looked at the check and saw that it was made payable to the mill. "What do you want me to do with this check?"

"Deposit it."

"I thought the mill would foot the bill for the furniture."

No," Mike said. "I want to do this, but I don't want Mr. Hood to know that I am doing it. He is already so beholden to me, and I don't want him to think that I am doing this on my own."

"Very well, I'll see that it's taken care of, but if you don't mind, I'll ask Sylvia to do it. She loves this kind of thing, and I think she's free this afternoon. The only thing is Philip. Do you think Addie would mind if he came to your house after school?"

"I know that would be all right. In fact, why don't you all just plan on having supper with us tonight? Addie always has enough to feed another family. She won't mind a bit."

Gerry made the arrangements with Sylvia, who called Addie and then the school to arrange for Philip to ride the bus home with Mary Margaret. With all these matters taken care of Mike was glad to return home even if he knew he had to face the wrath of Addie.

Reverend Cross pulled into the driveway and said he would just let his passengers out. He admitted that he was too chicken to face what was inside the house. They all laughed and the two men got out, and as they approached the porch Mrs. Applegate pulled up. She was surprised to see Mike up and about.

Reverend Cross tooted his horn as he left. Mrs. Applegate got out of her car and opened the rear door to retrieve something covered with a floral kitchen towel. From the size of it, it looked like a pie, and Mike soon discovered that he was not mistaken in his assumption. She had made a fresh strawberry pie with berries she had grown in her own small garden.

Her presence did not deter Addie from chastising both Mr. Hood and Mr. Smith. "The both of you are old enough to know that you can't go gallivanting about. Neither of you has good sense when it comes to taking care of yourself. You're barely out of the hospital bed, and you think you can just go off. Well, don't expect me to coddle you if you have a set back because of this. I just won't do it," Addie continued as she hugged Mrs. Applegate and relieved her of the pie.

The two men sheepishly grinned and went up to their respective rooms to rest knowing full well that they had escaped a more tortuous wrath by Mrs. Applegate's timely arrival.

Mrs. Applegate and Addie went into the kitchen where Addie put on a pot of tea and began making cucumber sandwiches. She got out the cream cheese to soften and began peeling a cucumber. They talked as her nimble fingers chopped the vegetable into tiny cubes. Then she got into the refrigerator and brought out her stash of pecans. She removed about a handful, carefully rewrapped the remainder, and placed them back into the darkness of the fridge. Addie expertly chopped the pecans into equally small pieces. An onion was then removed from the pantry where it was hanging. After Addie had minced about a tablespoon of this sweet Vidalia onion, she removed the mayonnaise from the refrigerator. All of her ingredients were ready to be mixed. She soon had a mixture which was aromatic, creamy and the palest of green. Her deft hands removed the bread from the wrapper, and she cut away the crusts. The filling was spread on half the slices and they were topped by the remaining ones. She then cut the sandwiches into halves diagonally, and mounded them on a platter.

The women didn't even realize that lunch was being prepared. The conversation was seamless as Addie went from one task to another, and soon plates were filled with sandwiches for the wayward patients who had taken to their beds, and the table was set for the two good friends who were enjoying being in the same room together.

Their conversation went from Addie venting over the adventurous patients to school being out the next day. Addie confessed to Mrs. Applegate that she had some concerns about Mary Margaret having so much unfilled time during the summer months, and they discussed a schedule for Mrs. Applegate to help fill some of that time as she and Mary Margaret worked on their quilt, and they continued their lessons in crochet.

After lunch was taken to the men in their rooms, Mrs. Applegate and Addie sat at the table and discussed the upcoming holiday week-end. Memorial Day is a time they both take seriously. They visit cemeteries where their family and friends are buried, and especially where their husbands have been laid to rest. Sometimes they go together to the cemeteries around the area because they both had loved ones in several places. This year, however, they realized that their children would be visiting them, and they would not be able to make the pilgrimages together.

The visits by the children while always welcome and enjoyable did cramp their Memorial Day visitation somewhat. The children do not share the memories, and do not see the relevance of the visits or the solemnity and reverence placed upon them. These graves represent mostly names and not the memories that the two friends shared. Of course, they all visit the graves of their fathers, and usually those of their grandparents. Maybe an aunt and uncle would be remembered, but more out of obligation to their mothers than to the memory of the deceased relative.

Flowers are always taken in cans which have been collected throughout the year and are placed in vases in the headstones at the cemetery or sometimes just left in the can on the grave if no vessel is provided. To Addie and Mrs. Applegate this honors their departed loved ones, but to their children, it represents a day they spend in the heat getting sweaty, slapping at gnats or worse yet, bees and wasps, and trying to remember how many more stops they have to make before returning to their respective mother's home for a shower and some dry clothes. The children share the running joke that this becomes the trail of tears.

Lunch was over and Addie started to clean up the kitchen and put a pot roast on for dinner. She invited her friend to stay explaining that the Gilberts would be joining them as well. Mrs. Applegate thought for a moment and decided it would be a wonderful way to spend the rest of the day.

The two women worked together as they peeled potatoes and carrots to be cooked with the roast, which was already in the iron Dutch oven with onions and was creating an aroma in the house equaled only in fine restaurants, as the meat seared against the hot iron and the juices caramelized along with the onions. Finally beef broth was added and the pot went into the oven. Addie got out a huge head of cabbage and with her knife shredded it into fine ribbons. This was placed into a big bowl and carrots were grated in with it. Addie again removed the mayonnaise from the fridge and placed two large scoops from the jar into a bowl. She then carefully measured a quarter cup of vinegar and a half cup of sugar into the same bowl. Two pinches of kosher salt were added, and a large dash of pepper. She expertly whipped this mixture with the same spoon she had used to scoop the mayonnaise. She stuck her pinky finger in to taste. "Perfect," she announced and dumped the dressing over the cabbage. She began stirring, and the ribbons of cabbage and flecks of orange from the carrot paled as they were enveloped by the homemade cole slaw dressing. The overfull bowl now seemed as though the contents were shrinking as the cabbage wilted in the wonderfully flavored sauce.

With this completed, Addie moved on to make something else for dessert. The strawberry pie was more than plenty for her family, but with guests coming something else needed to be added. After thinking for a few minutes, she announced that she knew what she was going to make. She had gotten a recipe from a friend who had eaten in a restaurant in Savannah. She had told Addie about a gooey cake, and said it was wonderful. Addie retrieved the crumpled piece of paper which held the recipe from her purse. A quick perusal and she knew she had all the ingredients. She read over the instructions and began the first layer of the cake which was a combination of cake mix and other ingredients she had gotten from the refrigerator and pantry. Soon she had a cake in the oven which by all accounts from the aroma as it cooked should prove to be an excellent addition to the evening's fare.

With the meal well underway, Addie and Mrs. Applegate went about setting the tables. They had so many people coming they would need both the kitchen and dining room tables. What would seem like a struggle to most people came as second nature to these veterans of the kitchen and soon that chore was completed.

At about the same time Addie glanced at the clock and realized that time had gotten away from her and she should be down at the bus stop. Before she could get out the door, however, she saw Mary Margaret and Philip walking up the driveway. Philip walked backwards as the two engaged in conversation. Addie smiled to herself and knew that with Philip she should not have been concerned with Mary Margaret's safety, but it did seem that this child had trouble all around her since the day she arrived. She stepped onto the porch and Philip stumbled as he turned to see where Mary Margaret's gaze had taken her.

At the edge of the woods were the mother deer and her twins. Their tails twitched as they stood to watch the children walk by. The mother's ears moved like radar, ever listening for any sound of danger, but at this moment in time she was only cautiously concerned for her babies. She did not feel any real sense of danger for either her or them. They slowly moved toward the woods and disappeared among the tree trunks.

The children reached the porch and Addie welcomed them and told Philip how glad she was to see him, and that he and his family would be having dinner with the Smiths. Philip immediately showed concern in his face and Addie asked him what was wrong. He said that he needed to care for the horses, and Addie assured him that his father was taking care of that before he came over. Philip's face relaxed and the two followed Addie into the house for a snack of apples and peanut butter, and a big glass of lemonade.

Mrs. Applegate, Addie, Philip and Mary Margaret were talking about the next day being the last day of school, when the voices of Davis and Jordan could be heard before they could be seen. Immediately after the yells, the footsteps could be heard on the porch. Addie yelled for them to come in, and they obeyed.

Soon Mike joined the group in the kitchen, and it was determined that this was a perfect day for fishing. Davis and Jordan had brought their poles and an extra one for Philip, and Mr. Smith told them to get what they needed from his garage. The boys ran off, and Mary Margaret went in to change her clothes.

Little by little the rest of the dinner party arrived. First, Sylvia came from her quick trip to Charleston. Actually, she had stopped at a mall near the city and had been able to do all her shopping in one store. She brought pictures of the furniture and announced that it would be delivered the next day. Mike clapped his hands in delight as he realized that his dream for his new friend was finally coming true. They discussed all the other things Mr. Hood would be needing and it was decided that Addie and Mrs. Applegate would go shopping the next day to get sheets, towels, dishes, glasses, pots and pans, silverware, kitchen utensils, food, paper goods, and all the other things they could think of to make this building a home. The excitement as this plan came together was contagious, and each seemed pleased to be able to participate in some way.

Cindy was next to arrive, and she was startled as she drove into the driveway and recognized both Mrs. Applegate's and Sylvia's cars. Her heart jumped, but she told herself that they had probably just come by to see how Mike was recuperating. They all greeted her as she came in, and she soon learned the reason for the gathering. She was so pleased to be having friends over for dinner, but she didn't feel quite right. She was certain that she was still exhausted from the previous nights' trials and excused herself to go freshen up.

The shower felt good, and she enjoyed the special soap Addie had gotten. It was a gel and the aroma and silkiness felt good and fresh against her skin. She stood there after bathing and let the water wash over her from head to toe. She got out of the shower and wrapped herself in one of her new large sage green bath towels, which had been delivered from Rowell's Department Store. It felt good as she rubbed her skin. The pile was soft, but absorbent. She dried her hair and put on a new shorts outfit. Her sandals were beside the bed, and she sat down to put them on. She thought she would just rest for a few minutes but was surprised when Mike came to get her an hour later. She was embarrassed and almost cried as she realized she had fallen asleep with guests in her home. "What'll they think of me?" she asked her husband, who replied, "They think you're exhausted. Don't give it another thought. Come on, dinner's almost ready."

They came into the kitchen to find that dinner was indeed ready. Addie and Mrs. Applegate had prepared a feast which was being served buffet style on the kitchen counter. The pot roast was surrounded by oven roasted potatoes and carrots, and the whole platter glistened under the rich brown glaze of sauce. The big bowl of cole slaw looked fresh and inviting, and a bowl of green beans had been added. A basket of rolls anchored the end of the serving line. The desserts had been placed on the bar between the kitchen and the eating area. The strawberry pie was piled high with large, red, ripe strawberries, and each berry was surrounded with a rich, red glaze as shiny as glass. The chocolate cake had been cut into squares and its aroma had overtaken the room. Cindy was even more self-conscious that she had not even offered to help as she surveyed the offerings. When she attempted to apologize, her comments were met with protests, and she was encouraged to fill her plate.

Gerry was asked to say the blessing, and the plates were soon filled. Mr. Hood stood back, but was encouraged to join right in and have a seat anywhere in the kitchen or the dining room. He chose the dining room, where it seemed that the other gentlemen found themselves along with Philip. The ladies and Mary Margaret stayed in the kitchen and nearly filled that table. Mrs. Applegate took note that the men were in one room and the women in the other. She said, "Some things never change. It's been this way as long as I can remember." The women laughed and set about eating the wonderful food.

Cindy ate a few bites and decided she wasn't as hungry as she had once thought. She moved the food around on her plate, and while this didn't go unnoticed by Addie and the other ladies, nothing was said about it.

When the meal was finished and the dishes cleared, the Gilberts went home and Addie and Mrs. Applegate soon followed. Mr. Hood went into his room, and Mary Margaret and her parents sat on the front porch for a few minutes. As the swing swayed back and forth, Cindy decided that she was going on to bed saying that she was exhausted. Mike said he was tired, too, and Mary Margaret realized that she had no choice but to follow suit. She had been excited to have company over this evening, and her mind was not ready to be quiet, but she didn't want to stay on the porch by herself, and she didn't think her parents would have allowed it if she had. Still, it was very early, and she couldn't remember any time that her parents went to bed almost before dark.

Chapter 60

This Friday morning dawned with dark clouds and thunder. Lightning flashed in the predawn skies, and Mary Margaret pulled the sheet up under her chin. The storms in the south seemed so much more violent than she had remembered in New York. She knew it stormed there, but the construction of her apartment had muffled the thunder, and the flashes of lightning were hidden by the towering buildings. Being absolutely exposed to the elements with nothing to protect you was frightening to this little girl. The rain pounded against the windows, and the wind howled through the trees. Nobody seemed to be up, so Mary Margaret stayed in her bed until she looked at the clock and realized that it was 6:45. Her parents were usually up and Addie was often even here by this time. Still the house remained silent except for the outside forces beating upon it.

What is going on? she wondered, as she got up and opened her bedroom door. She saw that her parents' door was closed, but a light was on in the kitchen. She tiptoed down the stairs to find her father sitting at the table. "Daddy, what's wrong? Why isn't Mama up, yet?" He looked at her and said that Mama didn't feel well today, and she was staying home. He told her not to worry, and that she had better hurry to get ready for school.

The storm died down almost as quickly as it had roared to life. Distant rumblings could be heard, but the sun was quickly evaporating the remaining clouds, and the birds were into their characteristic choruses when Addie arrived. She again attempted to apologize for being late which was met with objections. Mike and Addie discussed that Cindy was not feeling well and would be home today. Mary Margaret had toast and chocolate milk before she ran out the door to catch the bus. Her father attempted to keep up with her, but settled for keeping her in sight as they traversed the long driveway to the road. The bus stopped, Mary Margaret got on, and waved to her father. This was a new experience for them. He had not witnessed her riding the bus, and now here he stood in his jeans and t-shirt and shod in his house slippers. Addie and Charlene had been her constant companions as she made the treks to and from school, and the last time Mary Margaret remembered her father seeing her off was her first day of school in New York. He wore a suit and tie on that day, and she smiled in spite of the pang of sadness that struck her in the stomach as she thought of Charlene and missed her instantly.

There was not time for sadness today, however, and the mood was evident when she stepped on the bus. The driver had hung crepe paper and balloons. While all the students were in their seats, the noise level was high. She sat in the empty seat beside Jordan even though there was now another empty seat which Allison Kincaid had formerly occupied. Nobody even looked strangely at her today. It didn't seem foreign to be getting on the bus, and sitting next to Jordan was an everyday occurrence. Her family had been here six weeks, and finally she was beginning to feel a little at home.

Mrs. Calhoun met every bus and greeted the students as they got off. She handed them each a piece of paper, and instructed them to go immediately to the cafeteria. Mary Margaret looked at the pink piece of paper she had been given. On it was a number. Her number was 42. She wondered what this meant. The boys ran on ahead, and she went into the school alone. The cafeteria was orderly chaos. Teachers were waiting by the double doors and instructed the students to find the seats with the corresponding numbers on the paper.

Mary Margaret took a quick look around and immediately assessed that changes had been made. There were no tables. Only chairs occupied the floor, and a portion of the room had been left empty. On the floor were taped lines creating boxes and in the boxes were numbers. Each row of numbers had a different color. She walked past the boxes and took her seat in the third row near the end. Each row had 20 seats. A younger boy sat to her left, and a younger girl soon joined on her right. They seemed to know each other, and talked around her. She could see her friends in various rows, but none was close enough to talk with. She quickly counted the rows and determined that there were 10 rows of 20. As she multiplied she knew that was 200. The seats soon filled up. An occasional chair was empty as she looked throughout the room. The bell rang and the students began to get quiet. However, the lights in the lunch room had to be turned off to get total silence. This is the way it was at lunch when the noise level got too high, the lights were turned off, and the students knew it was time to be silent. The process worked again. Silence filled the room, and Mrs. Calhoun took the stage.

"Good morning, students," she began. A chorus of good mornings echoed across the room. The microphone squawked and squealed as she began to speak again. Adjustments were made, and she continued. "This morning we have planned some activities to help us get acquainted with one another. All year long we have been pretty much isolated in our classrooms with little opportunity for interaction. Today, we are going to see if we can find out something about each other and learn that while we are of different ages we can work together to accomplish a goal. The first thing we are going to do, however, is see how well we communicate. A teacher is going to hand the person on the end of the row a piece of paper with a sentence written on it. That person is to read the sentence and whisper it into the ear of the person next to them. The person on the other end will be asked to stand and repeat what they heard."

One by one the teachers handed the pieces of paper to the students on one end of each row. Mary Margaret was glad that she was not the last person on her row and would not have to stand and repeat the sentence. The young boy to her left said, "The state bird of South Carolina is the California Wren." Mary Margaret listened as he whispered this in her ear and wiped away the spit he left behind. He seemed to have some kind of lisp which sprayed his saliva as he spoke. She turned to the girl on her right and repeated, "The state bird of South Carolina is the California Wren." The girl continued the process and soon the message had made its way to the opposite end of the row. One by one the students rose to repeat their findings. The first row was manned by Nancy Miller, and she rose and said, "The state animal of South Carolina is the white tailed deer." Mrs. Calhoun told her that was absolutely correct. The person next to stand was a stranger to Mary Margaret and he said, "The state spider is the Carolina wolf spider." Again, Mrs. Calhoun congratulated that row. Now it was time for Mary Margaret's row. Again, she did not know the student on the opposite end who stood and said, "The state bird of South Carolina is the California Wren." Mrs. Calhoun asked him to repeat what he had said, and again he said, "The state bird of South Carolina is the California Wren." Mrs. Calhoun asked the student to his left, and he again repeated the sentence. This continued and each student said "California Wren," until it finally reached the young boy to Mary Margaret's left. He said in a loud voice, "The state bird of South Carolina is the Carolina Wren," emphasizing Carolina and looking directly at Mary Margaret as he spoke. She knew he had said California. She heard him distinctly. Her knowledge of South Carolina history was limited, and for all she knew it was the California Wren. She had repeated exactly what he had slobbered in her ear, and now she was embarrassed. The last day of school was turning out to be almost as bad as the first. Will it never end, she wondered.

The exercise continued through the 10 rows, and each row completed it perfectly except, of course, Mary Margaret's.

Next Mrs. Calhoun asked the people with blue, pink, green, yellow and white numbers to line up at the back of the room. One hundred students snaked their way out of the seats and found their positions at the rear of the cafeteria. The teachers assisted and held up pieces of paper of the respective colors. Mary Margaret soon realized that there were 5 rows of 20 people. Again she was in the third row, second in line. As they stood there, Mrs. Calhoun explained that there were going to play a form of bingo, and the students in the rear of the room would be the pieces which indicated the numbers that had been called. The noise level in the room was rising as the students, both seated and standing, started discussing what was to happen next. The lights were flicked off and on 2 times, and the room became quiet. Mrs. Calhoun continued. Two games were being called simultaneously, and cards and markers were passed out to the students who were seated, and the standing students waited until their number was called. Then they moved into the proper square on the floor. After about 10 minutes, two students simultaneously yelled, "Bingo." Groans could be heard throughout the chairs as disappointed students looked to see who had won. After it was determined that there were two official winners, they were given the opportunity to choose a new book from a rack on the stage.

Mary Margaret's interest was piqued when she saw the prizes. She enjoyed books, and suddenly realized that she had not gotten any new books since moving to Left Fork. She and Charlene often walked to the neighborhood bookstore, and she took great pleasure in selecting the latest award-winning books from the shelves. *A new book would be a great way to start the summer*, she thought.

The students changed places and a second round of Bingo began. Mary Margaret played to win. She listened and watched intently so as to not miss a number nor to put a mark on a square that was not called. She didn't want to be embarrassed by yelling "Bingo" only to find that she had marked Black 4, which in fact had been Black 14. The squares on her card were quickly filling, but there was no place that all five squares were filled in any direction. She just needed Black 4, Red, 23, Orange 47, Brown, 68, and Purple 99. She listened and waited for a shout as each number was called. Finally, she heard "Orange 47" and she yelled "Bingo" only it was much louder than she had intended. Unfortunately, she also jumped as she yelled, and much to her dismay, her chair tilted backward, and took the empty one beside along as it clamored into the aisle behind her. The unwary students in the fourth row were jumping to escape the avalanche of chairs, and they, too, upset their chairs in the melee.

Embarrassment reigned again. Mary Margaret felt as though a black cloud was hanging low over her head. She felt no joy in winning the prize. She wanted to run, but remembered the trouble she had created when she did that on an earlier occasion and realized she could only remain where she was and hope that soon the day and the school year would be over. Maybe over the summer the students would have forgotten about all of her misfortunes and somebody else besides her would be in the spotlight.

She chose her book and was glad to hear that she was being dismissed to her classroom. At least there she knew the routine and normally was inconspicuous.

Mrs. Stancil was standing by the door and placed her hand on Mary Margaret's shoulder as they walked down the hall. Inside the room it looked different. The bulletin boards were empty, and rolling shelves were standing in the corner. The students took their seats, and Mrs. Stancil began the task of taking up books. First was English, then Math, History, and Geography. The books were soon neatly arranged on the shelves, and it was time for lunch.

Mary Margaret had not brought her lunch today. However, it was brown bag lunch in the cafeteria. As she went through the line she was given a bag which contained a peanut butter sandwich, a resealable bag with 2 baby carrots and 2 pieces of celery, an apple, and another resealable bag which contained a large oatmeal cookie. The difference today, however, was that lunch could be eaten outside. Mary Margaret and Nancy Miller soon found themselves seated on a wall overlooking the history garden. The garden was remarkably beautiful. The warm weather and special care given by the students had produced a weed-free, healthy bounty worthy of the effort which had been put forth.

The two girls were soon joined by Davis, Jordan and Philip. Mary Margaret felt left out as the other students discussed their plans for 4-H Camp and Bible School. Philip said that he was going to Atlanta to a riding camp, and Davis and Jordan were going to visit grandparents. She was glad no one asked her what she was going to do this summer, and she was nearly in tears when she realized the only plans she had were for the 4th of July, and that was weeks away. How was she going to spend her time? It was going to be just Mary Margaret and Addie, and those prospects didn't seem too exciting.

The remainder of the day somehow passed, and it was time to board the bus for the ride home. Mrs. Stancil stood at the door and hugged each student as they left the room. She wished them well and handed each of them a small box. Mary Margaret wondered what was in the box, but she didn't look until she had taken her seat on the bus. The bus was hot, and the students were damp with perspiration as the bus roared to life. Philip was going home with Davis and Jordan and the three of them moved to the rear. Mary Margaret took a seat by herself. She was still holding the box in her hand and was anxious to open it. An envelope which contained a note from Mrs. Stancil was on top.

Mary Margaret,

I know that this year has been a year of changes for you, and not all of them have been good. However, I hope the summer will be a time of hope and anticipation. Please keep this journal to remember your first summer in Left Fork. This is a wonderful place, steeped in tradition and community love. I look forward to watching you and your family become a part of that tradition and know that you will someday find the peace that is here.

Fondly, Ann Stancil."

Mary Margaret removed the book from the box. The hard cover depicted pink, white, and yellow roses, and inside the bound pages were lined. She absently turned the pages, but each was as empty as the one before. She didn't know what she expected to find, but she continued until she reached the back. She closed the book and placed it back in its box. Mary Margaret suddenly remembered the slam book that Allison Kincaid had on her first day of school and realized that the journal given to her by Mrs. Stancil was an exact duplicate of that book. The jolt in her stomach came as a surprise, and she was glad when she realized the bus was coming to a stop at the end of her driveway. Her mother was standing beside the mailbox, but even that could not make her feel happy. The school term at Left Fork ended much as it began as Mary Margaret stepped off the bus and upchucked at her mother's feet while the bus pulled away.

Cindy was not expecting the explosion she felt at it spattered her lower legs. She had anticipated greeting Mary Margaret with a wonderful expectancy of a lazy summer filled with gatherings of their new-found friends and the surprises that she and her father had planned for her. A pedal boat had been ordered, and a dock was going to be built the next week. Construction was to begin soon on a barn, and the first surprise was scheduled for Saturday. Instead, however, she found herself also gagging as she attempted to clean as much of the mess off herself and Mary Margaret as possible while hoping she wasn't going to add to it. The nausea she had felt earlier in the day had subsided, but it suddenly reared its ugly head.

Mary Margaret was crying as they approached the house, and Mike was surprised at what he saw. He had expected to see the two loves in his life walking hand in hand up the drive, but instead, he saw two very distraught people racing toward the house. As they got closer, he could see that the front of Mary Margaret's clothing was soiled and Cindy was taking off her shoes before she stepped onto the porch. Mary Margaret ran into the house and to her bathroom, and her mother went to get the hose to clean off her legs. Mike didn't know which direction to take, but opted to go with his wife to find out what had happened.

She could not offer any explanation except the obvious, that Mary Margaret had gotten sick as she stepped off the bus. She hosed down her legs. The water in the hose was warm, but it soon turned cold as it was emptied of its stored contents and began a flow from underground. She decided that she had cleaned off enough, and she needed to go check on Mary Margaret.

Inside they found her daughter's bedroom door open, and her book bag and the box from Mrs. Stancil were on the floor. The bathroom door was closed, and the water in the shower could be heard. She yelled to Mary Margaret to see if she was okay, and she attempted to say she was. However, the hiccups had taken over, and most of what she attempted to say sounded much like a wounded frog attempting to croak.

The parents decided that she was safe for the moment and Cindy said she would go take a quick shower. They would attempt to determine what the problem was after that.

Within 15 minutes the three Smiths were in the kitchen. Mike was preparing a cup of tea for Cindy, and he and Mary Margaret were having lemonade.

"I'm sorry, Mama, she apologized and explained about the entire day, ending with the journal from Mrs. Stancil being an exact duplicate of the one Allison Kincaid had used. She explained that it was so unexpected when she became sick, and she was sorry it had happened. Mike and Cindy offered to replace the journal with a different one, but Mary Margaret declined. "This will be a reminder to only write nice things and to try to find the best of summer to write about."

A horn blowing in the driveway jolted this family meeting back into day to day happenings. The sound was obviously from Addie's truck, and Mike jumped from his chair. However, he slowed considerably as his body reminded him that he was still recuperating from surgery. Addie and Mrs. Applegate were waving as the family reached the porch. They had been shopping for items to fill Mr. Hood's new home, and the bed of the pickup was loaded. Mike said they would follow them to the new house as soon as he got his keys.

Cindy and her daughter went toward the garage after waving to Addie and Mrs. Applegate. Mary Margaret wondered where Mr. Hood was, but didn't ask anybody. She just got into her place in her mother's new van and took a deep breath of the new-car smell. Cindy secretly wished that the smell was already gone, but remained silent as she slipped behind the wheel.

The short trip to the mill took the two-car caravan through town where it seemed a new spirit had been infused. Children were riding their bicycles in the streets, and people were walking around the square. The aroma from Grammy's filled the air and was almost at once overpowered by the smells from the bakery.

At the mill, it was obvious which was to be Mr. Hood's new home. A fresh coat of whitewash made the house appear to stand a little more proud than the others. Even a few shrubs had been planted around the foundation. The concrete front porch had been painted grey, and the shutters were painted black. A red front door beckoned the visitors. Sylvia's van was already parked in the drive. She opened the door and came out to assist in unloading Addie's truck. A sort of assembly line was formed with Mike at the truck, then Sylvia, Cindy, Mary Margaret, Mrs. Applegate and Addie at the front door of the house passing each item from one to the other until Addie finally put it inside the house as near where it would remain as possible. In no time at all, the truck was unloaded and the workers went inside.

The transformation was unbelievable. The new furniture though sparse had been delivered earlier in the day. Sylvia had been there to receive it and instruct the deliverymen in the placement. She had scrounged her own attic and basement the night before to supplement the items she had purchased. Old pictures, lamps and books had been brought from her home to fill the empty spaces for the new tenant. The new sofa and chair filled much of the small living room. The coffee table and end table would have been bare had she not brought a lamp and flower arrangement from her own home. A small bookcase had been placed in the corner and several books and pieces of bric-a-brac warmed up the spot. The bedroom held a double bed with new mattress and box springs. A small table had been placed by the bed, a salvaged piece from Mrs. Gilbert's basement, and a clock and lamp looked right at home. The new chest of drawers matched the maple headboard, and a picture of a sea captain manning his wheel graced the wall above the bed. The kitchen had a small, white, drop-leaf table and two arrow-back chairs. An African violet looked right at home in the middle of the table in the sunny kitchen.

As the visitors looked around, Addie was busy putting away the groceries she had purchased. Soon the cabinet was filled with canned vegetables, tuna, canned chicken, soup, and canned fruit. She remembered the peaches she had served Mr. Hood just a few days prior and had made sure that he had those.

Mrs. Applegate and Cindy started unpacking the set of dishes. They had gotten a 16-piece set, and in a few minutes they were washed, dried and placed in what the women thought to be an appropriate cabinet. It was near the dishwasher Mrs. Applegate had said; and, therefore, it was the logical place. Glasses were unwrapped, washed and also placed in the cabinet. A small set of silverware was treated likewise before being placed in the clean, freshly lined drawer.

Sylvia had brought sheets from home, and in no time had made the bed and was covering it with a new blanket and bedspread. Towels were stacked in the linen closet, along with bath soap, cleaning products, and toilet tissue.

Back in the kitchen Addie was filling the cabinet under the sink with dishwashing detergent, cleanser, window cleaner, and a freshly lined new trash can.

Within a short time, a broom, mop, bucket, dust pan and other cleaning products had been put away. The bed was made, the refrigerator was filled with perishable items, milk, sausage, lunch meat, cheese, fresh fruit, juice and any other thing Addie and Mrs. Applegate had deemed necessary to make this house into a home.

As they looked around, Mike said that he wanted to ask Reverend Cross to come and bless this home before Mr. Hood moved in. They all agreed that a little celebration the next afternoon would be a good way to welcome Mr. Hood, and get him started in the right direction as he began this new time in his life. It was agreed that they would contact Reverend Cross and see if the celebration could be held at 2:30 on Saturday afternoon. Secretly, they all were anxious to see Mr. Hood's response to this house that had been prepared especially for him.

Chapter 61

Gerry and Mr. Hood had gone to the mall near Charleston to shop for some work clothes. It was decided that he should wear a uniform of sorts as he made his rounds so that he would be easily identifiable as the night watchman and not mistaken for an intruder.

They left at noon and were expected to return about 5:00. Gerry was taking him to lunch and was purposely making the afternoon a long one so that the others could make the house ready. They ate lunch at a seafood house and enjoyed fried shrimp, baked oysters, cole slaw, hush puppies and iced tea. He allowed that Mr. Hood's stomach was beginning to grow as his diet had been greatly improved since he identified himself to Mike just two weeks earlier. He silently pondered the happenings of the past two weeks and marveled at the amount of excitement and activity that had occurred in that time.

When the two men finished eating and the check arrived, Mr. Hood removed his wallet which was attached to a belt loop by a chain. From it he pulled a $20.00 bill and handed it to Gerry. He refused the money, but Mr. Hood insisted. He said, "Gerry, I'm a proud man. I've chosen to live a different kind of lifestyle, and I've worked to keep myself going. I've always paid my own way. It may have been a meager life compared to what you're used to, and sometimes a can of beans was the best I could do, but it's my life. I would never have eaten the food if I hadn't anticipated paying for it." Gerry was embarrassed that he had put this gentleman in the position of having to explain his lifestyle. He accepted the $20.00 and placed his own $20.00 with it. When the waitress returned the change, he divided the money, and Mr. Hood quickly calculated that his portion had been $13.75 and left a tip of $2.25 for the waitress, which Gerry quickly matched.

They continued on their journey until they reached the mall. They went to a store that specialized in work shoes. The two men determined that an ankle high boot with a firm, but flexible sole would be best for walking around the mill. After trying several, one was decided upon and 5 pairs of heavy socks were also selected. Mr. Hood protested that he only needed 2 pairs of socks, and that he was willing to wash a pair by hand every day to always have a clean one. This fell on Gerry's deaf ears. He used the company credit card, and soon the transaction was complete. As they chatted while going back to the truck, he explained that at one time the company had maintained a shoe area where workers could come and get steel-toed boots. However, he explained the machinery had become more sophisticated and that type of footwear was no longer necessary.

The next stop brought them to a store specializing in uniforms. After looking over the inventory, it was decided that khaki pants and shirts would be ideal. Again, Gerry insisted on 5 uniforms, and Mr. Hood attempted to protest. The clerk said they could monogram the logo and Mr. Hood's name on the shirts in an hour, and Gerry thought that was a fine idea.

The two men left to spend the next hour in a nearby coffee shop, having a muffin and coffee. "Hood, this is my treat," Gerry announced before going in. His guest agreed. However, his next comment made the host smile, "I believe I could drink coffee for a week for the $3.75 that one cup costs in this place." He figured that this was Mr. Hood's first trip to a yuppie coffee shop.

After returning to the uniform store and starting back toward Left Fork, Gerry asked, "Hood, is there anything you need before we go back?"

"If you don't mind, I'd appreciate it if you could stop at a flower shop or a gift shop."

"That's not a problem," and he pulled into a strip shopping center where he noticed a sign indicating flowers and gifts were available. He started to get out, too, but Mr. Hood said he would like to do this shopping alone. Gerry closed his door and watched as the old man limped through the door.

Inside the aroma reminded Mr. Hood of a funeral home. The fragrance of the flowers and moldy soil enveloped him. However, it was bright and cheerful, with pleasant music playing throughout. He stopped and looked around to get his bearings and finally headed in the direction of the small figurines he saw in the corner. He surveyed them, and picked up a few and turned them over. He whistled and quickly put each one back. His gaze was then drawn to the greeting cards where he searched the headings until he found Thank You. He read a few and nothing really matched his thoughts. He put each card back as he read, and then he noticed a sign which read, "Roses, $1.00." This fit his budget, and he selected 3 pink roses. The clerk added a sprig of baby's breath, wrapped them in green waxy paper, and tied a pink ribbon around the middle.

Timidly, Mr. Hood returned to the truck, placed the roses on the back seat, and the two men continued their journey to Left Fork.

The company truck turned in the Smiths' driveway just behind Cindy's van. Both vehicles came to a rest near the house and the occupants got out and greetings commenced. Mr. Hood was busying himself with the purchases of the day, and almost immediately disappeared into the house along with Mary Margaret. She helped him carry some of the packages to his room. He returned a few minutes later and bade Mr. Gilbert good-bye as he was pulling away. He yelled his thanks to the man who had purchased him more clothing at one time than he had owned in many years.

He turned and impulsively hugged Mike, taking him totally off guard. He nearly lost his balance, thereby causing Mr. Hood to put added weight on his injured leg. The pain shot into his body, and he went to his knee almost dragging Mike to the pavement with him. Cindy was witnessing this and stepped forward to catch the two men before they completely collapsed. Just the touch of her hands on their backs was enough to prevent another catastrophe, and soon they were both standing. Mr. Hood was embarrassed and the pain continued. He attempted to apologize, but could not complete the words as he held his thigh where Allison had inflicted the injury. A quick look revealed that blood had seeped through his trousers, and the nurse in Cindy reacted to the situation.

She told Mike to get Mr. Hood onto the porch, and she ran into the house to get the first-aid kit. A quick glance revealed that it contained everything she would need. When she got to the porch, Mr. Hood was seated on the steps and Mike was squatted beside him. The blood stain had enlarged in the few seconds which had elapsed, and Cindy assumed that he had probably torn loose the stitches.

She removed the scissors from the kit and started to cut the leg of Mr. Hood's trousers. He caught her hand and asked her to not cut another pair of his pants. He had lost one to Allison Kincaid, he explained, and this was his only pair of pants. Both Mike and Cindy could see the look in his eyes as he explained this and knew he was being further embarrassed to have to give them this explanation.

"I'll get you something else to wear," Mike said as he headed into the house. He soon returned with a pair of shorts and a large bath towel he could use for privacy as he changed his clothes on the front-porch steps. Mike held the towel as Mr. Hood exchanged his trousers for the shorts. Cindy busied herself with the first-aid kit until his dignity could be salvaged, and she then returned to her work. The dressing on the wound was saturated with blood. She put on the latex gloves she found in the kit and carefully removed the bandage. She expertly sprayed the area with sterile bottled water and was soon down to the source of the bleeding. She explained that all the sutures seemed to be intact. As she examined the wound, she surmised that a hematoma, or small pouch of blood, had formed along the suture line and had burst during the mishap. She cleaned the area and applied a new sterile dressing after applying an antibiotic ointment. Overall, she was pleased with the healing of the area and soon pronounced Mr. Hood to be *fit*. However, she told him that she planned on examining the area again the next day.

As she cleaned up the steps, she glanced at the whole patient. The old man was still wearing his long-sleeved shirt which hid his frail body, but the tennis shorts Mike had provided could not hide the long, thin limbs which seemed to grow from the wide legs of the shorts and disappeared into the folds of the too loose socks. Her first impression was newsreels she had seen of people dying in third-world countries. Their frail bodies were basically skin stretched over bones, and Mr. Hood was not much removed from that.

Tears welled in her eyes, but she averted them to her task. Mr. Hood was attempting to again stand and Mike reached to help him. She recognized that another accident was in the making and asked them both to please just wait. The two men exchanged glances and knew she was right. Mike folded the towel, and soon his wife was able to assist Mr. Hood to his feet. He walked around in a small circle and declared that he was much better. He attempted to again apologize for being so much trouble, but both Mike and

Cindy shushed him with loving words, that they should be apologizing to him for the injury he received while trying to keep their family safe.

Addie's truck could be heard before it was seen as she drove into the driveway from the road. She pulled up to the house and was puzzled by the site she beheld. A quick explanation and she was satisfied that all was well. She carried a bag of groceries into the house, and said that she had seen Mrs. Applegate's daughter, Beverly, when she took her home. It seemed that the holiday week-end had officially begun with the arrival of the first visitors.

Mary Margaret joined Addie in the kitchen, and they discussed her day at school as they set about getting dinner on the table. A casserole had been prepared and was heating. The salad was pulled from the refrigerator, and Addie was filling the iron skillet with a corn bread mixture to bake alongside the casserole.

Mary Margaret set the table and answered the phone when it rang. She was obviously excited and it just took a few seconds for Addie to realize that the person on the other end was her friend, Alice, calling from New York.

As she listened to her side of the conversation, Addie felt that Mary Margaret was still on the border of being at home in South Carolina. She would tell Alice something positive, which was immediately followed by a negative. Perhaps, she wondered, Mary Margaret was attempting to hide her true feelings of her new home from the old friend to make her feel more missed.

Mary Margaret soon called her mother to the phone to speak with Alice's mother. After the initial small talk about settling in, Alice's mother explained that Darlene had taken another position, and that Charlene was their new nanny. Again, from the one side of the conversation Addie and Mary Margaret were hearing, this was working out nicely, but only the two would be coming to South Carolina. Darlene would not be able to be off work for that week.

As Mary Margaret listened, she became resentful that Charlene would go so easily into somebody else's home. Her mind raced as she imagined the two people she had most cared for in New York doing the things without her that they had once shared. She was jealous. She thought of the long looming summer and immediately wished she was back there with them. She imagined the busy sidewalks as they went shopping, and the museums she and Charlene visited. She even knew some of the artists and here all she had to look forward to was swatting gnats and mosquitoes, both of which were plentiful in South Carolina.

The two mothers continued their conversation and soon it was apparent that a third person had joined in. Cindy laughed gaily as she and Charlene shared the few minutes on that Friday evening and planned for the upcoming visit. A quick glance at the calendar revealed that July 4th fell on Wednesday, and it was determined that a Saturday-to-Saturday visit would work best for everyone. Finally, plans were made to pick up Alice and Charlene in Charleston at 11:47 a. m. on Saturday, June 30. Summer was underway.

Soon dinner was on the table and Cindy shared her conversation with everyone. Mike was excited at the prospect of seeing Charlene again, and Cindy was animated as she relayed the news. Addie felt a little misplaced as they laughed and carried on a personal conversation to which she could add nothing. They both related the merits of Charlene and how much they had missed her.

Mr. Hood watched the dynamics of the room. Addie busied herself around the kitchen and failed to join the family at the table. Mary Margaret seemed to sulk as she moved the food on her plate but failed to eat much of it. He considered himself to be a study of human nature. He had spent much of his life on the outside looking in. His own family never understood him, as he always wanted to do and see more. His travels took him away from the people who would probably have loved him most, and he never stopped long enough to see if others could love him, too, until now. He had spent a lifetime watching others and saw that this room was filled with uneasiness.

Addie wiped off the counters and cleaned the stove top. She was fervent in her swipes. She listened to the carefree conversation regarding their former nanny and the upcoming visit and felt out of place. This was foreign to her. Addie was accustomed to being the center of attention and thrived on taking that position. She didn't do it as a diva, but more as a facilitator, who was adept at making things happen. She relived the past few weeks in her mind and all she had accomplished for this family up to and including this very day. Why she had taken the day to set up a house for an old man they had adopted from the woods. One phone call and she seemed to be forgotten, her mind wandered on and on through pits that were getting deeper with each thought.

Soon, the only two people in the room who were enjoying the conversation realized that nobody else was joining them, and the subject got around to the activities of the week-end. Addie said she was spending the week-end with her family and would probably see them in church on Sunday.

Mike and Cindy were shocked at her sudden change in attitude and were even more shocked as she picked up her purse and started toward the door. Before they could comprehend it, she was out the door, and Mike stood on the porch and waved as she backed her truck up and roared down the drive.

Mr. Hood started clearing the table and Cindy helped. Mary Margaret asked to be excused and went to her room. Mike returned to the kitchen and the three of them silently completed the evening tasks.

Mr. Hood went to his room, and Mike and Cindy went onto the porch.

"What do you suppose got into her," Mike asked.

"I'm not sure, but I intend to find out," said Cindy.

"Did we say something that offended her?"

"If we did, I don't know what it was."

They continued swinging for a few minutes, and Cindy went inside to phone Addie's house. The phone rang several times with no answer. She returned to the porch and the two continued to swing.

In Addie's apartment, she looked at the phone as it rang. *What has gotten into me*, she wondered as she continued to revisit the dark thoughts. Fatigue swept her body, and she went toward the bathroom to shower. After stepping into the bathroom, she knew it was more than fatigue as her stomach seemed to lurch from inside her, and she barely made it to the toilet. She was on her knees, and she reached for a cloth to wipe off her face. The cloth was out of her reach, and she was going to have to get up. However, that was impossible as another wave of nausea swept through her. This continued for what seemed to be an hour but in actuality was little more than 20 minutes. Dry heaves followed and soon her body seemed at peace with itself once again.

During this time, the telephone continued to ring. She knew it was Cindy, and now she was ashamed for the way she had acted. *Why wouldn't they be excited that Charlene is coming to visit? She was somebody very dear to them.* As she sat on the cool tile of her bathroom floor, Addie realized that she had been ill and that was what caused her bad behavior. She remembered that Cindy and Mary Margaret had both been ill in the previous 24 hours, and she deducted that a virus was going through the house. This disappointed her, as she had secretly hoped that Cindy was expecting a baby and that had been the reason for her sudden illness and fatigue.

Addie struggled to her feet and ran the washcloth under cool water. She held the cloth on her forehead with one hand and rested the other on the sink. The telephone rang again, but Addie did not feel strong enough to take the few steps to answer it. After several rings, the room was silent again.

She put down the toilet seat and sat down. Her body was trembling, and the bedroom seemed a mile away. More time passed, and she felt she had gained the strength to reach the bed and picked up the trash can and wash cloth as she headed in that direction. The telephone began to ring anew, but she knew she would not be able to stand up and answer it. She hoped it would still be ringing once she had landed, and she was not disappointed.

Cindy heard the trouble as Addie whispered, "Hello."

"Addie, are you all right?"

"No. I need your help."

"I'll be right there, Cindy said."

She had never been to Addie's apartment and realized that she didn't know where it was. She phoned Mrs. Applegate and asked her to please be ready and explained the situation. Mrs. Applegate said she would be on the porch. Cindy explained to Mike as she gathered her purse and put on her shoes.

"I'll go with you," he offered.

"No, you stay here with Mary Margaret and Mr. Hood," she said while truthfully, she wished he could go with her as she was uncertain what she would find when she arrived.

Mrs. Applegate was standing by the street and directed Cindy to Addie's apartment. The two climbed the stairs and found the door to be locked. They banged on the door, and could not hear the faint response as Addie tried to yell, but found herself too weak to be heard. Mrs. Applegate produced a key from her purse, and Cindy stood back as the tiny woman deftly unlocked the door and began yelling for her friend.

The unmistakable stench could be smelled when the door was opened. Mrs. Applegate ran into the bedroom to her friend and was quickly followed by Cindy. Both women were appalled at the pallor of Addie's skin. Cindy took her pulse, and found it to be racing. She went into the bathroom to look for a thermometer and found one in the medicine chest. She returned to the bedroom where Mrs. Applegate was applying a fresh damp cloth to her friend's forehead. The thermometer showed a near normal temperature. Cindy assessed the situation and went into the living room to call 911. She gave the information to the dispatcher, and yelled back into the bedroom to ask for Addie's specific address. She soon returned to say that paramedics were on the way.

Addie attempted to protest, but was too weak. Her arms felt heavy, and she was cold and clammy.

"I think you may have suffered a heart attack," Cindy explained. "You need immediate attention at the hospital."

Tears streamed down Addie's face, and her friend held her hand. Cindy became the professional that she is and began making way for the paramedics to get to Addie in order that they could begin the lifesaving measures immediately.

She looked at her watch and realized that it had been about 50 minutes since Addie had abruptly left their home. It was good that no more time had elapsed. She figured that Addie had probably been home about 35 minutes, and from the look of things she had gotten sick immediately upon arrival.

The siren could be heard in the distance, and Cindy opened the front door. She returned to the bedroom, and Addie motioned for her to bend over. When Cindy bent over Addie's face, she kissed her. She was so overcome that tears she had been holding back fell freely.

"I'm sorry that I left in such a huff," whispered Addie.

"Don't think about that," said Cindy.

"I just suddenly felt jealous about Charlene, and I didn't want to share you with anybody."

"Addie, you were feeling sick and vulnerable. You know you have no reason to feel jealous. You are the best thing God could have sent into our life. We love you and are grateful for all that you have done for us and our friends. Now, just focus on yourself, and we are going to pray that God will give you and us peace as we get you through this."

She began—

"Dear Lord,

I am new at praying publicly. You probably don't even know who I am, and I don't know you very well myself. However, I am standing over somebody who is one of your children, and I ask that you reach down and touch her with your healing hand and your hand of mercy. This woman loves you and places you first in her life. This is apparent as she ministers to everybody she meets. She has a presence like none other I have ever seen, except maybe for her friend who stands here beside me. God, these two ladies and I need peace right now that you are in charge in this situation and will bring Addie through this and back as a vibrant part of our life.

We thank you, God, and pray this in the name of your son, Jesus. Amen."

The paramedics raced into the bedroom just as the prayer was completed. Cindy and Mrs. Applegate stepped back and gave them room to work. A portable EKG machine is attached, and vital signs are taken. A bag is hung, and soon fluids are running into the veins as this woman who is accustomed to being in charge lay helplessly in their care.

Cindy monitored the situation from the corner of the room and knew from the conversation between the paramedics and the hospital via two-way radio, that her diagnosis was somewhat correct and her decision for immediate care was appropriate.

Soon Addie was loaded onto the gurney that allowed them to negotiate the small rooms and stairs to the waiting ambulance. Several neighbors had gathered outside, and Mrs. Applegate shared a brief explanation as Cindy quickly gathered some personal belongings and locked the apartment.

The siren wailed and the lights flashed in the near darkness as Cindy and Mrs. Applegate proceeded to the hospital. Their fears could be heard in the sound of their voices. Their dear friend had experienced a near death episode, and they truly knew that only God was in control.

Mrs. Applegate said, "I can only handle this because I know that God is carrying Addie through this." Her voice broke, and as Cindy looked across the seat, she could see that Mrs. Applegate's face was wet with tears.

She opened the console of the van and removed several tissues. She handed some to her friend and used the rest herself.

"Addie and I have been friends for nearly all of our lives. Her mother worked in my family's home. Back in those days it was not unusual for families to have help, and they often brought their children to work with them. Addie's mother took care of me and my family. She cooked, cleaned, did the laundry, and for a while, she and Addie lived with us. I loved Addie's mother. She was a large, gregarious woman, who always wore a crisp white apron. She made them herself, and took great pride in them. She starched them stiff. She ironed them so that there were no wrinkles. At the end of the day, she still looked clean. She would sing as she worked and often danced with us in her arms. She was full of joy. She would pick me up, and I felt lost in her vast lap. She would tell me wonderful stories of living on a plantation and picking cotton. Addie's grandparents worked on a farm that was owned by a wealthy man. He was kind to them, and gave them a little house to live in. Addie's mother loved her parents and spent much time in the fields with her father and even more time with her mother tending to the house. She told me there was always plenty of food, and she was adored by the plantation owner."

"She married a young man from another plantation, and he didn't want to stay there. He wanted to move to the city and to be quite honest with you, that was not a good place for them in those days. Discrimination was rampant, and soon he found himself in a place where others thought he ought not to have been, and he was beaten to death. Addie's mother came to work for my family, and Addie was just a tiny baby as was I. We both grew up on her mother's knee. I could not have loved a sister, had I been blessed with one, more than I love Addie. My parents saw to it that she had the best they could give, and her mother repaid them by working the rest of her whole life in their household."

"She was eventually able to move out, but she remained in their employ until she died one day taking down laundry in our back garden. Addie and I found her there when we came home from school."

"Addie went to a school for Negroes, and I attended Left Fork Elementary, right where Mary Margaret goes. Of course, it was much smaller then. We would meet on Main Street and walk the few blocks to my parents' home. When Louise, Addie's mother, was not in the kitchen when we came home one day, we ran into the back yard and found her covered by a sheet she had been taking from the clothes line."

"Addie moved into our home, and offered to take her mother's place. My daddy wouldn't hear to it, and he continued her education until she met her husband and they married. She moved to Michigan for a while and then returned. We have always been so close, and our children have become close as well."

"Cindy, Addie is one of the finest women I have ever known. I have never heard her complain without cause, and she is devoutly Christian. I don't want to say she is religious, because sometimes people go through religious motions and don't know Christ. Addie knows Christ, and He knows her. I pray selfishly for her to survive, but know in my heart that angels are around her to take her to God's right hand if her time on earth is through."

They pulled into a parking spot in the emergency room parking lot. The ambulance was empty, and Cindy knew that measures were already being taken to sustain the life of this patient. To those working in there, she was a patient. They could be objective and follow the directives for the best care.

She settled Mrs. Applegate and went to the registration area to complete the paperwork for Addie's admission. She had gathered up Addie's purse and prayed that her Medicare information was in her wallet. She was not disappointed. Her social security number and all other pertinent information were relayed to the clerk, who irritatingly popped her chewing gum while asking the computer generated questions.

Cindy was soon released to go sit with Mrs. Applegate which she did after first calling home. Needless to say, Mike wanted to come to the hospital, but she asked him to please stay with Mary Margaret and advised that she would keep them updated.

Thirty minutes and then an hour passed before a doctor finally came out. He asked for the Adalaide Jones' family. Cindy remained seated and may have missed the call had it not been for Mrs. Applegate who recognized her longtime friend's name and jumped before he had completed saying Adalaide. Cindy Smith was ashamed that she had never once said the name Adalaide Jones. To her it was Addie, and Mike had always written the checks. *How insensitive and self centered have I been*, she wondered as she made her way to the doctor.

He explained that Addie had indeed had a heart irregularity and that preliminary test results indicated it might be something that could be regulated with medication. They wanted to keep her, monitor her progress, and would do further evaluations as necessary.

Mrs. Applegate and Cindy both breathed a sigh of relief and asked if they could see her. The doctor said that someone would be out to get them in a few minutes, and they could go with her to the Coronary Constant Care Unit.

True to his word, a young woman came and spoke to them directly announcing that they were ready to take Mrs. Jones to her room. They obediently followed and soon found themselves at Addie's bedside. Her color had returned to her cheeks, and her eyes were beginning to show their familiar glint. Her voice was stronger, and she thanked them for coming to her rescue.

The procession started, one medical person at each end of the bed, along with Cindy and Mrs. Applegate trying to negotiate the halls and elevator.

Finally they made it to the 4th Floor and the doors of the elevator opened. Cindy was shocked to see Reverend Cross waiting for them. A short conversation allowed that he had been called by Mike and had come immediately to the hospital. At Information he was told that Addie was in the Coronary Constant Care Unit; and when he arrived there, he was told that she was being transported from the emergency room.

The medical personnel asked the visitors to wait until they had settled her in bed. While they waited, Reverend Cross was brought up to date on the occurrences of the evening. He was relieved when Cindy reached the part where the doctor felt the condition was treatable with medication.

A nurse joined the other medical personnel in the room, and soon the two transporters from the emergency room left. The three visitors went in and the nurse continued her assessment of the patient and the medications hanging much like cow's udders from a pole on the head of Addie's bed. When she completed her assessment and started to leave, Addie asked her to explain to Mrs. Smith what was happening. She appeared cordial, but looked at her questioningly. Cindy explained that she was a nurse in the surgical unit, and the nurse immediately began to explain the medications and the treatment plan for the next 8 hours. She said the doctor would be there in the morning to reassess the situation. She told Addie to call her if she needed anything and left.

Reverend Cross took Addie's hand in his and gently kissed the back of it. He continued holding her hand and started to pray.

"Dear Lord, we thank You for the mercy You have shown this gentle child of Yours. We thank You for knowing that You are her Father, but You didn't see fit to call her home at this time. We thank You for our love that we share for You and the love that we share for each other. Please guide us in Your way. We ask in Jesus' name. Amen."

Tears streamed down the faces of these four friends. Addie wiped hers with the corner of the bed sheet. Cindy looked around for tissues as she noticed the moisture from Addie's nose about to roll down her cheek. None were readily available, so she retrieved a roll of toilet tissue from the bathroom, and after tearing off a section for Addie, she passed the roll around. First Mrs. Applegate wrapped a small section around her hand and tore it off. Then Reverend Cross unwound a long piece and blew his nose. Finally the roll was returned to Cindy who laughed uncontrollably as she looked around the room and noticed the varying lengths of toilet tissue dangling from each person's hand. The laughter came more as a release of stress, but soon they were all laughing and holding up their toilet paper.

The laughter must have triggered one of the monitors attached to Addie because an alarm sounded, and the room was immediately filled with nurses. They were puzzled when they found everybody laughing and soon suggested that Addie needed to rest and their visit was over.

After being assured by the nursing staff that Addie would be all right overnight without a chaperone, Cindy agreed to go home. Reverend Cross said he would drop off Mrs. Applegate. The three walked to the parking lot and the Reverend watched Cindy to her van.

When she arrived home, Mike was on the porch steps, and Mr. Hood was at his side. Mary Margaret was lying in the swing and appeared to be sleeping. She parked the car and walked around to the front of the house. She explained to them all that had occurred, and they were relieved at the message she brought. Thunder rolled from the west, and they decided that it had indeed been a long day, and they were all tired.

Chapter 62

Saturday morning dawned with heavy dew from the previous night's rain. Mr. Hood made his way to the kitchen and put on a pot of coffee. He brought his sheets with him and soon the washing machine was running. He took a cup of coffee to the front porch and sat on the steps. The morning still was broken by the concert of the birds. They seemed happy to be alive this beautiful May, Saturday, morning and wanted everybody to know it. He sat there and pondered the new life that was about to begin for him. The past two weeks had been a prelude to something even better.

He felt so blessed to be taken in by this family, but better still, he felt blessed that he was going to be self-sufficient and an asset to society. He had a job. He no longer had to wonder how he would be able to buy his next supply of beans or kerosene to run his heater. He had more clothes than he could ever remember having even if they had the company logo on them, and he was going to have a roof over his head every night, not just the ones where he stayed in a motel to keep from freezing to death. He would have an address. He had only been able to use General Delivery if he stayed in one place long enough to matter. For the first time in a long time, he felt proud. Tears streamed down his face as he began to silently pray.

"Dear Lord,

We haven't talked much, but I have always known You were there, and Your angels have protected me more times than I care to remember. Thank You for bringing me to this place in my life and for surrounding me with these loving people. I guess it's been a roundabout way of getting here, and a long time in coming, but I know that it's only because of You that it's happening.

Also, God, take care of that Addie woman. I know she's a handful and can be contrary at times, but she has a heart of pure gold. She has cared for me even though she didn't want to. You and I both know I'm no axe murderer, but she wasn't too certain. You have used her on earth as an extension of Your love, now she needs Your help to get better and to come back to us and to continue Your work.

Thank you, Lord, for all You have done. In Jesus' name. Amen."

He didn't realize that his silent prayer had turned into a verbal one and was surprised when he heard, "Amen," from behind him. He turned to see Mike standing in the door with tears streaming down his eyes. His coffee cup was steaming in the cool early morning. He walked out and sat down beside Mr. Hood, and said, "You know what?"

"No, what?"

"I never once thought you were an axe murderer either."

Cindy joined them and wanted to know what they were laughing about. The explanation brought giggles from her as well and the jovial mood swept them into the kitchen for breakfast prepared by Chef Hood, as he came to be known for a few minutes that morning.

After checking the refrigerator and pantry, he decided that he would wow them with eggs benedict. He substituted ham for the Canadian bacon, but everything else was in the kitchen. Within minutes he had eggs poaching and a Hollandaise sauce was being kept warm in the blender container placed in a pot of hot water. Mike and Cindy set the table and poured juice. The kitchen hummed in anticipation of this meal while the tall, thin old man moved quickly around the stove. He asked that the plates be placed by the stove instead of on the table, and one by one he plated each dish which Mike delivered to its appropriate place. Cindy clapped as her breakfast was placed before her. Mr. Hood bowed gently at his waist and tipped an imaginary hat.

Breakfast was completed and the dishes were whisked away into the dishwasher. The washing machine had completed its cycle, and Mr. Hood transferred his sheets into the dryer.

Cindy marveled at his ability to handle himself in the house. She remembered that he had done many things in his life and had prepared himself for nearly anything that came his way. She smiled as she went to get dressed for a day of new beginnings.

At the hospital Addie found herself tethered to the IV lines and unable to move from the bed without assistance. She again pressed the button for the nurse to help her to the bathroom, and groaned as she waited. She felt fine, and muttered that this was a waste of time, just as Mrs. Applegate stuck her head in the door. The two friends embraced.

"You sure gave us a scare last night."

Addie wiped an invisible hair off her face. "I'm sorry I was so much trouble."

Mrs. Applegate took Addie's hand and held it to her face. She kissed it gently and told Addie, "Adalaide Louise Jones, you are my best friend in the world. I would give my life for you, and for me to take a couple of hours to take care of your needs is nothing compared to the love and affection you have given me through the years. We raised our babies together. You sat with me while my husband was sick; you sat with me when he was gone. You have prayed for me every day of our adult lives. Why truth be known, you have probably done more for the people of Left Fork than anybody else, and you apologize for needing me. Shame on you! Giving is a two-way street. You can't always give. Sometimes you have to be willing to receive, and that's not easy for you, I know. But, now is the time for you to be on the receiving end."

Tears were running down the faces of these two friends when the nurse arrived to help Addie to the bathroom. She mistook the tears as tears of concern and assured Mrs. Applegate that Mrs. Jones was going to be just fine, never knowing that these ladies knew they were both just fine, no matter what happened.

Breakfast arrived and Addie lifted the lid on the tray to find a pale egg white omelet, one piece of dry wheat toast, orange juice, and stewed prunes. There was no salt on the tray, and only the tiniest package of sugar free jelly. Decaffeinated coffee with no cream and artificial sweetener rounded out the fare. Addie was hungry and began eating, but she complained with every bite she took. Mrs. Applegate could be heard trying to encourage her, "Now,

now Addie, it's for your good. We both know we still cook like in the old days of the south with too many egg yolks and too much butter. We eat too much red meat and do enjoy our fried chicken. We both need to change how we eat, and I promise I'll change the way I eat, too."

Addie looked at her little friend who probably weighed in at 95 pounds and nearly spit out her food as she laughed. She was quick to catch it though because she was not certain when or what her next meal would be, and she wanted to get every bite they brought her. "Why, Sharon, you could eat a pound of butter every day, and never gain weight. You have been the same size you are today since you were 18 years old. I'll bet you can still wear your wedding dress, and you talk about watching what you eat." Her laugh echoed into the hall.

Mrs. Applegate was just trying to be a good friend. Addie was right; she had remained the same size through all of her life no matter what she ate. She was right about another thing, too. Her wedding dress still fit. *It seems Addie is always right about everything.*

The doctor arrived soon after breakfast and explained to Addie what had happened with her rapid heartbeat. "I don't want to minimize the importance of it. It is very serious. However, with medication taken as prescribed, I feel you can continue your everyday activities with no ramifications from this episode." However, he cautioned her that she would need frequent monitoring and dedication to her medical regimen—including not only the medication but diet and exercise. He said he would release her, but that she had to rest for the next two days.

She thanked him and buzzed the nurse to come in and remove the IV's. She was going home. Before the nurse could get into the room, the alarm on the heart monitor sounded as the beats rose while Addie was attempting to prepare herself for departure. The nurse arrived and turned off the alarm. She looked at Addie and reprimanded her. "Mrs. Jones, I know the doctor told you to rest for a couple of days, and he means for you to rest. Let others do things for you. I can tell that's not going to be easy, but it's necessary. If you don't, you may find yourself back in here and the outcome may not be as good."

Sharon Applegate was at her side agreeing that she needed to relax, and Addie rolled her eyes and said, "Oh, yeah, me, relax?" and laughed as the nurse removed the needles and allowed Addie to sit on the side of the bed.

Cindy and Mrs. Applegate had decided the night before that it would be better for Addie to come to the Smith house for her recuperation. Addie began to protest when Mrs. Applegate related the plan, but knew in her heart that she would be better off there. Why *do I have to be in control all the time*, she thought as she reluctantly gave in.

Mrs. Applegate had stopped by Addie's apartment before coming to the hospital and brought the necessary clothing. She didn't want Addie being so anxious to leave the hospital that she was willing to leave in a hospital gown with her backside hanging out. She helped her friend into the slacks and shirt she had brought. She had forgotten her shoes, but the gripper bottomed socks provided by the hospital were sufficient.

Mrs. Applegate called Cindy to prepare her for their arrival and soon the nurse returned with dismissal orders, prescription forms, and a wheel chair.

Addie didn't attempt to balk at riding in the wheel chair. She knew that was her only way out of there, and she was taking it. Mrs. Applegate went ahead and pulled the car near the doors and soon Addie was loaded in.

They stopped by the pharmacy, but it wasn't open. A glance at her watch surprised Mrs. Applegate. It was only 8:45. She had not slept much, and had left her home at 5:00 to go by Addie's to clean up and gather her belongings. She knew that another trip would be necessary, but that could wait she thought. She was suddenly very tired.

The arrival at the Smiths' was welcoming as Mike, Cindy, Mary Margaret, and Mr. Hood sat on the porch. They rushed to the car and seemed to surround it as Addie was attempting to get herself out. Cindy was there offering an arm, but Addie insisted that she was fine and could make it by herself. She was right, she made it by herself. It was slow going, but she did it alone. Cindy and Mrs. Applegate rolled their eyes as she let them know by her actions that she was in control. They just thought they were.

She sat on the porch swing and declined breakfast or other refreshments. She advised, "Such as it was, I had breakfast. Food wasn't much." Nothing further was said.

After a few minutes, Cindy insisted that Addie go in and lie down. She knew that rest was required to recover completely from this type of episode. She convinced Addie that the guest room was ready for her, and together they climbed the stairs, slowly but surely. Addie went into the bathroom before going into the bedroom and in a few minutes returned with the sleep washed from her eyes and feeling refreshed after brushing her teeth. She was again glad that she had brought some of her belongings here not for situations like this, but they came in handy now, too.

Cindy had pulled back the sheets and removed Addie's nightgown from the drawer. Addie changed into the gown and sighed as she reclined on the clean sheets she had put on the bed just 2 days before. The smell from the fabric softener reminded her of clothes that had been dried outside, and her mind raced suddenly to her mama. She immediately remembered finding her in the garden under the warm, freshly dried sheet and wondered if something had happened to her like she had experienced the night before. Tears puddled in the corners of her eyes, but she said nothing and Cindy handed her a tissue.

What about your children, Addie? What time are they coming?"

Addie's heart jumped enough that an alarm would have sounded if she was still in the hospital. She had forgotten this was Memorial Day week-end, and her children were coming.

"Oh, Cindy, I forgot all about that. They should be here about noon. They'll be upset if they get to my house and I'm not there." Panic was beginning to show in her voice.

"Don't worry, Addie." We'll take a note over and leave it on the door. They can all come here, and if you don't mind we'll share them with you. To be honest, I wasn't looking forward to a weekend without all of you, and now it has worked out just fine."

Addie smiled. She knew that Cindy was using her best bedside manner to put her at ease, and it was working. She not only loved this woman, she liked her. *She is a good person*, Addie thought.

She left Addie in the cool room, as the sun filtered around the blinds leaving soft hues, not unlike the first whispers of light on a bright new day. Addie closed her eyes, and thanked God for the house in which she found herself, for the doctors and nurses who had tended her, for the researchers who found the medication that would treat her without surgery, for the paramedics who so gently treated her, for her friend, Sharon Applegate, and . . . She dozed off—exhaustion finally taking over the body of this fearless woman who had found out once again, what she had known to be true for many years that God is in control. The rest of her thanksgivings would have to wait as she slept deeply.

Mrs. Applegate went to the pharmacy and then to Addie's apartment where she placed the note on the door along with directions to the Smith house. Her wording was brief, as she didn't want to alarm the children needlessly. "Am at the Smiths'. Please come there. Love"

She returned to the Smiths' and left the prescriptions. She needed to get home to her own company and said they would be at the dedication of the house at 2:30.

Reverend Cross came along shortly after Mrs. Applegate left. He had called the hospital and was told of Addie's discharge. He knew the plan to bring her here, but was surprised that she had gone along with it. "Did you have to hog tie her?" he questioned Mike with a smile.

"I don't think so—at least I didn't see any ropes when she got here." He explained that she was resting and they went inside. Mr. Hood was again manning the kitchen having just made a fresh pot of coffee and the aroma of a coffee cake wafted from the oven. Mary Margaret was attempting to fold the sheets which she had taken from the dryer, and Reverend Cross joined in as the two of them wrestled the fitted sheet to submission. Mary Margaret knew it would not meet Addie's standards, but felt quite good that it was at least in some sort of folded state. She took them to the study where Mr. Hood had been staying and placed them on the shelf next to the neatly folded blanket he had placed there earlier.

Mary Margaret looked around. The blinds were still closed. The room was cool and almost dark. She suddenly felt comfortable in her home. It felt as though the room had been totally transported from another place. Nothing seemed changed. The room was filled with things from the New York apartment. Her father's desk was in the corner. Pictures from his college days and family photographs were grouped on the walls. Her parents' diplomas were displayed. The sofa bed was hiding its identity as it had been folded up. *May is nearly over*, she thought. *It has been only six weeks since we moved, and I had almost forgotten what it was like in our old apartment.* For the moment, however, she was many miles away in a familiar place. It felt good. The only thing different she noticed were 3 pink roses in a water glass on a table beside the sofa bed. *I wonder where those came from,* she said to herself.

Shouts from outside brought her back to reality as Jordan's unmistakable voice reached her. She opened the blind and looked outside to see him, Davis and Philip riding their bicycles up her driveway. Their fishing poles were being held against the handlebars. With the magical moment broken, she went into the hall and could hear Addie snoring through the closed door. She quietly went downstairs to join the rest of her family, Mr. Hood, Reverend Cross, and the boys.

Davis asked about Miss Addie and was pleased when he heard she had been released from the hospital. "My mom is bringing something over in a little while, a cake or something," he said before he joined the others on the trek to the pond.

Mike opened the garage door and gathered up his fishing gear. He offered poles and Mr. Hood and Mary Margaret accepted. Reverend Cross said he would love to, but he had better stay near the house so that he'd be there when Addie woke up.

Cindy and Reverend Cross sat on the swing while the others could be heard by the pond. "With all that noise they'll scare away the fish," said Reverend Cross. She agreed, but added that it was good to hear the joy after the week of chaos they had been through. Reverend Cross concurred, and said, "I can't remember a time when so much has happened to so few in such a short time."

Cindy took this opportunity when no one else was around to inquire about Allison Kincaid. She knew Reverend Cross was in touch with her parents and would disclose anything he felt he could.

"Well", he drawled. "Let me see, now. She has been taken to Charleston and is in a medical facility. She has been put on medication that is used for treating people with anger, and is undergoing psychotherapy. You understand," he continued, "I am not at liberty to share much about the situation, but her parents are concerned about the underlying reason for her behavior. They're not just interested in making the situation here go away. They want to help her get better, and I commend them for that."

Cindy acknowledged his position and thanked him for being as candid as he was.

A vehicle could be heard turning onto the drive and soon Jennifer's SUV could be seen. She stopped near the garage and removed a cake saver from the rear of her vehicle. She walked around and looked like sunshine itself in her coral cropped pants and shirt. Her feet were exposed as she wore flip flops matching the color of her outfit. Her long hair had been pulled back. The sun glistened off the highlights, and her smile radiated as she greeted them.

She explained that she wanted to bring something over to share. It seems that the telephone lines had been buzzing all morning, and the ladies of the church had lined up people in the congregation to bring food the entire weekend. She didn't know who was bringing what, but she allowed that if it was true to form they would be able to feed any army in a short while. She said she wished she could stay, but she needed to go open the store. "I don't know why I bother on holiday weekends, but I guess I need to be there for those few who need shoes today. In this town, this weekend marks the time to take shoes off and not put them on. Oh, well, at least I'll be closed tomorrow and Monday for the holiday. It won't be too bad." She yelled and waved to the fishermen as she walked to her car and was gone almost as quickly as she had arrived.

Cindy excused herself to put the cake in the kitchen and to begin a list for thank-you notes she knew Addie would insist on writing. Before she returned, another car had pulled in, and a lady she didn't know was on the porch with Reverend Cross. She was carrying a ham. Cindy walked out and extended her hand. The lady introduced herself and explained that she was Joey's mother, Barbara Daniel. It was obvious from the look on her face that Cindy was not acquainted with Joey, and the name was not ringing any bells. "My son, Joey, is in Mary Margaret's class at school and is in Betty Tyler's Sunday school class with her as well. They don't really know each other yet, but he has been telling me about all the problems she has encountered since y'all moved here. When I received the call that Miss Addie had been taken ill and was here to recuperate, I wanted to bring this ham to help out. I know her children will be coming here today, and Miss Addie is bound to be having lots of visitors. We all love her so. My husband lost his job at the mill a few months back, and Miss Addie has been so kind during that time. We will never be able to repay her for all she has done."

"Husband lost his job at the mill!" Those words were echoing through Mrs. Smith's head. *Nobody had lost their job at the mill since they moved here, what was this woman talking about*, she wondered.

"Mrs. Daniel it is so kind of you to come by and bring this generous gift. I'll be sure to tell Addie that you were here. Let me put it in the refrigerator. Won't you come in and have a cup of coffee? Addie is asleep right now, but I'm sure she'd love to see you when she wakes up. You say your son's name is Joey. I'm sure I've heard Mary Margaret speak of him before." Her nervousness was obvious as one sentence lapped over the other and she barely took a breath.

Mrs. Daniel and Reverend Cross followed her as she carried the ham into the kitchen. She was struggling to get the refrigerator door open, and Reverend Cross reached around to assist her. Together they managed to find room for the meat, and Mrs. Daniel continued to stand in the middle of the room.

"Oh, please, please, have a seat," Cindy Smith stammered still trying to get her thoughts together to come up with a reason why this woman was saying her husband had lost his job at the mill.

Mrs. Daniel sat at the table and Reverend Cross filled three coffee cups. He carried them to the table and returned to the refrigerator for the milk. Cindy realized that he was carrying on in her mental absence and apologized to him. "Oh, I am so sorry. Here, let me get that." He said he was used to doing this at home and was happy to help out here. "You'll have plenty to do as the weekend goes on. Let me help when I can."

Finally, the coffee was on the table and the milk and sugar. The silence hung in the air, and Cindy knew nothing else to say except what was on her mind. "Barbara, you said your husband lost his job at the mill. When was that? I didn't think anybody had lost their jobs since my husband arrived. In fact, I thought he was hiring new people."

Barbara Daniel felt the tears welling in her eyes. "This had nothing to do with your husband, Cindy. In fact, I feel certain it would never have happened had your husband been here. You see, as best as I can say without being so ugly that you wouldn't want me back in your home, the person who headed up the mill before your husband arrived was not completely honest. No, I'd like to say he was not honest at all. He was the main reason the mill was about to close. Not only was he not honest, he was a thief, and he insisted that my husband sign off on some of his misdeeds. When he refused, he was fired. No, that's not right. He quit! He couldn't stand by any longer, and he knew he would be fired, so he just quit. This man was so powerful that no one could help my husband. Eventually, the man resigned, but not before he lined his personal coffers and nearly bankrupt the mill. He has moved on to another source of revenue and will probably do the same to them. Meanwhile, my husband has his integrity, knowing he did the right thing, but our family has struggled. I have gone to work teaching at the county high school, and my husband finally got a job as the custodian at the new Shop-Mart. This is a college educated CPA who cleans toilets at night and quite honestly is glad to have the job. At least he feels some accomplishment at the end of his shift."

Cindy thought she was nervous before, but now she was outraged. "Can you wait here just a minute? I want you to tell this to my husband. He needs to know everything." She was out the door even before Barbara could respond knowing in her heart that this woman would still be seated in her kitchen when she returned.

The two returned in a few seconds. Mike was winded as he had run when he heard Cindy's frantic calls to him. He couldn't imagine what crisis had befallen them now, but he knew he was needed in a hurry.

Cindy introduced her husband to Barbara Daniel and asked her to tell her story again. She repeated the words, and Mike was somewhat dumbfounded when she finished, but not altogether surprised. His analysis of the business indicated that it should have been at least borderline profitable if not totally profitable, but the books showed it severely in the red. He had called in outside auditors who concluded that the books as presented were correct. However, they had placed some sort of disclaimer on their report regarding fraud. Now that disclaimer flashed in his brain.

Mrs. Daniel, this is the first I've heard of this. I promise you and I will promise your husband that I will get to the bottom of it. His mind was racing. He knew he had to be careful what he said. He couldn't make promises nor hurl accusations until he completed his investigation, but now missing pieces to the puzzle were beginning to fall into place. Profitability had come quickly once he took over the mill. Manufacturing had changed, but not to the extent that would allow the quick climb out of the hole. *Why didn't Gerry Gilbert tell me about this,* he wondered, but quickly turned his attention back to the tearful lady sitting at his kitchen table.

She was wiping her eyes with her napkin, and she looked at him squarely. "Mr. Smith, I have heard nothing but good things about what you're doing at the mill, and I know you can't promise my husband a job. However, I do hope that you will be able to give him back his pride. He feels like he has let his family down to keep his integrity intact. To me he is my white knight, and I couldn't love him more."

"I just wish I had known about this sooner, and I promise that the day will not end before I have a better handle on the situation."

Mary Margaret and Mr. Hood had come into the house to get drinks for everyone and to see if anything was wrong. It was obvious that the conversation didn't concern them, but the interruption led to Mrs. Daniel's departure. She explained that she had errands to run and thanked them for their time.

Mike and Cindy walked her to her car, thanked her for the ham and assured her that they would tell Addie of her visit. Mike shook her hand and again promised a complete investigation.

Reverend Cross and Mr. Hood filled a box with cold drinks they found in the refrigerator. "This is good," the Reverend said. "We need to find some empty space in this refrigerator, and we need to find it fast."

He was right. Car after car came up the driveway, and members of the congregation introduced themselves, inquired of Addie's condition, and left testaments of their visit—freshly baked bread, fried chicken, potato salad, macaroni salad, deviled eggs, green beans, more cakes. On and on it went until noon.

The cars that arrived after noon were first Mrs. Applegate and her daughter, Beverly. They couldn't wait until the dedication at 2:30. They wanted to be a part of everything, they explained. Beverly was a mirror image of her mother probably 35 years earlier. She radiated the same warmth from her tiny body, and soon ingratiated herself into the mix as she moved seamlessly into the kitchen duties. Next to arrive were 2 of Addie's sons, who were obviously distressed when they learned of their mother's illness. Cindy's professional manner and explanation put them at ease, but they would not be satisfied until they saw for themselves.

They were taken upstairs and Cindy listened. It was still. She quietly opened the door, and Addie was sitting on the side of the bed. She had heard the footfalls and was anxious to see whose they were. Cindy stepped aside, and the concerned faces of her sons were the next things she saw. "Don't look so down in the mouth. I'm not dead yet. It's three strikes and you're out. I'm nowhere near that." They smiled broadly and immediately went in to hug her.

Cindy honored their privacy and left them alone. However, within minutes she could hear them in the hallway and knew that Addie had been kept down as long as she could stand it. She was coming out.

They reached the kitchen and Addie took a seat at the table. Her sons stood, but Cindy insisted they sit after they properly greeted Beverly and Mrs. Applegate. They had spoken upon arrival, but that was overshadowed by learning that their mother was ill. This was a true greeting. They hugged like family. Nothing was contrived about the feelings these folks shared for each other. Cindy could feel the tears welling in her eyes as she witnessed family cohesion. It was like a family reunion.

Addie was at a loss for words as she learned of the food gifts which had been brought on her behalf. "Why would you feel like that?" chastised Mrs. Applegate. "Woman, you have fed nearly every family in this town. The least they want to do is feed yours." Addie knew it was true, but she felt unworthy of such an outpouring. "They don't need to do this anymore. You just call and tell them to put a stop to this. I'll be on my feet in a day or so, and I can take care of everybody here."

Mrs. Applegate just flung her hand in the air as she knew there was no talking to this stubborn woman. Anyway, she thought, *the deed has been done, and food will arrive for 2 more days. Ha. Ha.*

After lunch Reverend Cross said he needed to go prepare for the festivities and would meet them at 2:30. Addie asked, "What time is it?" Somebody said it was 12:45, and she started to rise from her chair. "Where do you think you are going?" asked her son, Leonard.

"I'm going to Mr. Hood's house," she responded.

"Well, I don't know who this Mr. Hood is, but you aren't going anywhere."

"Who's going to stop me?" asked Addie, and everyone in the room answered, "We are!" She knew she was overwhelmed and would miss the day's festivities. "Okay," she said, disappointedly, but I want to know all about it, and I want to know how he likes everything.

Mr. Hood had remained at the pond with the boys and had missed lunch in the kitchen. Mary Margaret brought sandwiches to them, and told Mr. Hood they were getting ready to go to his house, and he needed to come along in a few minutes. Butterflies seemed to stampede in his stomach, and he refused the sandwich she brought. He was not accustomed to being the center of attention and liked being on the outside looking in. This was uncomfortable to him. He had anticipated this time, but now that it was here, he wished it could happen without his being present. He knew it couldn't, and he also knew he would not do anything to jeopardize his position with Mike. He felt Mike would understand how he felt, but still he wanted him there, so he was going to be there no matter how awkward it felt.

He made his way to the house and went into his room. He unfolded the waxy green paper and removed the three pink roses from the glass on the table beside the sofa bed. He dried the stems and along with the baby's breath gently placed them on the paper. He wrapped the paper around the stems and attempted to retie the pink ribbon in a bow. After several attempts, he deemed that a square knot would have to do. He changed his clothes and went into the kitchen where Addie and her two sons were still sitting. He introduced himself, and Addie introduced her sons forgetting that Jim had met Mr. Hood on Mother's Day.

Then he began, "Addie, I'd planned to give you these at my new house today to thank you for being so kind to me when I knew you really didn't want to. It's not that you didn't want to, but, you know, you didn't know me, and for all you knew, I could have been an axe murderer. Anyway, I know you took good care of me and saw that I got my medicine and fed me well, and, you know, you did more than you had to. Well, everybody has done more than they had to, but you really seemed to take a personal interest in getting me better even if it may have been to get me out of the house sooner. I don't know, but anyhow, I wanted you to have these."

With his speech completed, he bowed and handed Addie the roses. Unfortunately, he had been so nervous that he didn't realize he was holding the wrong end of the package. His calloused hands failed to recognize the bulge of the buds, and when he handed the wrinkled green paper to Addie the heads of all three roses fell onto the floor.

Addie was touched by his speech and her son bent over to retrieve the broken buds. He placed them in his mother's hands, and she graciously accepted them in the manner in which they had been given.

"Mr. Hood, you have proven yourself to be a man of honor. Yes, I was concerned when Mike brought you into this house, but I knew him to be a man of character who would not knowingly jeopardize what was dear to him, his wife and daughter. I probably was not as gracious to you as I could have been, but as the housekeeper I treated you as I would any guest. In the few days since you have been here, however, I don't consider you a guest, you are a friend, and I thank you for this lovely token of friendship. By the way, I really didn't think you were an axe murderer."

The sons stood as the two friends exchanged compliments. They looked at each other and wondered what the story was behind this, but felt for now it was better left untold.

Chapter 63

Soon they were in the van heading toward the mill. Mr. Hood had placed his belongings in the rear, and he was wearing his new uniform. His tall frame looked handsome, and the clothes hid his frail limbs. Perspiration stains circled under his arms. Water ran down his face and dripped on his shirt. He couldn't remember being more nervous. He had been coming to terms with the fact that he now had responsibilities, and he was scared. He had run away from the responsibilities of marriage and parenthood. Work challenged him as responsibilities grew with each passing day. He hid his fears under the guise of being a wanderer, but for the first time in his life he had to admit that he was afraid of failure. He was at a time in his life when most people his age were accepting fewer responsibilities. He, however, was maybe for the first time in his life, accepting them. Not only for himself, but for a whole company. He was going to be responsible for keeping people out of a mill from 11:00 p.m. until 7:00 a.m. *What if I fall asleep? What if somebody climbs over the back fence when I'm in the front? What if there is a fire?* His mind raced over and over for the few minutes until the van was parked in the drive beside the newly whitewashed house.

The doors opened on the van and Mr. Hood asked Mike to stay with him for a moment. Cindy and Mary Margaret got out and closed the doors. Mike turned in his seat to see the perspiration soaked old man. His clothes no longer looked crisp and fresh. They appeared to be more like a dirty bath towel at the bottom of the laundry basket.

"What is wrong, old friend?" Mike asked, and Mr. Hood lowered his head. "I don't know if I can do this. I just don't think I can. For the first time in my life I have come against something that I don't want to run away from, but I don't know how to face it. I'm afraid I'll let you down, just like I've let down everybody else in my life."

"Who have you let down?" Mike asked innocently, not really prepared for the answer he was about to be given.

"First of all I let my parents down. I ditched school, and I disappointed them. Then I married, and I was not the husband I should have been to my wife. I was always off somewhere else. She had to make the way for our family. We had our two sons, and they must have been terribly disappointed in their father who was never there for their birthdays, Christmas, to see them graduate high school, to teach them to fish or to do anything at all. I've had good jobs over the years, and I've let down every employer I ever had. Just when they would feel they could depend on me, I would jump ship so to speak and leave them high and dry. Now you come along, and you're like a son I never knew. You've treated me with respect, and I love you for that. You took me into your home, and made me a part of your family. Now I don't want to disappoint you, too, and I'm afraid that if I do this I will."

Mr. Smith continued to look into the pooled eyes of this old man and loved him even more. He knew that the old Mr. Hood would have jumped ship and left him high and dry, but this was a new man sitting before him. Yeah, he was scared, but for the first time instead of running from his fears, he was facing them. After pondering those words, he shared them with Mr. Hood, who seemed to sit a little straighter in the seat when he finished. Then he said, "Mr. Hood, anytime you feel that you need to leave, I want you to know that you have my blessing to go as your spirit leads. However, I don't want you to run because you feel you can't do this, because I feel you can, and I know you won't let me down. My expectations for you are high, and I know you will satisfy them. You can come to me at anytime, and together we can find a solution for any problem you have. Come on now, friend; let's bless this new beginning in your life."

Reverend Cross and Gerry Gilbert had been standing on the porch and wondered what was transpiring in the van. No clue was evident when the two men stepped out and hugged each other before walking toward the porch.

Reverend Cross began at the stroke of 2:30. Gathered around him were Gerry, Sylvia, Mike Cindy, Mary Margaret, Mrs. Applegate and her daughter, Beverly, along with a few employees from the mill who were probably nosier than anything thought Mrs. Applegate as she recognized them. She had heard comments around town that Mike seemed to be getting carried away about hiring a night watchman. She knew it was the usual gossip of a few and had not seen fit to repeat it. Their presence confirmed her thoughts. These were folks who loved nothing better than a feud.

Reverend Cross took notice of their presence as well. He began by welcoming the guests to the blessing, not only of a new home, but a new beginning for the mill. He continued—

"This mill has provided not only income for many families through the years, but it stands as a place of integrity. These walls are constructed of bricks and mortar, but the interior or the heart of this building has been built by the blood, sweat and tears of men and women who have worked there. They came day after day, year after year to provide for their families in the only way some of them knew how. They were honored to be able to work here. They were able to not only support their families but the community as well."

"We faced a time when it appeared this legacy was going to end. A few short months ago the rumor was the mill would be closing. The town was in mourning. Our futures appeared bleak. We were sent a man from New York whose purpose it was to turn this mill around and not only maintain the employment of those already there, but to increase it in an industry where many of the jobs are being sent overseas."

"This man had a vision. His vision included not only the people who worked in the mill, but the community as a whole. He wanted to see prosperity in every business. He wanted to see growth in the entire community. He wanted only the best for the people of Left Fork, South Carolina, and this mill."

"We have been blessed by this man's vision. In less than six months, the rumors are different. Now we hear in the grocery store that the mill is hiring. We hear that somebody is building a new house. We hear it's a good place to work."

"A part of this man's vision is to utilize the mill and its properties to their fullest. These houses here were once filled with workers who couldn't afford to live anywhere else. Now they're filled with junk. They were company houses, and a portion of the employees' pay was held as housing expense

for the people who lived here. Those days have long since passed, but with the influx of new people, and the limited amount of housing in Left Fork, these houses will one by one be refurbished and rented to the employees. His vision is endless, and we need to be thankful that we have him."

"Let us pray.

Dear Lord,

We have come here today and stand before You in this heat to praise Your name and to thank You for the hand You have played in turning this mill around. We thank You that our families now have a more secure economic future. We thank You that You have sent someone with a vision that will benefit all the community and not a chosen few."

"We ask, Lord, that You bless those who have gathered here today to join in this celebration and those who were unable to attend.

"And, finally, Lord, we ask that You bless this house and turn it into a home to provide not only shelter but comfort and joy to all who enter into it. May it be filled with peace and thanksgiving.

"We ask these things in the name of your precious son, Jesus.

Amen."

The listeners wiped tears as Reverend Cross completed his prayer. The words had touched their hearts but each in a personal way. Mrs. Applegate was thanking God not only for the economic boon to the community, but also for the relationship she had developed with this family and the friendship she felt for them.

Gerry and Sylvia Gilbert held hands as they prayed, which had been their practice for many years. They not only felt closer to God when they prayed, but they felt united in their love for God with this simple gesture. She was thanking God for the revitalization of the community and the character of the man who had been brought there.

Gerry Gilbert was looking forward to a future of friendship with a man he had grown to admire.

Mr. Hood was overcome by the enormity of it all. He was standing on the threshold of his own home. He was prepared to sleep in his sleeping bag, but knew that he would have a roof over his head. He would be able to go to the bathroom in proper facilities and would no longer have to walk to the nearest fast food restaurant or gas station or worse yet find a secluded area as he hitched along a highway. He could go into the kitchen and fill his tin cup with water. He could flip a switch and have light. He would have heat in the winter. He could prepare decent food. The basic necessities of life that those around him took for granted had not been available to him, and he was now thankful. If that wasn't enough, he was going to be able to support himself financially. He would have money in his pocket. He was going to be a contributing part of this community. He stood a little taller and remembered Mike's words to him, "My expectations for you are high, and I know you will satisfy them. You can come to me at anytime, and together we can find a solution for any problem you have." He was thankful to finally have somebody in his life who told him they believed in him. The words sang over and over in his head, and he liked the tune he heard.

Cindy did not think she had could remember a moment when she was more proud of her husband. She had always honored him, but to hear his praises from someone like Reverend Cross, whom she had come to admire immediately for his sincerity, she felt like she was going to burst with pride. She knew him to be a man of honor and integrity, but to hear that his vision was being brought to fruition not only made her proud to be his wife, but proud for him that he was accomplishing what he set out to do.

The other visitors were clustered together talking about the other houses that would be available for rent. This concept had never occurred to them. They could not conceive that the company would be not only willing but desired to assist employees. "Do you think they'll really do it?" asked one. "If Reverend Cross says it, I believe it," answered another. They also had to admit that the future of not only the mill but the community was brighter because of this man's vision.

Mary Margaret stood apart from the grownups. She didn't know how to be a part of this occasion. It was more her daddy's business, and he had always intentionally kept her out of that part of his life. Yes, she knew where he worked, and sort of what he did, but he had never shared much else. He had always kept his work out of the home, except when it was absolutely necessary to bring it there. Now she was in the middle of something that seemed almost like a family function, but she knew deep in her heart that it was her daddy's professional life that was happening here. She listened to the words Reverend Cross spoke, and with each syllable she stood a little taller. She realized that her daddy was not only important to his family, he was important to the people who worked for him and to this whole town. She was taken back to the day when he asked for her support. After hearing the praises of her father, she hoped that she had not made it too difficult for him to fulfill this dream he had for his family and the community he told her about that day.

Reverend Cross pulled out a pair of scissors, and together Mr. Hood and Mike cut the ribbon which had been placed across the door. The screen door was opened, and Mike stepped back to allow Mr. Hood to be the first to enter the home he had not seen since its completion. He walked in expecting an empty house, but instead found a fully furnished home. He gasped as the reality of it swept over him. He couldn't seem to walk and dropped to one knee.

Mike was at his side and reached down to assist him, but Mr. Hood raised a hand. "I am okay," he whispered. "Just give me a moment." In that moment tears covered the wrinkled cheeks of this man. They dripped on his uniform and large wet circles formed on his chest and shoulders. He wept openly. His friends wept as well.

He finally stood and faced those who had formed a semi circle around him. His voice was weak, but he began with, "Thank you, God, for finally bringing me home. I don't deserve any of this. My life has been a disappointment to you and everybody I've known before, but I promise You, God, and all these people gathered here that I'm a changed man. I'll spend the rest of my life working not only for my benefit, but for Your glory. Amen."

By this time the tissues everybody had been using after the dedication were soaked and were nothing more than compressed wads. Noses sniffed, and eyes were averted as the folks in the room attempted to gain their composure.

Nobody had seen that others had entered the room, and their presence went unnoticed for a few seconds until a clear unmistakable voice was raised and the words echoed through the house. They turned to see Addie and her 4 children. Addie had begun to sing and the words melted the hearts of all those present. She began singing the prayer of prayers from Matthew 6:9-13, the Lord's prayer. Her voice filled the tiny house. Her eyes closed as she prayed for God's blessing on earth as it is in heaven. She asked for forgiveness and the ability to forgive. She asked that they be delivered from evil and temptation. Finally, she proclaimed God's kingdom and power and glory now and forever.

She was weeping as she finished and said she needed to sit down. Needless to say, no one reprimanded her for being there. Instead, they all commented that it would not have been the same without her.

Her daughters greeted Cindy and Mike Smith and thanked them for caring for their mother. Carolyn said to her sister, Louise, "See, I told you that you would like them."

With introductions over—everyone toured the beautiful little house. Mr. Hood was still overcome and ran his fingers across each piece of furniture. He touched the bedspread. He turned on the new kitchen faucet. He even flushed the commode. *I must be dreaming*, he thought to himself.

The table had been covered with platters of cookies and Sylvia had brought a punch bowl. Refreshments were served, and the icy mixture of orange juice concentrate, pineapple juice and ginger ale was refreshing after the ceremony in the hot May afternoon in Left Fork, South Carolina.

Mrs. Applegate and Beverly were the first to leave each wondering what the grandchildren had done while they were gone.

Addie's children insisted that she leave. Mr. Hood came over and took Addie's hand to help her from the sofa. "Addie, I can't begin to tell you how much I appreciate your being here today. It's a comfort to know that God is watching over me as I live here."

Everybody laughed at his comment, knowing he was intentionally relieving the enormous amount of emotion that had accumulated during this process. It worked, the mood was immediately lighter and conversations overlapped each other until only the good-byes could be discerned as the vehicles pulled from the drive.

The Gilberts, Smiths and Mr. Hood were all who remained. Cindy and Sylvia began clearing the table and picking up the cups and plates which had been left around the rooms. Mary Margaret held the trash can and walked around with her mother.

Mike told Mr. Hood that he wanted to meet with him the next afternoon at about 4:00 o'clock so that they could go over his duties and asked Gerry to join them to show Mr. Hood how the surveillance equipment worked. The butterflies were now just fluttering in his stomach instead of stampeding as they were earlier, and he agreed to the meeting.

Mike turned to Gerry and told him that something had come up on another matter and asked him to walk to their office with him. Gerry was surprised but readily agreed.

It was determined that Sylvia would ride home with Cindy and Mary Margaret and the two men would come along shortly.

Mr. Hood suddenly found himself alone in his not only empty house, but his silent house. The noise of the previous hour had filled the home, but now in its emptiness he felt lonely. Loneliness had never been a problem for him. Unless he was under self analysis, he usually found himself to be good company. As he pondered this, he laughed. "I am just an egotistical old poop," he said out loud and looked around to see if anybody heard. He often talked to himself as he traveled. At least he rarely had an argument. He usually agreed with what he had to say.

He walked over, sat on the sofa and then moved to the chair. He slightly repositioned it so that his feet could rest on the coffee table. *That is much better*, he thought. He relaxed in the chair and soon was snoring.

Chapter 64

In the office at the adjacent mill, Mike and Gerry had each gotten a soft drink and were now in Mike's office. Gerry had never seen his business associate so intense. It was obvious that they were about to discuss a matter of a serious nature, and as he searched the cobwebs of his mind, he could not come up with anything. Things were going good at the mill. For the first time in nearly three years, they were going to post a small profit for the second quarter. He was expecting a celebration in a few days when the figures were disclosed. The renovations of the houses were underway, and it was expected that each one would be filled in the next two to three months. There was a surplus of applications for the positions which were available and would be available in the near future. *What could be so serious as to warrant a private meeting on this particular holiday week-end, Saturday afternoon,* he wondered.

Mike was removing financial reports from the file cabinets and opened the ones dated January 1, 2000 through December 31, 2000. The bottom line indicated a deficit of $1,487,256.12. He noticed the disclaimer, and the word fraud jumped out at him.

"Gerry, I want you to tell me about my predecessor."

"Well, he was nothing like you. He did not delegate authority. He was more of a dictator. He held his power over the employees, and was not loyal to anyone. If you didn't follow his mandates, you were fired. I think I'm still here only because I knew the mechanics of the mill, and he knew nothing about that. He was not pleasant to be around and the morale was very low as you saw when you arrived. He created a distrustful atmosphere. What else do you want to know, and may I ask you why you want to know this?"

Mike was pondering these words and a brief silence filled the room. Gerry moved nervously in his chair and wondered if he had been too candid in his response. The man about whom they were speaking wielded a wide sword when he was in this company, and he now felt blessed to have missed its blow, although there were times when he almost left what he considered to be his home forever. He was a little man who lived in Charleston and commuted. He was never a part of the community and considered himself above it. His life seemed lavish when compared to those around him. "He was just plain hateful," Gerry said to fill the emptiness.

Mike began to tell his co-worker the story that had unfolded in his kitchen earlier that day. It was obvious that he was distressed that somebody had not only mistreated employees of the company he had come to love, but had possibly stolen millions of dollars in the process.

"I heard about that back in 2000 and my heart ached for Rick. I always found him to be honorable. However, my duties didn't include preparation of the financial reports although I always questioned why the mill was not profitable. The quality of our work had allowed us to garner the higher prices necessary to pay the wages, but somehow it never filtered out onto paper. Before you got here there was talk that the health insurance plan would be completely dropped but instead significant cuts were taken. You know yourself; the health insurance was almost a joke with the high deductibles and lack of other coverages. You personally changed that."

"Gerry, we've got to get to the bottom of this, and I'll do that with the internal auditors from New York. I've already placed a call, and they will be here on Monday afternoon. Before that, though, we've got to right what I believe is an unconscionable wrong. We've got to go see Mr. Daniel and attempt to mend this man's credibility. I've always felt something was wrong, and until now couldn't identify the source of the loss of funds. I think you have just opened my eyes. Mr. Daniel is cleaning toilets at the Shop-Mart, and while there is nothing wrong with that, this is not the man who should be doing it. I want him on our team, and I want him here to meet the auditors on Monday. I'll meet with our accounting staff on Monday morning, and hopefully, we won't find any rotten apples here. I haven't seen anything suspicious since I have been here, but we still have to look."

Mike rose, and Gerry followed suit.

"Gerry, I can't drive until tomorrow, and I hope that you will be my chauffeur."

It was agreed that they would go to Mike's house and plan their strategy on the way.

They walked back to the company truck parked in Mr. Hood's driveway. The front door was open and Mike went up to say good-bye. He could hear the snores from the front steps and laughed heartily as he walked back to the truck.

Chapter 65

The Smith house was full, and folding chairs had been brought over from the church and placed on the porch. Davis, Jordan, Philip and Mary Margaret were drinking lemonade under the weeping willow. The boys were curious about the house Mr. Hood had moved into. Mary Margaret described it to them, and told them about the furniture. When she appeared to have finished, Jordan asked where the television was. Mary Margaret thought and responded that there wasn't one.

Jordan jumped to his feet, "No television!" he stammered. "How can anybody live without television? At my house the TV is on all the time."

Philip said, "Well, Jordan, just think about it for a minute. He didn't have a television when he lived in his tent. He probably won't miss something he never had."

Jordan thought about this, but still it didn't seem right. "I know what," he said. I saw a 13-inch color TV in Mr. Rowell's window just yesterday, and it only cost $119.95. I have about $50.00. How much do you have, Davis?"

Well, now, this was serious to Davis. His money was precious to him. He didn't like to spend his own money, and he was caught off guard. "Uh, I, uh, I don't know, maybe $10.00 or so."

"Oh, come on Davis, I know you have more than $100.00. Can't you divvy up some of it? It's for a good cause, and besides, he saved your girlfriend's life."

Into Addie's Arms

With those words, all heck broke loose. Davis and Jordan were soon a mass of flailing arms and legs. Philip just stood back and laughed, and Mary Margaret was so disgusted she wanted to pour the pitcher of lemonade on them. Fortunately, Addie's son, Jim had decided to come see how the fishing was going. He was just in time to break up the fight and attempted to determine its cause. He couldn't understand what Davis and Jordan were saying as they continued to shout at each other, and Jordan seemed to be crying that Davis had punched him in the eye. He was holding his right eye, and was spitting mad.

After all explanations were finished, he sat the boys down and he joined them. He looked around at the 4 sweaty children, and said, "This is a perfect example of something good going bad. Jordan, you had a wonderful idea. However, if Davis doesn't want to be an equal partner of that idea, it's okay. I'm sure he has his ideas, and you don't want to be an equal partner in them. Instead of fighting, you need to accept what the other person is willing to do, and move along. If you can attain your goal, good for you, but if you can't, don't consider it a failure. You guys are brothers and have a lifetime bond. It's important that you respect each other, and it's never too soon to do that."

Davis hung his head and said, "It's not that I didn't want to help. He said that Mary Margaret was my girlfriend. That's why I hit him."

Jim tried to control his lips as they wanted to curl into a smile, but he maintained his serious face and said, "Well, you know what. I think you would be a lucky man if Mary Margaret was your girlfriend. She is one fine lady."

With this Mary Margaret blushed and wanted to run away, but she felt pulled in by Jim's charm.

"I'll tell you what. I'll put in $25.00 toward that television set. Jordan, how much are you in for?"

Jordan scratched his head, and the shiner was becoming obvious. "Well, I said I had $50.00, but I'd like to keep some of it for when we visit our grandparents. I'll put in $25.00.

"Davis, would you like to participate in this?" Jim asked.

Davis said, "Oh, okay, I'll give $25.00, too."

Jim looked him in the eye and said, "Davis, remember God loves a cheerful giver. Do you qualify?"

Davis smiled and said, "Yeah, I qualify."

Philip said, "I don't have any money with me, but I can get $25.00 at my house if someone will take me there."

Mary Margaret was already standing. "I'll get my money, too," she said, we have to pay tax.

It was agreed that they would get permission to go to Mr. Rowell's after stopping by to get Philip's money and purchase a new 13-inch television for Mr. Hood.

Jim took his dirty brood to the house and after the idea was explained, and a phone call was made to the Raver household for permission, it was agreed that the trip could commence.

It was nearly 5:00 when they had gathered all the money and ventured into Rowell's Department store. The wooden floors creaked under their feet and a cool fragrant smell greeted them. This area was for perfumes and colognes, and to one side could be seen purses and scarves. On the other side mannequins were modeling the latest junior summer wear.

The store seemed empty of customers except the three dirty little boys, one little girl and a tall, handsome man. They walked through the store, and clerks were busying themselves with the day's tallies. They nodded and acknowledged the presence of the customers, who seemed to know where they were headed which thankfully the clerks thought was not to them. It was almost 5:00, and they didn't want to be kept late waiting on somebody who couldn't decide on a $2.00 scarf.

The customers took the stairs to the lower level and found themselves in the Furniture Department. Jim and the boys knew where to go as their parents had shopped in this store many times. Davis and Jordan often came over when they had to stay at their mother's shoe store. They were considered *regulars* to the clerks.

Jim knew Lew Rowell and looked forward to seeing him again. He had worked for Mr. Rowell when he was in high school. He helped make deliveries and did whatever was necessary on week-ends and summer vacation. Mr. Rowell had been a good role model for Jim, as he watched him treat his customers with care, and lived by the words he taught on Sunday morning.

They found him where he often was in the Furniture Department. For a town this size, the stock was on par with Charleston. Mr. Rowell and his wife, Jerry, went to market in High Point every year and maintained high quality, reasonably priced merchandise. After greetings, Mr. Rowell learned the purpose of their visit. He was touched by the generosity and led the way to the electronics. The television displayed in the window was right there. It was a 13-inch color TV, and it was $119.95. Right above it was a 19-inch remote control television for $159.95. The wadded up money was already being pulled from pockets which had until a short time before held fishing worms. Mary Margaret's money was folded nicely in her hand, but was damp from perspiration. The children put the money on the table. And Jordan began counting. When he reached $100.00, he looked at Jim, who withdrew his money clip and placed two $10.00 bills and $5.00 bill on the pile.

"One Hundred Twenty-Five Dollars, Mr. Rowell. That's what we have. Is that enough?"

Mr. Rowell looked at the money and said, "Well, today is your lucky day and winked at Jim Jones. The sale on that TV was already over at 5:00 and it's now precisely 5:04. However, this 19-inch is on sale for tomorrow only at the same price. It's a Memorial Day Special."

"Do we have to wait until tomorrow?" Jordan innocently asked, never realizing that tomorrow was Sunday and the store wasn't open.

"No, I think we can complete the transaction right now," said Mr. Rowell. "Come on into my office."

They followed him to the back of the store where he unlocked the soda machine and offered its contents to his customers. Jordan was carrying the money. He held Mr. Rowell's hand in his and the exchange took place. Mr. Rowell completed the paperwork, including an extended warranty at no charge just for this one-day special, and offered to deliver the television himself. Jim agreed, stating that he didn't think it would fit in his car, but Davis countered that they should deliver it themselves.

"It's only a few blocks away, and my wagon is at my mom's store. We can pull it there."

Jim knew this was important, so he agreed. Mr. Rowell phoned Jennifer at her store, and she said she would bring over the wagon at once.

She looked at her boys and cringed. They were as dirty as she had ever seen them and then she noticed the shiner. "What happened to you?" she exclaimed, but stopped Jordan before he could begin his explanation. "Never mind. We will discuss this at home later."

The television was loaded at the front door of the now empty department store, and the journey to Mr. Hood's began. The box was too large to fit in the bed of the wagon, so bungee cords had to be fastened around to hold it on. Each child took a turn at pulling, and the other three steadied their cargo. Jennifer followed along on the street in her SUV in case the journey proved too difficult for anyone. She needn't have worried. They would all sleep well tonight, but right then the adrenalin could have carried them to the moon.

Mr. Hood heard the commotion before he saw his visitors. The wagon rattled down the street and bumped over the break in the pavement onto the drive. The children shouted as they worked to steady their cargo. He walked to the door and laughed at the sight. The caravan of the wagon, children, tall handsome man, and the SUV driven by the pretty woman made its way up the drive and stopped at the steps leading to the porch.

He stepped outside and welcomed his guests. Of course, he knew everyone except Jennifer. After a quick introduction, Jordan got down to business. "Mr. Hood, we heard you didn't have a TV, and we wanted to give you one. We all put our money together, even Jim, and we bought you this one. We wanted to get you the 13-inch model, but Mr. Rowell said the sale ended at 5:00 o'clock, so we had to take this 19-inch one for the same price. We guessed it would be all right."

Mr. Hood was touched by the sincere generosity showing on the faces of these young people. Tears were again welling up in his eyes, and he attempted to stifle them, but to no avail. They streamed down his face and again circled on his already tear-wrinkled shirt. "I don't know what to say, he blubbered. Today has been a day filled with so much joy that I am about out of words, so I guess that thank you is all I have left."

Jim said, "You don't have to say anything. It was something they wanted to do. However, I could use some help getting it in the house."

They attempted to pick up the box, and after some struggle they decided that maybe it would be simpler to unbox it before attempting to carry it in. Mr. Hood got out his pocket knife and cut the strapping tape. The styrofoam was removed along with the other corrugated packing material. Finally, the top of the TV was exposed. Jim attempted to lift it from the box, but the perspiration on his hands and arms made it impossible. He finally sat down on the steps to catch his breath. He secretly wished Mr. Rowell had not been so generous. The 13-inch model would have been much easier to deal with. Mr. Hood went into the house and came back with a glass of ice water which Jim gladly accepted. In a few minutes he was refreshed enough to finally snatch the TV, while Jennifer pulled the box away. Davis hurriedly opened the door, and Jim carried the TV into the house. He immediately recognized another obstacle. Where was he going to put it now that it was inside. His back was aching. The muscles in his legs were quivering when he decided that the coffee table looked to be the best place to him. With a thud he placed it on the table. Glad to be free of it, he collapsed onto the sofa.

After a quick discussion it was decided that for now the coffee table would be moved to the wall until a more appropriate stand could be obtained. Within minutes a blurry picture could be seen on 3 separate channels. Joy filled the room as the children felt at last a part of the celebration.

Jennifer said it was time to head toward home. Mr. Hood invited them to stay, glad for the company, but she loaded up her 5 sweaty passengers for the drive back to pick up Jim's car. The mission was accomplished.

At Jim's car Mary Margaret and Philip got in. Jennifer said she would just take her boys on home to soak in a tub for a few hours to see if the grime would come off. Jordan looked down. "I'm not that dirty, mom. I washed my hands off in the pond, and I haven't touched any worms since then." She cringed as she waved and headed home.

Chapter 66

Mike and Gerry had determined that Rick Daniel was not working at Shop-Mart that night, but instead was washing dishes at a seafood restaurant located on the road to Charleston. They called and arranged to meet him at 9:00 o'clock when he got a break.

The only people left at the Smiths were the Gilberts and Addie's children. After dinner everyone pitched in to clean up, dusk was falling, and Addie said she needed to go on up to bed. Her daughter, Carolyn, went up and pulled back the sheets on the bed that Addie insisted be made up when she left it earlier in the day. Addie finished in the bathroom and came into the bedroom, and hugged her daughter. "I am so glad you are all here," she said. "I thought about you last night and realized that it could have been a different outcome. I want to tell you how much you mean to me. You've always made me proud, and I'm just so sorry your daddy didn't live long enough to see what upstanding, productive people you and your brothers and sister have turned into. Carolyn, you have the gift of compassion. You see beyond the surface of people and somehow can see into their soul. You have a caring heart. You're a wonderful daughter, and will someday be a wonderful wife and mother. I love you, and I don't want to die and wonder if you realized that."

Carolyn was startled at the compliments her mother poured forth. She loved her mother, but felt that in her mother's eyes anything below perfect was unacceptable. Compliments were few and far between but felt like warm chocolate chip cookies on a cold winter's day when they were infrequently bestowed. She hugged her mother. Tears stung the back of her eyes. "Thank you, Mama. I love you, too. I feel that the best of my qualities I learned from you. You have been the most generous person I've ever known. Your love abounds for everybody. You always look for the good."

Then in an attempt to lighten the mood said, "You're a tough old bird. You'll be around forever."

They laughed and Addie climbed into bed. Carolyn closed the door and knew that her mother would spend the next minutes praying—thanking God for caring for her, for the Smith family, for her children, for the preacher, for the church, all of her friends. She knew the list would be nearly endless. She might ask for something, but Carolyn would almost bet it would be for somebody else.

Cindy offered the sofa bed to Addie's children, but they insisted on going back to Addie's apartment. They explained that the sofa was a sofa bed there, and the girls said sharing their mama's bed reminded them of the old days when they had to share a bed. They related that growing up they never had a bed to themselves until one of them went away to college. They laughed as they told stories one after the other of antics they had pulled.

Louise embarrassed Carolyn by reminding her how slow she was at not wetting the bed at night. "She wet that bed every night until she was 7 years old. Mama would just get out the old wringer washing machine every day and hung the sheets in the bathroom so that nobody outside the family would know." With each story, Addie's love for them was apparent as they told of her sacrifices and dedication to their success.

They left and Mike and Gerry were soon behind them. Mary Margaret showered and put on her night gown. Cindy opened her bedroom door after getting ready for bed and turned on the television. Mary Margaret joined her, and in a few minutes she remembered her mother's statement from the day before that there was a surprise for tomorrow. The day had been full of surprises, but Mary Margaret didn't think any of them was what her mother was referring to. "Mother, what was the surprise for today? Did I miss it?"

Her mind raced, and she gasped. "Oh my gosh, Mary Margaret, in all the excitement I forgot all about it. However, I can't tell you what it is. I need to make a phone call and see when we can arrange for another time for the surprise." Mary Margaret went into her room while her mother looked in her Day-Timer for a phone number. She was tired and ready to go to bed.

The two men pulled into the nearly empty parking lot just off the main highway. Mike was exhausted, but felt the need to complete this mission. His purpose was twofold. One was to apologize for somebody else's alleged bad behavior, and the other was to see if this man was willing to come back and assist a company that had let him down as they unraveled the misdeeds.

It almost seemed clandestine as the three men huddled in a corner booth. Rick Daniel provided a pitcher of tea and large glasses filled with ice. They each poured their own as they became acquainted. Within minutes it was obvious that Rick was sincere in his belief that Mike's predecessor had been dishonest. He said it started out casually. He was asked to change a figure here or a figure there, and "I didn't want to rock the boat with my new boss, so I did what he asked. Then his requests began to substantially alter what I thought I knew to be correct. However, I was not aware of the countless dollars he was siphoning off for his personal use. I heard rumors of lavish parties he was giving in Charleston which I assumed were company related, but they turned out to be for his wife's birthday or his son's graduation. He took his family on trips, which I was told were business trips. He rented private jets for the entire trip and would supply me with names of customers who had allegedly accompanied him. I accidentally, well, maybe not so accidentally, mentioned a trip to one of the customers; and it was obvious he knew nothing about it. When I refused to sign a report I knew had been altered, he fired me. No, I quit before he could fire me."

"Why didn't you contact the New York office?"

"He told me he would ruin me if I crossed him in any way. By this time he had browbeaten and intimidated me and most of the other employees, so that we felt we didn't have a leg to stand on. I figured I was well rid of that job, and wanted out. However, when I would apply for a new job, and my previous employer was contacted, I was no longer given consideration. He somehow ruined my reputation. I never could learn what he was telling them, but I could not get a job in my field."

Mike considered what he had heard and began by saying, "I believe what you are telling me. I smelled a rat shortly after I arrived, but I have to give him credit, he covered his tracks very well. I apologize for the injustice I feel you've suffered, and I would like to ask for your assistance in helping us uncover what he did. We may never know everything, but I want to uncover enough that at the very least he'll know we have found him out. Moreover, though, I would like to put him behind bars."

A smile spread across Rick's face, and he asked, "When do we begin?"

"Monday morning, 8:00 o'clock sharp. I have a team of internal auditors arriving around noon, and I'd like for you to work with them. They're the best, but your knowledge will help immensely."

The men shook hands and Rick returned to the kitchen to finish his shift. Gerry took an exhausted business associate home, where the soft glow told them that the family was sleeping.

Chapter 67

Mr. Hood awoke early Sunday morning. The sun was rising, and the birds had begun their concert, but nothing else around him seemed to be awake. He felt a chill in the tiny house upon leaving the warm bed. He realized, however, that in a short time the house would be warm, and there was no need for heat. He went to the bathroom, and enjoyed the comforts he found there. He had unpacked his back pack and his medicine cabinet held the personal items he had carried on his journey. His razor, shaving cream, tooth brush and paste were all neatly stored away. He had placed his shampoo on the bathtub edge, and his soap was in its dish. His towel and washcloth were in the laundry basket, as he had used the ones Mrs. Gilbert had provided. They were soft and smelled fresh compared to his which had been infrequently washed at the laundromat.

He showered and was met with a dilemma. What should he wear? This had not been an issue with him for a long time. He had either his clean jeans and plaid shirt or his dirty plaid shirt and his jeans. The choices were limited. Now new uniforms had been entered into the mix. It was Sunday morning, and he was going to church, so he decided to look his best and wear one of his new uniforms.

Breakfast was a joy. The night before he had investigated the contents of his cabinets and refrigerator. He had prepared himself a breakfast meal for supper, and had enough left over for breakfast. All he had to do was make toast and reheat the sausage and eggs, and he was set. However, he decided to mix the sausage and eggs and add some cheese. He put this in the oven for a few minutes. He made coffee and was on his second cup when the aroma indicated his breakfast was ready. He smacked his lips as he removed it with a hot pad he found in the drawer.

He placed a paper towel over the front of his shirt and started to eat. He stopped, and placed his fork on the table. He folded his hands, and in the stillness of his home, he thanked God for the bounty he has about to receive.

He cleared the table and placed the dishes in the dishwasher after rinsing them. Soon his kitchen was once again tidy, and he moved on to make his bed. With that done, he decided he would walk over to the church. He hoped to be able to speak with Reverend Cross before the services began, but realized that this was his busiest day.

Truthfully, every day was busy for Reverend Cross. He was the only minister in the church, and it fell upon him to fill the needs of his entire congregation. If someone died, he was there. If a baby was born, he was there. If someone was sick, he was there. If there was any family need which called for a minister, his congregation knew he would be there. However, many failed to remember this and often it was discussed that he really only *worked* one day a week, especially when it was time for the Finance Committee to discuss his salary.

Mr. Hood started walking the few blocks to the church on the clear Sunday morning and was at total peace with his world. The aroma of the roses filled the air as he passed by the garden in the park. The sun glistened on the dewdrops until they shone like diamonds.

He stepped onto the grass with his new work boots. The tan leather immediately turned dark as the thick, wet Bermuda grass hugged them and he sank into its dense turf. He looked down, but undeterred continued on to cup several large roses in his hand and breathe in their fragrance.

He recommenced his journey, nodding at two other men who appeared to be on a morning run as they passed him.

He arrived at the church and nobody else was there. He pulled his pocket watch out and realized it was only 7:30. The church sign indicated that services started at 11:00 a.m., with Sunday school at 9:30. Well, *I might as well have a seat*, he thought as he reclined on a bench nearly hidden in the azaleas.

The warm morning sun soon surrounded him and sleep came unexpectedly. He dreamed fitfully as his head drooped, and his body rolled, causing his chin to rest upon his chest.

"Move along, move along," he heard the voice say, and realized that somebody was shaking him. The cobwebs cleared quickly as the unfriendly voice and shaking brought him to immediate consciousness. He found himself looking into the eyes of a Sheriff's Deputy, and he could see the patrol car pulled to the curb with the lights flashing.

"I'm sorry," he heard himself saying, but couldn't think what he had to be sorry for.

"Get on out of here, you can't sleep here," said the Deputy.

Mr. Hood was able to look quickly around and realized that he was at Eastside Baptist Church, and that his purpose for being here was to attend church, not to sleep. "You don't understand . . ."

The policeman didn't want any explanation, he just wanted this man out of his area, and soon had his hand on Mr. Hood's shoulder and was attempting to lift him from the bench.

Mr. Hood was not attempting to protest, but the gesture was causing him pain as he tried to stand, and the policeman's knee was directly against his injured leg. He fell back onto the bench. By this time the policeman was removing an aerosol container from his belt.

Reverend Cross arrived at the church somewhere between Mr. Hood's attempt to stand and when he fell back onto the bench. He witnessed the altercation and stopped his car behind the police car and began blowing his horn. He jumped out and started yelling, "No, no, don't do that. Don't do that."

The policeman's attention was diverted long enough for Mr. Hood to pull away, and the Reverend was soon at his side.

"What's going on, officer," Reverend Cross asked, as he placed his hands on Mr. Hood's shoulders.

"I got a report that we had a vagrant sleeping at the church, and I came over to get him out of here before church started. If you don't mind, I'll go ahead and put him in the car. You go ahead and look around to see if everything is all right, and nothing is missing."

Reverend Cross paused and in a barely visible gesture bowed his head and silently prayed, "Forgive him, Father, for he knows not what he does."

To the officer it must have appeared that he was taking a deep breath before thanking him for ridding the area of this unwanted man. Then he addressed the officer. "Officer, I appreciate your diligence this morning, but you have made a terrible mistake. You see, this is the new night watchman at the mill. He, I am sure, is here at this early hour to meet with me before our services begin. The warm sun must have given him such comfort that he fell asleep. He's not a vagrant. He has a beautiful home. He lives in one of the mill houses."

Mr. Hood remained silent as he glared at the officer. He had not been given an opportunity to explain his presence, and there had been a time when he would have tangled with this man. However, his increasing age and his new look at life had spared him a needless altercation.

The officer dejectedly walked to his vehicle as Reverend Cross continued standing by his new friend keeping his hand on his shoulder. He waved at the officer and turned to Mr. Hood.

"Are you okay, old friend?"

Mr. Hood smiled and said he was.

Reverend Cross said, "Come on inside and we'll have a cup of coffee." Together they went into the darkened church foyer. The large windows in the sanctuary bathed the room with light, and the stained glass likeness of Jesus glowed as the sun rays danced across it.

They entered Reverend Cross' office which reminded Mr. Hood more of a living room than an office. A desk anchored one part of the room, but the remainder held a small sofa and 3 chairs. There were tables and lamps, knick-knacks, and books all around the room. The coffee pot was on a credenza behind the Reverend's desk. All the supplies were hidden behind the doors. After a trip to the bathroom for water, Reverend Cross was asking Mr. Hood if he wanted cream or sugar.

They had chatted as the coffee brewed. Reverend Cross was curious about his first night at the house. The conversation was predictable. Mr. Hood was overjoyed with everything.

Finally, Reverend Cross asked Mr. Hood. "What brings you here this fine Sunday morning?"

He gets right to the point, thought Mr. Hood. "Well, I'm not sure how to say this, but I want to know if I can join this church."

Reverend Cross smiled at the innocence of his new friend. "What makes you think you want to join this church? Do you like my coffee that much?"

Mr. Hood was caught a little off guard at his attempt at humor. "Well, Reverend Cross, this is a serious matter that I have put off way too long, and I don't want to die without knowing that I'm going to heaven."

Reverend Cross was embarrassed at his attempt at humor when this man was obviously serious about his mission. "Mr. Hood, I hope you weren't offended by my remark about the coffee. That was my poor attempt to break the ice. However, it's obvious that you are serious and I want to respect that. The first thing I have to say is that being a church member alone won't get you to heaven. Getting into heaven, however, is a simple thing. You must first recognize that you are a sinner. Then you have to accept what John 3:16 says, that God loved us enough that He allowed His Son, Jesus, to die on the cross for our sins so that we can have eternal life. Then you have to ask God to forgive you of your sins. Once that has taken place, a change will come over you, and you will want to change your life. You will want to do good things. But it won't be the good things that will get you there, it will be knowing Jesus died for our eternity and accepting a personal relationship with Him. Many people attend church and go through religious, ceremonial things, but they never have that relationship with Jesus and come to accept that He is their Savior. When they reach heaven's gates, their names won't be written in the book. He will say, 'I know you not.'"

Mr. Hood said, "Many years ago in Huntington, West Virginia, an evangelist from New Orleans came there. He told about salvation, and I knew that night I wanted it. I went down when the invitation was given, and I accepted Jesus as my Savior. However, I can't say I developed too much of a relationship with Him. I pray a lot or I suppose it's praying. I talk to somebody, and I think it's God. I've had times when I felt a presence around me, and knew I was safe when everything else said I wasn't. I always felt it was my guardian angels watching over me. I haven't lived a life like Addie or Mrs. Applegate, and of course, not like you, but I did feel a change after that. I don't drink or smoke, and while I enjoy a pretty woman, I don't chase after them. I pretty much keep to myself and have been on a kind of journey most of my life. Now, I feel that I have reached my destination, and I want to make sure I do it all right from this point on."

Reverend Cross stood and walked across the office to the credenza behind his desk. "Mr. Hood, do you have a Bible?" he asked expecting a negative answer.

Mr. Hood immediately started reaching into his front pocket and retrieved a small dog-eared New Testament. "I have this one," he proudly stated.

Reverend Cross was touched. He quickly decided to wait before giving him a Bible. He wanted to purchase a large print version and have his name embossed on it. He returned to his place next to Mr. Hood.

The room filled with silence. Finally, Reverend Cross spoke. "Mr. Hood, I believe that you had a born again experience when you heard salvation explained to you in West Virginia. Did you follow that up with baptism?"

"No." he said.

I'll tell you what. Why don't you and I have a prayer and you repeat after me, if your heart tells you it's right."

"Okay." said Mr. Hood.

"Dear Lord, I come to You humbly this morning and I bring my friend, General Sherman Hood. Mr. Hood knows a time when he asked you to forgive him of his sins, and he acknowledged that Your son, Jesus, died on the cross for his sins. As a rededication of his life to You, he wants to make certain that he spends eternity with You, so he is going to repeat the following prayer."

"Okay, Mr. Hood, repeat after me. Dear Lord, I am a sinner."

The words echoed, *"Dear Lord, I am a sinner."*

"I have chosen to believe that Your son, Jesus, died on the cross for my sins, so that I can be forgiven and spend eternity in heaven."

"I have chosen to believe that Your son, Jesus, died on the cross for my sins, so that I can be forgiven and spend eternity in heaven."

"Please forgive me of my sins."

"Please forgive me of my sins."

"I will live my life as Your son and want a relationship with You."

"I will live my life as Your son and want a relationship with You."

"In Jesus' name we pray. Amen."

"In Jesus' name we pray. Amen."

"Is that all there is to it?" Mr. Hood innocently asked.

"Well, as Baptists, we believe in baptism by immersion. How do you feel about that?"

"Do you do it in a creek or river?"

"Neither, we have an indoor baptistery."

"When can we do it?"

"Is today too soon?" Reverend Cross inquired.

"Not for me. I want to get myself ready for heaven, and if that's what it takes, then that's what I'll do."

Reverend Cross loved his innocence. He had come to realize that many adults were stubborn and would not accept the ease with which salvation came. They attempted to weigh the pros and cons, and wanted proof. Mr.

Hood entered into this with childlike, but not childish, faith and it was refreshing.

Reverend Cross explained that he would make some arrangements, and asked Mr. Hood to wait in his office. He went to begin filling the baptistery, and hoped that the job would be done before the congregation arrived. Usually a deacon took care of this and a committee arranged for the robes, towels and saw to it that the folks being baptized were briefed on everything. Today, in addition to holding a Memorial Day celebration, he was totally in charge of baptizing a wonderful old gentleman. "God is good," he shouted as he called his wife, Nina, and asked her to bring some clothes for Mr. Hood to wear under the robe.

He waited in Reverend Cross' office. It was obvious that people were arriving at church. The voices could be heard in the hallway. The telephone rang endlessly, and nobody seemed around to answer it. Through the window Mr. Hood noticed some young men practicing marching and flags would occasionally come into view. The door opened and a young man came in not seeing Mr. Hood in the high winged back chair. He went into the closet obviously on a mission. He was muttering under his breath. ". . . Can't count on anybody. These should already have been put up. Mumble, mumble." He removed a large box marked "American Flags." He was retreating when Mr. Hood sneezed. The young man jumped and yelled, "Sh . . ," and then remembering where he was quickly changed his word to sugar as he threw the box and the contents, 12 unfurling American flags, across the room. The young man blushed, and went about picking them up. Mr. Hood jumped and joined in. No words were exchanged and the young man soon had his cargo safely returned to its box. Mr. Hood took his seat and the young man retreated, embarrassed.

Finally, the halls were quiet. Mr. Hood looked at his watch and it was 9:30. Sunday school had begun. Reverend Cross returned, and was carrying a grocery sack which his wife had brought. He handed it to Mr. Hood, and explained that these were clothes he could wear under the robe. He said that the robes were transparent when they got wet and without something on underneath they would be having an X-Rated baptism. Mr. Hood laughed uneasily. Reverend Cross realized that he had again attempted humor at a time Mr. Hood was taking very seriously.

He explained that he would be taken to a changing room, and a deacon would assist him with the robe and take him to the baptistery. Reverend Cross explained what he would say and do while he was in the water. "When you get in there, you will notice a bar on the floor and a box. Sit on the box and put your toes under the bar. I will say some words, and ask you if you have accepted Jesus as your Savior. You will answer that you have. I will ask you if you have sinned and asked Jesus to forgive you of your sins. You will answer that you have. I will ask you if Jesus died on the cross for your sins, and you will answer that he did. I will then place my right hand on your nose and my left hand on your shoulder. I will quickly lower you into the water. It is important that you keep your toes under that bar to keep your feet down and to help me pull you back up. Do you understand that?"

"Yes," he said.

"I will begin by telling the congregation that you have accepted Jesus. I will say General Sherman Hood, my brother, I baptize you in the name of the Father, The Son, and the Holy Spirit. As I lower you, I will say, Buried in the likeness of Christ. As I raise you I will say, Raised to walk in the newness of His life."

"I will then hand you the handkerchief."

"Handkerchief, what handkerchief," asked Mr. Hood.

Reverend Cross realized that he had left that out of his instructions. He explained that he would be holding the handkerchief in his right hand when he placed his hand on Mr. Hood's nose. Mr. Hood seemed to understand, and together they walked to the changing room.

He was left in the changing room for what seemed like an eternity. He needed to go to the bathroom, but didn't feel he could leave. *What if they come for me while I'm gone,* he wondered.

Addie's children arrived at the Smith's house at 8:30 as arranged the night before. Mr. Smith had gotten up at 7:30 and put a breakfast casserole someone had brought the evening before into the oven. The aroma filled the house. A bowl of fruit salad had been placed on the counter, and throw-away plates, bowls and glasses were arranged buffet style. Blueberry muffins were in a basket, and pitchers of juice and milk sat in a bowl of ice. Two cereal boxes rounded out the meal.

Into Addie's Arms

Mike and Cindy were dressed when the children arrived, and Mary Margaret was already on the porch. Addie had showered and put on a pant suit her daughters had selected. It was agreed that Addie could attend church, but she was not to sing in the choir. Nobody was going to Sunday school. There just didn't seem to be enough time.

After eating and clearing the kitchen, they started to church. Mike asked Cindy to drive by to see if Mr. Hood wanted to go with them. When they arrived, he wasn't at home. Mike secretly prayed that he had not run away in the night, but he didn't have time to dwell on that. They were about to be late.

They arrived and Addie and her children were all on one row. It was easy to spot them because a crowd had gathered. Her friends were glad to see she was there, and the friends of the children were catching up on news. Mike, Cindy and Mary Margaret took seats in the row behind Addie's family. Soon the music began. *The Battle Hymn of the Republic* was followed by an introduction of the armed forces along with a song for the Army, Navy, Air Force, Coast Guard and Marines. As each song began the veterans were asked to stand and remain standing during their song. Across the sanctuary, men and women, old and young stood. Tears streamed down their faces as they were honored that day and they remembered the reasons for the honor. As the *Star Spangled Banner* was played, the congregation all stood. Music filled the church to the highest rafters. Twelve American flags were held in the front of the sanctuary by veterans dressed in their uniforms. Down each aisle marched ROTC cadets from the Regional High School carrying flags representing each branch of the Armed Forces. Patriotism was high, and nobody was untouched. Across the auditorium men and women wept, noses sniffed, and at that little church in that small town in South Carolina veterans were honored for their service to this great nation.

Reverend Cross began his service and his message entitled, "The Armor of God." He asked his congregation to turn to Ephesians 6:10-17. He asked them to stand for the reading of God's word. After the reading and the congregation was seated he began by reminding the congregation that this day was originally meant to honor the fallen soldiers and over time had also come to commemorate the living ones who had sacrificed for our country.

"These men and women went forth in both peace and war to keep our country free. We are able to be here today because many years ago people were willing to fight for religious freedom. We often fail to honor those, but without their courage we would not be able to assemble on this beautiful morning in the midst of the dew and the smell of the roses to praise the name of our Lord and Savior, Jesus Christ. Our freedom has come at a high price to many."

"Our soldiers fought bravely and knew their foes. Each one of us goes into battle every day, and we face a foe without a face. Oh, yes, we see the faces of our foes, but they are disguised, often as friends. However, I don't want you to let down your guard for one instant, because the evil one is out there each and every day we live, and he is ever vigilant that our guard will be dropped, and he can attack. He may attack from our right flank as we decide to watch a movie that we know we really shouldn't be watching. He may attack from our left flank as we go to a computer site that offers pornographic material. He may attack from the rear as a friend offers you marijuana or cocaine, or maybe even a legal drug. He may attack directly from the front when you are confronted by your friends to do things that you know to be wrong. Let me assure you, friends, if it feels wrong, chances are *IT IS WRONG!* The first time you feel led to do something that must be done in secret *RUN*, I said *RUN* in the opposite direction," he said pounding the podium each time he spoke the word *RUN!* Nothing done for God's glory needs to be hidden under a basket. It will be like a beacon to shine even in the bright of day. Anything else is evil and needs to be stricken from your life."

"Gird yourself with truth and righteousness and put on the full armor of God each day before you leave your home, better still before you get out of bed."

"I heard a story about a woman who said 'God, it has been a good day. I haven't lied. I haven't gossiped, I haven't committed adultery, I haven't cheated, and I have not done anything wrong today. But, God, I'm really going to need your help now, because I'm fixin' to get out of bed."

"We need to begin each day with proper adornment. We need to have truth, which we find in the Gospel. We need to have righteousness, and we need to shod our feet with the righteousness of the gospel of peace, and take up the helmet of salvation and the sword of the Spirit. Roman soldiers wore sandals and the soles of their shoes had what we would call spikes. These were essential for strong footing in battle. They symbolize the strong footing we need today. We need to stand for the righteousness of the gospel. God is the same yesterday, today and tomorrow. His *stand* is steady and strong. We need to be properly shod to equip ourselves for that righteousness. Evil is lurking. Before each day begins, we need to be properly armored to face the enemy. If we don't plan on that, we will find ourselves unprepared when evil arrives. And as I said when I began, that comes from the Gospel."

"Today is a wonderful day to take up the helmet of salvation. Why wait until tomorrow. Who knows if we will have a tomorrow? Today is what we have, and I would hope that nobody will leave this place today without the peace of salvation. I can't offer you peace in the workplace. I can't offer you peace at school. I can't offer you peace at home. I certainly can't offer you peace in the world, but I can offer you the peace of salvation. With that peace, my friends, I promise you that you will find more peace in your workplace, at school, at home and even in the world, because you will be a changed person. You will see each of those things with new eyes. You will see them through God's eyes, and His perspective is perfect."

When he finished and the invitation was given, he announced that he was deviating from the program. He explained that there would be a baptism and motioned to the choir director to continue. Soon music filled the air, and the Reverend dashed back to remove his jacket and put on his robe. He gave the signal to the deacon that he was ready, and when the song was finished, the stained glass was moved aside thereby exposing the baptistery. Reverend Cross stood on the backside of the baptistery. He explained that he had been met that morning at the church. He left out the part about the Sheriff's Deputy. He said that a man told him he wanted to know he would spend eternity in heaven. He said that he and the gentleman discussed all this, and the man knew in his heart that Jesus died on the cross for his sins, and asked God to forgive them. "He also asked for immediate baptism," the Reverend explained, "and I can get much more immediate than this. Please step down here, Mr. Hood."

Addie gasped loudly, along with her children. Mike and Cindy were almost too stunned to breathe, but finally air escaped their lungs. The frail arm reached out from behind the wall as he walked down the few steps into the water. Reverend Cross took his hand and patted it gently. He guided Mr. Hood to the proper place to sit and looked to see that his toes were under the bar. All the while he was stroking this gentle man's hand. Mr. Hood was introduced and the baptism began just as it had been explained, and within seconds his head was above the water, and a smile spread across the face of a new man in Christ.

Rarely, was Reverend Cross brought to tears any more at a baptism. At one time he cried with every one. However, when Mr. Hood reached out of the water and embraced him, not only Reverend Cross wept, but the congregation wept as well. The man had stolen their hearts as his sincere love filled the Sunday morning, Memorial Day service.

Mr. Hood climbed the steps on the other side of the baptistery and went into the arms of a deacon holding a towel. That deacon wrapped the towel around him, and together they went back to the changing room.

The service ended, but nobody left. Clusters of people gathered throughout the auditorium. Reverend Cross changed and joined them. Soon, the man of the hour, General Sherman Hood, was escorted out by his deacon. One by one the congregation came over and shook his hand, welcoming him into their family, God's family.

Mr. Hood came home with the Smith's for lunch. Addie and her children got there first, and they had begun setting up for the next meal with Addie at the table giving directions. Casseroles were in the oven, the fried chicken was on the table, and the salads were being lined up on the counter. Soon, the feast was ready, and the diners were hungry. Addie asked to say the blessing.

"Dear Lord, it is with great joy that I come to You this afternoon. To be here with my family is a blessing. I thank You for this time. I thank You for my life, and the things that have made it possible for me to continue living it. I thank You for my new brother in Christ, and ask that you bless him as he begins this new walk and encounters things of the world which will challenge him. Give him grace and mercy to handle each thing as it comes his way. Thank You for the home in which we are about to eat. Thank you for the food we are about to receive and the hands that prepared it, and bless it to the good of our bodies, and our bodies to your service. In Jesus name we pray, Amen."

Around the room, "Amen," was echoed.

The room was soon filled with conversation as the plates were filled and this group of family and extended family sat down to enjoy a restful meal.

When it was over, the kitchen was cleaned and the food put away. Mr. Hood seemed anxious. Mr. Smith looked at his watch and saw that it was already nearly 3:00. "I'll tell you what, old friend, let's go on down to the mill and wait for Gerry there."

Mr. Hood was on his feet in a flash, and together they left.

Addie's children were going to take her to one cemetery, the one where their father was buried, and they were doting on their mother as she prepared to leave with them. Addie had finally had enough pampering.

"Okay, okay. Let's get one thing straight. I love having you all here. I know that I had a spell the other night and need to take it easy. But, you are smothering me. I won't die of a heart attack. I'll die of suffocation if you don't step back and let me breathe."

The children stepped back. Addie looked slightly embarrassed at her outburst. Carolyn broke the ice. "Well, one thing is for sure. She's feeling better. Come on. Let's wait for her in the car." The children all marched out of the house and went directly to Leonard's car. Addie watched them and laughed out loud. "They know their mama," she said, and she went out behind them.

Mary Margaret and her mother were left home alone. The house was still.

Chapter 68

"Mary Margaret, is there anything you want to do?"

"What about the surprise?"

Cindy was thoughtful for a few seconds then said, "It is a family surprise, and since daddy is working this afternoon let me see if we can do it this evening." She went to her room, and returned in a few minutes to say that they had an appointment at 6:00 o'clock. "Surely, daddy will be home by then. In the meantime, let's see if we can go visit Mrs. Applegate and meet her grandchildren."

Mary Margaret was overjoyed. It was always a pleasure to spend time with Mrs. Applegate, and her daughter seemed nice. Mrs. Applegate was not at home when Cindy telephoned. The disappointment was obvious. "I guess it's just the two of us." Let's go down by the pond and lie in the hammock.

They had only gone a few yards down the hill when a car could be heard coming up the drive. It was a white Ford van, and neither Mary Margaret nor her mother recognized it. They stopped and waited for the occupants to get out, and immediately recognized Lew Rowell and his wife, Jerry.

Cindy was so glad to see them as she had wanted to invite them to the house, but needless to say, the chaos had kept it from happening. This would be a perfect time, but she realized that her husband would have enjoyed it, too. They greeted each other with the customary hugs Mary Margaret was beginning to take for granted, and Cindy invited them into the living room. "Mike had to go to the mill, and he'll be disappointed that he missed you. Maybe he won't be long and can join us."

"By the way, Lew, thank you for the generous donation to the television," she said as a sincere afterthought.

"Oh, it was nothing. I was glad to do it. It gave me so much joy to see the faces on those children. We never read about kids like these in the newspaper. We only hear about the bad things on the news. These young people are our future, and yesterday, they gave me a renewed hope. I do hope they stay a little cleaner when they grow up, though."

Now, Lew, you know the prettiest flowers grow in dirt. I saw them go by the beauty shop as I was closing up, and I had to laugh at the sight. Mary Margaret was pulling, and she was immaculate. The boys, however, put me in mind of my own grandchildren. Then Jim was right behind them looking like their protector. The funniest thing though was Jennifer coming behind in her SUV. It reminded me of a parade where rescue vehicles come after the bands to pick up the casualties. I don't suppose there were any casualties were there?" Jerry asked.

"No. They did just fine. I think Jim had a hard time getting it into the house, but it all worked out."

"I offered to deliver it, but they refused.'

"I know you did, but Jim realized it was important for the children to handle it. It gave them more ownership. His back will heal in a few days."

They all laughed and accepted the iced tea Cindy offered. When she went into the kitchen to get it, Mrs. Rowell asked Mary Margaret how she liked being in Left Fork. Cindy listened discreetly from the kitchen.

"Well, it's all right. I loved living in New York, but I didn't have anything else to compare it too. I enjoyed taking walks with my nanny, Charlene. We went to museums and plays. I miss my friend. We played together many days on our rooftop playground. We would have Rook tournaments. I loved going shopping with Charlene, and we would have lunch in neat little restaurants. I was scared about a new place, and since I've been here I've been more scared than I ever was in New York. It seems that bad things keep happening to me and my family, and nothing bad ever happened there. I always felt safe."

Lew and Jerry thought this was a mature little girl, but felt this was a strange thing for her to be saying. They considered Left Fork to be one of the safest places on earth. Nothing bad ever happened here in their opinion. When they visited New York, they always were cautious. They never walked on the sidewalks any more than they had to. They took taxis everywhere. They watched their wallets and purses, and never, never, never rode the subway. They had read that the crime rate was down, but they never felt completely safe on the streets of New York, or Atlanta, or any big city they visited. They enjoyed the quiet peaceful place they called home, but after a quick reflection of the Allison Kincaid incident understood Mary Margaret's reason for concern.

Cindy returned with the tray of ice-filled glasses and a green plastic pitcher of sweet tea. She asked Mary Margaret to go get the bowl of lemons she had left on the counter. She returned with a large bowl of whole lemons, and her mother gently said, "No, sweetie, the cut wedges in the little bowl." The adults never disclosed the humor they saw in this as they continued discussing the Smith family's new home.

The subject soon turned to church. "We missed y'all this morning," said Jerry Rowell.

"We missed being there, but you can imagine how hectic it was. Addie is recuperating here, and her children came over to have breakfast with us. By the time we were finished, it was too late for Sunday school, so we just went to church, and are we glad we did."

"Yes. I'll bet you are. Did you know that Mr. Hood was going to be baptized this morning?"

"No, it was a complete and wonderful surprise. He has become so dear to us. There's something very special about that man. Usually, you would not be so ready to accept a homeless man into your life and home, but he has a quality that is irresistible. Not only that, he saved our family from the attack of Allison Kincaid. We will never forget that."

The conversation turned to the Sunday School class, and the people in it. Jerry and Lew told Cindy about every family. It was obvious that it was more than just people they knew, they loved them. It was apparent that this was a small *family* in the church. They shared the joys, heartaches, and miracles of the others. "We've all been together for several years, and we hope that you and Mike will someday feel comfortable enough to join our class on a permanent basis. We think you'll find it an easy group to fit in with."

Cindy thanked them and said she was sure they would, but they were still trying to *find themselves.*

Cindy told Jerry Rowell that Addie was going to bring Mary Margaret in to have her hair trimmed but with all the commotion of the preceding week, there had not been time. "I'll have Addie call this week when she's feeling better."

"Never you mind calling for an appointment. I can trim that child's hair right now. Lew, honey, will you go out to the car and get my scissors box. We can take care of this right here."

Before Cindy could protest, Lew was up and out the door and Jerry was directing Mary Margaret to go upstairs and wet her hair. Cindy just decided to sit back and take advantage of some unusual southern hospitality in her own living room.

Within minutes the hair cutting station was set up with Mary Margaret being placed on a tall bar stool. The scissors box held more than scissors, and a cape had been placed around Mary Margaret's neck. The comb and scissors were removed from the box, and Jerry had put on a smock Lew brought in from the van.

As the hair cutting commenced, the conversation returned to Mr. Hood's new television set. "Mary Margaret, how was the picture on the TV?" Mr. Rowell asked.

"It was fuzzy, and he only got 3 stations," was the reply.

"Well, I'll take him over an antenna and we'll get him a couple more stations, and they should all be fairly clear. It's so flat here; an antenna still does a pretty good job."

The hair fell quickly and the conversation continued without pause. The Rowells shared anecdotes about their family ending with Jerry saying, "Tell her the story about the beef stew."

Already laughter had erupted before the first word of the story was spoken. "Well, it was right before we got married. We, Jerry and I, had been out on my day off to do some things for our wedding, and we came in after my mama had cleaned up the kitchen. There was a bowl of beef stew sitting in the middle of the table and since everybody else had eaten, Jerry and I each got a fork and started eating out of the bowl. We had been there a few minutes when my sister came in. She looked at the scene, and dryly said, 'If you dig down a little further you'll find some cole slaw. You're eating out of Sport's bowl,' we were eating from the bowl with everybody scraps in it that was intended for our dog."

Laughter erupted! Cindy wasn't sure if the story was so funny or the people sharing the story were funny as they shared it with her, but she was enjoying the time she was spending with them.

Too soon Mary Margaret's hair was in a perfect bob, and her face was framed in beautifully trimmed bangs and the guests announced they needed to leave. They were going to see their grandchildren, Nicholas, Benjamin, Harrison, and the princess, Makenzie.

They were off and once again Mary Margaret and her mother were alone. Together they swept up the hair and Mary Margaret followed her mother's directions to go and gather up the dirty towels. Addie always made it seem like magic when clean towels and underwear appeared miraculously in their proper places. Charlene, too, had never let them down. Now, she realized she needed to see where that magic came from, she thought.

Soon the washer was humming, and a quick glance at the clock showed it was 5:15. The phone rang, and after a brief conversation, Cindy told Mary Margaret that Addie and her children were going to a restaurant for dinner. "They invited us to join them, but I declined. I'm not sure when daddy will be home, and we do have an appointment at 6:00."

At 5:30 Cindy phoned her husband's private line at the mill. He answered on the second ring and said he would be home in time for them to make the 6:00 o'clock appointment.

The afternoon with Mr. Hood had gone well. The paperwork that was needed for his employment was completed, and Gerry arrived to explain the workings of the surveillance equipment. Mr. Hood was to spend most of the night in the guard house, with walks around the property at predetermined intervals. There was a sequence used for his walks so that he would not be in or out of the guard house at the same time every night. Sunday night he was to walk the property hourly. Then on Monday the walk would begin on the quarter hour. On Tuesday, it was hourly, but on the three-quarter hour. Wednesday, hourly, but on the half hour. Thursday had its own schedule as well. He was off on Friday and Saturday, and for the time being, that was going to be manned by a private agency.

When Mr. Hood heard this, he protested. "I can work on Friday and Saturday night, too," he said.

"No, you can't. It would be too much for you, and anyway, we would have to pay you too much money. This will work out for now. If it doesn't, we'll change things."

The men said their good-byes, and Mike asked Mr. Hood, "Do you need anything?"

Mr. Hood looked him squarely in the eye, which is one of the qualities Mike so liked about this man, and said, "How could I need anything. You have thought of everything."

"I didn't do this by myself. Mrs. Gilbert, Addie and Mrs. Applegate all helped. In fact, they did most of it. I'm just sitting back taking all the credit."

He hugged his friend, and thanked Gerry for taking time away from his family on the week-end to help him out. "I appreciate you and your dedication to this endeavor. None of it would be possible without you. I consider you to be the top player on the team at the mill. You make me look good."

Gerry was unaccustomed to such honest glory except from his wife. He blushed, "You make it easy. Thanks for being here."

The two men drove off in the same direction until they reached the square where one went left and other right.

Chapter 69

Mary Margaret and her mother were on the porch when Mike arrived. Mary Margaret found it hard to contain her excitement, even though she didn't know what she was excited about. Secretly she was thinking, "I hope it's a horse, I hope it's a horse."

Cindy was smiling as she watched her little girl show enthusiasm for something. It had been a long time since she had seen her excited, and she enjoyed it. *I hope she's not disappointed. It's not like she's getting a horse,* she thought.

They got in the car, and soon were heading away from Left Fork. Mary Margaret sat in the back seat and listened as her parents discussed Mr. Hood's new job. Cindy told her husband that the Rowells had been to visit. His disappointment was obvious, and he said they needed to plan a time to get together with them. "Jerry even cut Mary Margaret's hair," she added and Mike looked in the rear view mirror at his precious daughter with her fresh hair cut.

She could feel the car beginning to slow and heard the turn signal begin to click. She looked first to her right and then her left. Disappointment struck immediately. There was nothing in the landscape that indicated horses were nearby. Back from the road on the left side she could see a house with a chain link fence around the back yard. On the other side there were just trees. As they began to turn to the left and went up the driveway, Mary Margaret's mind raced. *What are we here for,* she wondered. She sat up in the seat as far as the shoulder harness would allow. No people were outside and nothing indicated surprise to her. The car came to a stop, and her father said he would be right back. He knocked on the door, and an old man came out onto the porch. He was wearing jeans and a brown stained white t-shirt. Suspenders held up his jeans, and his feet were bare. His white hair was wild, and he spit over the porch railing and wiped his mouth with the back of his hand.

When he spit, and Mary Margaret saw the large brown liquid splat on the dirt, she gagged. Her mother turned to her, and felt sorry for her. She, too, had felt queasy. "What is he doing?" Mary Margaret asked her mother.

"He's chewing tobacco, and when he accumulates a lot of liquid in his mouth, he spits it out."

"It is absolutely disgusting. Why would anybody want to do that?" asked the nauseous little girl.

"It's a habit, just like smoking."

"Oh, no, it's not like smoking, it's worse. This is the worst thing I have ever seen. I don't care what the surprise is. I don't want anything this nasty man has," cried Mary Margaret."

"Be careful what you say," said her mother. "You might be fooled by his cover. Sometimes ugly packages hide beautiful treasures."

Mary Margaret could not imagine this man having anything beautiful. She just wanted to leave here and go back home. *No surprise is worth this*, she thought."

Her father was motioning for them to get out of the car, and Mary Margaret reluctantly joined her mother, quickly holding her hand and being careful where she stepped. The old man had gone back inside to put on his shoes. He came out of the house through a back door and was soon yelling for them at the gate. The high green grass in the back yard was in clumps, and it was soon apparent that there was dog poop scattered throughout.

This has to be a nightmare, thought Mary Margaret as she stepped in a fresh pile, and it squished around the edge of her sandal and onto her toes. She started hopping on one foot, and to her dismay landed squarely in another equally large pile.

The old man continued walking toward another fenced area, and said, "You might wanna' watch your step. I had them out a little while ago while I cleaned the kennel, and they seem to like to poop out here instead of in there."

Mary Margaret looked up at her mother with questioning eyes. "What do I do?" she asked between clenched teeth, and her mother seemed to not hear what she asked and continued walking.

The old man opened the kennel, and out came a beautiful black lab. She was obviously accustomed to having visitors, and she walked up to each one and stood until she was petted. She looked at them with golden eyes that seemed to see into their souls. She sniffed, sometimes in embarrassing spots, and after circling the trio several times deemed them worthy to continue.

They walked into the kennel and Mary Margaret attempted to wipe the dog mess as best she could in the grass. Some remained on her toes, but the sight that she saw soon made her forget all about it. Inside the fenced kennel was a large shelter, much like a dog house. Inside that was a child's plastic swimming pool which held puppies. Some of the puppies were black, and some were black and white spotted. Most of the puppies were sleeping in a mass. One, however, was standing with its feet on the top edge of the pool attempting to see the visitors.

"Are we here to get a puppy?" she breathlessly asked looking first at her mother and then her father.

"Did you want a puppy?" asked her father teasingly. "I thought you wanted a horse."

"I do want a horse, but a puppy is almost as good," she admitted.

Her mother said cautiously. "We are here to look at puppies. These puppies are too young to leave their mother, but if you feel that you can take good care of a puppy, then we are willing to let you try it. However, you must realize that this is *your responsibility*, and I emphasize your responsibility. Daddy and I will help when you can't do something, but Addie is not to be burdened with anything else. She has enough to do. Do you understand that?"

Into Addie's Arms

"Yes, I can do that. Addie won't have to do anything. I'll do it all."

The puppies started to wake up and one by one came over to look at the 3 strangers. The Smiths took turns holding them, and it soon became apparent that it would not be easy to make this decision. The old man in the t-shirt helped make it a little easier. "Do you want a boy or a girl?"

"I want a girl," said Mary Margaret. Her parents concurred.

"Well, then, we'll separate them that way. I have 4 girls and 4 boys." One by one he lifted them and looked at their underside. Soon there were two groups. One inside the swimming pool and one outside. "The girls are out here," he motioned and turned to spit through the fence. Spray dripped on his shirt, and Mary Margaret and her mother averted their eyes.

The puppies waddled on the concrete pad and soon attracted the attention of Mary Margaret. There were two which were all black and two were white with black spots.

"The father of the litter is a Dalmatian. He belongs to my brother, and one day he carried that dog over here to visit. I didn't realize she was in season, and now we have these puppies. It was a disappointment. I was planning on a litter and hopefully making $4,000.00. I usually get $500.00 a pup, and she has about 8 pups each time. This is her third litter. I hope to make enough to pay for the feed and vet bills, but I doubt I make that much. I was only goin' to breed her a couple more times."

Mary Margaret could hear the conversation, but her job was to choose a puppy. She squatted down. She wanted a white with black spots, and both of them were cute. One had an all black ear, and the rest was white with lots of small spots. The other had a large spot which covered her right ear and eye. Most of the rest of her was white with very few spots. She held each one, and the puppy breath was sweet. The licks and nibbles on the ears made the decision even harder. She was finally tired of squatting and decided it was all right to sit on the concrete. She crossed her legs and from the other side of the kennel a black female ran, or rather tumbled over to her, and nosed its way under her leg and into her lap. The other three females explored the kennel. This puppy seemed to have found a home. Mary Margaret caressed the soft fur, and the small black puppy licked her hand, and gently nibbled on her fingers. The golden eyes stared at her with total adoration and trust. Mary Margaret had chosen a puppy, or had it chosen her?

Arrangements were made to pick up the puppy in two weeks. Money changed hands, and a collar was placed loosely on the puppy's neck. A handwritten tag on the collar said M. M. Smith, indicating this was Mary Margaret's dog.

The old man offered the use of his hose to clean Mary Margaret's feet before they got back into the car. Mr. Smith helped his daughter as she removed her sandals and the warm water which was stored in the hose washed away the yuck. The shoes were hosed off as well, and they were soon on their way.

Mary Margaret was too excited to talk. She sat in the back seat and planned her days with the puppy. She could envision them playing Frisbee, and knew that Davis and Jordan would love her. She could swim in the pond and would chase away dangerous animals. She imagined her dog sleeping in her bed, but knew that probably wouldn't happen. Her mother had taken a giant step in agreeing to a dog. She wasn't sure it would make it into the house, let alone into her bed.

They stopped for bar-b-que and arrived at their home in time to bid Addie's children farewell. They would be by in the morning to tell their mother good-bye, but declined an invitation to breakfast. "We all need to get an early start, and if we stay for breakfast, it will turn into lunch," Leonard explained. Cindy knew they were right, but also knew that Addie would want to spend as much time as possible with them. She would be sad when they left.

Darkness was falling, and the family was getting ready for bed when the telephone rang. Sylvia invited Cindy, Mary Margaret and Addie over for lunch the following day. "I understand our men folk will be working, and I thought it would be nice if we spent the day together. Mary Margaret and Philip can ride the horses, if she would like, and we can just sit around and do nothing."

After checking with Addie, Cindy accepted the gracious invitation. She had hoped to spend some time with Mrs. Applegate over this extended holiday week-end, but it appeared that would have to wait for another time.

Again, the phone rang, and it was Jennifer Raver inviting the Smith family over to swim on Monday afternoon. Cindy explained they had already made other plans; but thanked her for the invitation.

"How about dinner then? I would like for the children to spend some time together before they go visit their grandparents on Tuesday. They'll be gone for almost 2 weeks. I wouldn't let them come over today since they had gotten into a fight on Saturday, and Jordan has quite a shiner, but they want to see Mary Margaret before they leave, and of course, we'd enjoy an evening with you."

"Let me check," and after a quick conversation said they would be delighted to come. "You realize that Addie is staying with us right now, and I don't want to leave her alone just yet. Would it be all right if she came, too?"

"Of course, how thoughtless of me not to remember that. Addie is always welcome. Do you know that when I had my boys she came and stayed with me in the evenings for a week with each one and wouldn't take any money for it? Alan was working 12 to 14 hours a day, and I don't know what I would have done without her. She has been a Godsend to this town. We're looking forward to it. How about around 6:30?"

"That sounds good. See you then. And, thanks."

"You're welcome. Bye."

"We have quite the busy schedule tomorrow, said Cindy to her husband. I'm so glad the hospital didn't schedule any elective surgeries. It's been nice having the long week-end, even if I was sick one of those days."

"Yeah, about that. How are you feeling now?"

"I'm feeling better, but there is still an undercurrent of nausea, and when that man spit his tobacco today, I thought I was going to puke right in the car."

"You and me, too. I prayed that the wind was away from us, because I could just imagine it blowing back on me. That was awful."

They both laughed and Addie said goodnight through their open door before she turned in for the night.

"Oh, Addie. We have been invited to the Ravers for dinner tomorrow night, and you are included in the invitation. I accepted for you, and I hope that was all right."

"I thought I might go back to my house tomorrow after lunch with Sylvia. I don't want to be a burden here," said Addie as she turned to walk back toward the Smith's bedroom.

"I'll hear nothing of the sort. We can talk about it in a week or so, but I don't want you staying by yourself while your body is adjusting to the medication. Mrs. Applegate is coming over this week and staying with you and Mary Margaret, and that's that."

Addie was startled. She wasn't accustomed to being told what to do. She usually told others what to do even if she worked for them, or she did what she wanted and made them think if it was their idea. This was a new concept, and she must be tired, because for now she acquiesced and said it was probably for the best.

Soon the house was quiet and everyone slept well.

A few miles away in a puppy pen a black puppy was remembering the sweet little girl who allowed her to comfort her gums, even if just for a short time, as she cut her milk teeth and chewed on her fingers. She remembered the clear brown eyes, and the familiar smell of her mother's poop on her feet.

Mr. Hood locked up and walked to the guard house. The mill didn't operate on week-ends, and it was deathly silent. Even the mosquitoes seemed to be missing. He unlocked the guard house, clocked in, and switched on the new surveillance equipment. A battery of 6 screens gave him 4 vantage points at each end of the mill and 2 near the middle—one in the front and one in the back. These 2 cameras could be moved to see from side to side. The entire perimeter of the mill was visible from inside the guardhouse. He observed each screen, one after the other. He made appropriate entries on the time sheets. It was soon midnight, the time for his appointed rounds. He left the guard house and locked the door behind him. He walked from the north to the south, then west, back north, then east and was again at the guardhouse. He checked the doors as he passed by, and all were secure. All was well. This has taken 25 minutes. He unlocked the guardhouse and made the appropriate notes. He was beginning to relax. A car drove by; he watched the camera on the opposite end of the mill until it was out of sight. The night watch continued until 7:00 a.m. Mr. Hood was tired. He had not rested on Sunday, as he knew he should have, but the excitement kept him moving forward. Now in the early hours of dawn, he longed for his bed, and was glad it was just a few steps away. The watch was changed with the arrival of the day guard. After introductions were completed, Mr. Hood made the short trip to his house for sustenance and sleep, both of which he badly needed. He had forgotten to bring something to eat during the night, and had only eaten a can of peaches for his dinner. He was starving.

Chapter 70

Monday morning dawned clearly. The bright sun shot across the horizon and it was soon apparent that it was going to be a scorching hot day. Mike was up at 6:00 and watched the sunrise from the porch. Addie joined him in a few minutes. They sipped coffee. It was early, and words were few.

Cindy turned over in bed and felt the empty place where her husband should be. The clock said it was 6:30 and she knew he had a big day ahead of him. She got up to fix him a good breakfast and was surprised as she went down the steps and the aroma of French toast filled the air. She looked into the kitchen and saw the oven light was on. She walked over and opened the door. A casserole was bubbling. It smelled like Vermont at the syrup mills. As a child her family visited Vermont and purchased cans of pure maple syrup, enough to last for the whole year. The trees were tapped, and buckets of liquid were carried to the mill in wagons and boiled into the sweet elixir she had come to love. She remembered the delivery of the casserole and was thankful that God had sent them to a place so filled with love that people not only shared, they shared their best to help out a friend. She knew she was not the recipient of this gift. It was intended for Addie, but right now, right here, she was glad she was Addie's friend.

She poured herself a cup of coffee and carried the carafe to the porch to refill Mike's cup. She was surprised that Addie was there, too. The cups were filled, and now the three of them sat there, Mike on the steps, and Addie and Cindy on the swing, watching the sun rise and listening to the serenade of the birds. Off in the distance a woodpecker was busy with his breakfast as he tapped bugs from a tree.

Mike's watch alarm sounded, and he announced that the casserole was ready. They went inside and Cindy insisted that Addie sit down while she set the table. Addie attempted to protest, but it was more out of habit than anything else. She was tired and didn't have her usual morning vitality. She had always enjoyed morning and looked forward to completing most of her chores before noon. After that, she felt like she could relax and maybe have a rest if necessary. Today, however, she felt tired when she woke up, and now, an hour later, still didn't feel much like facing the day.

Mike removed the hot aromatic casserole and served them each a portion. Cindy served small bowls of fruit salad.

Mary Margaret joined them saying the smell woke her up, and her stomach was growling. They all agreed that the smell was wonderful, and after Addie's blessing of the food and asking for God's guidance on their day, they ate their breakfast.

Mike excused himself and went to get ready for work.

Cindy cleaned up the kitchen with Mary Margaret's help, and Addie went upstairs to make her bed and get dressed.

"Did you tell Addie about the puppy?" asked Mary Margaret.

"No, I didn't want to tell her just yet. Let's let her get better and then we'll spring it on her. How about that?" she laughed.

"Okay," said Mary Margaret disappointedly. She wanted to talk about the puppy, and now she couldn't. "I think I may burst if I don't tell someone."

"I'll tell you what. In a little while why don't you call Alice and tell her. The puppy will be here when she gets here, and it'll be something she can look forward to."

"Yeah, it's so exciting. I don't know if I can wait."

Mike arrived at the mill and noticed the front door of the little house was closed, and the window air conditioning unit was humming. He smiled as he thought of his friend spending the night in the gate house and wondered how it had gone. He stopped by to say hello to the day guard and casually looked over the report from the night before. He was not disappointed. Each entry was clearly and concisely recorded. It looked as though the first night went well.

He went on to the office building and was greeted by Rick Daniel, who was waiting by the front door. Mike unlocked the door, and they went in together.

"Rick, I want you to know how much I appreciate your being here today, leaving your family on a holiday, to help us try and straighten this out."

Rick Daniel looked at Mr. Smith and wondered if he was for real. He had never met a man with such grace and humility. "Don't thank me, sir; I want to thank you for giving me another chance. I thought my chances were over and I was doomed to a life I never planned for. You've made me look at the human race in a different light again. My morale was about as low as it could get. My mother always taught me that the only thing you have in life is your integrity, and once it's lost, you probably will never get it back. I lost mine because of someone who was dishonest. I hope when this is all said and done I have mine back."

"As far as I'm concerned, you did nothing wrong in this matter. You were victimized and harassed. You were put in a hostile work environment. Not only do we want you back, but I intend to see that you get something for the time you weren't working. We'll have our attorneys look into what we can do there."

Gerry arrived and was glad to see Rick Daniel was already there. The three men met in Mike's office to begin a strategy to best assist the internal auditors when they arrived. It was determined that Rick would be their liaison and would supply all the documents needed. He was given complete access to company's records, and was put in an office so that he could begin his personal review.

"It looks like our old friend did all right last night," said Gerry.

"Yeah, I checked it out too. It looks like his house is closed up. I'll bet he's sleeping. He had a busy day yesterday."

"He sure did. Did you hear about the Sheriff's Deputy hassling him before church?"

"Nooo. Tell me about it, and don't leave out anything."

He related the story as he had heard it from Reverend Cross the night before. When he finished, Mike just shook his head. "I know the man was just doing his job, but Mr. Hood did not look like a vagrant yesterday. We both saw him at church. I think the deputy may have been a little overzealous. I am so thankful that the Reverend came by when he did."

The two men went their separate ways and in no time it seemed it was noon, and the brigade of accountants was filling the reception area. Mike stepped out and greeted them individually. He called in Rick, and they all went into the conference room, which was going to be Command Central for a while until something better could be worked out. The story was related, and they all looked at Rick with pity in their eyes. He was embarrassed, and didn't want their pity. He wanted the jerk that did this behind bars, knowing in his heart of hearts that he may never see that, but at the very least, he would have the opportunity to make his life miserable for a while, and that power felt good.

They were left with strict instructions that this matter was very confidential, and was not to be discussed with anyone outside this room. It was agreed and acknowledged that all financial and personnel matters were kept in the strictest confidence. No other employees were at the mill this Memorial Day holiday which gave everyone the perfect opportunity to begin the investigation without interruption.

Mike ordered lunch from Grammy's. He and Gerry went to pick it up. This aroused curiosity. As the food was brought from the kitchen Grammy wondered who was at the mill to eat it all.

"I thought the mill was closed for the holiday"

"It's just a routine audit and the accountants arrived today to get an early start," he explained. He was not a good liar. He had no experience at it, and the awkward words stuck in his throat. He hated this. He hated the idea of malfeasance. He hated the idea of personal corruption. He hated that an honorable man had been dishonored. More than anything though he would hate himself if he didn't get to the bottom of it.

The accountants had made themselves comfortable, and were ready for the delicious smelling food when it arrived. There was not, however, a formal lunch hour. These men and women filled their plates and returned to their tasks. These were the cream of the crop, and they had a job to do. As much as Mike hated this, they loved it. They loved uncovering dishonesty. They hated the deed, but lived to right a wrong.

Mike and Gerry ate lunch together. They exchanged small talk and both had their minds on unspoken things. They had agreed to not discuss the matter privately. They would hear what each day's updates brought, and would be part of any open discussions. Privately, however, they agreed it best to steer clear of the matter. They didn't want to muddy the water with preconceived notions. The facts were all they could deal with, and they both anxiously awaited that information.

Addie's children arrived at the house at about 8:00 a.m., each in his or her own car. One by one they spent time with their mother in her room. She requested this. She already had said her few words to Carolyn, but she wanted to know that her children knew she loved them. She had to individually acknowledge the ways in which she cherished them. Jim was first.

He hugged his mama. She was nearly as tall as he. She rested her head on his chest and patted him gently on the back. She leaned back and held her hands on his shoulders, looking him squarely in the eyes.

"You look just like your daddy. When I look at you, I see him. He was handsome and lean just like you. Your daddy was a fine man. He worked hard for his family. He loved all of you. Your character is much like his. You love the Lord. You are gentle while being strong. What you did with those children—getting that TV for Mr. Hood, made me so proud of you. You took your precious time off and spent it with 4 children you hardly knew before that day to do something for an old man you just met. That speaks volumes for your character. Why, for you to come here to satisfy an old woman's longings to have her children visit their daddy's grave with her is unbelievable. Some of my friends say their children are too busy for such as that. You never once told me you are too busy. You respect me and my wishes. I want you to know that when you look in the mirror, you can be proud of the man you see looking back. I love you, James Raymond Jones. You and your brother and sisters make me proud. I know I don't usually take time to say these things to you, but now it seems important to me that you know that if I die tomorrow, I love you and am proud of you."

Jim pulled his mama to him, and tears streamed down his face. She was right, she didn't often take the time to say these things, and he was grateful that she had. However, without saying the words, he knew her feelings. He knew that Addie was a woman who showed her feelings with actions, not words. He gained his composure and said, "Mama, if you had died, I would have known that I was loved unconditionally by you. You have shown me every day of my life that you loved me. I am the man I am because of your love for me. You were a task master. You never allowed anything but perfection, but even in my imperfection you gently nudged me in the right direction. You had high expectations for me, and I would rather have died than disappoint you. You set the bar high with your life, and my hope was to be half as good as you. As for the TV thing, if those children are a part of your life, they are a part of mine. And, Mr. Hood, well, I witnessed his admiration for you. He has joined your fan club in this town. I love you, Mama. I do want to know what this thing is about an axe murderer though."

Addie released her son and leaned back her head in laughter. "Oh, that's nothing—just the mumblings of a silly old woman."

Leonard was next. Addie hugged him and they sat down on her bed. She held his big strong hands, gently patting them as she spoke.

"Leonard, I wanted to spend a few minutes with each of you. I usually stand at the door and yell, 'Good-bye. I love you.' as you leave, but this heart episode made me realize that I might not live forever. I'm not totally convinced of it, but just in case, you need to know some things. First of all I do love you. I want to begin and end each day in the knowledge that you know that. Secondly, I want to tell you how proud you have made me. You are a man of character. You, like Jim, remind me so much of your father. You're generous. You're focused, and you're dedicated to your Christian walk. You have made me very proud to be your mother. You are possibly the most generous of my children, but I don't want you to get uppity in that belief. Each of you has wonderful qualities. I love you Leonard Thomas Jones, and I am proud to be your mother.

Leonard continued holding hands with his mama, and for the first time realized that there may come a time when she isn't going to be there. He searched for the exact words to respond to her unexpected and unforeseen verbal display of affection.

"Mama, I can't believe there will be a day when you aren't here. But if that day comes, I will never doubt for one moment that you loved me. Yeah, you usually yell it as we leave, but you have shown it in more ways than I can begin to count. Even when you caught me skipping school, and I was smoking behind the mill, I knew you loved me when you marched me to school and made me apologize to every teacher there for not appreciating their work and taking full advantage of it. I hated doing it, but as a teacher now, I understand why you did it. Mama, you showed me and the others love every day when you went off to work, and became not only our mama, but our daddy when daddy died. You worked hard and then came home to see that we had a clean place to live, decent clothes on our backs, and good food to eat. You held us when we cried. You nursed us when we were sick. You applauded us when we succeeded, and picked us up when we failed. The words I love you were written in bold letters on each of those actions. I am the man I am today because you loved me so much. Before you loved me, though, Mama, you loved Jesus. We never ate a meal without praying. We never missed church or Sunday school unless there was vomit or blood involved, and maybe not even then. Mama, you laughed with us and you cried with us. You cared for other people. I never understood how you could work all day, take care of your children, keep your house, and still find time to tend to somebody's new baby or a sick friend, or a widow in her time of grief. I can only hope to achieve half the greatness you have. When, or maybe if, God comes to get you, I will grieve not for you, but for me. You have accumulated so much wealth in heaven, that you'll probably forget us poor people here on earth. God has many rewards waiting for you."

Addie was openly weeping. She was wiping her tears with one hand, still holding on to her son with the other. He let go and reached around her shoulders and pulled her close. "Mama, how could you ever think any of us didn't know we were loved? Why in the dictionary, your picture is right next to the word *love*. It sure is. You just need to go look for yourself."

As with the others, the conversation ended with humor, not from disrespect, but to allow each of them the freedom to part gracefully.

Finally, it was Louise's turn. She by this time had learned the reason for the private visit with her mother. Her siblings shared the message. Addie knew this was happening, but each child deserved her own time. Louise came in and sat in the chair while her mother sat on the bed. Addie quickly began.

"Sharon Louise, I'm sure you know by now that I wanted to spend time with each of you to make sure that if I die you will know that I love you. I love each of you as my children, but each of you has qualities that makes you unique and endears you to me in a special way. When I named you after my mama and my lifelong friend, Sharon, I didn't know what your character would be. As I watched you grow, however, I knew I had not made a mistake. You are so much like them both. You laugh easily, you love life, and you have an inner joy. You are meticulous. You helped raise your brothers and sister. I could not have worked like I did had I not been able to depend on you. At times I felt I was asking too much, but you never disappointed me, and you never, never complained. You seemed to know what was needed and usually did it before I could even ask. You excelled in school, and you have always made me proud."

"There is one thing that worries me though. You never accepted Jesus Christ as your Savior, and I hope that I will someday know that we will be together in heaven. You have had the same exposure as the others, but for some reason you have resisted, not the teachings, but the acceptance of the teachings. I'm not saying this to pressure you, but to ask you to think about it, or talk with somebody about it. Just open your heart and let Jesus come in. Do something so that we can all spend eternity together. No matter what decision you make, I will always and completely love you. You have brought me so much joy. You are so talented and creative. I could never have expected a better person as my daughter, but being good is not enough to get you to heaven. You have to accept that Jesus died on the cross for your sins. You have to admit you are a sinner and ask Jesus to forgive you of those sins. You have to believe in Jesus Christ and ask Him to be your Savior. You already have a life that would develop a relationship with Him. You're just missing the first part of asking for and receiving forgiveness."

Louise sat across the room from her mama. She knew when she called her by both names, the discussion was serious. She knew the conversation would probably lead to her salvation, and she had attempted to mentally prepare herself for it. However, she knew she would never be totally ready to say what she had to say.

"Mama, you have loved me in so many ways that words aren't necessary to say it. You could hire an airplane and write the words in the sky, and that wouldn't mean as much as the time you did without work shoes when yours had holes in the soles so that I could have the ballet slippers and tutu that

I needed for dance class. I never understood how you managed to pay for the lessons, much less the things that went with it. Not just for me, either. You did it for all of us. I know you wore underwear that was barely held together by the elastic. You didn't have a new dress for the whole 4 years I was in high school. Every cent you earned went to support us, and to see that we had everything we needed to feel the same as our friends. You never wanted us to know that you worked an extra job cleaning the library after we went to bed. I woke up one night and found the note you left telling us where you were. I was awake when you came home and put it in your purse only to replace it the next night when you went out. You worked there 3 hours a night 6 days a week. Mama, your love is so apparent. When you love somebody, you love them completely. I love you, too. That's the reason I have not been able to accept Jesus as my Savior. That didn't sound right. Let me say that again. Because you are such a good woman and so filled with love and such a wonderful person in the Lord, I can't understand how a loving God would have put so much heartache in your life. Why would he have filled your life with situations that required you to work like a dog to supply your family's needs? Why did he take Daddy and leave it all on your shoulders? When I know the answers to those questions, maybe then I can believe."

Addie looked across the room and had never felt so close to yet so distanced from her first-born child. She stood up and walked over to her. She stood beside the chair and stroked her long dark mane. "Child, child. You are looking at this all wrong. Yes, I had a life of heartache, and hard work. But you're missing the point that Jesus was my Savior through all of this. He gave me you to be there when I couldn't. He gave me 4 good children whom I could trust to behave when I was working. He gave me health to work and provide for my family. He took my husband, and only He knows why, but for the years we had together, we loved each other, and I am thankful to have had the man I did for the time we had. Dear, child, everyday I thanked God for the gifts I was given. I never looked at them as hardships or punishment. I always knew that if I trusted in the Lord with all my heart and didn't ask for my understanding of life, he would make my path straight. That's right from the Bible, Proverbs 3:5-6. Maybe I didn't have a new dress for 4 years, but I was very thankful for the one my children gave me when you graduated from high school. It was a blessing. My cup runneth over. Goodness and mercy follow me every day of my life."

"Please, Louise, don't use my hard life as a reason to keep you away from God. I look at it as a blessing. I am so filled with God's love as He led me through everything I encountered in my life. If I ever did anything to make you feel otherwise, I apologize."

"No, you never complained, Mama. You always somehow got done all you needed to do and we always seemed to have what we needed to have. I just felt you missed out on so much and I wanted more for you. I didn't see how your loving God could ask so much of you."

"You missed the point that He didn't ask so much of me. He gave so much to me."

Louise stood and hugged her mama. "Sharon Louise Jones. I love you," Addie said as the embrace ended and Louise opened the door. "Please think about what I said, child of mine. I will love you no matter what, but I think you are missing the best part of life, and I want to share that with you."

Downstairs the other children were anxious to get on the road. They all had stops to make on their journey home, but they didn't want to leave without one more hug and a good-bye. They were on their feet as they heard Addie and Louise approaching. Addie knew their departure was imminent and she always disliked this part of their visit. One by one they hugged her, kissed her, and said, "I love you." She responded in like actions and words. Cindy stood back and marveled at the dedication of these grown children to their mother but knew it was deserved. Addie stood on the porch and wiped her tears as their cars proceeded down the long drive and finally went around the bend and were out of sight.

Cindy invited Addie in for a cup of tea, but she declined saying she wanted to rest before they went to lunch. Mary Margaret heard Addie close the bedroom door and was certain she heard a sob.

Chapter 71

Lunch with Sylvia was enjoyable. She had prepared finger sandwiches and a green congealed salad with pineapple and pecans. Her sweet tea hit the spot as the temperature was in the high 80's. The ladies sat on the screened porch and the ceiling fans whirred. Goldie and Freckles lay in the shade of the porch and snored as the ladies talked.

Mary Margaret waited patiently for Philip to invite her to ride. She had put her boots in her mother's van. After the table was cleared, Sylvia came back to the porch with a bunch of carrots. "Philip, why don't you and Mary Margaret go see about the horses? I bet she'd like to ride, if it's not too hot."

Philip had been invited to spend the day with Davis and Jordan, but his mother said he had to stay home with Mary Margaret. He was pouting.

"I think it's too hot. This is the hottest day of the season, and they aren't used to it yet."

His mother knew he was making excuses, but chose to allow him his moment.

"Mary Margaret, would you like to go feed the horses these carrots. I'm sure they'd welcome your visit."

Mary Margaret was on her feet in a flash but before she could get out the screen door, Goldie decided to move to the other side of the porch and walked directly in her path, causing her to stumble. She crashed to the floor with a thud. The carrots flew apart and scattered in every direction. Freckles joined the fray and began circling Mary Margaret as she attempted to stand from her prone position. Everybody laughed, especially when the dogs each picked up a carrot and began to gnaw. Mary Margaret's embarrassment heightened and soon turned to tears as she realized her elbow was hurting. She attempted to move it to support herself, but the pain shot through her like a bolt of lightning. She couldn't get up. Her mother realized that there was a problem and she, Sylvia and Addie were immediately at her side, lifting her to her feet.

Philip was embarrassed, too. He was feeling bad that he had not agreed to go riding when his mother suggested it. He felt responsible for the accident.

Mary Margaret continued to cry, and it became obvious that her arm was broken.

Cindy used a magazine and duct tape to immobilize the injured arm. Philip was very helpful as the supplies were gathered. Sylvia was apologetic. Cindy professionally handled the situation and was soon ready to transport her child. Sylvia offered to drive but Cindy said she would take her if Addie could have a lift home. Addie protested that she wanted to go with her to the hospital, but Cindy insisted that she still needed to rest. A phone call was made to Mike at his office, and he said he would meet them at the emergency room.

This is getting to be a habit, thought Cindy when for the 4th time in a week someone in her household was being seen at the hospital. Just a short week ago, Mr. Hood was treated. The very next day Mike had appendicitis and then on Friday Addie had her near heart attack. Having Mary Margaret here was the furthest thing from her mind, but then nobody actually plans to visit the emergency room.

The room was full, but one look at her arm and the Triage nurse determined she could go ahead of the person with poison ivy and the earache patient. They glowered as her name was called ahead of theirs. The child was in pain, but her mother marveled at the way she was handling it. Mike arrived and was directed to the cubicle they occupied. He was obviously upset, but attempted to comfort his child.

"I'm all right, Daddy. Don't worry. It's probably not broken. I probably just sprained something," she said in an effort to be the comforter.

Cindy knew better. The skin was not broken, but an obvious compound fracture had occurred. *The first day of summer vacation and a broken arm. What a rotten thing to happen*, she thought.

An orthopedic surgeon was called in, and he confirmed the diagnosis and further said that surgery would be required to set the arm. Mary Margaret was admitted to the hospital and the surgery was scheduled for the next morning. While still in the ER a bag of fluids was hung, and soon another nurse came in to insert a needle in a vein to begin hydration. She explained to Mary Margaret what she intended to do, and her mother held her hand while the process took place. The IV nurse was experienced, and within minutes the needle was inserted and the fluids began to drip undetected into the tiny vein. A pain reliever was inserted into the same tube and soon Mary Margaret was resting comfortably.

Phone calls were made to advise Sylvia of the status and Jennifer that they would not be able to join her family for dinner. Mary Margaret was moved to a room. Her mother helped her change into a hospital gown, and the round of nurses and aides began. Her temperature and blood pressure were taken. A pitcher of water and ice were brought in. She dozed throughout the afternoon, and didn't know that Philip and his mother had come by and brought a vase of beautiful roses. Jennifer dropped by with a new book, and a box of mint wafer candy.

Mike went home and had dinner with Addie. He insisted that she stay there when he returned to relieve Cindy to go home for dinner. Addie was totally unaccustomed to standing by while somebody was sick or hurt. She was beginning to feel useless until she saw Cindy walk up on the porch. This woman was drained. She was pale.

"You look awful. Are you sick?" Addie asked her.

"I don't know what's the matter. I can't seem to get over that virus I had last week. I still feel nauseous."

"I know it's none of my business, Cindy, but I wondered this last week until Mary Margaret got sick, and then when I first got sick I thought I had a virus too. Do you think you have something other than a virus?"

Cindy looked at her questioningly. "What do you mean?"

486

"I guess I have to spell it out. Are you pregnant?"

She laughed, "I wish you were right, but after 9 years, I don't think there's much chance of that happening now."

"Stranger things have happened. If you ask me, you are, but I only had 4 children, so I'm no expert."

Again, Cindy Smith laughed at this wonderful woman, and wondered if it could be true.

After eating dinner and drinking some of Addie's sweet tea, she began to feel better. Over Addie's objections, she gathered up some personal items and went back to spend the night at the hospital so that her husband could come home and get some rest. Tomorrow would be a tense day for both of them, and she knew the hospital room had a bed for her. She would rest there.

Mary Margaret relaxed peacefully through the evening and drifted into a sleep which was interrupted regularly as nurses were in and out of the room. Her mother reclined on the chair which pulled out into a makeshift bed, but she never slept. She dozed occasionally, only to wake with a jerk. Her heart would race momentarily until she realized where she was. A quick glance at the sleeping child would reassure her, and she would attempt to rest again.

Chapter 72

Morning finally arrived, and the activity increased. Mike arrived along with Addie, who would not hear to staying home. Nurses were in and out of the room. Doctors came and went. Papers were read and signed. Permission was given to put their precious child into the hands of strangers, knowing in their heart that it was all right, but as a parent the fears were mounting. Mrs. Applegate arrived, and soon after Reverend Cross appeared. His presence was calming. His demeanor exuded care and comfort. He was truly their shepherd. After greeting everyone including Mary Margaret, he asked for a moment of prayer.

"Dear Lord—We are gathered here today in Your presence to ask that You be with this child as she undergoes surgery. Give her peace, comfort and quick healing of her arm. Be with her parents as they turn her over to the doctors and nurses and wait for her swift return to them. Give them peace and comfort. Be with the doctors and nurses and everyone who touches this child's life that they may be prepared for their job. Clear their minds of anything but the needs of this child. God, You are the ultimate healer, and we place Mary Margaret Smith in Your hands with the complete knowledge that You are her Heavenly Father and love and care for her as we do. In Jesus' name we pray. Amen.

Around the room Amen resounded.

Mike and Cindy sat on the side of their daughter's bed, stroking her hair, her hand, straightening the covers, nervous gestures that made them feel needed.

Mary Margaret was slightly sedated, and was enjoying the attention. Mrs. Applegate was telling her that they would spend time together in the garden when she was better. Addie said they would go to the library and select books and read them together. Her parents told her that her cast would probably be off about the time the New York visitors arrived. The conversation was meant to pass the time, and it did. However, somewhere in the mind of the bright little girl a question was ringing.

What if I die? she thought, over and over again. She attempted to push it away, but it kept returning. Finally, she could contain it no longer, and she spoke the words that everyone else was just thinking. "What if I die?" she asked out loud.

Mike and Cindy were startled and both started saying, "Now, now, don't worry about that. This is done everyday. You'll be all right."

Mrs. Applegate sweetly said, "Child, God will take care of you, now put that out of your mind."

Addie and Reverend Cross looked at each other, and he began. "Mary Margaret, do you want to know that you will go to heaven if you die?"

"Yes," she responded.

"Well, I believe that God has a place for you at this young age, but to be absolutely certain, are you willing to pray for salvation?"

"Yes," she whispered.

"Do you believe in Jesus," he asked.

"Yes," she said.

"Do you believe he died on the cross for your sins?" he continued.

"You say every Sunday he did and Ms. Betty says it, too," she whispered.

"It's not enough that we say it, you have to believe it."

"I do," she said.

"Do you want to acknowledge that you have sinned, and ask Jesus to come into your heart, to forgive you of your sins?" He asked as he lifted her hand.

"Yes," she admitted. "I wanted to since the first time I heard it in Ms. Betty's class, but I didn't know what I should do about it. It seems that I am scared all the time, and I want that to go away."

"I'll tell you what. I'm going to pray, and I want you to repeat after me, okay?" he said with tears burning behind his eyes.

"Okay," she whispered as tears began to roll down her cheeks.

"Dear Lord—

I know that I am a sinner. I know and believe that You love me and gave Your only Son so that my sins could be forgiven both in the past and in the future. Please come into my heart so that we can develop a relationship where I can depend on you for my daily needs.

Amen"

As he said a line, the tiny girl in the hospital bed repeated it with fervor. Every witness to the scene was crying, and the orderlies who had arrived to take her to surgery were touched as well. They stood back and wiped the tears from their eyes with the backs of their hands.

They carefully exchanged the tiny body from the bed to the gurney. Mike kissed their child, as did Addie, Mrs. Applegate and Reverend Cross. They all promised to be waiting when she returned after the surgery.

The gurney began to move, and Mary Margaret said, "Please wait a minute." The men stopped, and she attempted to prop herself up on her good arm. "Mama and Daddy I don't want to be in heaven alone. Will you be there someday, too?" she asked in childlike innocence.

Her parents were struck silent. Here in the hallway of this hospital their child was asking them to make a life altering decision.

Reverend Cross stepped forward and whispered, "In Matthew 18 the disciples asked Jesus who is the greatest in the Kingdom of heaven. Jesus replied,

'Truly I say to you, unless you are converted and become like children, you will not enter the kingdom of heaven. Whoever then humbles himself as this child, he is the greatest in the kingdom of heaven. And whoever received one such child in My name receives Me . . . 'The gift is yours to accept as your dear child has. The decision is yours."

Her mother was the first to respond. "Yes. I will be there. I know that Jesus died for my sins, and I openly ask that I be forgiven of those sins and that He come into my heart for eternity. I want to know that we will spend eternity together." She was sobbing as she finished and had her arms around her child.

Mike stepped forward and too acknowledged his faith and belief in Jesus Christ, and asked to be forgiven of his sins. "I want my family and me to have a relationship with God. I, too, want to spend eternity in heaven."

By this time a crowd was forming. Sobs were heard through the hallway. One of the orderlies asked, "Will God forgive me, too?"

Reverend Cross attempted to take control of the situation and assured the young man that God would hear his profession of faith as well. They agreed to meet in the chapel when he got his break for lunch.

"Mary Margaret and her parents exchanged professions of their love for each other, and she was slowly being rolled down the hall. Again, she said, "Wait. Reverend Cross, does this take now, or do we have to be baptized first?"

"It takes right now. We'll get to the baptizing when your arm is better."

Satisfied, she lay back and disappeared through the double doors.

The family was taken to the surgical waiting room. Cindy was experiencing what the families of the patients she tends to go through. They were told to sign in and that they would be called when any news was available.

The chairs in the waiting area began to fill. Sometimes a single person would arrive, and occasionally whole groups of 5 or 6 would come in. As they waited their group enlarged. Sylvia was the first. Betty Tyler was next. Mrs. Stancil had received a call from Addie, and brought a large basket of muffins when she came. Jennifer stopped by for a moment before she opened the store.

One by one the good news was shared. Tears were shed, and the general consensus was that while it was a bad thing that Mary Margaret's arm had broken, life's greatest gift had come from it.

After nearly 4 hours the doctor came out to announce that Mary Margaret had come through the surgery with *flying colors*. He discussed the surgery with her parents and explained that a plate and screws had to be used. "They will be removed at a later time, and she should be good as new in a couple of months. By the way," he continued, "You have one remarkable little girl there. She came into that operating room with a big smile and didn't show the least fear. With children it's not always that way. Sometimes restraints are needed, but she was a trooper. She is special."

Her friends and family knew the secret, but the doctor was off to his next surgery before he took time to hear what it was.

Reverend Cross led the group in a prayer of thanksgiving, not only for the good outcome of the surgery, but for the new bodies in Christ which had been born that day. He looked at his watch and realized the orderly was hopefully waiting in the chapel. He didn't want to let him get away.

He needn't have worried. This young man's heart was ready to receive Christ. He had been trying to handle life on his own, and it wasn't working. He knew he needed another solution, and his mama and daddy had tried to get him to go to church. He had resisted. However, when he saw the faith of that little girl, he wanted that same thing. He and Reverend Cross prayed together, and the plan of salvation was presented. He told Reverend Cross that his life had been so filled with sin that he didn't see how he could be forgiven of it all.

Reverend Cross said, that in Romans 5-8 we are told that, "God demonstrates His own love for us in this: While we were sinners, Christ died for us." He was assured that not only his past sins would be forgiven in God's eyes, but any future ones as well.

"That doesn't mean that you're being given permission to continue the life you've been living. When you truly accept Jesus as your Savior, you will want to change your life. You will be a new man. You will want to tell others of the joy. Your friends will see a change in you and ask you what's going on. You may even become obnoxious about it.

He accepted that plan and for the fourth time in one day, and it wasn't even a Sunday, a new soldier in God's Army was enlisted. He promised to come to church and get into a discipleship program Reverend Cross was developing. "I want to thank you for the change you made in my life today."

"I didn't make the change in your life, you did. God only put me in a place to catch you when you were ready to fall into his arms. He used me to place you where you need to be. This decision and this new life you have ahead of you is yours. I expect you to use it for great things and for God's Kingdom here on earth."

"I promise I will, but I have to do one thing before I do anything else. I have to call my mama and daddy. This decision has been their prayer for me since I was born, and I can't wait to tell them about it." Tears streamed down his face and he hugged Reverend Cross clumsily. He closed the door on the phone booth and shared the good news of his new life with the ones who gave him life and had prayed for it to be eternal.

Mary Margaret was soon in her room, and each of her visitors stayed to greet her. Mrs. Stancil and Betty Tyler just said hello and wished her well before they left. Reverend Cross gently kissed her on the forehead and said good-bye.

Mike, Cindy, Addie and Mrs. Applegate stayed in the room and watched the child as she slept.

"Nothing is more precious than a sleeping child," whispered Mrs. Applegate."

About 1:30 a gentle knock was heard. Mike opened the door and Gerry was standing there holding a picnic basket. From behind him came Mr. Hood holding a gallon of tea. The aroma gave away the contents. He explained that when he took the accountants to lunch at Grammy's, she asked about Mr. Smith's whereabouts. When she heard about Mary Margaret, she insisted that he bring lunch to the hospital for the family, "And anyone else who might be there," he repeated her words.

I saw Mr. Hood when I took the accountants back to the mill, and asked him to ride here with me.

Mr. Hood placed the tea on a table and went over to Mary Margaret's bed. He picked up her small hand in his large rough one and gently kissed it as she slept. Tears ran down his face, and he was too moved for words. So was everybody else. The room was utterly silent.

A nurse broke the spell when for the umpteenth time that day she came in to check on Mary Margaret's vital signs.

Conversation began anew, and the hungry visitors were grateful for the food. None had wanted to leave, but each had felt the grumblings in their stomachs. Addie took the basket and began to unpack its delicious smelling contents. "Fried chicken, mashed potatoes, gravy, green beans, cole slaw, and deviled eggs," she announced as she removed each container. Paper plates, napkins, plastic silverware, and cups were sandwiched around the food, and a cardboard box holding a whole chocolate pie was on the bottom.

Gerry asked about the patient and said he had heard about the other good news, too. For a split second, nobody understood, and then Mike and Cindy Smith realized he was talking about their decisions.

"Thank you," they said. "God uses us in various ways, but I never dreamed he would use my child to lead me to Him" Mike said, his voice quivering.

Gerry said he needed to get back to work since the boss was away, winking at Mike.

They each began to fill their plates, and were so thankful for Grammy with each morsel they consumed. Soon, their stomachs were full, and the chocolate pie was set aside for a mid-afternoon snack.

Mary Margaret began to arouse, and complained of pain. A nurse was called and a dose of pain medication was administered through her IV line. She was thirsty and was given ice chips. In a short while the medication took effect, and she felt better. Her request for food produced red Jell-O, her favorite. After a few bites, she slipped into a restful state.

Mrs. Applegate was the first to leave, and she insisted that Addie come with her and rest. "I'll bring you back later this evening. You come home with me now, and we'll both take a nap." Addie agreed that a nap sounded good after a restless night the night before.

Mike and Cindy remained in the darkened room watching their child's chest rise and fall with each gentle breath. He reached over and took her hand. "You know, the decision we made today is one I have wanted to make since I first heard Lew Rowell talk about his mama and how he prayed for her renewed relationship with Christ. That touched me so deeply. Then each time I heard about salvation since then, I had to use restraint to stay in the pew.

"Why did you feel you had to sit there and not go forward?" Cindy asked.

"I didn't want to go without you, and I didn't know what you would think about it," he said.

"Why didn't you ask me? I was waiting on you," she replied.

Throughout the remainder of the day nurses and aides came into the room. They checked the patient often as she slept.

Visitors returned. Sylvia brought Philip. He stood back and looked at Mary Margaret as she lay sleeping. His conscience was bothering him. He felt guilty. He should have taken her to the horses when his mother asked. He felt this was his entire fault. Reverend Cross arrived while they were there, and Philip asked to speak with him alone.

Reverend Cross was sensitive to him and suggested that they go to the chapel. He felt the young man may have a crush on Mary Margaret or something like that and wanted to assure him privacy as he revealed his love. However, when Philip began to speak, he was unprepared for the admission of guilt he produced.

"It's my entire fault," He gushed out. "I was mad that I couldn't spend the day with Davis and Jordan, and I wouldn't go with her to see and ride the horses when my mother asked. I knew she wanted to go, but I didn't like having to stay home with her. She's all right and everything, but Davis and Jordan left today to visit their grandparents for 2 weeks, and I wanted to go swimming at their house. If we had left when mother asked, none of this would have happened."

Reverend Cross listened to the confession and let him get it out. He believed that confession is good for the soul. When Philip was finished, he said, "Philip, none of this is your fault. Yeah, you were pouting, and maybe you weren't a good friend to Mary Margaret, but you didn't hurt her. She tripped over a dog. That's all that happened. Don't beat yourself up about her injury. You are guilty of being a boy who knew he would miss his friends and used momentary poor judgment. I know that in the past you have been a friend to Mary Margaret, and unless I am a poor judge of your character, I'll bet you'll continue to be a good friend. I'd be surprised if you're not at her house nearly every day being her friend as she recuperates. She can hold a fishing pole if you bait the hook. She could ride a horse with you. You two can take adventures in books, and I'll bet she's a decent card player. I don't think anybody holds you responsible, and I don't want you to either."

"But nobody knows . . ."

"Nobody needs to know. You are not guilty of hurting her. You are now and will continue to be her friend."

"Are you sure?" he asked with relief beginning to spread across his still wrinkled forehead.

"Yeah, I'm sure. Come on. Let's get back before they send a posse for us."

Addie and Mrs. Applegate had returned and Sylvia and Philip said their good-byes and offered assistance when needed as they left.

Mary Margaret was fully awake, and she was hungry. After a consultation with the nurse, a bowl of chicken noodle soup was brought in. Addie fed her the noodles while Mary Margaret sipped the broth through a straw. "We're going to get to be good buddies, my sweet little friend," Addie said, as she spooned up the last bit of noodles. "One handed living might be tough for a while, but I'll be there to lend the other hand."

Mike and Cindy were separately sharing much the same thought, but Mike expressed it best when he said, "God sure had his hand on our lives long before we knew it. He brought us here and put us right into Addie's Arms."

Epilogue

Epilogue means conclusion, and we are concluding this book, but not the story.

We have many loose ends to tie up as this family *attempts* to settle in their new home. Only six weeks into the move, and chaos has met them at every corner.

Will Mike Smith's predecessor be exposed as a thief? Will the mill prosper? Will the puppy fit into the household? Will Mary Margaret recover from her injury? Will the visit from Alice and Charlene go well? Is there a horse in Mary Margaret's future? Is there a new addition to the Smith household? How will the lives of these new Christians be impacted as they begin their walk with the Lord and face new challenges?

These are only a few of the unanswered questions. A sequel will be forthcoming to shed light and hopefully inspire you as we unfold the next months in the life of the Smith family as they journey from New York to Left Fork.

If this part of the journey has touched you to make a decision to ask Jesus Christ into your life, I rejoice. This decision doesn't have to be made in a church pew, during summer camp, or in any edifice related to religion. Jesus can be found wherever you are as illustrated when Mary Margaret asked Him into her life in a hospital. Don't let your location deter your decision. He is ready, and waiting wherever you are, you only have to ask. He is available to every one of us. Your past life doesn't matter. He is willing to forgive.

Your first command after that decision, however, is to go and tell. I pray that you will find someone who knows and experiences the daily love of our Lord and Savior and ask that they disciple you. Discipleship is key to building the relationship you deserve after make this life-changing decision. I would appreciate hearing about this decision as well and you may contact me at addie@barbarahoodhopkins.com.